Psychological Perspectives on Social Issues and Human Development

About the Editor

Dr. Arun Kumar Tiwari, D.Phil.(Allahabad), is a Reader in Psychology at K.S. Saket P.G. College, R.M.L. Awadh University, Faizabad. He has written extensively on issues concerning organizational behaviour, health psychology and social psychology. He has to his credit a good number of research papers published in various journals of repute. Also, he has participated in a number of national and international seminars and conferences. He is Editor of a biannual journal entitled United Journal of Awadh Scholars. Presently, he is directing an NCERT sponsored research project on Work Values in Children. He was the Organizing Secretary of the NAOP convention held at Faizabad.

Email: fzdtiwari_ak@yahoo.com

Psychological Perspectives on Social Issues and Human Development

[Selected papers from the Proceeding of 15th Annual Convention of National Academy of Psychology (NAOP) India]

Edited by

Arun Kumar Tiwari

D.Phil. (Allahabad)
Reader
Department of Psychology
K.S. Saket P.G. College
Faizabad (U.P.)

CONCEPT PUBLISHING COMPANY, NEW DELHI-110059

ISBN-13: 978-81-8069-612-1 **ISBN-10: 81-8069-612-X**

First Published 2009

Published and Printed by

Concept Since 1974

Concept Publishing Company

Regd. Office:

A/15-16, Commercial Block, Mohan Garden
New Delhi-110059 (India)
Phones: 25351460, 25351794, *Fax*: 091-11-25357109
Email: publishing@conceptpub.com,
website: www.conceptpub.com

Editorial Office:

H-13, Bali Nagar, New Delhi-110 015, India.

Cataloging in Publication Data--*Courtesy:* D.K. Agencies (P) Ltd. <docinfo@dkagencies.com>

National Academy of Psychology (India). Annual Convention (15th : 2005 : Ayodhya, India)

Psychological perspectives on social issues and human development: selected papers from the proceeding of 15th Annual Convention of National Academy of Psychology, NAOP, India / edited by Arun Kumar Tiwari.

p. cm.
Includes bibliographical references and index.
ISBN 13: 9788180696121 ISBN 10: 818069612X

1. Social problems--India--Psychological aspects--Congresses. 2. Ethnopsychology--India--Congresses. 3. Social psychology--India--Congresses. I. Tiwari, Arun Kumar. II. Title.

DDC 302.0954 22

Foreword

Psychology in India has shown incremental growth in studying problems situated in its unique socio-cultural context in the last few decades. This is supported by various reviews of psychological researches in India, notably, undertaken by the Indian Council for Social Science Research. If one looks at the fields in which the Departments of Psychology are working under the Special Assistance Programme of the University Grants Commission, a similar picture emerges. Cotemporary psychological research in the world is driven, broadly, by six perspectives, namely, biological, cognitive, learning, socio-cultural, humanistic, and psychoanalytic. Be that as it may, a major shift came in psychological research in India after the call given by Professors Udai Pareek and Durganand Sinha in the 1960s to make psychology socially relevant to India. This resulted in change of emphasis on training of students in laboratory methods. Accordingly curriculum of psychology of UG and PG programmes also underwent change. In 1972, the University of Allahabad started a course in Psychology of Social Change, which for the first time sought to focus on developing psychological understanding of social problems in India. Although, this course was adopted only by a few other universities in India, it helped in emphasising the importance of studying individuals within their socio-cultural contexts employing indigenous methods as well as concepts. The idea was not to debunk the western models completely but to suggest that they have limited value in enhancing understanding of 'our' problems. Also that Cartesian approach employed by psychology to discover universal behavioural laws was not very appropriate and actually restricted understanding of phenomena which were culturally rooted. Consequently, a balance was sought between epistemological and ontological methods to study social cultural problems of India. The evolving research programme of psychology in India, thus, veered more towards problems of inclusion, be they the socially disadvantaged, minorities, poor, or people belonging to various other marginalised groups. It was in some ways an agenda for radical psychology sans its ideology.

The present volume based on papers presented in the Annual Congress of the National Academy of Psychology held at Ayodhya may be seen in this light. It may help the readers to evaluate how far psychology in India has moved away from the dominant hypothetico-deductive Cartesian model of mainstream psychology, if at all. Also, the success it has had in studying problems in the socio-cultural context of India; and how far psychologists have been successful in developing new psychological perspectives for studying social problems. It may also be asked what learning psychologists have derived by treating culture as an exogenous variable. Does it really help to view culture as a concrete product than view it as a process. Such a reflective glance is required, if psychology has to be meaningful for the community whose lot it seeks to improve. Psychologists often complain, sometimes rightly, of the disciplinary bias of policy makers in India for not involving them in making of social policy relating to economic, social and psychological well-being, as also in matters relating to education and health. The world over planners have moved away from the narrow paradigm of development, which assesses development of societies in terms of economic parameters, to assessing macro psychological states, such as Happiness, Quality of life, Societal safety, Social inclusion, Social integration and Harmony to mention a few important ones. The Nobel in Economics awarded in the last few years amply demonstrates the potential of psychology in playing a very significant role in enhancing our understanding of a wide range of social, economic and cultural problems as also the possible role it can play in policy formulation. This is an important challenge which is waiting to be met by psychologists in India. The present volume seeks to bridge this gap in a small way. It provides several excellent exemplars which provide new understanding of old social problems faced by India. Even studies included in this volume which have a micro focus have important implications at the macro levels. Although one may not find that there has been a noticeable shift in terms of methodology used by psychologists to study social problems, one is struck by the wide variety of social problems that have been studied ranging from social and personal identity to natural disasters, like Gujarat Earthquake. Quite a few papers focus on health, stress, and psychological well-being. Problems related to family, parenting styles, gender and schooling also find attention.

The articles included in this volume have depth and greatly add to our understanding of social problems within the Indian socio-cultural context. I am sure that this book will find acclaim which it richly deserves. Dr. A.K. Tiwari has done an excellent job as Editor of this volume. He deserves appreciation on behalf of the NAOP and other fellow psychologists in India.

R. C. Tripathi

Preface

Manopubbangma dhamma

—Buddha

(All human tendencies and actions are preceded by mind)

While Lord Buddha knew the role of mind in everyday life very well and many insights exist in classical literature, philosophical texts and epics systematic analysis of mental processes in the modern idiom is of fairly recent origin. The modern incarnation of the discipline of psychology that has established itself as a knowledge-specialty exclusively focusing on mental and behavioural life is a twentieth century phenomenon. During this period it has evolved and grown in many directions and has undergone nothing short of metamorphosis. Today it encompasses almost all the domains of life and has become without doubt a plural enterprise in its theoretical and methodological orientations. Against this backdrop the present volume exploring psychological dimensions of societal issues in the domains of self and identity, human development, organizational behaviour and health and well-being amply illustrates that Indian psychologists are becoming increasingly aware of their surroundings. They are now more eager to make sense of the happenings and relatively more prepared to extend a helping hand to ameliorate the problems encountered. The contributions to this volume address a range of social issues of signal importance at theoretical, methodological and applied levels and evince reflexivity and responsiveness. My dear friend Dr. Arun Kumar Tiwari, the editor of this volume, deserves special appreciation for taking pains in bringing out this volume. It's on his insistence that I have accepted this pleasant but challenging task. I feel privileged and honored in sharing some of my concerns on this occasion.

I find three distinct features of this volume that make it impressive and different from other related publications. First, it invites the readers to engage in dialogue with the minds of three generations of psychologists: the very senior stalwarts, the modern experts, and the upcoming younger colleagues. Second, it extends the boundaries of psychological discourse by incorporating diverse themes and concerns. Third, it documents methodological variety in treating psychological issues. Taken together this volume marks a new and welcome turn in the practices of psychology in India.

During major part of its disciplinary journey psychology has been inspired to emulate other more developed disciplines like physics for the sake of becoming scientific and gain entry to the group of royal disciplines. Most of such efforts have not met success and the strategies of reductionism, mechanization, quantification and objectification have not served much purpose for generating basic psychological elements and enduring grand theories comparable to those found in the physical sciences. It is quite clear now that psychology has many facets, levels, and concerns that cannot be framed within the disciplinary designs following physical sciences. Psychology's conversation with reality does not allow any unitary enterprise as psychology does not deal with fixed entities in static environments. Also, there is considerable diversity and variety in concepts across theories from various psychological traditions as they are located in disparate metaphors of mind. There are many competing paradigms and discourses which go beyond the simple physicalistic and deterministic causal analysis.

Notwithstanding the above struggles society has developed expectations that psychology must offer guidelines for a happy and meaningful life. The responsibility and task before the psychologist is enormous as we stand at a point where our world is torn by conflict, terror and strife and impact of globalization is spawning its problems - thereby creating its pressures and demands on the individual. The rapidly changing scenarios continue to be a drain on the mental, social and psychological well-being of the individual. It is the psychologist who realizes the intimate and reciprocal connection of psychology with society. This creates challenges that psychology has to be generative or creative and attend to solving various problems. Also, psychology is informing the minds of people. Terms like unconscious, reinforcement, conditioning, archetype, personality, IQ etc. are used as heuristics to create a meaningful world to live in. This has led to tremendous pressure for applications. The same is visible in majority of the contributions to this volume. A close perusal of the present set of contributions indicates a turn in the discipline's general orientation.

The turn being witnessed in psychology is remarkable in the context of Indian psychologists' long drawn preoccupation with a universalistic stance and absolutism in its meta theoretical assumptions. The psychological applications have to be closely tied to the local conditions, historical context, and cultural practices. Applied endeavors cannot afford to be culture free, abstract, and trans-historical. The solutions for real life problems demand cultural sensitivity. Such sensitivity is often reflected in the various themes such as self and identity. The centrality of the questions of self and identity evident in the contemporary social, political and psychological discourses also underline the interplay of culture and psyche in the formation of our concepts and nature of understanding. The portrait of self is undergoing shift. The blending of independent and interdependent self construals and individualistic and collectivist orientations are leading to new modes of experiences and one's well being and health are being redefined. This is often related to conflicts which are aggravated by economic and technological developments.

The economic development coupled with increase in amenities, has resulted in the increase in leisure time and enjoying freedom from ethical/moral principles and obligations. It is nurturing egocentrism, and neglect of the common good. The growth of shrinking self is taking place at the cost of social welfare. The moral standards, social obligations and values of compassion, empathy and forgiveness are receding to background and are replaced by conflict, distrust, competition and short term gains.

The advances in technology are bringing change in the habits of mind and body. Our experiences are mediated by technologies of different kinds. The use of mobile, computer, Internet, fax, I-pod etc. are changing the demands on cognitive functions and bring in change in the life style. The distinction between real and virtual is becoming blurred. The changing technologies are reconfiguring the functions of memory, perception and motor behaviour by deployment for various purposes and with different goals. The strong presence of electronic media is signifying the decisive role of representation and construction in our lives. We learn to think, emote and act under the overpowering presence of these representations.

In the social life the 'other' is becoming anchor for self presentation. Although being a mirror that informs the market value of one's self worth 'others' are important but they are subjected to manipulations. We are becoming too self-absorbed and use technology and other resources for building self-esteem which delimits our sense of being unique and curtails the relational space. It's reflected in the diminishing value of the institutions of family and marriage and leading to experiments such as live-in relationships.

The fast pace of life , increased mobility of people across cultures, global nature of the patterning of economic and environmental influences accentuate the demand for a knowledge system not only sensitive to the cultural roots but sufficiently responsive to the happenings in the outside world. But that may not be sufficient enough. Humans are multilayered conscious beings. A comprehensive understanding demands us to consider the physical, social as well as spiritual aspects of life in a comprehensive manner. The present volume shows a move in that direction. Indeed it extends the concerns raised in earlier volumes based on the NAOP proceedings. Since its inception the NAOP as a professional body has been making efforts to rejuvenate the teaching and research in psychology and bringing together the fragmented works of Indian psychologists to a point of consolidation. I am sure this volume would go a long way in establishing the identity of psychology in India as a vibrant and socially responsive discipline.

I take this opportunity to congratulate Dr. Tiwari for taking up the challenge of bringing out this volume and hope that the community of Indian psychologists will own the responsibility and respond to the contemporary issues in creative and constructive manner.

Girishwar Misra
Professor of Psychology
University of Delhi

Introduction

Society as a congregation of various entities that form a collectivity, is a dynamic structure. As such it has life with ups and downs. The ideal state (or a *Ram Rajya* free from *daihic, daivik and bhautic tapas*) is really an idea conceived by all the civilized societies, which inspires to move on the path of progress. Of course such ideals are also varied (e.g. Communism, Capitalism, Democracy, Feudalism, and Military Rule) and their ecological validity is time and space bound with no ultimate verdict. The events in different countries like erstwhile USSR, China, USA, Pakistan, South Africa, and more recently in the neighbouring country of Nepal amply attest this idea. They also indicate that societies are dynamic in nature, need local models and capturing its reality is a quite complex and gigantic task.

The social problems and issues are inevitable and intrinsic part of any living society. It is like any living body or organism. It is equally true for non-human species. It is often said that the human beings are social animals. However, one should not miss the point that other animals also do have social order. In fact, as ethological and evolutionary psychological scholarship is showing, each and every animal, be it an insect or a cattle, has some kind of social order or system of some complexity. It is true that in cases of some animals, it is loosely knitted, but in case of some other animals, it is relatively strict. Naturally the humans represent highest level of social order. Be it society of humans or other animals, the members, in general, respect and obey their respective scheme of social order. It gets expressed as acts of co-operation and competition. But whenever any element of social order is violated, it creates conflicts and sometimes physical clashes among the members. We often see the insects and other animals cooperating and fighting on different occasions. However, since the social order in animals is not very complex, the problems in their societies are of simple nature. Contrary to it, the human societies are complex in nature, therefore, the social problems in these societies also are very complex. Sometimes it needs serious kinds of interventions. The complexity at human level is largely owing to greater intellectual capacity, ability to communicate and ability to develop and nurture culture. Humans are endowed with the power of self-reflexivity. They are capable of subjecting themselves to their own reflection. This kind of dialogue is central to human existence for its problems as well as solutions.

While ancient India pursued *para* and *apara vidyas* — spiritual and material modes of knowing — modernity brought in the centrality the idea of (empirical !) science (alone) as dependable source of knowledge. As a result the development of the institution of natural sciences as well as social sciences has taken place. It has practically grown under the societal pressure for problem solving. The social lives came under the scientific scrutiny. They were subjected to careful analysis and systems of social, psychological and other kinds of data collection and analyses were established. Research methods became an essential ingredient of social science teaching programmes. Theories and principles were developed to describe, explain, control and create the reality in the social arena. Obviously the main impetus for the emergence and development of the enterprise of social sciences has been the social problems and issues, which inhibit the smooth flow of the social system.

The social problems weaken not only the social system but by doing this, damage groups, communities and sometimes the nation, region or the entire world. Therefore, the social issues that precipitate these problems become relevant subject matter for investigation and scientific intervention in almost all the social science disciplines. In fact, every society expects from different scientific disciplines to come forward with such inputs of knowledge, which may be utilized in resolving the multifarious problems faced by the society. Psychology, as a responsible scientific discipline, owned its responsibility and attended to various problems of Indian society.

The psychological perspectives on social issues and problems assume that the social and psychological processes are intertwined in developing a socio-psychic system. It may occur either at individual level or at group level, and sometimes at both the levels. It is these socio-psychic systems that initiate, nurture and give direction to the social relationships. MacIver has defined society as 'the web of social relationships'. Therefore, one can argue that any strategy to deal with a social issue/social problem would need to necessarily address the nature and quality of social relationships in the society. It can be done by understanding the process of development of sociopsychic systems among individuals or groups. The same was reflected in the papers presented in the 15th annual conference of National Academy of Psychology (NAOP). These papers tried to comprehend the dynamics of socio-psychic systems. This volume contains a set of selected papers, which were presented at this conference. These papers were updated by the authors to make it publishable articles.

The conference was organized at Ayodhya (Faizabad). The delegates from all the corners of the country along with a few delegates from abroad participated in the conference. Ayodhya and Faizabad are twin adjacent cities, situated in Uttar Pradesh (India). Ayodhya is known to be birthplace of Lord Ram and, therefore, has recognition of place of worship for Hindu pilgrims. Faizabad had been capital of Nawabs of Awadh, who had been Muslim kings of this area for a very long period. Therefore, entire area including Ayodhya and Faizabad has been a best site of multicultural and multiethnic traditions of so-called '*Ganga-Yamuni Tahjeeb*'. Unfortunately, many of us now view Ayodhya as a place of dispute between two communities, but the real natives of this area do not think so and continue to live with full fraternity with each other. Since the conflicts between Hindus and Muslims have dominated the entire Indian subcontinent as a major social problem, therefore, Ayodhya was a valid place to discuss various aspects of indigenously relevant social problems and issues.

Organization and Themes of the Chapters

The book is divided into two parts. Part-I presents articles, which have dealt with the development of group level sociopsychic system as the determinants of social problems and issues. The articles of Part-II have taken same approach, but with specific emphasis on individual level development of sociopsychic system. Most of the articles of Part-II have taken psychopathological approach in dealing with some specific issue. In fact, the social relationships get expressed in three ways in society. They are, relationships between/among individuals, relationship between an individual and a group, and relationships between/among groups. Therefore, both individual and group level interpretations would always be needed for perfect understanding of social problems and issues at different occasions.

Prof. L. B. Tripathi authors the first article of Part-I. It is based on his keynote address, delivered at the conference. He notes that the psychological contribution in solving the real social problems has been limited. It is because of certain "meta theoretical biases, blind spots, and neglect of well documented facts and facets of social reality in planning, execution and drawing conclusions from the data obtained". The article explains these factors in detail and suggests that all the disciplines associated with social issues should come together so that the investigations of these issues may proceed beyond the boundary set by each of these disciplines as its subject matter. It would broaden the perspective of the study. Then the united social sciences would be able to plan for successful intervention and provide the techniques of solving the social problems. Also, it would facilitate social engineering.

More or less, similar concerns were raised in the presidential address by Prof. R. C. Mishra. According to him psychology has been searching for its relevance in solving social problems for many years. So his article discusses and suggests the ways through which the psychology can act to establish its relevance in the social context. In fact, psychology has produced data on the basis of empirical and academic studies, but it has not been gauged from the angle of society due to various factors. Some of these factors are associated with psychologists themselves. However, sometimes the agencies having responsibilities to implement the schemes, neglect such data due to their practical limitations. Lastly, the article calls psychologists to use data to develop intervention programmes for solution of the problems of society. They should develop direct contact with communities to implement these programmes. It would be beneficial for the society and it would enhance the usefulness of psychology also.

The two articles, referred above, provided the context and identified the ways in which psychology can relate to social problems in future. In other articles of the volume, some specific kinds of social issues have been psychologically interpreted. Among them the two articles, one authored by Nick Hopkins and other by R. C. Tripathi have focused upon the development of social identities among various ethnic groups of a society and its psychological and behavioural consequences in the context of pluralistic cultural backgrounds. Nick Hopkins dealt with the social identities of people of Muslim community residing in Britain, whereas the article by R. C. Tripathi investigates social identities of Hindus of India in the context of Ram Janam Bhumi-Babari mosque controversy. Nick Hopkins collected the inputs from Muslim ideology that play important roles in shaping the social identity of members of Muslim community of Britain. He found that all the Muslims did not have similar social identity. It indicated the possibility of multiplicity in the social identities of members of a particular community. He opined that since all the members of a community do not perceive the role of culture in their day-to-day social relationships in the same way, therefore, their social identities might differ with that of each other. According to him, psychologists should take note of this fact, as it has serious behavioural implications. (These arguments by Nick Hopkins seem to provide logical support to the contention that all the members of a community should not be equally treated for so-called 'Islamic terrorism', which is being currently regarded to be a major social problem of global nature).

The article by R. C. Tripathi sets the example for—how a social problem can be addressed with a behavioural scientist's approach. This article analyzes the roots of a current burning problem of the country related to Ram Janam Bhumi-Babri mosque controversy on cognitive grounds. Taking inputs from the historical facts and information obtained through the interviews of activists of *Mandir* movement, the article suggests that the controversy is mainly caused by the faulty development of social identities due to imagined perception of past. The imagined perception of past distort collective memory, which consequently affect the social identities. Therefore, the problem should be addressed through dialogue and strategic communication. Also, the article emphasizes on the need to create new space by positive recollection of past to assimilate and integrate so that a syncretic culture may be created.

Immigrants having cultural attributes different from that of native people of a country sometimes create serious social problems. These problems can be solved by synchronizing the cultural attributes of different groups. It is possible only when the immigrants and native people have positive attitudes towards one another. It is depicted in the article of Jyoti Verma. She has reported a study of the acculturative experiences of Indian immigrants living in Paris. She notes that these immigrants perceive the French culture and people in very positive manner. This information can be utilized to create better intercultural relations between the countries. Braj Bhushan has traced the role of culture in the attempts of cognitive interventions by psychologists in the schemes for attaining the objectives set at national level. One such aim is to provide education to all. He opines that the behavioural scientists can share larger social commitments through the application of research-based knowledge in this area. It can be done by developing culturally acceptable concept-specific artifacts that are user friendly. Furthermore, the article illustrates suitable cognitive artifacts looking at the nature and content of mathematics curriculum. M.B. Sharan collects indigenous points of view from Indian culture to understand human mind, *karma* and behaviour. He distinguishes between Indian and Western approach regarding these issues. He differentiates between *karma*—as conceptualized in Indian culture and behaviour as described by American psychologists, on the basis of the sense of righteousness/wrongness of one's action. Further, Sharan advocates to accept Vedantic approach and to believe in the divine aspect of one's *karma*. It would save oneself from the wrong deeds. It would automatically check the social evils.

The characteristics of one's family structure and other dynamics including the generational gaps affect each of us. It determines the development process, more particularly among the children. Some articles of the book have approached the issues associated with family and development. One of such article by Abha Mishra and Janak Pandey deals with an important problem of changing family structure. The study, reported in this article has shown the serious impacts of changing family structure on the development of various aspects of self and values of the adolescents. The article by B. Patnaik is of conceptual nature. It discusses the paradigms of children's thinking and its implications for their schooling and social competence. The generation gap has always been recognized as the potent factor in social relationships. The article by Shubhra Sinha and R.C. Mishra focuses on this issue. It discusses various factors associated with generation gap, particularly in the context of our country.

Disasters, whether manmade or natural, affect the lives of many people psychologically, physically and socially. Apart from the other types of rehabilitation, the people need psychological rehabilitation also in such unfortunate situation. With these preliminary notes, T. Vijayakumar in his article, reports his study on psychosocial dimensions of Gujarat earthquake disaster. The results are of wide nature and can benefit the people working in disaster management area.

The diseases, particularly chronic diseases of the individuals raise social issues many times. It occurs in two ways. First, the diseases make the individual somehow defunct in establishing inter-relationships with different persons, which is micro unit of one's social behaviour. Second, the patient individual needs all types of social support such as supports from family, friends, colleagues and community for the purpose of all-round recovery including physiological, psychological, economic and social recoveries. Some of the articles of the book have addressed the issues related with different kinds of diseases of individuals. The article by Ajit K. Dalal is one of them. It focuses on the role of cultural beliefs in managing a chronic disease. This article is qualitatively sound on both theoretical and empirical points of view. It collects the insights from the results of five studies conducted by the author and his associates, to explore the health promoting cultural beliefs. It is noted in the article that even some of the delusional beliefs contribute positively in the recovery process of patients. The author has critically analyzed Indian belief system also to underline its specific relevance in the context. Lastly, the article proposes an interesting cultural belief model of health. HIV/AIDS has emerged as a global pandemic and the number of people infected keeps rising every year. According to WHO estimates, the male-female ratio of newly infected people is now almost equal. In this context, the article by Mrudulla and Vindhya seems to be very relevant. This article reports a study, which attempted to explore the dynamics of how widowed women infected with HIV/AIDS by their husbands cope with the situation. Neena Kohli, in her article, presents a very systematically and scientifically conducted study on cervical cancer patients to assess their psychological recovery during different phases of treatment. Counsellors, working in hospitals, can utilize the results of the study. In an interesting article, Nishi Tripathi has presented the study that elaborated the problems of the physically disabled girls and their coping styles. The role of family support in the cases of these girls has been highlighted.

Development of an infant to be an adult being is determined by a large number of factors. Thus it proves to be of very complex nature. Through the process of development the child earns cognitions about his/her identity. Some of the articles have tried to investigate the process of development along with the factors that determine this process. One such article is by G. Chauhan and J. Shastri, which deals with the process of development of gender identity among preschoolers. Gender plays an important role in our social life. It creates several types of social problems also. Therefore, the issues related to gender have been a major area of interest for many researchers. The article by Chauhan and Shastri suggested that the boys and girls spread across three to six years of age, were able to describe their gender according to the gender stereotypic norms, activities and other social expectations. Mendiratta, Bhargav, Jasrai and Mohite, in their article, focused upon the development of self of 18-20 months old infants. It is a relatively less explored area. Therefore, study reported in the article proved to be very relevant. The results of this study established that infants of 18-20 months were capable of identifying the parts of their body. Also, the infants showed the concern towards others. On the basis of these findings, the authors opine that the infants are able to acquire self-knowledge up to certain extent. Swati Shah and Hina Mankodi studied the sense of sharing and conflict resolution behaviours among children of three to four years old. They report this study in their article. The results of the study are utilized to understand the process of social moral development and its determinants.

Stress is now not restricted to the working professionals only. It has spread over each and every field of our lives. The increasing rate of suicides by adolescents and several young people has shaken the society up to a great extent. Psychologists have taken note of this and started researching this area to find out the precipitating determinants of increasing stress proneness. Jigisa Gala and Sangeeta Chaudhary have presented one such study in their article, which have investigated the adolescents' perceptions of coping with stress in general and under specific situations. The results revealed the nature of stressors for adolescents and also the ways they adopt to cope with these stressors. M. Pradhan and P. Pandey describe an empirical study, which revealed association of high level of spiritual orientation with very low level of stress vulnerability. On the basis of this result, they recommend to include protective factors like spirituality in the schedules for psychological interventions in cases of such people who are more vulnerable to stress.

The article by Sweta Srivastava and Arvind K. Sinha is based on their study to explore the relationship of certain organizational level variables with organizationally relevant outcome variables. It suggests that in any organization, various types of supports (which are social in nature) associate with positive consequences. The last article of the book, authored by Archana Shukla, is based on her experiences attained in the workshops on cognitive behavioural interventions for emotional well-beings, which she has been organizing at different occasions. It can be presumed that the emotional well-beings of the people would automatically save the society from many problems. Thus the article has social implications also.

The twenty-two articles constituting this volume provide glimpses of the mental make-up of the Indian psychology fraternity. It shows their preparedness to respond to the societal needs. They also demonstrate a range of theoretical and empirical strategies to tackle different issues and problems. Here it would not be of place to mention that various governmental agencies as well as several NGOs have been working to solve the problems of our society. Several legal provisions to eradicate problems like illiteracy, poverty, untouchability etc. have been made. Protective reservation schemes have been launched to arrest the feelings of relative deprivation among the backward and deprived people. However, it is now being felt with full sincerity that most of these schemes and provisions have not benefited the real targets. Here one can be reminded of the famous statement by late Prime Minister Rajeev Gandhi, who had commented that only a few paise of every one-rupee reach to the real target and how the same is further publicly endorsed currently by Sri Rahul Gandhi, the Secretary General of ruling Congress Party. This demands answer by us. Why is it so? More often, the system is blamed for it. However, now it is being conceded that along with lacunae in system, certain psychosocial mechanisms are also responsible for this pathetic situation. We take this opportunity to humbly draw attention of the students, researchers, peers and scholars towards some of the pressing problems that need attention on a priority basis.

Some Social Problems Challenging the Discipline

Some of the key problems that need our attention are as follows :

- Corruption in almost all walks of life including political, business, judiciary, education and military sub-systems of society.
- Prevalence of unethical and immoral practices as core constituents of modern (and practical !) life-style.
- Preference for short-term orientation and neglect of long-term future leading to potentially disastrous planning.
- Preoccupation with materialistic goals and avoidance of social and transcendental goals, which are more encompassing.
- Consumerism and politicization of anything and everything (including religion and God !).
- Legitimization of antihuman/terrorist strategies which demonstrate the relevance of violence and aggression.
- Fuelling of excessive egoistic aspirations (by the media) at the cost of societal concerns.
- Unconcern for the society or community, particularly rural, agricultural deprived, aged, women folk, and disadvantaged sections.
- Unmindful imitation in the national planning with greater emphasis on the urban sector, industrialization and high technology.
- Education for producing elites with an alien orientation having little concern for Indian values and ethos.

These are some of the obvious trends that are individually and globally problematic. They are posing serious threat to the sovereignty of the country, its heritage and development. They need serious reflection and action on our part. But we hardly recognize them as legitimate themes in teaching of psychology courses. Perhaps psychology is more preoccupied with mental processes more than their implications at behavioural level. That too is framed in such a way that the whole exercise remains at an abstract level. The Western theories have become more as goals than tools or heuristic for problem solving. It is unfortunate, perhaps, that the call for culturally relevant and indigenous psychology could not get responded and we are still entrenched in a mental frame that refuses to open eyes toward the society, which is nourishing us. We believe that the articles of the book have provided much information that can be used by policy makers in solving various social problems but that is not enough. We have to stand up to the cause and realign ourselves as researchers for a better society.

At last, I use the opportunity to thank all of those who helped me in preparing and publishing this book. At the outset, I must concede that if the book is a reality now, it is due to continuous encouragement and active support from Prof. Girishwar Mishra. He guided me at every step. In fact he taught me how to edit a book. Prof. Mishra not only took pains to read all the articles but also provided his critical comments on each of them, which were later utilized by the authors to update and modify their contributions. Prof. Mishra is a real 'Guru' who has a hobby to motivate his students to work hard to strengthen the discipline. I express my hearty gratitude to him. Prof. R.C. Tripathi was generous once again to me and wrote Foreword for the volume on my request. Also he provided valuable suggestions on different occasions. I am highly grateful to him. I am thankful to all the authors also, who contributed their articles for the book. Further, they showed admirable patience as the publication of book was somehow delayed.

The 15th annual conference of NAOP was organized at K.S. Saket P. G. College, Ayodhya. The faculty members of Department of Psychology of the college and some of their colleagues from other departments did praiseworthy job to make conference successful. The then principal of the college Dr. H. B. Singh provided all kinds of support. Dr. R. P. Singh, Head of Department, acted as one of organizing secretary. Dr. R. K. Tiwari and his son Shirish Tripathi worked for 24 hours of the days of conference. Other colleagues from the department Dr. P.C. Tripathi, Dr. S. N. Dubey, Dr. R. S. Tiwari, Dr. P.K. Tripathi, Dr. K.N. Pandey, Dr. A.K. Srivastava, Dr. S.K. Rai and Dr. Radha Saxena also worked very hard as the members of various committees. All of them deserve high appreciations. Furthermore, on behalf of my college, I wish to bring on record the financial supports provided by UGC and ICSSR, New Delhi for the conference and thank them for the same.

Sri Shailendra Yadav, Swati Agarwal, Naveen Mani and Awadhesh Tiwari assisted in the tedious task of proof reading. They deserve our blessings for the same. I also thank the Concept Publishing Co. and its proprietor Sri A. K. Mittal for their warm reactions to our request to publish the volume.

Finally, it is hoped that the book would enhance our understanding about the dynamics of social cobweb.

Arun Kumar Tiwari

Contents

PART - II
CULTURAL, SOCIAL AND DEVELOPMENTAL INTERFACE

Contributors

G. Mishra : G. Misra is Professor of Psychology at Delhi University, Delhi. Earlier he had been faculty at the universities of Gorakhpur, Allahabad and Bhopal. He has published numerous papers in national and international journals. Also he has written or edited several standard books. These books are recognized internationally. Prof. Misra was a Fulbright Fellow at Swarthmore College and the University of Michigan. He has received Radhakrishnan Award in1991 and Dr. Hari Singh Gaur Award from Madhya Pradesh Government for contributions to social science teaching and research in 1992. Presently he is Editor of Psychological Studies. His current areas of interest include cognitive psychology, cultural psychology, and applied social psychology and human development. He has been member of various committees of UGC, ICSSR and NCERT.

Email : misragirishwar@gmail.com, misragirishwar@hotmail.com

L. B. Tripathi : Professor L.B. Tripathi has retired from Gorakhpur University as Professor and Head, Department of Psychology where he started his career as Assistant Professor in 1957. He held various Academic and Administrative positions at Gorakhpur University and University of Jodhpur, Rajasthan. He served as Dean, Arts Faculty and Pro-Vice Chancellor and Acting Vice Chancellor. He was a Commonwealth Scholar in Canada at McGill University where he completed his Ph.D. degree in the area of Experimental Psychology. He was a Visiting Professor at Psychology Department and Centre of Behavioural and Cognitive Sciences, University of Allahabad. He published a number of research articles, monographs and chapters in national and international journals/books. Professor Tripathi has authored several books. Some of his books include *Psychological Consequences of Prolonged Deprivation* (With G. Misra), *Calibration of Verbal*

Material in Hindi and *Psychological Consequences associated with Severe Iodine Deficiency* (With B.D. Tiwari). His book in Hindi brought about a paradigm shift in learning and teaching of Psychology in Hindi speaking States of the country. The standard scientific terminology in the discourse on psychology became prominent after publication of his books in Hindi. He has translated *Psychology of Learning* by Hulls, Deese and Egeth in Hindi. He has been a prolific writer and passionate speaker. Collection of his Papers and Essays were brought in the book on Psychological Theory and Teaching Profession (G. Misra, Editor) in 2006 by Concept Publishing Company, New Delhi.

R. C. Mishra: R.C. Mishra is Professor of Psychology at Banaras Hindu University. A D.Phil. from Allahabad University, he has been Post-Doctoral Research Fellow, Shastri Research Fellow and Visiting Professor at Queen's University, Canada. He has also been Visiting Professor at University of Geneva and Jean Piaget Archives, Switzerland. His principal interest is in cultural influence on human development, and he has published articles in the fields of cognition, acculturation, schooling, and cross-cultural studies. He has extensively contributed chapters to books, including the *Handbook of Cross-Cultural Psychology* and *Handbook of Culture and Psychology.* He is the co-author (with J.W. Berry and D. Sinha) of *Ecology, Acculturation and Psychological Adaptation: A Study of Adivasis in Bihar,* and co-editor (with J.W. Berry and R.C. Tripathi) of *Psychology in Human and Social Development: Lessons from Diverse Cultures.*

Email: rcmishra_2000@yahoo.com

Nick Hopkins: Nick Hopkins is a Senior Lecturer at the University of Dundee, Scotland, UK. He studied as an undergraduate at Oxford and as a post-graduate at Cambridge and Exeter. His interests revolve around identity and action. In particular he is interested in the construction of social identities and the implications of such constructions for behaviour. He has a strong interest in national and religious identities and uses a variety of methods (e.g., interview and ethnographic) to explore the strategic and argumentative construction of identity. So as to explore the consequences of such constructions he uses experimental research paradigms.

Email: n.p.hopkins@dundee.ac.uk

R. C. Tripathi: Ramacharan Tripathi is former Director of G.B. Pant Social Science Institute at Allahabad and also Professor of Organizational Psychology at the University of Allahabad. He was also Chair of the Department of Psychology for more than two decades. Prof. Tripathi has served on important bodies of higher education in the country. He was member of the UGC and ICSSR. He is presently a member of the Indian National Commission of Cooperation with UNESCO. He received his doctorate in Organizational Psychology from the University of Michigan. He has been a Fulbright Fellow at the University of Michigan. He has been a Visiting Professor at Tilburg University, Wake Forest University, Recanti Management School Tel Aviv University, and University of Haifa. He was President of the National Academy of Psychology, India; and also one of the Regional Presidents of Indian Academy of Applied Psychology. He also served as Secretary General of the section of "Psychology and National Development" of the International Union of Psychological Sciences. He is the founding editor of Psychology and Developing Societies: A Journal (From Sage) and served on the editorial boards of *Indian Journal of Psychology*, *World Psychology*, *Psychological Studies* and half a dozen other journals. Among his books are: *Environment and Structure of Organizations; Deprivation: Its Social and Psychological Roots; Norm Violation and Intergroup Relations; Psychology in Human and Social Development; Understanding Academic Underachievement.* His work on organizations has focused on Organizational Values, Organizational Influence processes and Organizational Change. He has consulted for Merril Lynch, Pierce, Fenner and Smith in U.S. and a number of organizations in India. More recently he has completed CSR studies for Honda-Siel Cars and for Mawana Sugars.

Email: ramacharan.tripathi@gmail.com

Jyoti Verma: Jyoti Verma is Professor of Psychology at Patna University. She has been awarded gold medals from Banaras Hindu University and Patna University and visited USA as the Post

Doctoral Fulbright Fellow. Dr. Verma visited Paris under the Indo-French Social Scientists' Exchange Programme; on the fellowship of the French Ministry of Research and Higher Education and as a collaborator of Observatoire Cidil de l'Harmonie Alimantaire project. She has to her credit around 50 papers in national and international journals and a number of research reports. She has been Consulting Editor of a couple of international journals and was the regional representative for South East Asia for the International Association for Cross-Cultural Psychology.

Email: jyotiverma_us@yahoo.com

Braj Bhushan: Braj Bhushan, Ph.D., works as Assistant Professor at the Indian Institute of Technology, Kanpur (India). He has served the Indian Institute of Technology Guwahati as a Senior Lecturer and Kyushu University, Japan as a Visiting Professor. His primary areas of interest include study of laterality from ergonomic and evolutionary perspectives, post-traumatic stress and growth. He has published over 25 research papers/book chapters/books in peer-reviewed journals/books.

Email: brajb@iitk.ac.in, brajbhushan1@yahoo.com

M. B. Sharan: M. B. Sharan is now Emeritus Professor at Purushottam Institute of Engineering and Technology (PIET), Rourkela. Earlier, he served as Principal of RIMS, Rourkela. Before that he was retired as Professor and Head in 2005 from IIT, Kharagpur where he worked for more than thirty years. He was President of NAOP in 2006-07.

Email: mithilasharan@yahoo.co.in

Abha Misra: Abha Misra is a D.Phil. in Psychology from Allahabad University, Allahabad. She specializes in personality and developmental psychology.

Janak Pandey: Janak Pandey (Ph.D. Kansas State University) is currently Professor of Psychology and Head, Centre of Behavioural and Cognitive Sciences, Allahabad University and has earlier held important positions like HOD Psychology and Co-Ordinator, Centre of Advanced Study, Allahabad University, Allahabad, Director G.B. Pant Social Science Institute, Allahabad. He is a reputed social and Cross-Cultural Psychologist and has been widely published in national and international journals. Recently he has been elected member of executive committee of International Union of Psychological Sciences (IUPsyS).

Email: janakpandey@usa.net

B. Patnaik: Bhaswati Patnaik is currently Assistant Professor in the Department of Humanities and Social Sciences, National Institute of Technology, Rourkela. After obtaining Ph.D. Degree in Psychology as a UGC Research Fellow at the Centre of Advanced Study in Psychology, Utkal University, Orissa, she pursued teaching in the area of Organisational Behaviour and Human Relations. She has a number of publications in and has presented papers in national and international conferences.

Email: pbhaswati03@yahoo.co.in

Shubhra Sinha: Shubhra Sinha is a U.G.C. Senior Research Fellow in the Department of Psychology, Banaras Hindu University, Varanasi. She is interested in the study of the dynamics of parent-child relationship and transmission of values across generations.

T. Vijayakumar: T. Vijayakumar is Assistant Professor in Centre for Equity and Social Development at National Institute of Rural Development, Hyderabad. He is a Post Graduate in Psychology and Education, with Ph.D. in Eucational Psychology from Osmania University. He attended a certificate programme in Development Management from Asian Institute of Management, Manila, Philippines. He has been working in the areas of community mobilisation and empowerment, as well as behavioural dimensions of Rural Development.

Email: tvk@nird.gov.in, vijayakt2002@gmail.com

Ajit K. Dalal: Ajit K. Dalal is Professor of Psychology at the University of Allahabad. He has obtained his doctoral degree from the Indian Institute of Technology, Kanpur, and has published in the areas of causal attribution, health beliefs and indigenous psychology. He received the Fulbright Senior Fellow and worked at the University of California, Los Angeles, and at the University of Michigan, Ann Arbor. He is also a recipient of the UGC Career Award, Rockefeller Foundation Award and ICSSR Senior

Fellowship. He was a visiting faculty at many places, including the Queen's University, Canada; the National Institute of Health and Family Welfare, New Delhi; the Indian Institute of Management, Ahmedabad; and the Calcutta University, Kolkata. He has published about 60 research articles and book chapters, in addition to eight books, including *Attribution Theory and Research, New Directions in Indian Psychology* (Vol.1), *Social Dimensions of Health and Handbook of Indian Psychology.* Presently, he is editor of the journal '*Psychology and Developing Societies*' published by the Sage.

Email: ajitdalal@hotmail.com

Mrudula Akki : Mrudula Akki has completed her M.Phil. in Counselling Psychology from Andhra University, Visakhapatnam.

U. Vindhya: U. Vindhya is Professor of Psychology, Andhra University, Visakhapatnam and is currently on lien at Centre for Economic and Social Studies, Hyderabad. Her research concerns are located in the interface of psychology and feminism and include mental health of women, domestic violence, the psychological dynamics of women's political activism and the linkages between reproductive health and psychological well-being. She has edited the volume *Psychology in India : Intersecting Crossroads* and has published widely in national and international journals. She was the recipient of the South Asian Visiting Scholarship at University of Oxford and the Fulbright Visiting Lecturership. She was Convener, National Academy of Psychology and is presently its President.

Email: u.vindhya@gmail.com

Neena Kohli: Neena Kohli is a Senior Lecturer in Department of Psychology, Allahabad University, Allahabad. She is doctorate from Allahabad University. Her Post-Doctorate is from the Institute of Psychiatry, London. She has worked on factors involved in psychological recovery following tragic life events. Her current research interests include illness cognitions, coping with chronic disease, adherence to medical regimen and factors facilitating return to work following illness.

Email: drneenakohli@rediffmail.com.

Nishi Tripathi: Nishi Tripathi is M.A., D.Phil. in Psychology from Allahabad University. She served at the Counselling Centre, Department of Psychology, Allahabad University, Allahabad. At present she is a faculty of MBA programme at the Allahabad Agricultural Institute, Naini (Deemed University).

Email: tripathi_nishi@yahoo.com

Gargi Singh Chauhan: G. S. Chauhan is Doctoral Student (Development Professional), Department of Human Development and Family Studies, Faculty of Family and Community Sciences, The Maharaja Sayajirao University of Baroda, Vadodara, Gujarat.

Email: Gargisingh79@gmail.com

Jigisha Shastri: Jigisha Shastri is Reader, Deptartment of Human Development and Family Studies, Faculty of Family and Community Sciences, The Maharaja Sayajirao University of Baroda, Vadodara, Gujarat.

Email: jigishastri@yahoo.co.in

Ankita Mendiratta: A. Mendiratta is a doctoral student from the Department of Human Development and Family Studies, Faculty of Family and Community Sciences, The M.S. University of Baroda, Vadodara. She was adjudged as the "Best Young Scientist" in the Young Scientist Award session, conference of the National Academy of Psychology (NAoP), at Utkal University, Bhubaneshwar. (January 27-31, 2003).

Email: ankita_mendiratta@yahoo.com

Shruti Bhargava: Shruti Bhargava is Senior Lecturer, Deptartment of Human Development and Family Studies, The Maharaja Sayajirao University of Baroda, Vadodara. Also she is Superintendent, Chetan Balwadi, The Laboratory Nursery School, Department of H.D.F.S.

Email: Shrutib20@gmail.com

S. Jasrai: Sucheta Jasrai is Education and HIV/AIDS Specialist in UNICEF, Gujarat.

Email : sjasrai@unicef.org

P. Mohite: P. Mohite is the Professor and Dean, Faculty of Family and Community Sciences at M.S. University Baroda, Vadodara.

Swati Shah: Swati Shah is professional associated with Department of Human Development and Family Studies, M.S. University Baroda.

Hina Mankodi: Hina Mankodi is Senior Lecturer, Department of Human Development and Family Studies, The Maharaja Sayajirao University of Baroda, Vadodara. She is former Superintendent, Chetan Balwadi, Department of Human Development and Family Studies.

Email: hina_njmankodi@yahoo.com

Jigisha Gala: J. Gala is a doctorate student, Department of Human Development and Family Studies, Faculty of Home Science, Maharaja Sayajirao University, Baroda.

Email : g.jigisha@gmail.com

Sangeeta Chaudhary: S. Chaudhary is Lecturer at Department of Human Development and Family Studies, Faculty of Home Science, Maharaja Sayajirao University, Baroda.

Email : schaudhary_13@yahoo.co.in

Madhurima Pradhan: M. Pradhan is Reader at Department. of Psychology, Lucknow University. She did her post graduation from Kanpur University and Ph.D. from Lucknow University. She is U.G.C. NET qualified and also did Post-Graduate Diploma in Counselling from IHCA, Chennai. At present she is undergoing a UGC sponsored major research project on "Promoting Spirituality to Enhance Subjective Well-being among Young Adults."

Padma Pandey: Padma Pandey did her M.A. in Psychology from Lucknow University, Lucknow and now she is a research scholar there.

Sweta Srivastava: Sweta Srivastava is currently an Assistant Professor at the FORE School of Management, New Delhi. An alumnus of the University of Allahabad, and the Indian Institute of Technology Kanpur, she has had a brilliant academic record. She had earned her Ph.D. degree from the Indian Institute of

Technology, Kanpur. She had worked earlier at the Indian Institute of Management, Kozhikode, Calicut, Kerala. She also has to her credit the Dr. P. Deivasanapathy — IAAP Young Scientist Award, 2004, at the 39th National and 8th International Conference of the Indian Academy of Applied Psychology.

Email: swetasriv@yahoo.com

Arvind K. Sinha: Arvind K. Sinha is a Professor of Psychology in the Organizational Behaviour area in the Department of Humanities and Social Sciences at the Indian Institute of Technology, Kanpur – 208016 (India). Earlier, he was associated with the Department of Psychology, University of Allahabad, Allahabad, and the A.N.S. Institute of Social Studies, Patna. He has had a brilliant academic record and earned his Ph.D. degree in Psychology from the Patna University, Patna. He has spent about 30 years toward teaching and research both at UG and PG levels. He has about 100 authored and co-authored research articles to his credit in journals of repute, and in national and international conferences, and has guided ten research scholars leading to their Ph.D. degrees. He is on the reviewers' panel of reputed national and international journals, and is a member of various high powered committees in academic organizations. He has also been the President of the National Academy of Psychology (NAoP), India for the year 2008-2009.

Email: aks@iitk.ac.in

Archana Shukla: Archana Shukla is Professor in Psychology and teaches Clinical and Counselling Psychology and Motivation and Affective Processes at Lucknow University, Lucknow. She is a consultant to various organizations such as NCERT, IGNOU, NIPCCD, NABARD, UPSC, National AIDS Control Organization (NACO), and Staff Selection Commission (SSC). She is a master trainer on HIV/AIDS counselling for prevention, care and support. She has published 35 articles in various national and international journals and has several chapters in books on Psychology.

Email: archana1942@sify.com

Part - I

Concepts, Concerns and Issues

1 Reflections on Psychology and Social Problems

L.B. Tripathi

It is a matter of common knowledge that the contemporary Indian society is afflicted with innumerable social problems, such as widespread poverty, deprivation, illiteracy, child abuse, communal disharmony, rampant corruption in governance, increasing incidents of rape and abduction, demand of dowry, bride bashing and burning, casteism and communalism in politics etc. Psychologists in India realized long back that these problems give rise to varied stumbling blocks in smooth functioning of the democratic form of governance and social development. Naturally enough a good number of social psychologists in this country directed their efforts, either individually or in teams, at studying some of such problems with a view to finding out scientific answers to three basic questions. (1) What are the manifest features and deleterious effects of the chosen problem, (2) How does the social problem manifests with what frequency that disturbs peaceful and progressive social life, and (3) What are the specific sources and causes of the targeted social problems?

Since mid-fifties of the last century a number of social psychologists have investigated, and still are doing so, various types of social problems. During the past four decades numerous research articles, monographs and edited books have been published. A critical review of these publications reveals a number of meta theoretical biases, blind spots, and neglect of well documented facts and facets of social reality in planning, execution and drawing conclusions from the data obtained.

The present author aims at pointing out these biases and blind spots that have made psychological studies of chosen social problems ineffective in providing sound scientific understanding of the origins and the causal factors of a single social problem. Thus it is no wonder that no effective and dependable intervention programme or technique has been developed for solving a single social problem in any part of the Indian territory.

Bias of Environmentalism

The first half of the twentieth century was an era of different schools in psychology. Studies of mental processes and behaviours were conducted within the diverse frameworks of meta-theoretical assumptions. The most prominent meta-theoretical perspective was initiated by J.B. Watson and promoted by Hull, Skinner, Mowrer and a host of others. They forcefully argued that psychology as a science must focus on objectively observable behaviours. They emphasized that all behaviours are caused by stimulations reveived from the environment in which organisms are born, brought up and have their ambience. Environmental features were accepted as the determinants of all behaviours, Watson (1926; page 10) stated that 'give me a dozen healthy infants, well formed and own specified world to bring them up in, and I will guarantee to take any at random, and train him to become any type of specialist I might–select a doctor, lawyer, artist, merchant-chief and yes, even into beggar man and thief, regardless of his talents, penchant, abilities and vocations and race of his ancestors.'

The Watsonian environmentalism was further enlarged and promoted by Hull (1943, 1951, 1952), Mowrer (1947), Skinner (1938, 1953) and a host of others under the rubric of 'learning paradigm'. They argued that all living organisms including human beings learn various kinds of habits, habit-family hierarchies through stimulus-response associations. This kind of behaviouristic school had become the most dominant and popular approach among psychologists of USA and some other countries as well as in India. It is worthwhile to note that it was in fifties and sixties of the twentieth century that a large number of young scholars and teachers of psychology went to USA for their doctoral degree or for advanced research on various scholarships and fellowships. Due to rapid and wide expansion of psychology in Indian Universities, these psychologists made environmentalism one of the most popular meta-theoretic approach. This trend is still continuing in a large number of psychology departments. During the last four decades of the last century owing to newer developments in the mainstream of psychology influence of environmentalism and the learning paradigm has waned and many of their principles have been modified and incorporated in cognitive psychology in American Universities. However, it continues to dominate and shape social psychological researches in Indian Universities.

At this point it is worthwhile to note that the environmentalism and learning paradigm dwindled and was left behind, and some of its insights were duly incorporated in the mainstream cognitive psychology. For a fairly large number of psychologists from all over the world, environmentalism had a fresh incarnation in the corpus of cross-cultural, and indigenous psychologies during the last three decades of the twentieth century. A fairly good number of psychologists assumed that culture constitutes the man-made environment, and it determines human behaviours and cognitions. However, when the question of providing a substantiative definition of culture was raised, there were as many definitions as there were cross-cultural psychologists. Now culture is conceptualized as 'some force out there to be studied' (Segall *et al.*, 1992), 'as an all encompassing context' (Pandey *et al.*, 1996). Some psychologists conceptualize culture as a medium in which individuals grow psychologically. It is intuitively clear that such conceptualizations are rephrased form of environmentalism.

Any context, be it cultural or eco-cultural, assumed as the main determinant of the origin and growth of psychological functions is misleading. Such accounts remain limited to phenotypical aspects of psychological functioning. The genotypical facets of behavioural origin and development are either deliberately or unconsciously left out. Validity of such as an assertion becomes self-evident, if and when one considers the methodology employed by environmentalists or cross-cultural psychologists. These researchers draw two samples from two highly different kind of context, measure some features of mental or behavioural characteristics, and calculate significance of data differences between the two sets of data. However, they ignore within group differences as error variance. It is in this error variance that spontaneously manifested genotypical effects present but are ignored.

To illustrate the above point, let us take an example from agricultural sciences. An orchard man decides to plant saplings of four or five types of mangoes in the same kind of fertile plot. He provides same kind and quantity of irrigation, fertilizers and pesticides on all of the plants. After a few years the plants become trees and yield fruits. However, *prima facie* all the fruits are more or less similar in shape and tints. But different varieties of mango seeds bear fruits of different sizes, shapes and taste which are easily discernible in spite of the fact that the mango seeds grew and came to bear fruits in the same kind of environmental background. Social psychologists all over the world in general and in India in particular have shown blindness for the realities and importance of the role of seeds (biogenetical contributions) in human development.

Neglect of Biogenetic Perspective

More than three decades back a sizeable number of social psychologists came to realize the importance of the role of genetic factors' play in psychological development of every individual. Jensen (1968) asserted that environmental determinants of human behaviour and psychological traits do not provide a balanced picture of social behaviour. Biological inheritance as a source of psychological traits is of vital importance. The nature and nurture controversy arose a long time ago, and passed through a variety of vicissitudes owing to faulty questions raised by those who were endeavouring to resolve the distinctive roles, genetic factors and environmental variables played in psychological development of human beings. Even though they were convinced that genetic potentials along with environmental factors jointly determine human development, they raised wrong questions in the context of intellective functions. It is a well-accepted dictum that wrong questions never yield right answers. Two questions were mainly addressed to, i.e. which is more important in psychological development, environment of birth, existence and growth, or genetic potentials inherited from parents and ancestors? The second question was about relative contribution of genetic potentials and environmental variables. After a prolonged debate and research efforts for providing a valid answer it was unanimously realized that both genetic potentials and environmental variables are absolutely essential for human organisms to come into existence, survival and development. Psychological development is thus joint function of genetics potentials and environmental components. Both are simply necessary and jointly sufficient.

Psychological trait variability is a two-facet function, i.e. genotypical and phenotypical. The term genotype refers to genetic constitution of an individual, meaning thereby genetic base of human being. It may be considered as inherited potentials for specified traits, behavioural features observed in human beings. On the other hand, phenotype refers to observable outward characteristics resulting from simultaneous influence of genotype and environmental conditions. It is worth noting that the strongest the genotypic potential, the more pronounced is its manifestations in the form of phenotypical characteristics. It happens to be so even if the person is born and brought up in highly impoverished environment. On the other hand the weaker are the genetic potentials, the phenotypical characteristics remain weak even though the person concerned is born and reared in enriched environment.

Murphy and Kovach (1972) have elaborately discussed the relationship between genetic potentials and behaviour development. They conclude that 'the gradual disappearance of the classic nature-nurture problem, and its replacement by various complex issues of interdependence between organism and environment required more sophisticated use of behavioural analysis....' In the light of numerous research findings, Hirsch (1969) called for a complete reorientation of psychology. It has to follow the route charted by life sciences and has to accept its legitimate roots. At present widespread realization of complex and fine interplay between unfolding genetic potentials and individual experiences is at the centre of newly emerging biogenetic outlook in psychology.

At this point it is pertinent to note that numerous studies have been conducted on schizophrenic cases, and yielded results that demonstrate that blood relations of schizophrenics are more prone to become schizophrenic than are random controls even when detailed exclusion of environmental effects are achieved. It has also been empirically shown that chances of becoming a psycho-pathological case remain great even if the offspring from pathologically affected parents is removed (Kety, 1970).

A number of studies in the area of psychogenetic and genetics of behaviour development have been reported in which genetic manipulation of some major behaviours such as learning drive and emotion were emphasized. Other studies laid emphasis on strain and genotype dependent differences in the process of behavioural development. Such studies have strongly proven that genetic factors are of vital importance in behavioural characteristics and their origin as well as development.

In an article on 'Code of Behaviour' in the *Times of India*, it was stated that scientists at the Institute of Psychiatry, London, have been scanning human genome for answers to the behavioural questions. According to them, most behavioural traits are results of interaction between nature and nurture. They have concluded that bad behaviour free of psychopathic stains had relatively little genetic component whereas psychopathic trait seems to be gene related, this finding is significant. If socially unaccepted behaviour is programmed into a person's genes, with a conscious effort to modify behaviour would prove effective? The findings of London scientists suggest that inherited criminal or psychopathic behaviour could be attended to with medical intervention. Tweaking genes should not be seen as answer to dealing with aberrant behaviour, because inheriting a tainted gene is not the same as the disease or disorder manifesting itself. It is well known that psychopaths are those who have different shades of criminal and unethical tendencies even though they are generally socially pleasant, amiable and not easily detected. Such psychopaths are responsible for initiating social problems, and their perpetuation is mostly due to environmental precipitators and modelling.

With a view to illustrating the preceding account of the role of genetic potentials in psychological development and behaviour let us take up an example of a social problem and analyze it. It is a matter of common knowledge that fairly frequent communal tension and clash occur in India. One community organizes a religious procession, which passes through an area in which mostly members of another community have their residences, shops, and places of worship etc. The processionists shout slogans, use noisy musical instruments and loud speakers in large size vehicles. While the procession moves on through the areas of the other community, some residents of the area raise objections against the clamorous activity because it appears to be offensive. Gradually, it turns into confrontation between the two communities. While verbal exchanges are going on, the whole atmosphere hots up. Suddenly some members use firearms from both the sides. The crowd created by the two gets transformed into mobs. 'A good number of' members of the two sides become de-individuated and violent behaviours occur. Some persons are shot at causing serious injuries, shops are looted, doors are broken and put on fire. After a while police force intervenes, violence is suppressed, and tension filled calm is restored.

If one analyses the constituents of the two communities it would become self-evident that all individuals in the two groups are not fanatic members of their communities. Some being orthodox members are attired in clothes indicative of community customs. Such members become aggressively vocal and adamant about their action plans. They may be considered as the front liners and leaders. A sizeable number of participating persons in the two groups, who are there as community members with superficial interest in the matter and follow others without involvement in the issue. Another set of person in the two groups are followers of their leaders and conform to what their leaders dictate and suggest. The third set of participants in the two groups, who are there is community members with superficial interest in the matter and follow others without involvement in the issue. Another set of persons in the two community groups do not feel comfortable in this kind of tension and possibility of violence. They are there because they do not want to be isolated in the community. When the situation becomes violent, some individuals stealthily walk away. However, some members of both the groups predisposed to get involved owing to their bad genetic potentials for illegal/criminal predispositions. They perceive the situation fit for manifestation of their latent psychopathic traits. Such persons would be present at any layer of the crowd. It is this fringe that initiates illegal/criminal disruptive actions. Once such activities begin, the crowd turns into mobs. Now individuals become deindividuated and there is large-scale use of firearms, shop-looting and property burning etc.

Proper understanding of different kinds of social problems warrants through analysis of various layers involved in them. Such analysis is bound to differentiate the role of environmental features and genetic factors. Apart from this, in order to develop effective social technology for solving problems, it is essential to determine the level of human evolution of people who are beset by social problems.

Importance of Human Evolution

Theory of biological evolution deeply influences the sciences of anthropology, sociology and economics. Owing to this influence studies of social, cultural and economic activities came close to the interest of psychologists in general and social psychologists in particular. Now it is a matter of common knowledge that nowhere in the world social life remains static. Easily perceptible changes occur from one generation to the other in the forms of social rites and rituals, traditions, customs and relations. Changes in the substantive aspects of social activities and thinking occurs relatively more slowly and lead to onset of a different stage of human evolution. The six volumes of August Comte (1830-42) on Systems of Positive Polity became a source of profound influence in theory of human evolution. According to him there are three stages of human evolution, i.e. (1) theological, (2) metaphysical, and (3) positive or scientific. It is rather a very broad classification

Theological Stage

This stage began during that period when human beings became capable of simple perceptual discriminations, retention, storage and retrieval functions of memory and constructive imagination. According to Taylor (1871), onset of this stage was characterized by animism. In this context he presented a vivid account of primitive mentality. Primitive man, according to him, thinks of this world as a place of animated beings existing on this terrestrial sphere. They are either inimical or friendly to man. In the other natural forces, products and objects are either benevolent or malevolent. Rivers, clouds, mountains, trees, yielding, eatables, timber or firewood are considered benevolent, while snakes, carnivorous animals, poisonous plants are considered to be malevolent. Primitive man made a distinction between body and soul. The former being mortal and perishable, while soul is immortal and non-perishable. It is primitive mentality that a religion originates. All benevolent entities are worshipped for their blessings. On the other hand all malevolent ones are either to be avoided or to be approached and offered suitable sacrifices. Gradually such religious practices give rise to different kinds of theologies.

All theologies are rooted in tenacious faith, rituals and rites which are prescribed and promoted by priests and clergymen, *pundits, purohits, imams* and mosque keepers, *rabbi* for whom their work is vocation providing means of decent livelihood. In theology there is little scope for dissent. Dissenters are ostracized and often tortured. Theological principles along with prescribed rites and rituals are shaped by ecological conditions of the territory in which a particular religion thrives. In all theological theories and assumptions of omnipotent and omnipresent god is conceptualized and accepted as supreme power that controls the universe and rules over the destiny of human beings.

Metaphysical Stage

As there is increase in cerebral activities, thinking capacity and reasoning power by virtue of biological evolution, some individuals find contradictions in untenable assumptions in the theologies concerned. Such individuals raise voice against the controlling power of the guardians of theology; they propound their self-created theory of life, time, space, identity, nature etc. Thus newer philosophies are created with diverse kind of principles and precepts, some woven in theism and others in atheism. It must be noted that all types of metaphysics are rooted in *a priori* reasoning and thinking. As the quantum of metaphysical thinking increases theological practices undergo drastic changes. In each religion diverse types of sects and sectarian programmes are launched. History provides authentic evidence to prove that well educated individuals, developed in prevailing system of education endeavour to bring about changes in the style of life for the masses. Some of those entrenched in certain metaphysical ways of life do not feel fully satisfied and become restless for more dependable understanding of life on earth. This kind of restlessness paves the way for moving toward the positivist or scientific way of understanding and knowing.

The Positive or Scientific Stage

This is the final stage of human evolution. This stage is rooted in the empirical methods. During this stage social reconstruction is affected through emancipation of mankind from *a priori* reasoning based bondage of metaphysics in favour of the practice of direct and objective experience of natural phenomena. So acquired insights are available for experience to the public. Scientifically tempered persons neither accept nor reject any statement about natural entities. They put a question mark against it. If and when their interest is aroused they examine such statements on the touchstone of objective or controlled observations. In this stage quite often efforts are made to identify and define specific antecedent conditions and note down their consequent outcomes. This is done to discover the laws and principles of natural features. Scientifically oriented researchers assume that Nature functions according to specific laws. If these laws are correctly understood, they not only explain but also lead to their control and predictions. However, this positive stage is in its infancy and it is still to go a long way in order to understand numerous mysteries of Nature.

It is important to note that there is no clear-cut transition from one stage to another. At present all the three stages exist simultaneously all over the world even though they originate in a sequence. It is so because human evolution depends on ones genetically endowed intellective ability, environmental enrichment or impoverishment, and upbringing including education. All over the world there are communities and social groups, which are still living, in the theological stage. Lots of communities educated in traditional school and having spiritual interests are in metaphysical stages and are following saints, swamis and scholars of scriptures. A fairly sizeable number of individuals have entered into the scientific stage.

Origin and Solutions of Social Problems

Before an effective intervention programme or remedial measures or social technique is developed, it is absolutely necessary to have scientific answers to three basic questions, i.e. (1) what are the salient features of social problems and specific behaviours that characterize the problem, (2) what is the level of human evolution of those who add to the problems and those who gets affected by it, and (3) what kind of upbringing, socialization the initiators and propitiators of the problem have as well as what kind of ambience they have. Answers of these questions are necessary requirement for developing an effective remedial technique.

With a view to finding reliable and valid answers to these questions so that an effective technique is developed is a stupendous task. It requires a long-term plan to be implemented by a team of social psychologists. Such plan should have several steps to be sequentially implemented. First the problem-afflicted segment of society must be identified and delimited. Second step should be identification of the initiators and perpetuators of the problem. Third step calls for development and standardization of effective testing techniques for ascertaining the relative contribution of environmental background including upbringing, schooling and areas of ambience, family history including ancestral antecedents, and level of psychological development. In the light of research findings reported so far it is reasonable to assume that the relative contribution of these factors would vary from problem to problem as well as from person to person in society.

How to determine the role of these factors is a complex task, and a single researcher, no matter how competent and hard working he is, it would not be possible for him to complete it in his lifetime. Such a task calls for a teamwork. Here, what is warranted is that various councils, commissions and organizations established by the central/state government should take interest and initiative. They should launch all India level seminars on specific problems and research projects. This task should be main theme of deliberations in the annual conferences of the professional organizations of psychologists, sociologists and anthropologists. The governments on their own cannot solve social problems by enacting laws and trying to implement them.

In this context the next but the most important task is concerned with development of effective remedial techniques for solving different types of social problems. Notwithstanding the fact that a number of psychologists and other social scientists have studied a variety of social problems in India, and have endeavoured to develop intervention programmes, no effective and acceptable social technique has been prescribed. In an article entitled, 'Is the study of society science?' Alan Ryan states that the most familiar implication of the absence of general laws on a par with natural science is that there is nothing one could properly call social technology.

Whatever techniques are available for social engineering are not properly utilized. A fairly large segment of Indian society is against the use of such technologies because it is considered to be violation of the freedom of choice. It is argued that to treat other people's behaviours, beliefs and practices as objects for technical manipulation would amount to transgression on God's domain, and violation of the democratic principle of the freedom of choice. However, what is valued as freedom of choice is nothing more than leaving every improvement to random and ill-understood programming by the environment. Now the relevant question is : would it not be better that programming is made rational, controlled and effortfully aimed at maximizing mental peace, social harmony and happiness. At present what is needed is that the social psychologists, sociologists, anthropologists and psychiatrists get together and concentrate on some selected social problem with interdisciplinary framework and discover the causal factors, and develop some effective techniques to solve that problem. Medical sciences have done so in the areas of prevention and betterment of physical health.

REFERENCES

Comple, August (1830-42). *Course de philosophies Positive* [System of Positive Polity] 6 vols., Paris: Bachelier.

Hirsch J. (1967). *Behaviour-Genetic Analysis* (ed), New York: McGraw-Hill.

Hull, C. L. (1943). *Principles of Behaviour.* New York: Appleton Century-Crofts.

Hull, C. L. (1951). *Essentials of Behaviour.* New Haven, C. T.: Yale University Press.

Hull, C. L. (1952). *A Bechaviour System.* New Haven, C. T. : Yale University Press.

Jensen, Arthur (1968). Biogenetic Perspective: Introduction in Martin Deutsch, Irwin Katz & Arthur & Jensen (eds) *Social Class, Race and Psychological Development.*

Kety, S. (1970). Genetic Environmental Interaction in the Schizophrenic Syndrome. In R. Concro (ed) *The Schizophrenic Reaction,* New York : Brunner-Mazel.

Mowrer, C. H. (1947). On the dual nature of learning: A re-interpretation of conditioning and problem solving: *Harvard Educational Review,* 17, 102-148.

Murphy, Gardner; Kovach; Joseph K. (1972). *Historical Introduction to Modern Psychology* (Sixth edition) p. 366. London Routledge & Kegan Paul Ltd., Broadway House, 68-74 Carter Lane. E. C. 4.

Pandey, J.; Sinha. D.; & Dhawuk, D. P. S. (eds) *Asian Contribution to Cross-Cultural Psychology,* New Delhi: Sage Publications.

Seagull, Marshal; Lonner J.; & Berry J. W. (1998). Cross-Cultural Psychology: A flowering discipline. *American Psychologists.* Vol. 55, No. 10, 1101-10.

Skinner B. F. (1938). *The Bechaviour of Organisms.* New York: Macmillan.

Taylor, E. B. (1871). *Primitive Culture.* London, Murray.

Times of India (Lucknow Edition) Code of Behaviour. June 11, 2005, page 9.

Watson, J. B. (1926). Experimental Studies on the Growth of Emotions. In C. Murchison (Ed), *Psychologies of 1925,* Worcester, M.A. Clark, University Press.

2 Psychology and the Challenges of Social Problems and Issues

R.C. Mishra

Psychology today has sophisticated methods, enormous data, excellent models and fanciful theories that help us to understand, predict and explain behaviour both at the micro and macro levels. However, the responsibility for dealing with social problems of human beings is largely attributed to social psychologists. They have widely studied how people perceive and evaluate individuals, how they form and change attitudes, how they develop attractions, repulsions, co-operations, competitions, prejudice and tolerance, how they resolve conflicts in family, society or work place, and how they react to and deal with environmental and health problems. While some of these problems have been studied mainly in laboratory settings, others have been examined in wider field settings.

Along with this understanding, we are also aware of research in other disciplines of science that has taken people on moon, provided cure for many dreadful diseases, and has produced technology, which makes today life easier and more comfortable than the one people experienced in previous decades. The question is: Does psychology also possess potential for similar contributions to the well-being of individuals or society? Do we have enough understanding of behaviour that can justify our interventions into people's life to help them solve their problems? We may ask many crucial questions like these for which we do not seem to have a clear answer.

Relevance of Psychology

It is not for the first time that we are asking the question about the use of psychology in solving social problems. This question has been asked in one way or another in virtually all meetings of psychologists no matter whether they were held in this country or elsewhere. Sometimes the question has been fairly explicit: sometimes it has been relatively implicit. Sometimes the voices were fairly strong; sometimes they were relatively weak. In spite of the experience of these bright and dark shades, we all seem to agree (may be to variable extents) that psychology carries enough potential for promoting human welfare.

In this context, one can be reminded of George Miller's (1969) presidential address to the American Psychological Association (APA). In that meeting he remarked, "I can imagine nothing that we could do that would be more relevant to human welfare, and nothing that could pose a greater challenge to the next generation of psychologists than to discover ways to give psychology allway." A few years before Miller's address, Prof. Durganand Sinha (1966) has made a similar remark in his presidential address to the Section of Psychology and Educational Sciences at the Indian Science Congress Association meeting. In that meeting he strongly urged upon psychologists to come out of their narrow grooves and work with real problems of people to make their subject socially relevant. A volume entitled, "Psychology in Human and Social Development: Lessons from Diverse Cultures" edited in honour of Professor Sinha (Berry, Mishra, & Tripathi, 2003) has brought together scholars from different parts of the world who have shown us the way in which psychology can contribute to the broader issues facing human and social development.

From these and other similar efforts one is likely to develop quite a positive impression of psychologists and also of psychology they do around the world. On the other hand, considerable debate and controversy exists on the issue of involvement of social psychologists in applied research, and more so about their involvement in social intervention. There are many who argue in favour of the pursuit of scientific knowledge just for the sake of knowledge. They believe that the pursuit of scientific knowledge is a good activity in its own right. Baumrin (1970) remarks, "...scientific knowledge is an absolute good apart from its consequences". On the contrary, those who feel more concerned with the application of knowledge believe that their science must study problems in order to work out acceptable solutions and determine consequences of various actions. If a science cannot do this, it is good for nothing. Arguments and activities have flourished between these two polar positions ever since psychology started taking a definite shape. More than two decades ago Carol (1982) pointed out this conflict particularly in social psychology when he indicated that"... social psychologists quite often wear two hats, one is that of the scientist who constructs theories based on empirical research, and the other is the hat of the behavioural engineer who uses this basic knowledge to solve practical problems outside the laboratory". This dilemma is evident even today.

In spite of many difficulties and threats to professional identity, relevance of psychological research has shown growing concern over decades among all those who view the progress of discipline through the eyes of application. The position is well described by Sants (1980) when he observes, "...it would be reasonable to assume that psychologists in their everyday life nourish within them, like everyone else, some concept of better world. Few of them, however have said very much about the consequences of their work for social policy. The present achievements of psychologists are not, however, entirely trivial or irrelevant. A great deal has already been discovered, although in the absence of generally acceptable unifying theories, no single psychologist is able to identify or present what is here to stay".

The Search for Relevance

The search for a better world seems to be one of the strong motivations underlying the search for the relevance of psychology. The nature of problems may vary across groups defined by social, cultural or national boundaries, but the goal is generally the same (i.e., the search for better). If we consider the work carried out in India, we will find a distinct orientation among psychologists towards the application of psychological knowledge at least during the last three decades. The Second Survey of Research in Psychology (Pareek, 1981) comprises ten major areas representing the work of psychologists during the 1970s that has direct bearing on the problems of the Indian society. These include: communication and rural social change, teacher behaviour, organizational development and change, student activism and protest, elections and voting behaviour, poverty, inequality, population and family planning, and dynamics of social change.

Studies relating to the real problems of our society have proliferated over the last two decades, so much so that in the third survey of research (Pandey, 1988) a full section has been devoted to researches in Applied Social Psychology. Pressing social problems of the nation, which include development and change, family planning and fertility behaviour, health behaviour, social disadvantage, poverty and deprivation have been in the main focus of these studies (Tripathi, 1988). Other applied areas such as environment, social justice, ethnic identities and relationships have been widely covered in volume 3 of the fourth survey of research in psychology (Pandey, 2004). This gives clear indication to us that psychology has been brought down to the level of Indian social reality, and today there is not as much of Western bias in our thinking and research as it happened to be in the earlier decades. It is also evident that the basic psychological principles of perception, attribution, reinforcement, and feedback may be brought into effective use in searching out solutions to most of these problems.

What Psychology and Psychologists can do

Larger social problems of the kind discussed above often require social programmes and some form of social intervention if their solutions are to be worked out. Looking at the nature of research carried out in psychology in general and social psychology in particular, one easily gets the impression that most of it has been at a basic level. It has largely put emphasis on the production of knowledge leaving its use to the natural processes of dissemination and application.

On the other hand, relatively limited research of applied kind generates the feeling that psychology can contribute to the solution of social problems at least in three ways:

(1) by documenting the problems that exist in our society,
(2) by evaluating the costs and gains of various social programmes aimed at solving people's problems, and
(3) by providing people with means for changing their world into a better world (i.e., developing and using intervention programmes).

In the following section we will examine these activities in some detail.

Documenting Social Problems

Documenting the problems that exist in our society has been (and currently constitutes) a fundamental contribution of psychologists. Initially these problems were sampled on the basis of observations and collection of opinions. In recent years, however, social indicators have been developed, which provide us not only with estimates of the severity of the current problems, but also often serve as most direct measures of human welfare. Statistics on child birth, longevity, incidence of diseases, access to medical care, literacy, educational problems of children in various social groups, job opportunities and limitations, acceptance of new technology, social crimes, and environmental and health hazards, etc., serve as indicators of the problems of our society. Precise knowledge of such problems including their causative factors and underlying dynamics is prerequisite to any attempt at their solution, and from this viewpoint, the pursuit of psychology appears to be relevant.

Evaluation of Social Programmes

Whether social scientists define or do not define a particular social problem and its magnitude, the solutions are often devised by politicians, bureaucratic machinery and many others who may be directly involved in the problem. Often the solutions are ridiculous, and are imposed upon people without involving them into the process (Mishra, Sinha & Berry, 1996). Several years ago Donald Campbell (1969) expressed his discontentment with this approach and argued that "...modern nations should be ready for an experimental approach to social reform, an approach in which we try out new programmes designed to cure specific social problems, in which we learn whether or not these programmes are effective, and in which we retain, imitate, modify or discard them on the basis of apparent effectiveness on the multiple imperfect criteria available".

Evaluation research, which Campbell advocated, has nowadays become an active field of social psychology. The purpose is to assess or evaluate the effect of a given social action or programme (Hornstone, 1974; Tripathi, 2003). While this purpose apparently appears to be simple, the process is fairly complicated because of the often hazy, ambiguous and hard to pin down nature of the goals set under the programmes (Tripathi, 2003). A social psychologist is capable of operationally defining and translating such goals into specific criteria and his methodological knowledge may be quite useful in properly designing evaluation studies. Unless we know how a social programme is working, we cannot begin to develop better means for the solution of problems facing any society.

Evaluation studies of the Integrated Rural Development Programme (IRDP), National Adult Education Programme (NAEP) and Mother-Child Health Programme (MCHP) provide us with a number of points to increase the effectiveness of such programmes (see Mishra & Vajpayee, 2000). For example, they suggest that integration of individuals with organization is a key factor in effective functioning of any programme (Prakash &

Mishra, 1987). To a large extent this can be ensured by achieving consistency between organizational and individual goals, but "how will that be possible" is a big question. Social psychology can contribute enough to exploring these possibilities.

Designing Intervention Strategies

To provide people with means for changing outcomes in a particular setting is the most difficult task that social psychologists have to accomplish. Some of the projects on health, education of the disadvantaged/deprived children, and social change have represented a beginning effort in this direction. They are helpful in identifying issues directly related to intervention in social problems.

Studies on various aspects of health (e.g., immunization, nutrition), family planning, child care, and community development have identified conditions (factors) that lead to success or failure of a given programme. Social psychologists have been using their tools to compare the efficacy of different approaches to the solution of specific problems (e.g., health, change, education and family planning), and in this process they are creating the basis for a new social technology (Tripathi, 2003). Summarizing the efforts of social psychologists in this direction several years ago Varela (1977, 1978) has observed, "...we already have most of the technology we need to solve an enormous range of problems, from personal miseries to organizational conflict, from the marriage bed to the conference table". He further argues, "...just as there are several methods for doing research, there are also variety of responses to the outcomes of research, and no single response or tactics can have an exclusive claim on the truth. Hence, social psychologists must continue to do research the way they have been doing, for such research will definitely add to our knowledge and form the basis for some future social technologies to handle the contemporary social problems".

With enormous problems of poverty, unemployment,

education, health, and social conflicts facing a large percentage of Indian population, all of us realize the need to forge immediate ameliorative measures and intervention programmes. In view of the support currently available from various international organizations, one can expect even greater involvement of researchers in intervention research. Two related goals in this context are: (a) development of proper intervention strategies, and (b) monitoring and evaluation of intervention programmes.

Problems with Intervention Programmes

Intervention research poses a number of complex methodological problems. Sinha and Mishra (1993) have discussed these problems in detail. The important ones are briefly described in the following pages.

Less Sophisticated Design

Psychological research emphasizes the control of variables so that the effect of experimental manipulations can be maximized. This is possible only if the situation permits the use of control groups. A serious limitation of intervention research is the non-availability of appropriate "control groups" for making comparisons. Hence, inferences about the effects of intervention become tenuous. Even when the "control groups" are constituted by selecting people who do not participate in the intervention programme, psychologists find it difficult to accept them as controls because of the diffusion of many of the effects of the programme in the community at large. In real life situations the manipulation of variables and exercise of controls, considered as ideal in scientific enterprise, are neither available nor feasible. Studies (e.g., Dubey *et al.*, 1987) indicate that even without participation in an intervention programme people tend to derive considerable benefits from the programme through other community members who participate in it. An intervention study, thus, cannot be cast in the mould of a neat experimental design.

Variable Outcomes

A related difficulty arises with regard to intervention programmes, which are organized on a nationwide scale. For example, we may consider the ICDS programme. The interventions under this programme made in different parts of the country, though essentially part of the same programme, are not identical. Their outcomes have shown considerable variations probably because of differences in the target groups, the personnel involved in implementing the programme and the actual content of the programmes themselves. Thus, one cannot be sure that the same intervention (manipulation) would produce comparable outcomes (effects) everywhere. This forms a naturalistic experiment and provides us with an opportunity to identify the specific conditions under which specific programmes will work.

Absence of Empirical-Theoretical Base

An important limitation of the large scale intervention programmes (e.g., the ICDS) is that they have not been designed on any particular theoretical or empirical base. Consequently, most of these programmes have been incapable of making specific predictions regarding the effect of interventions. A major reason for the 'negligence' of psychological research in designing intervention programmes is that our research is mostly concerned with micro-level analysis of behaviour and determination of variables of proximal (micro-level) environment influencing behaviour. Except for those studies in which ecological or eco-cultural perspectives have been adopted, macro-level environment and distal variables have been either ignored or not conceptualized systematically. Such variables have usually not been measured and their influences not analyzed. The analysis of this context can suggest the possibilities and also the levels of the system where intervention can be effectively applied.

Nature of Intervention

The schemes for intervention developed during the past decades may be broadly classified into two groups, namely structural and behavioural. While structural intervention requires changes in the basic structure of the society such as family, community, economic system and the school, representing a kind of long-term goal, behavioural intervention may be directly introduced into the lives of the concerned individuals, and may yield the desired outcomes even in a shorter time frame. Both types of interventions are currently in practice, although in psychological research greater emphasis seems to have been placed on behavioural interventions (Mishra & Vajpayee, 2000). However, the importance of the former is generally recognized, and relevant suggestions have been advanced in the context of education of socially disadvantaged children. For example, Chitnis (1979) has argued that 'structural changes' are necessary in the educational set-up to achieve educational goals set for them. Singh (1983) has advocated for the establishment of *ashram*-type schools for socially disadvantaged children in order to counteract the adverse effects of unfavourable conditions of their families. These proposals contain the belief that for success of any intervention programme, structural change is a necessary condition.

While these propositions exemplify ideal situations, their translation into objective reality appears to be difficult, because the process involves long-term planning, political will and commitment (Mishra, 1990) for bringing about socio-cultural changes. This is something on which psychologists can have no direct control. Hence, many of them have tried to search for alternative strategies, which are generally of a short-term nature. One such strategy is to provide people with specific experiences and training, which can produce desired changes in a short span of time within their existing socio-cultural conditions. Such intervention programmes have shown considerable improvement in behaviour of individuals. Short-term evaluations of their effects indicate remarkable gains in the domain of cognition (Mishra,

1990; Mishra & Vajpayee, 2000). These psychological gains can be predicted as lasting provided it is ensured that improvements in family setting and educational environment of the child are of an enduring nature.

The lesson of behavioural intervention programmes is that: (a) these strategies can be used on a very limited scale depending upon the resources available to researchers; (b) intervention periods are likely to be brief, as researchers may not have necessary support available for a longer period of time; (c) evaluation of intervention effects is likely to be of a short-term nature; and (d) the stability and the criterion validity of these effects cannot be guaranteed. Changes are required in research-funding policies for overcoming some of these difficulties.

Dilemma of Roles

Research aimed at application of findings and development of policies for improving conditions of people's life, also poses a dilemma for researchers in respect of their role as a scientist and that of an advocate of policies. On the one hand, there is the obligatory requirement of scientific objectivity. On the other hand, the researcher's involvement in the success of a programme policy seems to be of prime value. The roles of an objective researcher, interpreter and evaluator of results, and that of the social advocate of policy do not easily go together. The urgent need for the application of the findings and a commitment to the programme tend to create a socio-biological climate that is not conducive to the maintenance of objective detachment, an attitude of critical examination, scientific skepticism and openness to record negative results. Confronted with such a dilemma, the researcher has to exercise cautions in performing his roles. Real life situations often yield ambiguous results and are not conducive for yielding outcomes that are uncontaminated by negative pointers. Therefore, identifying the 'contaminating forces' and searching out the ways in which these could be eliminated from the situation appear to be the major tasks before researchers. Traditionally established techniques of experimental control are not likely to work, and the researcher has to show his innovativeness in evolving new techniques, which may also be acceptable to the target group.

A general problem associated with government sponsored programmes (e.g., the ICDS) is with regard to the time frame that is generally granted for evaluation purposes. There is considerable pressure, often quite implicit, on the researcher to produce quick results and document the effectiveness of the intervention. This time constraint does not permit the researcher to utilize the theoretical and methodological knowledge of his discipline in a satisfactory manner. Problems also arise if the researcher comes out with negative results which indicate serious limitations of the programmes. These limitations, instead of being taken as guidelines for improvement and modification in the programme, are generally considered as failure of the evaluation itself. Therefore, there exists a pressure on the researcher to provide positive outcomes and to tone down the negative findings. On the other hand, the wide publicity often given in the press to negative or even ambiguous outcomes of the intervention is likely to seriously threaten the continued support for an important social programme. The researcher is confronted with difficult alternatives of whether to report his findings in full with both negative and positive implications stated, or to reveal only with the brighter side of the picture. Since the funds for research and evaluation are arranged by the government or the private agencies engaged in implementing the programme, there is a tendency to provide with evidence only of the effectiveness of the programme. This tendency can be changed by accommodating scientific evaluation as an integral part of the programme so that through formative evaluation, there is a constant feedback for its modification and improvement.

Looking into Future

In the foregoing paragraphs we have examined what psychology and psychologists are capable of doing with respect to social problems. While there is hardly any doubt about the potentials of the discipline with regard tc handling social problems we face today, a serious effort is required in the direction of application of empirical knowledge for intervention into problems. However, as we move forward into the new century, we also apprehend quite a few more (and perhaps novel) problems, which we might confront. Hence, it is quite in place to do a bit of exercise in respect of the future that we are likely to face after a few years.

Astrology believes that all people seem to be concerned about future and that one plunges into future with one's past. Looking forward to what will come, and attempting to propose solution to those future challenges is known as *futuristics*. Cornish (1977) argues, "If anything is important, it is the future. The past is gone and the present exists only as a fleeting moment. Everything that we think and do from this moment one can affect only the future". If we look at future from this perspective, then preparation for future should constitute the most essential activity on our part at the present time.

Social scientists in general feel that the range of our problems is hardly going to change from what we confront today, yet there are indications for the experience of future shock (Toffler, 1970) or "culture shock" (Berry, 1990) produced by the currents of social and cultural changes. Such experiences are more likely to be encountered by people in developing nations particularly in response to the rapid process of modernization and acculturation going on there. Toffler pointed to a variety of experiences in today's world that might lead to the experience of future shock. Increased transience of people and products, novelty, greatly increased diversity in products, life style with over-choice, and a date deluge produced by high speed computers and genetic innovations are some of the prominent ones. Human beings may not be able to adapt to these changes so readily, and hence, they are likely to develop symptoms of confusion, anxiety, hostility, physical illness, senseless violence and self-destructive apathy. Such behavioural problems often appear when people try to negotiate life with new cultural systems (Berry, 1997). The situation may be dramatic in Third World nations where many of the traditional values and norms are still functional, but stand at the risk of being eroded or transformed radically.

Looking forward to people's life in the twenty-first century, members of the World Future Society predict that people from different countries will be more unified in a world community or global village (although worldwide conflicts rooted in some form of euthenist may present a paradox here), people will have a relatively higher standard of living and more leisure time, families will be less stable, and people will be more mobile and educated. Such predictions involve both risks and challenges, nevertheless, they may be helpful as far as they are able to clarify our goals and provide with alternative policies.

Where and how does psychology fit into the study of these problems? There are contrasting viewpoints on the issue. With respect to social psychology, Garden (1973) argues that it primarily reflects a kind of historical inquiry; it deals with "facts that are essentially non-repeatable and which fluctuate markedly overtime" and hence, it will never achieve the success of natural sciences in building a cumulative structure of knowledge. If we consider our discipline to be like this, then our conclusion is quite obvious. The principles of social behaviour developed today will be of little use in predicting and comprehending social behaviour in future. Many others also have not been happy with the progress of social psychology over the years. However, scholars like Schlenker (1974) and Berry (2003) have expressed faith in the application of the principles of social psychology. The argument is that although some of the facts (problems) may change over time, most of the problems and the processes determining them will generally remain invariant. As an instance we may consider the problem of unemployment. Some 500 years ago the great saint poet, Tulsidas, encountered the problem in the same way as we experience it in today's world. In the 97th verse of *Uttrakand* in his famous treatise *Kavitavali* he observed that "the farmers were not able to pursue agriculture, the beggars did not get easy alms, the businessmen did not have scope for business and those searching for employment did not happen to have it; having no means of livelihood and being ridden with anxieties and depressions, people were asking each other where do we go and what do we do"? To quote him :

> *"kheti na kissan ko bhikhari ko na bhikh, bali vanik ko vanij na chakar ko chakari jeevika vihin log seedyaman sochvas kahain ek ekan son kahan jaya ka kari"*

In spite of our best attempts to drive it away, we find that the problem is still with us, and in somewhat greater magnitude than before. If the basic problems are not going to change, if the historically provided social structure is not likely to be easily altered, then we may assume that many of our principles will be useful even in years to come.

Conclusion

Summarising his chapter on 'Applied Social Psychology', Tripathi (1988) observed "...though the number of research studies has gone up considerably, there has been dearth of systematic problem-focused studies" (p. 142). Pointing to a number of limitations of social psychological studies he further observed, "...If psychologists have not been able to come up with specific solutions, they have certainly generated enough data, which should force policy makers to examine the various assumptions they make in the formulation of public policy" (p. 143).

These statements provide us with the best assessment of our standing as psychologists. We have been able to identify and conceptualize our social problems, offer suggestions towards their solution in better ways, and evaluate the efficacy of various programmes that have already been at work. What we have not been able to do is the delivery of the fruits of our studies to the community either directly or indirectly through our collaboration with government or other agencies. The time ahead would demand not only a vigorous attempt towards designing intervention programmes, but also our direct involvement in the application of those programmes in the community at large. An early preparation in this direction will enhance our usefulness. Let us pledge that we will meet these challenges more effectively than ever.

REFERENCES

Baumrin, B. H. (1970). The immortality of irrelevance: The social role of science. In F. Korten, S. W. Cook & I. Lacey (eds.), *Psychology and the problems of society.* Washington : APA.

Berry, J.W. (1990). Psychology of acculturation : Individuals moving between cultures. In R. W. Brisline (Ed.) *Applied cross-cultural psychology*. Newbury Park: Sage.

Berry, J. W. (2003). *Experience of acculturation: The case of tribals and native peoples.* Personal Communication.

Berry, J. W.; Mishra, R. C.; & Tripathi, R.C. (2003). *Psychology in human and social development: Lessons from diverse cultures.* New Delhi: Sage.

Berry, J. W., & Sam, D. (1997). Acculturation and adaptation. In J. W. Berry,; M. H. Segall, & C., Kagitcibasi (eds.), *Handbook of cross-cultural psychology*, Vol. 3. Boston: Allyn & Bacon.

Campbell. D. T. (1969). Reforms as experiments. *American Psychologist*, 24, 409-429.

Carroll, J. S. (1982). What is this thing called "Applied Social Psychology", *Contemporary Psychology*, 27, 772-773.

Chitnis, S (1979). The education of the socially disadvantaged children. *Indian Journal of Social Work*, 40, 267-282.

Cornish, E. (1977). *The study of future: An introduction to the art and science of understanding and shaping tomorrow's world.* Washington, D. C.: World Future Society.

Dubey, V. K., Mishra, R. C.; & Pandey, K. N. (1987). Radio in support of women's empowerment for child survival, protection and development in India. *Interaction*, 5, 1-14.

Gergen, K. J. (1973). Social psychology as history. *Journal of Personality and Social Psychology*, 26, 309-320.

Hornstein, H. A. (1975). Social psychology as social intervention. In M. Deutsch & R. A. Hornstein (eds.), *Applying social psychology: Implications for research, practice and training.* Hilisdale, N. J. : Erlbaum.

Miller, G. (1969). Psychology as means of promoting human welfare. *American Psychologist*, 24, 1063-1075.

Mishra, R. C. (1990). Cognitive stimulation, training and perceptual–cognitive task performance by socially deprived children. *Indian Journal of Current Psychological Researches*, 5, 1-9.

Mishra, R. C.; Sinha, D.; & Berry, J. W. (1996). *Ecology, acculturation and psychological adaptation: A study of adivasis in Bihar.* New Delhi: Sage.

Mishra, R. C. & Vajpayee, A. (2000). Intervention for cognitive performance of disadvantaged children. In A. K. Mohanty & G. Misra (Eds.), *Psychology of poverty and disadvantage* (pp. 214-229). New Delhi: Concept.
Pandey, J. (1988). *Psyclology in India : The state of the art.* New Delhi : Sage.
Pandey. J. (2004). *Psychology in India revisited : Development in the discipline*, Vol. 3. New Delhi: Sage.
Pareek, U. (1981). *A survey of research in psychology, 1971-76.* Part II. Bombay: Popular.
Prakash, A., & Mishra, R. C. (1987). Integration of individual with organization : A study of Anganwari workers. *Interaction*, 5, 15-27.
Sants, I. (1980). Developmental psychology and society. In. I. Sants (ed.), *Developmental psychology and society.* London: Macmillan.
Schienker, B. R. (1974). Social psychology and science. *Journal of Personality and Social Psychology*, 29, 1-15.
Singh, A. K. (1983). Parental support and academic achievement. *Social Change*, 13, 9-14.
Sinha, D. (1966). *Psychologists in the arena of social change.* Presidential address, Section of Psychology and Educational Sciences, 3rd Indian Science Congress, Chandigarh.
Sinha, D. & Mishra, R. C. (1993). Some methodological issues related to research in developmental psychology in the context of policy and intervention programmes. In T. S. Saraswathi & B. Kaur (Eds). *Human development and family studies in India: An agenda for research and policy* (pp. 139-150). New Delhi: Sage.
Toffler, A. (1970). *Future shock.* New York: Random House.
Tripathi, R. C. (1988). Applied social psychology. In J. Pandey (ed.), *Psychology in India: The state of the art.* New Delhi: Sage.
Tripathi, R. C. (2003). Culture as a factor in community interventions. In J. W. Berry, R. C. Mishra, & R. C. Tripathi (eds.), *Psychology in human and social development: Lessons from diverse cultures* (pp. 235-259). New Delhi: Sage.
Varela, J. A. (1977). Social technology. *American Psychologist*, 32, 914-929.
Verela, J. A. (1978). Solving human problems with human science. *Human Nature*, 1, 84-90.

3 Organising Action
Citizenship, Identity and Culture

Nick Hopkins

Contemporary societies are complex. Within any national community there are any number of groups differing in status, and there has been increasing social scientific interest in people's needs for 'recognition', and the painful experiences of 'misrecognition' (Taylor, 1994). Indeed, as analysts have become increasingly aware of the social and psychological significance of such needs, the conceptual analysis of many taken-for-granted ideas on such issues as 'citizenship' has undergone immense change. Thus, rather than simply considering an individual's relationship with an overarching political body, researchers increasingly recognise "a more diffuse social-cultural form of citizenship" that is "wrapped up in questions of who is accepted as a worthy, valuable and responsible member of an everyday community of living and working" (Painter and Philo, 1995: 115). Of course, institutional arrangements still matter. However, more informal notions of citizenship have the capacity to shape many aspects of people's lives (e.g., the use of public space). For example, Painter and Philo

Note: The author would like to thank the organisers of the NAOP conference in Faizabad (2005) for their generous invitation to participate in this conference and for their kind welcome. The preparation of this paper was greatly facilitated by my participation in the Advanced Social Psychology Research Refresher Course jointly organized by the UGC Centre for Advanced Study, University of Allahabad and the University of Dundee, U.K. (held in Allahabad, March 7-21, 2005). Particular thanks are due to the British Council for funding, and to the course director, Prof. Janak Pandey.

observe that 'if citizenship is to mean anything in an everyday sense it should mean the ability of individuals to occupy public spaces in a manner that does not compromise their self-identity, let alone obstruct, threaten or even harm them more materially" (p. 115).

Associated with these developments is a growing interest in the diverse, everyday, contexts in which, as Purvis and Hunt (1999) put it, "alternative identities vie for instantiation in the political institutions and discourses of society" (p. 458). Such struggles have many features. Thus when Muslims seek to establish mosques in Australian, European, or North American cities they often find themselves involved in complex controversies (Dunn, 2001). When their opponents argue that such buildings would compromise the local environment's character they are typically talking about more than architectural aesthetics. So too, those behind the projects are rarely simply seeking to establish gathering places for prayer. Rather, both are involved in a struggle over the symbolic definition of space, place and belonging, and in their clashes they evoke and imply different conceptualisations of who belongs and on what terms (Isin and Siemiatycki, 2002).

Typically, such struggles have attracted the attention of political scientists and sociologists. However, the social psychological dimension to such struggles is crucial and demands attention. Whatever their disciplinary background, all those wishing to analyse how communities organise collective action to either advance or rebut claims to material/symbolic resources, must invoke psychological concepts, and psychologists are uniquely placed to contribute towards developing a theoretical framework adequate for the phenomena before us. Certainly, wherever one looks, it is hard to avoid issues of identity. Identity features in the practice of exclusion and marginalisation. For example, the major far-right party in the UK, the British National Party (BNP), recently sought to construe Muslims as an alien other who could never identify with Britain. More specifically, it instigated a 'campaign against Islam' with a document using the words 'Intolerance, Slaughter,

Looting, Arson, Molestation of women' printed vertically to quite literally spell out what the BNP believes ISLAM stands for (BNP, 2002). However, the concept of identity is not only apparent in the everyday vocabulary of political exclusion. It is also apparent in the claiming of rights and struggles for change and much social psychological work inspired by Tajfel and Turner (Tajfel, 1978, 1982; Tajfel and Turner, 1979) has explored the identity processes through which minorities may reclaim the power to define themselves and assert more positive self-definitions.

In this chapter the author develops an analysis of some of the processes that may be observed in a minority group's responses to marginalisation. Whilst the author focuses on one particular group (Muslims in Britain), the broad logic is applicable to groups in general, and makes three points. First, social identities are crucial in the organisation of action. Second, definitions of identity are constructed and contested. Third, such contestation requires social psychology to more fully engage with cultural and political processes.

Social Identity

Central to social psychological explorations of identity is the concept of social identity as theorised by Tajfel and Turner (1979). Initially this concept was elaborated to conceptualise the processes involved in inter-group relations and their transformation. However, the concept has been developed through its application to a larger range of phenomena (e.g., social influence, the determination of collective behaviour, etc.: see Turner, Hogg, Oakes, Reicher Wetherell, 1987; Turner, Oakes, Haslam and McGarty, 1994).

The concept is crucial to any analysis of intergroup relations because it allows the theorisation of how group behaviour is possible. At its heart is the idea that the behaviour of people as group members cannot be reduced to the properties of the individuals themselves. Rather, the theory argues that our social identity derives from our knowledge of our membership of social groups and the meaning that such memberships have for us. Indeed, in the more general theoretical statement of how social identity makes group behaviour possible (self-categorisation theory), Turner and his colleagues argue that group members' action is shaped by their cognitive representation of who they are in relation to others (Turner, *et al.*, 1987, 1994).

One implication of this tradition is to challenge the widespread assumption that intergroup tensions and conflicts are the by-product of deep-seated irrational forces. Rather, conflict is understood 'as an outcome of the social, psychological, and historical processes which have shaped people's collective understandings of themselves, their ingroups and outgroups, and their relationships with other groups. It is an outcome of the collective theories and ideologies which they have developed to make sense of, explain, and justify intergroup relationships' (Turner and Reynolds, 2001, pp.146-47). This approach draws our attention to group members' representations of the intergroup complex within which they are located, and important progress has been made in investigating these beliefs and their behavioural significance. For example, experimental research has explored how beliefs about the legitimacy and stability of the group hierarchy and the permeability of group boundaries, individually and in combination, encourage strategies of individual social mobility (in which group members attempt to leave their group and enter higher status groups), or collective action to raise the relative status of their group (see Ellemers, van Knippenberg, and Wilke, 1990; Ellemers, Wilke, and van Knippenberg, 1993).

Identity : Some Problematic Assumptions

The fact that the concept of identity features in both the practice of political exclusion, and in the social scientific analysis of intergroup phenomena, imposes a particularly heavy burden on psychology. Importantly, it means that throughout our analyses we must be aware of how lay assumptions about identity are used to organise exclusion, and, in turn, ensure that our own use of the concept as an analytic tool does not reproduce such problematic assumptions, but indeed, facilitates their critique. So what are these problematic assumptions, and how may awareness of these help us develop our thinking about social identity processes?

One of the key problems of much lay (and indeed, much academic) discourse is the tendency to think of identities in highly essentialised terms. Again, this is well illustrated through reference to the academic depiction of Muslim societies, whereas Said (1978, reprinted 1995) puts it, a 'heterogeneous, dynamic and complex human reality' is typically approached from 'an uncritically essentialist standpoint' (1995: p. 333). The ahistorical nature of this essentialism is highlighted by Abdel-Malek (1963, translated 1981) who observes that the traditional analysis of Muslim activity "is at once 'historical', since it reaches back into the depths of history, and fundamentally ahistorical, since it fixes the being, the 'object' of study, in its inalienable and non-evolutive specificity" (p. 77). Unfortunately, this tendency to view Muslim identity as fixed and unchanging is not limited to academic circles and essentialised constructions of Islam and Muslims abound.

Clearly, such characterisations are unacceptable. However, it is not simply that such constructions are organised to exclude. Such essentialised images of group identity are also woefully inadequate analytic tools and face enormous difficulty in the face of evidence concerning the historical and geographical variation in Muslims' understandings of their religious identity. Indeed, such is this variation that Al'Azmeh (1993, p. 1) argues that there are 'as many Islams as there are situations that sustain it'. Furthermore, analyses of the contextual contingency of Muslim identifications have emphasised the innovation and creativity apparent in Muslim communities, and authors such as Ahmed and Donnan (1994, p. 5) increasingly conceptualise Muslim identities in the West 'as local, as indigenous not as the other, the exotic or the Oriental'.

However, for all this emphasis upon local variation and the dynamic nature of identity development, the concept of 'identity' is still associated with a number of connotations and assumptions that limit our ability to theorise such developments (Brubaker and Cooper, 2002). And, if social psychology is to fulfil its potential in this field it is important that psychologists are explicit about how they conceptualise the dynamic and changing nature of a group's identity.

Social Scientific Approaches to Identity: Towards a Cognitive Level of Analysis

As has already been hinted, social scientific analyses increasingly question the idea that it is possible to speak of identities as objectively given 'things' that have an existence independent of human cognition and practice. As numerous authors observe, national and ethnic identities, although often seen in essentialised terms, do not exist apart from or beneath their social representation or the conditions of their own making (Macdonald, 1993). Following this logic, rather than taking national and ethnic identities as our basic units of analysis, there are good reasons to explore the mundane and everyday group-making practices that bring particular self-categories into being (and without which they would not exist). Indeed, viewed from this angle, group identities are not so much 'things *in* the world, but perspectives *on* the world' and exist in and through 'our perceptions, interpretations, representations, classifications, categorisations and identifications' (Brubaker, Loveman and Stamatov, 2004, p. 45 original emphasis). However, this should not be taken to imply that such constructions are unimportant or without consequence. To foreground the social practices that make it possible to think about oneself in terms of a particular group membership does not mean that such an identity is not psychologically real. Indeed, as countless social psychological experiments have demonstrated, people can and do invest (psychologically speaking) in even the most 'minimal' of groups (e.g., the groups employed in Tajfel's 'minimal group' studies where it was found that group behaviour can arise in the absence of interaction, personal friendship etc.: Tajfel, 1978, 1982).

Furthermore, the fact that group identities are actively produced through everyday social practice does not stop ordinary people talking and thinking of identity in much more essentialised terms. Indeed, as we will see, there are good reasons why ordinary people should conceive of their social identities in essentialised terms. The key point is that as analysts we should not slip into such ways of construing identities, but rather, should explore the social and psychological significance of such essentialising talk.

To conceptualise identities as being constructed may, at first sight, appear to invite an individualism and voluntarism in which identity is simply the product of a lone individual's imagination. However, conceiving of identities as 'perspectives *on* the world' (Brubaker *et al.*, 2004) is not necessarily individualistic. As Brubaker *et al.* argue, the domain of the 'mental' and the 'psychological' is not identical with the domain of the individual. Rather, collective identifications are social in that they are socially shared and a key task becomes the study of the social practices that support and sustain such socially shared self-conceptions. In turn it follows that an emphasis upon people's cognitive representation does not necessarily imply a retreat to a psychologism in which what goes on in people's heads is privileged over what goes on in the social context or in public. Rather, the promise of a cognitive approach to ethnicity is that it 'may help connect our analyses of what goes on in people's heads with our analysis of what goes on in public' (Brubaker *et al.*, p. 46). That is, our attention is drawn to the social practices that facilitate the adoption of particular self definitions.

Group Behaviour and the Organisation of Collective Action

With these observations in mind, the social identity tradition in European social psychology holds much promise. The theory offers a cognitive definition of the group (Turner, 1982) which means that group members' action is shaped by their cognitive representation of who they are in relation to others. Indeed, according to the theory (Turner, *et al.*, 1987, Turner *et al.*, 1994) people do not only have single, individual identities. Rather, the self may be defined at different levels of abstraction. Sometimes, it may be defined in terms of individual uniqueness. Yet, at other times, it may be defined in terms of a specific group membership. This psychological shift from personal to social identity underlies the behavioural shift from inter-individual to inter-group action. Specifically, when in-group identity is salient group members' behaviour conforms to the contents of the in-group stereotype.

The theory also recognises that our identities are fundamentally social products. Identification (at whatever degree of abstraction – whether in terms of our unique individuality or as members of a particular group) is socially determined. Furthermore, social identities are not to be construed as superficial: rather social and personal identities are, as Haslam puts it, "equally 'real' and just as much a reflection of a person's 'true' self" (2001: 46). As we may self-categorise in terms of a number of groups (e.g., as British, as Muslim, as female), it follows that our sense of who we are is variable, and contemporary theorising draws attention to the contextual factors that support and sustain the salience of different identities. It is also clear that the theory emphasises the social determination of self-definition. Whilst social identities are profoundly felt, they are fundamentally social, irreducible to any individual: what it means to be British or Indian, Hindu or Muslim, academic or lawyer, is a product of wider social and cultural processes.

The social identity tradition does not make any assumptions about which identities may be adopted or the behavioural consequences of adopting any identity. Rather the theory specifies a limited number of generic processes, and argues that the behavioural implications of such processes are dependent upon the norms and values associated with the relevant collective identity. For example, the theory argues that an important social identity process involves the making of inter-group comparisons and the establishment of the group's positive distinctiveness in relation to other group identities. Whereas some have interpreted this as implying that the social identity tradition assumes group members to be motivated to derogate others and indulge in acts of out-group discrimination, this is misleading (Reicher, 2004; Turner, 1999). Inter-group differentiation is a process and not a specific behaviour, and the behavioural outcome of this process depends upon the norms and values of the relevant identity. Or, to put it another way, the behavioural consequence of the process depends on social and cultural factors. Indeed, Turner argues that process theories such as social identity and self-categorization require the incorporation of specific content into their analyses before they can make predictions either in the laboratory or in the field and are designed to require such an incorporation' (Turner, 1999, p. 34). In turn this means that in order to explore how minorities respond to their marginalisation we need to explore the cultural content to their group identity.

However, from what has been said thus far it must be clear that the cultural content of any collective identity is itself a complex issue. As hinted at in the earlier discussion of Muslim identities, a group's culture is not fixed but contingent upon context, and we need to conceptualise culture in a way that facilitates our analysis of this dynamic and malleable quality. Holy (1996) makes just such a point in an analysis of social movements and political change in Eastern Europe, especially Czechoslovakia. As he puts it, Czech culture 'must be conceptualised not as timeless and unchangeable attributes of the Czech nation, as Czechs themselves conceptualise them, but as constructions perpetually recreated and modified in political practice. Moreover, rather than as a harmonious, singular, and coherent ideational system, they must be seen as a system of competing values and concepts which are internally inconsistent and ultimately irreconcilable' (Holy, 1996: 201).

Reicher and Hopkins (2001) argue that one particularly helpful approach is to view culture in terms of a 'reserve' (Reszler, 1992) of symbols and meanings to be appropriated and deployed in the activity of identity definition. The advantage of such an alternative is that our attention is necessarily drawn to the issue of human agency and to how the meanings of cultural products undergo constant reconstruction in everyday interactions and routines. Central to this reconceptualisation is an emphasis upon argument and contestation: the nature of a group's culture is always contested, and even those elements of a group's culture that everybody knows and invokes as revealing something about the group's identity, are typically interpreted in many different ways (Hopkins and Reicher, 2005; Reicher and Hopkins, 2001 a, b).

At first sight the degree of contestation to be found around collective identities might be construed as revealing these identities' lack of substance, and this may lead some to question their psychological significance. However, it is also possible to interpret the degree of contestation surrounding such identities as actually testifying to these identities' social and psychological significance. People's understandings of how they could (and should) act is contingent upon their identity, and it is because of such behavioural consequences that controversies over the characterisation of identity are worth entering into, and so exist. In other words, it is precisely because collective identity definitions matter for behaviour that group stereotypes are so contested, with those seeking to organise different forms of collective action constructing group identity differently.

This emphasis upon practice and the strategic organisation of collective action is important. First, it invites us to rethink the concept of identity. Rather than conceiving of identities as 'things' with a determinate existence, much may be gained through viewing identities as 'projects' to be realised in the future. That is, what people say about their identities may usefully be viewed as having a performative and constitutive dimension, and as being organised to encourage the forms of action that would realise the proposed construction (Reicher, 2004; Reicher and Hopkins, 2001 a, b). Or to put it another way, identity may be usefully conceptualised as the basis for mobilizing people to act so as to bring into being future social realities. Second, it is for this reason that the active contestation of culture is so ubiquitous and demands serious investigation. As group members have different visions of the future that they wish to realise, and seek to organise different forms of collective action, it follows that quite contrasting constructions of group culture are to be expected as group members seek to represent their particular project as truly exemplifying and expressing group values. Third, and as a corollary, the reality of construction and contestation helps to explain why essentialising talk should be so apparent in ordinary people's constructions of their group identities. As we will see, it is not only non-Muslims who attribute a timeless fixity to Muslim identity, in-group members may also do the same as they seek to ground their construction of identity over alternative constructions offered by their in-group rivals. Indeed, unless the constructed nature of collective identity is obscured, and identity definitions given a semblance of transhistorical fixity and substance, it is unlikely that they will motivate group members' psychological investment and form a basis for mobilising collective sentiment and action. From this vantage point, just as racist exclusion and murder are dependent on 'collective objectifications' so too may claim for citizenship rights and multiculturalist agenda (Werbner 1997, p. 229). However, there are important differences between the essentialist rhetoric involved in exclusion (such as that evinced in the BNP's propaganda referred to above) and in-group members' own attempts to ground and warrant their own constructions. As Hopkins, Reicher and Kahani-Hopkins (2003) explain, whereas the former is organised to deny minority group members' agency, the latter evidences it.

Culture, Contestation and Action

So as to illustrate the ways in which culture is contested in the organisation of collective action, some examples arising from recent studies of how Muslims in Britain have oriented to their marginalisation and exclusion, can be discussed. Muslim identity in Britain is complex. Some retain identifications with diverse Indian, Pakistani and South Asian traditions. Yet many (especially those born and brought up in Britain) have questioned the relevance of traditions associated with their families' countries of origin (construing them as 'cultural' rather than 'genuinely' Islamic) (Lewis, 1994). In turn, many have engaged with the question of what it means to be a Muslim in Britain. An important feature of this engagement has been the establishment and growth of a number of Muslim organizations seeking to represent the interests of all Muslims in Britain. So too there has been the growth of an indigenous national British Muslim media articulating British Muslims' concern. Yet, if these organizational developments stand as testimony to the development of a distinctively British Muslim public sphere in which Muslims' interests are deliberated, these same organizations and media stand as testimony to the contested nature of this collective identification (Hopkins and Kahani-Hopkins, 2004 a, b). Simplifying enormously, it is possible to characterise some Muslim activists as encouraging British Muslims to participate in British social and political institutions (e.g., joining Britain's political parties, voting in elections etc.), and others as arguing that Muslims should express their political views through developing alternative institutional arrangements that would better allow them to realise their potential and contribute to British society. These controversies are part of a much wider debate about how Muslim identity could be secured public recognition.

Let us now consider how activists advancing different visions of how Britain's Muslims may secure a greater presence in the public sphere seek to recruit group members' support through constructing divergent constructions of Muslim identity. In particular let us examine the strategic invocation of key Islamic concepts and principles (including the principles derived from Prophetic example).

(i) Da'wah

Consider first the diverse constructions of the concept of *da'wah*. According to Denny (1987) *da'wah* refers to 'a religious outreach or mission to exhort people to embrace Islam as the true religion'

(p. 244) and Walker (1995) observes that its *Qur'anic* meanings extend 'to encompass concepts of summoning, calling on, appealing to, invocation, prayer (for and against something or someone), propaganda, missionary activity, and finally, legal proceedings and claims' (p. 343). In early non-*Qur'anic* usage, there seems to be two particularly important themes. On the one hand, there is a religious usage that refers to the invitation addressed to humanity by God and the Prophets to believe in true religion. On the other, in a politico-religious context it refers to a process of mission or propaganda (Canard, 1965). In more recent years *da'wah* has taken on complex political connotations and been construed so as to propagate Islamic unity. From what has been said earlier, it should be clear that whilst such definitions have a certain utility they are limited. It is only when terms and concepts are analysed in the context of their usage that they take on richer and more nuanced meanings with diverse strategic implications (Kahani-Hopkins and Hopkins, 2002), and it is to these that we now turn.

(i.a) Da'wah: Engagement with British Society

For some the concept of *da'wah* is invoked in order to encourage Muslims to become actively involved in addressing Britain's social ills. Speaking at a public meeting for students, one activist first spoke of the need for such an involvement in general terms :

> There is a need for creating a movement for creating a revival of Islam. Not just an Islam that is stuck in the text books, that you can see it if you study hard enough, but an Islam that is open in the market place, an Islam that can be seen by everybody, there is a need for people taking an interest, there is a need for [Muslim] students to be the first to stand and protest against student loans, there is a need for Muslims cleaning out the environment against drug dealing, against

> prostitution and so on, there is a need for Muslims to take care of the deprived in society, the elderly, the weak, the rejected, the poor. If we do not fulfil that obligation, we do not deserve the name Muslim, we do not deserve to be part of such a great enterprise.[1]

This argument was then developed and cemented through the invocation of the concept of *da'wah*. Specifically, Muslims' active participation in addressing Britain's social problems (including participation in political elections) was construed as:

> A perfect propagandistic opportunity of doing *da'wah*: inviting those who worry about the country's future direction to the truth and the sensible programmes stemming from it. Our proposed solutions were, and still are, radical for both the host society and the Muslims within it. We do not content ourselves with a superficial, cultural Islam, halal meat and turbans. Muslims need to be at the forefront of change.[2]

Thus the 'call to Islam' – a duty incumbent upon all Muslims– demanded practical engagement with the realities of Muslim and non-Muslim Britain. It was through such practical engagement that respect for Islam would develop and spread: 'respect for Islam would be an automatic result once the solutions Islam had to offer proved to be beneficial for all'[3]. Indeed, this group was highly critical of other approaches to *da'wah* that concentrated on the missionary activity. Real *da'wah* entailed 'talking to the ordinary man and woman in the country' and this 'meant talking their language (...) concentrating on issues which were considered of importance by them. It meant the exact opposite of academic missionary activity'. It meant dealing 'exclusively with practicalities and experiences which are common to any member of society, irrespective of his religious belonging'[4].

(i.b) Da'wah: Community Development

By way of contrast consider an alternative construction of *da'wah* propagated by a group that encouraged Britain's Muslims to develop their own independent political organisations. Rather than addressing themselves to the common problems faced by all (regardless of religious identification), Muslims were encouraged to develop an independent political consciousness and organisational structure before seeking to play a more active role in wider society. Central to this argument was the idea that Muslims' social and economic marginality meant that involvement in conventional British political institutions would compromise their Islamic identity. In turn it was argued that if the call to Islam was to be at all meaningful, Muslims needed to have a clear sense of Islam's own essence and the concept of *da'wah* was, therefore, construed in such a way as to require Britain's Muslims to focus on (Muslim) community development. Take, for example, the following:

> the absence of a living and dynamic model of an Islamic civilization makes *da'wah* very difficult. When you invite someone to your house, you vacuum clean the carpet, you put things right and make your house look attractive. Unless you put your own house in order, how can you invite somebody to it? (...) the first step in *da'wah* is to establish Islam as a working model of a civilization, of a system, and, therefore, we must use our stay in this country not to convert this country to Islam, but to establish Islam in the house of Islam. And once it is established there, then you will be able to establish Islam everywhere. That is *da'wah*. So, if we mobilize our resources in this country in order to support an Islamic movement overseas, ultimately this is *da'wah* in the non-Muslim world.[5]

Here, rather than *da'wah*, the overarching duty of Muslims, being invoked to encourage participation alongside non-Muslim Britons in addressing British social ills, it is invoked to encourage solidarity with non-British Muslims overseas to develop a distinctive Islamic political consciousness.

Thus far it is sought to substantiate the argument that the political meaning of Islamic concepts (and hence the nature of Muslim identity) is not a 'given' but is inevitably shaped by the political projects and strategic concerns of those who invoke them. As we have seen both sets of activists characterize *da'wah* in ways that challenge British Muslims to become politically active. Indeed, both characterized British Muslims as preoccupied with abstract ritual rather than concrete action. However, although sharing this condemnation of Muslims' failure to move beyond the ritualistic, these groups' characterizations of *da'wah* were strikingly different and shaped so as to advance their respective projects (Kahani-Hopkins and Hopkins, 2002).

(ii) Prophetic Example

Support for different forms of collective action was also mobilized through divergent constructions of the actions of Muslim prophets when Muslims lived as social and political minorities before the foundation of the First Islamic State in Madinah. The most important referred to when Muhammad and his companions lived as a minority in Makkah (where they were outnumbered by a non-Muslim tribe called the *Quraysh*), or when Muhammad sent some of his followers from Makkah to Christian Abyssinia for safety.[6] However, other examples referred to other Prophets (e.g., Yusuf) living in non-Muslim environments (in this case, in Egypt). In the examples below one can consider how Prophetic example was invoked in the context of a debate as to whether Britain's Muslims should vote in a UK General Election.

(ii.a) The Prophets and the Call for Britain's Muslims to Vote

One activist called for Britain's Muslims to participate fully in the election arguing that:

> we have a duty to work for the general welfare and interests of people as a whole and not just of Muslims. As citizens of Britain, our duty is the same as our duty as Muslims. To perform that duty it follows that we are not and cannot be a ghetto community. We are and must be an outwards looking community. We need to interact with people – people of different faith and no faith.[7]

For my present purposes what makes this characterization interesting is the way in which it was developed through a particular construction of the examples of both Prophet Yusuf and Muhammad. The piece continued:

> We derive this understanding of duty from what our Prophets were required to do and did. The story of the Prophet Yusuf (upon whom be peace) is told in great detail in the Qur'an. He was sold into slavery and ended up in the court of the Pharaoh where he was subjected to various trials, including seduction and imprisonment. He maintained his integrity and when famine and drought threatened the people, he took charge of the most important office in the pagan Pharaoh's government. He did not wait for the ruler and people to renounce their paganism before acting. He moved swiftly and served the people, fulfilling their essential needs and rescuing them from starvation. He did not remain aloof. We look also to similar examples in the life of the Prophet Muhammad (peace be upon him) (...) When the Prophet arrived in predominantly non-Muslim Yathrib [another name for Medina] after the *hijrah* [migration from Makkah], his first instruction to his companions was to spread the greeting of peace and attend to the welfare of the people.[8]

The significance of these Prophetic examples was emphasised when the author asked 'What has this to do with Muslims voting for candidates in general or local elections in Britain'? and concluded that it implied a duty to ensure the election of candidates with 'a genuine concern for the human condition and for equitable dealing'. Indeed, he continued, Muslims 'should not opt out of the political life of the country and voluntarily give up their social and political rights. Neither should they surrender their duty to make their opinions and advice known on matters that concern themselves and the wider society'.

In similar vein another activist argued:

> Islam exists to serve mankind, with or without an Islamic State. In Makkah, countless verses were revealed on feeding the poor and freeing slaves. These were not necessarily Muslims, they were humans. (...) There are numerous Islamic examples of Muslim involvement in non-Muslim governments. The most beautiful is that of Prophet Yusuf. It is worth noting that this young man who was imprisoned and mistreated, seized the moment when it was right and expressed readiness to take charge of the most important office in the Pharaoh's government, believing it was his duty to rescue many nations threatened by famine and drought. He did not wait for the Egyptian people to renounce paganism and embrace his Unitarian religion so as to form the foundation for an Islamic government. What that young man had in mind was the fact that religion had come to serve the people and fulfil their essential needs. Yusuf had the conviction that rescuing the people could not wait. He saw that he was able to help, and he did help.[9]

Again, the key point is that this identity definition is strategically constructed to organise a particular form of collective action, and this strategic aspect of identity definition extends to a key dimension of Muslim culture – Prophetic example.

(ii. b) The Prophets and the Call for Britain's Muslims Not to Vote

Just as some urged Muslims to vote through construing Prophetic example (and hence Muslim identity) as demanding such action, so those calling upon Britain's Muslims to boycott the election did the same. Thus one portrayed the invitation to vote as an attempt to subvert Muslim identity and drew parallels with the invitations of the non-Muslim *Quraysh* in Makkah at the time of Muhammad. For example, it was argued that: 'just as modern day politicians attempt to undermine our Islamic identity with half-baked promises to secure our vote (...) the *Quraysh* even went so far as to offer Muhammad considerable wealth'[10], and, just as Muhammad rejected such invitations, so too must contemporary Muslims. This call for an election boycott was further grounded through reference to Muslim experiences in Abyssinia. The same activist continued:

> There is a direct analogy with our situation here in Britain concerning participation in a struggle for power in a non-Islamic land. This occurred when some Muslims sought asylum from the oppression of the *Quraysh* in Abyssinia who were ruled over by the Negus. The Abyssinians revolted against Negus due to his leniency to the Muslims and challenged his rule. Ja'far bin Abi Talib, who led the migrants, and his companions did not interfere in any way in this power struggle. They could have easily put their voice (their vote) with the Negus which would have been of obvious benefit to them. Instead, they remained silent on this issue as was indicated by the Prophet. They stayed in Abyssinia without participating in local power struggles until the Islamic state was declared in Madinah and they then migrated to it. The clear message here is that such affairs like voting in elections do not concern us and whatever apparent benefit may be perceived by doing so is irrelevant to the correct way for change.[11]

In similar vein, another, urging action that would allow the creation of an independent Muslim political organisation called upon British Muslims to reject UK party and parliamentary processes in these terms:

> When becoming politically active, in a secular environment, we must follow a method in accordance with the Qur'an and Sunnah, not the political parties. You cannot be loyal to the Labour party and God at the same time. You cannot become integrated into an ungodly and unjust political system, and at the same time serve God and bring justice. There is a very simple principle in Islam, 'no man can serve two masters'. This is exactly what was meant when the Prophet (peace be upon Him) rejected the offer of the Quraysh to make him head of their order in Makkah. This does not mean that Muslims cannot live under an unIslamic system. The Prophet clearly did so in Makkah and accepted the protection of certain tribes, for a time. He and his companions lived and organised as a distinct community with their own identity and pursued their own agenda. They would interact with Makkan society, but never integrate into it.[12]

Here again, the Prophet's aiding of non-Muslims in Makkah and the example of Prophet Yusuf are construed so as to define Muslim identity in very different ways from those considered earlier. Whereas the former called upon Muslims to achieve a particular presence in the public sphere through full participation in British institutions, the latter called upon Muslims to achieve a very different presence through institutional and ideological autonomy. Yet again, the point is that the meaning of Muslim identity is constructed in the context of contemporary debates about Muslims' action. Common cultural resources are interpreted strategically to promote quite divergent forms of action.

Conclusions

The wider implication of this emphasis upon the contemporary construction of identity should be readily apparent. At a time when Muslims are increasingly construed in homogenising and essentialising terms it is important to observe that our data illustrate the point that far from group members simply 'acting out' a given identity there is contestation about the nature of group identity. In terms of social psychological theory, this underscores the point that identities are constructed and contested. It would be a mistake to assume that such controversies signal the absence of a sense of community. Indeed, unless the idea of community is potent, it is hard to see why people should devote so much energy to arguing about their commonality. The logic to self-categorisation theory emphasises this point. According to the theory, social self-categorisations motivate an expectation of agreement with in-group members and encourage an active striving to reach agreement on identity-related issues. That is, there is a process of consensualisation. However, this does not rule out dissension. Rather, an empirical reality of dissension and argument can co-exist alongside the dynamic of consensualisation. Indeed, the idea of commonality encourages dispute as to the nature of that commonality (Reicher and Hopkins, 2001).

The coexistence of a multiplicity of versions of Muslim identity alongside the idea of a singular Muslim identity illustrates the importance of viewing identity definition as controversial. Furthermore, it should be clear why such controversies are worth entering into (and therefore exist). According to self-categorisation theory, group members act in terms of their group identity through conforming to the ingroup stereotype and it, therefore, follows that those seeking to build support for any form of collective action may do so through advancing strategically organized identity constructions (Reicher and Hopkins, 2001). Even the most important concepts within a community's cultural reserve are open to interpretations that imply quite different forms of action. This is well illustrated in Tudor's (1972) analysis of the stories and narratives that communities tell about themselves. For Tudor, the key point is that such cultural products cannot be analysed so as to capture the real (singular) essence to a community's culture. Indeed, Tudor argues that their meaning and significance is only to be found when they are actively invoked and that their meanings are always shaped by the (varied) practical action that is being promoted. It could also be added that those aspects of a group's culture that are widely recognised as being important (and as revealing something about the group's identity) are particularly likely to attract alternative interpretations for they are the most potent cultural resources with which to ground and essentialise identity constructions.

Social psychology's neglect of culture and the cultural determination of behaviour has attracted considerable criticism from those working outside the limited confines of North America and Europe and has prompted many calls for the indigenisation of psychology (Sinha, 1997, 1998). Certainly the discipline's poor theorisation of culture (see Misra and Gergen, 2002) limits the applicability of much social psychological theory to India. However, the discipline's failure to take culture seriously has impeded social psychological research across the globe. Wherever we are located we need a theoretical vocabulary that demands attention to culture, and the concept of social identity has much to offer in this regard. Indeed, despite the well-founded concern about the culture-bound nature of social psychological theorising, I believe that the concept of social identity has an analytic utility beyond the (European) cultural context within which it was produced. As a model of social psychological processes, it requires the incorporation of content before specific behavioural outcomes can be specified, and this requires that social psychological research (whether conducted in Britain, or India, or anywhere else) pays due regard to the cultural content of group identities. Furthermore, if social psychology is to succeed in developing a culturally sensitive social psychology we need to move beyond the misleading assumption that cultures are internally coherent, fixed givens that exist above and beyond ordinary people's everyday activities, and the broad logic to the theory actually helps sensitise us to the practical (action-oriented) contestation of culture. Indeed, once we recognise that identity is a basis for mobilizing and organising action, it follows that any group's culture will always attract contestation and that it is through the dynamic of dispute that a group's cultural reserve is developed, transformed and re-vitalised (Hopkins and Reicher, 2005).

NOTES

1. Speech, given by General Secretary of the Islamic Party of Britain (IPB), Newcastle University, 24th February 1997.
2. IPB Newsletter: 'Elections and money', *Common Sense,* issue no. 20, 1997, p. 7.
3. IPB Newsletter: 'Islam taking root in Europe', *Common Sense,* issue no. 8, 1992, p. 10-11.
4. *Ibid.*
5. Siddiqui, K. (1996) *In Pursuit of the Power of Islam: Major Writing of Kalim Siddiqui* (Compiled and edited by Z. Bangash), London: The Open Press, p.125.
6. Siddiqui, K. (1996) *Stages of Islamic Revolution,* London: The Open Press, p.111.
7. 'Why you should exercise your vote,' *Q-News,* no. 255-259, 14th March, 1997: p. 26.
8. *Ibid.*
9. 'The 1997 Elections and the British Muslims,' *Trends* 7, no. 3 (1997): pp. 23-25.
10. 'Voting in non-Islamic election: a sinful diversion,' *The Muslim News,* no. 94, 28th February 1997: p. 5.
11. *Ibid.*
12. 'And why you should not' — a reply to 'Why you should exercise your vote,' *Q News,* no. 255-259, 14th March 1997: p. 27.

REFERENCES

Abdel-Malek, A. (1963). 'L'Orientalisme en crise', *Diogene,* Vol. 44 (winter): 109-142. Reprinted in translation as 'Orientalism in crisis', in A. Abdel-Malek (1981) *Civilisations and Social Theory: Volume 1 of Social Dialectics,* (pp. 73-96). London: Macmillan.

Ahmed, A. and Donnan, H. (1994). 'Islam in the age of Postmodernity'. In A. S. Ahmed and H. Donnan (eds.). *Islam Globalisation and Postmodernity,* London: Routledge.

Al-Azmeh, A. (1993). *Islams and Modernities,* London: Verso.

BNP (2002). *The Truth About Islam,* www.bnp.org.uk

Brubaker, R., and Cooper, F. (2000). Beyond 'identity'. *Theory and Society,* 29, 1-47.

Brubaker, R.; Loveman, M.; and Stamatov, P. (2004). Ethnicity as cognition. *Theory and Society,* 33, 31-64.

Canard, M. (1965). 'Da'wah', in Bernard Lewis, C. Pellant and J. Schacht (eds), *The Encyclopedia of Islam,* Volume II, Leiden: E.J. Brill, London: Luzac.

Denny, F. (1987). 'Da'wah', in Mircea Eliade (ed), *The Encyclopedia of Religion,* Volume IV, New York: Macmillan.

Dunn, K.M. (2001). Representations of Islam in the politics of mosque development in Sydney. *Tijdschrift voor Economische en Social Geographie,* 92, 3, 291-308.

Ellemers, N.; van Knippenberg, A.; and Wilke, H. (1990). The influence of permeability of group boundaries and stability of group status on strategies of individual mobility and social change, *British Journal of Social Psychology, 29,* 233-246.

Ellemers, N.; Wilke, H; and van Knippenberg, A. (1993). Effects of the legitimacy of low group or individual status on individual and collective identity enhancement strategies, *Journal of Personality and Social Psychology, 64,* 766-778.

Haslam, S.A. (2001). *Psychology in Organizations: The Social Identity Approach,* London: Sage.

Holy, L. (1996) *The Little Czech and the Great Czech nation: National Identity and the Post-Communist Transformation of Society.* Cambridge: Cambridge University Press.

Hopkins, N. & Kahani-Hopkins, V. (2004 a). The antecedents of identification: A rhetorical analysis of British Muslim activists, *British Journal of Social Psychology, 43,* 41-57.

Hopkins, N. &. Kahani-Hopkins, V. (2004 b). Identity construction and political activity: Beyond rational actor theory. *British Journal of Social Psychology, 43,* 339-356.

Hopkins, N. & Reicher, S. (2005) Culture, social identity and the organisation of collective action: developing a culturally sensitive social psychology. *Psychological Studies, 50,* 217-225.

Hopkins, N.; Reicher, S.; and Kahani-Hopkins, V. (2003). Citizenship, participation and identity construction: Political mobilization amongst British Muslims. *Psychologica Belgica,* 43, 33-54.

Isin, E.F. and Siemiatycki, M. (2002). Making space for mosques: Struggles for urban citizenship in immigrant Toronto. In S. Razack (Ed.) *Race, Space and the Law: Unmapping a White Settler Society.* (pp. 185-210). Toronto: Between the Lines Press.

Kahani-Hopkins, V. and Hopkins, N. (2002). 'Representing' British Muslims: The strategic dimension of identity construction. *Ethnic and Racial Studies*, 25, 288-309.

Lewis, P. (1994). *Islamic Britain: Religion, Politics and Identity among British Muslim*. London: I.B.Tauris.

Macdonald, S. (1993). Identity complexes in Western Europe: Some anthropological perspectives. In S. Macdonald (ed.) *Inside European Identities: Ethnography in Western Europe*. (pp. 1-26). Providence/Oxford: Berg.

Misra, G. and Gergen, K. (2002). On the place of culture in psychological science. In A.K. Dalal and G. Misra (Eds.) *New Directions in Indian Psychology, Vol. 1, Social Psychology*. New Delhi: Sage.

Painter, J. and Philo, C. (1995). Spaces of citizenship: an introduction. *Political Geography, 14,* 107-120.

Purvis, T. and Hunt, A. (1999). Identity versus citizenship: Transformations in the discourses and practices of citizenship, *Social and Legal Studies, 8* (4), 457-482

Reicher, S. (2004). The context of social identity: Domination, resistance and change. *Political Psychology, 25,* 921-945.

Reicher, S. and Hopkins, N. (2001a). *Self and Nation*, London: Sage.

Reicher, S. & Hopkins, N. (2001b). Psychology and the end of history: A critique and a proposal for the psychology of social Categorisation. *Political Psychology, 22,* 383-407.

Reszler, (1992). L'Europe a la recherche de ses symbols. *Les Temps Modernes, 550,* 209-220.

Said, E. W. (1978, reprinted 1995). *Orientalism: Western conceptions of the Orient*. New York: Penguin.

Sinha, D. (1997). Indigenizing psychology. In J.W. Berry, Y.H. Poortinga and J. Pandey (Eds.) *Handbook of cross-cultural psychology,* Vol. 1. (pp. 129-169). Boston: Allyn and Bacon.

Sinha, D. (1998). Changing perspectives in social psychology in India: A journey towards indigenisation. *Asian Journal of Social Psychology, 1,* 17-31.

Tudor, H. (1972). *Political Myth*. London: Pall Mall.

Tajfel, H. (ed.) (1978). *Differentiation Between Social Groups: Studies in the Social Psychology of Intergroup Relations*. London: Academic Press.

Tajfel, H. (ed.) (1982). *Social Identity and Intergroup Relations*. Cambridge: Cambridge University Press and Paris: Maison des Sciences de L'Homme.

Tajfel, H. & Turner, J.C. (1979). An integrative theory of intergroup conflict. In W.G. Austin & S. Worchel (eds.) *The Social Psychology of Intergroup Relations*. (pp. 33-47). Monterey, CA: Brooks Cole.

Taylor, C. (1994) The politics of recognition, in A. Guttman (ed.) *Multiculturalism: Examining the politics of recognition* (pp. 25-74). Princeton, N.J.: Princeton University Press.

Turner, J.C. (1982). Towards a cognitive redefinition of the social group. In Tajfel H. (ed.) *Social Identity and intergroup relations.* (pp. 15-40). Cambridge: Cambridge University Press.

Turner, J.C. (1999). Some current issues in research on social identity and self-categorisation theories. In N. Ellemers, R. Spears & B. Doosje (eds.) *Social Identity: Context, Commitment, Content* (pp. 6-34). Oxford: Blackwell.

Turner, J.C. and Reynolds, K.J. (2001). The social identity perspective in intergroup relations: Theories, themes, controversies. *Blackwell Handbook of Social Psychology: Intergroup Processes* (pp. 133-152). Oxford: Blackwell.

Turner, J.C.; Hogg, M.A.; Oakes, P.J.; Reicher, S.; and Wetherell, M. (1987). *Rediscovering the Social Group: A Self-Categorisation Theory.* Oxford: Blackwell.

Turner, J.C.; Oakes, P.J.; Haslam, S.A.; and McGarty, C. (1994). Self and Collective: Cognition and Social Context. *Personality and Social Psychology Bulletin, 20,* 454-63.

Walker, P. (1987). 'Da'wah', in John Esposito (ed), *The Oxford Encyclopedia of the Modern Islamic World,* Oxford: Oxford University Press.

Werbner P. (1997). Essentialising essentialism, essentialising silence: Ambivalence and multiplicity in the constructions of racism and ethnicity, in P. Werbner and T. Modood (eds.) *Debating Cultural Hybridity: Multi-cultural identities and the politics of anti-racism* (pp. 226-254). London: Zed.

4 Hindu Social Identities and Imagined Past

The Faceoff between Ram Temple and "Martyred" Mosque at Ayodhya

R.C. Tripathi

This article attempts to understand social identities in flux and in different context. It assumes that like multiple "selves" there are also multiple "social identities" which emerge and fade into background largely on the basis of social contexts. Most social situations are equivocal requiring sense-making. They are attributed meanings based on one's own lived experiences which serve as cues for the emergence of social identity of a kind. We assume unlike some, that persons may differ with respect to elements they choose to construct their identities with but once the core gets constructed, it is retained over a period of time. Our contention is that social situations determine the salience of elements, and the manner in which they combine to form social identity. Thus, traditional *vs* progressive, conservative *vs.* liberal may be false dichotomies. I have come across my liberal/Marxist Hindu and Muslim friends taking "communal/fundamentalist" positions during the 1990-92 period when the dispute relating to the Babri Masjid in Ayodhya had reached its vortex. We were taking out peace marches to keep the temperatures down only to find these "liberal/Marxists" staying away from these marches. It only goes to prove that secularists of today may turn out to be zealots of tomorrow. Then, I have seen my own *"Agnihotra"* (one who performed *Yajna* everyday) Brahman Father, a great believer in cleanliness/purity, coming out with a broom in hand cleaning toilets of his neighbours without the slightest qualm. An Idol worshipper, he went on to become a pure

"*Vendantin*" (believer in formless supreme being) in his later life. There have been occasions, when I had to evaluate my own reactions to other's position, on Hindu-Muslim relations and ask myself whether my own reactions came from the threat I saw being posed to my "Hindu" identity by others who constructed theirs in contradistinction to it. I continue to locate myself somewhere on a liberal humanist Hindu continuum who believes in the contextualization of social sciences and Convergence of social theory and social action. What kind of a Hindu identity do I have? But I too need to wait.

This article joins the discourse on "communalism" and its various shades in understanding the Ramjanma Bhumi tangle at Ayodhya. No where else in India's recent history, the past has surfaced so vividly as the present which potentially threatens the future of India's multi-culturalism or its '*Ganga-Jamuni Tehzeeb*'. I shall present data collected in the context of the recent "Sankalp Rally" held at Ayodhya organized by the Vishwa Hindu Parishad (VHPs) on October 17, 2004.

Historical Context

Vishwa Hindu Parishad's (VHP) "Sankalp Rally" was organized to put pressure on the Government to start building the Ram temple at the birth place of Lord Rama where stood until December 6, 1992 a mosque constructed by Meer Baqi, a noble in the Court of the first Mughal Emperor, Babar. The mosque was popularly known as Babri Masjid. This dispute between Hindus and Muslims has remained unresolved for many centuries. Hindus claim that at the site of the mosque stood an ancient Ram Temple built by King Vikramaditya which was pulled down in 1528. A mosque was built in its place by Mir Baqi. Hindus must have laid claims to it soon after, as Nandy, Trivedi, Mayaram and Yagnik (1995) point out, William Finch, who was one of the first foreign visitors to the place found that Hindu worship was possible within the mosque between 1608-1611. It is not known whether there were any idols inside the mosque or where within its precincts, the *puja* was performed. There are numerous instances of peaceful coexistence of Hindu-Muslim worshippers at Ayodhya facilitating each other in offering prayers, providing services at the religious places, Muslims tending to the temples and Hindus to the mosques. This continued to a very large extent till the Babri Masjid was finally pulled down, or as Muslims would put it "became a *shaheed* or martyr" on December 6, 1992.

It is unclear when the differences between the Hindus and Muslims over the Mosque took the shape of a "dispute". Initially the disputes was over property, i.e., who owned that particular piece of land. There was no religious angle involved. There was no acrimony between the Hindus and Muslims of Ayodhya. The Civil suit arose around 1950. In fact, when we visited Ayodhya, a few months before the demolition took place, we were informed that both the petitioner and defender of the legal suit would travel in the same car to Allahabad to plead their cases before the High Court. They had the best of personal relationships. The "dispute" over the temple/mosque began soon after the 1857 mutiny, in the 1880s: some allege that it was one of many instances of British's divide and rule policy. Through this, the British succeeded in creating a division between the Hindus and Muslims and sowing a seed of suspicion. Nothing seems to have happened over the next 50 years or so until 1936, when it is said that Hindus attacked it but little damage was done to the structure. The Muslims, stopped offering *Namaz* at the mosque. When that happened is not known. On November 22, 1949, approximately, two years after India had attained independence the idol of God Ram as a child suddenly appeared in the mosque, allegedly with the connivance of authorities. The Courts did not permit any prayers/worship to take place within the mosque. It was around this time that a political party called Ram Rajya Party and Vishwa Hindu Parishad emerged. Ram Rajya Party was a party which promised to restore glory of India which obtained at the time of Ram. Another party to come on the scene was Bhartiya Jan Sangh, the precursor of the present Bhartiya Janta Party (BJP). These parties took up the cudgels on behalf of Ram Lala (Child Ram) who they said had remained behind bars due to the Nehruvian secularists and due to their policy of Muslim appeasement. But Ram Temple or Ayodhya was never a political or election issue for almost 40 years after Independence.

Ironically, it was when Nehru's grand-son, Rajiv Gandhi was Prime Minister in 1986, the Court ordered that the doors of the Mosque be opened for the worship by the Hindus of Ram Lala. The Government did not go in for appeal. In 1989, adjacent to the mosque, unable to resist the pressure of the VHP, the Congress government allowed for the foundation to be laid for the construction of a Ram Temple. This then started a full-fledged *political* movement for the construction of Ram Janma Bhumi Temple at Ayodhya and emergence of various political formations for the mobilisation of the Hindus. Political analysts believe that by getting the doors of the mosque opened for the worship of Ram Lala, Rajiv was trying to garner Hindu votes, after he had burnt his hands by not accepting the order of the Supreme Court relating to personal law of Muslims in *Shahbano's Case.* In hindsight, Rajiv's gamble may have backfired on him, because the Hindu Nationalist party, BJP was quick to size upon this opportunity to mobilize its Hindu Vote bank with the help of VHP and its associates. The Congress led by Rajiv Gandhi promised during the 1989 elections to usher in "*Ramrajya*" (governance like that of Lord Ram) if elected. But how could he, asked Hindus. He was born to a Parsee father and married to a Christian and educated in England. The BJP had won only two seats in the 1984 elections. It shot up to 88 in 1989 and 117 in 1991 [after the *'Shilanyas'* (foundation laying) of the temple had taken place]. The BJP gained power in a number of States in 1991 for the first time. The Babri Masjid was demolished on December 6, 1992, when the Congress Government was at the Centre and BJP had its government in UP.

The event saw large scale reactions both within and outside India. Large-scale riots broke out. Buildings were bombed in Bombay. In Bangladesh, 300 Hindu temples were destroyed according to one news report. Since then, the demand for the construction of Ram temple at the site of Babri Mosque has been continuously raised which is stoutly opposed by various bodies of Muslims. The matter of demolition of the Mosque is being investigated by a National Commission. Other legal issues relating to various matters lie in various courts of the country. Attempts to resolve the issue through dialogue have remained largely unsuccessful, neither party yielding an inch of ground. Both parties are willing to accept the decision of the Courts but reserve their right to revise their views. Hindu leaders argue that it is an issue related to *'Astha'* (strong religious belief). Therefore, it cannot be decided by the Courts. Muslims argue that the whole matter relates to the title of land. To decide the issue, the High Court at Lucknow recently asked the Archaeological Survey of India (ASI) to excavate the Mosque site to determine whether any temple existed at the site prior to the building of the mosque. The ASI's report according to the newspapers, found the existence of some structure, which is disputed by the Muslims, which could have been a temple. This gave the VHP, BJP and their supporters a shot in the arm. Although, the Courts still have to give their final judgment, pressure has been mounted on the Government to permit the VHP to start construction, at least on the land, which is undisputed. It also wants the Government to bring in a legislation to facilitate construction of a temple, and put pressure on the Muslims to concede the title of the land to the Hindus. The Sankalp Rally was organized by the VHP and its militant wing "Bajrang Dal" as a show of strength and to put pressure on the Government to allow construction of the Ram Temple. Prior to the rally, VHP organizers, particularly, its General Secretary, Praveen Togadia, had gone around the country addressing large gatherings of Hindus, and organizing *"Trishul* (Trident) *Deeksha* (Training) *Karyakram* (Programme)". VHP had hoped that almost 1 million Hindus will come to Ayodhya in U.P. on October 17, 2004. About 2 months back the change of Government took place and Mr. Mulayam Singh Yadav became the Chief Minister of U.P. He was also the CM in 1990 when the VHP had organized the first "*karsewa*" in which a large number of "*Karsewaks*" had died in police firing. A similar situation was brewing. However, there were some major differences this time. Fewer people showed up than did in 1990 and 1992. The town I live in, Allahabad did not turn Saffron with buntings and head gears of the *Bhaktas* this time. The Central Government at Delhi, unlike last time, was headed by a BJP leader, Mr. Atal Bihari Vajpayee. The CM of U.P., this time was remarkably low on rhetoric and was not eager this time that the blood of the rallyist should 'flow in the drains and streets of Ayodhya' or that they should be "taught a lesson". Instead, explicit instructions were given to the police, not to get provoked or fire at the crowds under any circumstance. This time, because of the orders of the Central Government, the trains were not allowed to enter Ayodhya from any direction and were forced to change routes to avoid pilgrims coming to Ayodhya. Massive checking of the trains and buses was done to prevent pilgrims and people from reaching Ayodhya. Pilgrims were detrained at various places and stopped from travelling to Ayodhya and to its surrounding towns like Allahabad, the town, where this study was conducted. At Allahabad, a large number of the rallyists were arrested while alighting from the trains and buses and taken to "temporary jails" (25 local schools had been converted into prisons). Those not arrested came to VHP camps where they stayed and were taken care of by the VHP organizers. Allahabad is on the trunk route, a large number of rallyists had to pass through Allahabad. It is a major centre of Hindu pilgrimage. One does not know the exact number of rallyists who came to Allahabad. As usual, the figures reported in the media were at great variance with the figures put out by the organisers. Our guess would be that there were close to 35 to 40 thousand "Ram Bhakt" who were detained at Allahabad and stayed in prisons or camps. Approximately 15 thousand Bhaktas were lodged in the Temporary Jails. The rallyists did not resist arrests and the event passed off rather peacefully at Ayodhya and in other places with skirmishes here and there. A "Sankalp Rally" did take place in which rallyists who were able to reach Ayodhya participated but only on the next day, i.e., on October 18, 2004. Speeches were made and threats issued by the VHP leaders to the Governments of Delhi and Lucknow. The arrested rallyists were agitated but not too much, although, the arrangements at the schools where they were confined left much to be desired. The total period of confinement for the rallyists varied from one to four days. The rallyists had generally come from far off States like Karnataka, Andhra Pradesh, Orissa, West Bengal, Assam, Maharashtra, Konkan (Goa), Gujarat, Himachal Pradesh, Chhattisgarh, Rajasthan, Madhya Pradesh, Jharkhand, Sikkim, etc. Surprisingly, not many came from the neighbouring States of U.P., like from Bihar, Delhi, Punjab, Haryana and from U.P. itself.

Social Identity and Collective Memories

The concern with the issue of identity goes back to the very beginning of the civilization both in the eastern and western traditions. Identity forms the central question in the *Upanishadic* tradition as well as in the Greek tradition. "Know thyself" is found engraved on the front piece of the temple of Delphi. Indeed, it is so in most religious traditions. Man was called a social animal a long time back but concern with "know thy social self", perhaps, is a recent phenomenon. We are not suggesting that construction of social identity did not occur then but the epistemic concern may be of recent origin. In the ancient Indian tradition one comes across terms like *"Kul"*, *"Kutumb"*, *"Vansh"*, *"Gotra"*, *"Varna"*, "Jati", "*Parivar*" and *"Parampara"* and many other similar terms to suggest that an individual could use several kinds of social categories to define self and others. Even today, most caste Hindus, besides their caste would know their *"Gotra"* and marriage within the same *"gotra"* is considered incestuous. The contemporary discourse on Social Identity owes much to sociologists like Durkheim (1898) and Mead (1934) besides psychologists like William James (1890) and to the psychoanalysts. Modern Social Identity theory in Psychology owes much to the work of Henri Tajfel (1982) who argued that the psychological process of categorization was at the root of construction of social identity. Social identity implies an individual perceiving similarity with others in his/her group at the cognitive and affective planes while differentiating himself/herself from others in other groups. It is in the combination of similarity seen in own group and differences with other group members, that social identity emerges. An individual's social identity makes him/her see that she/he belongs to a group of people who are like him/her on important dimensions. She/he evaluates them positively and feels attracted towards them as opposed to the group of individuals, who he/she sees as different and not particularly in favourable light. According to Tajfel, development of a positive social identity is a function of the degree of favourableness attached to one's membership group (own group) which is achieved in contradistinction to the group which serves as a basis for comparison (out group).

Psychologists, like Marrisa Zavalloni (1973), have proposed a multilayered concept of Social Identity. Turner (1987) who was a student of Tajfel, too proposes three levels of social identification. At the supra order level one distinguishes oneself from other living beings as a human being; at the intermediate level as member of a particular group one distinguishes oneself from other groups and thirdly, at a subordinate level one seeks to establish differences between self and other members of one's own group which results in personal identity. Although, such comparisons made are unique to the individual and the three types of identities make conceptual sense, in reality, we suggest that there is a continuous interplay among these, such that one kind of identity feeds on the other two and *vice versa*. The relationship in which they stand to each other, their configuration at any juncture is more important than their independent existence. This we feel is important to understand because very often our understanding of social identity does not admit to the possibility of many social identities. Thus, when one talks of Hindu and Muslim identities, one takes them as uniform and homogeneous and does not admit to their various shades. Such constructions eventually become part of social representations and, therefore, end up influencing the nature of social interactions of groups and communities. Not only such shades are not admitted, few serious attempts have been made in post-independent India to develop understanding of multi-cultural identity. Attempts have been made to understand social identities that have developed only around caste, religion, regions and ethnic groups. It is because of inequitable distribution of scarce economic and social resources, the feelings of inequality have increased resulting in the perception of group differentiation and a movement towards uniform and rigid group identities. This is more so because members of certain groups cannot go out of their groups to become member of another group. This condition inevitably gives rise to myths, falsehoods and stereotypes relating to own and other groups and also its members. To give an example, one salient dimension of comparison used by Hindus to differentiate themselves from Muslims is on the grounds of their "not eating meat". However, more Hindus in India eat meat than there are vegetarians. The myth persists that because most Hindus are vegetarians that they are opposed to Cow slaughter. A number of studies have shown that other groups are seen as more homogeneous and treated as such compared to one's own group which is seen as heterogeneous. But, groups seeking solidarity may engage in some typical behaviours. For example, Worchel (1998) points out that groups which are seeking to re-establish their identity and raise the level of membership awareness may make impossible demand of the other group in order to prove that the other group is evil and unfair. He points out that groups for example, may demand for the return of land or other resources that were taken away from them at an earlier period in history. This is how it is happening at Ayodhya or for that matter in Jerusalem. The use of past memories for construction of social identities is a well recognised social practice.

However, memory is not mere recollection of the past. It is anchored in the present because of the use it is put to. It should also be noted that just as there is a functional aspect of memory, there is also a structural part of it. Memories related to episodes are subject to distortions which occur because distortions take place at the stages of encoding, storage and retrieval. The memory content that is retrieved is reconstructive because it is guided by the pre-existing schemas that a person may have developed based on his/her previous experiences. Interesting psychological experiments by Bartlett (1932) have shown that reconstructive retrieval is subject to loss of details (levelling), preconceived notions (assimilation), and embellishment of facts (sharpening) to make it into a good story. Episodes involving social groups get processed on the basis of social schemas which may contain attitudinal structures about groups and also their patterns of interaction.

Collective memory as Bar-Tal (2002) points out is common past of the group which is shared by group members for the purposes of self-characterization and, therefore, is often biased in the direction of own group enhancement. Collective memory is functional in the formation and maintenance of social identity as well as in social mobilization. It contributes in the development of social schemas of conflicts which enable unequivocal and quick understanding of conflicts in the light of past history. Bar-Tal points out that there are four themes which influence how a social conflict will be understood and managed. These are (i) conflict is justified because it threatens the very existence of the group; (ii) it gives an opportunity for self-glorification; (iii) leads to delegitimization of the opponent group; and (iv) presents own group as a victim of the opponent.

To the extent collective memories are reconstructed, they are false memories. Some interesting studies have been done by Loftus and her associates on how they come to be created. Garry, Manning, Loftus and Sherman (1996) used a 3-stage procedure to create false memories. In stage I, subjects were given a list of 40 events which could have occurred when the subject was a child and was asked how probable it was that the event actually took place. In the second stage, after 2 weeks, the same subjects were asked to imagine that the event had actually taken place. They were asked to engage in the visualization of the event and asked to write about it. The Experimenter then put questions based on the details they had provided. In the final stage, again after 2 weeks the subjects were called back in which they were asked to recall the events again (E pretended, S/he had lost the responses given in the II stage). Subjects who engaged in visualization reported that an incident, which they had said was unlikely to have taken place in their childhood, actually had taken place. The experiment showed how imagining an event actually leads to "imagination inflation" (a person comes to believe that a "non-event" had actually occurred). Another study by Goff and Roediger (1998) showed that the more often one "imagines" that an event had occurred, the greater was the confidence in reporting that the incident had actually happened. Most collective memories come to be acquired based on imagining and are subject to "imagination inflation".

Collective Memories are built around strong norms of the groups which have been violated by the other group. They spur anticipatory reaction when a similar situation recurs. Every time, a Ganesh or Tazia procession is taken out, the respective groups in India in certain regions fear trouble.

To the extent memories are rooted in material culture, groups make use of memories for making comparisons of their present state with other groups. The resulting feelings may be of contentment or resentment, of gratification or deprivation. In either case, memory is used for building a justification for entitlement for the group; which is governed by the values of the present. It is then that the question of entitlement gets raised and social identities come into play. Political use of the past cannot be made if justifications cannot be advanced for entitlement. However, different groups in different societies may not be able to use the past in the same manner. Groups in countries like U.S. and Australia formed with the help of migrants may use pasts differently than in countries like China, India, Egypt and Greece with hoary pasts. Even within a country/society, different groups may use different time frames in recalling episodes. The history of Muslims in India is only a few centuries old compared to Hindus. It is not expected that the two groups will use the same periods for making recalls.

Social identities are a function of the manner in which the memories of present intersect with the memories of its past. Different groups may not use different time frames, the events of past used by them may change as a function of the situation, yielding different intersections used for identity formation. In this sense, making and unmaking of social identities is a continuous process.

Historical constructions of the past serve the purpose of providing justification for the competitive and sometimes conflictual relationship with other groups in society. There are at least two ways in which past can be used. The group can argue that it had a glorious past and was in an advantageous position compared to the other groups in society but has been unjustly denied possession of *X* (goods, status, power, etc.) or it never was allowed to possess *X* in the first place because of the unfair social structure. It is left to the groups to decide the time frame they want to use for purposes of comparison. Muslims while comparing themselves to Hindus may go back to the times of Mughals when they possessed everything, power and pelf, which they deserved, but now have nothing in comparison to Hindus. The Hindus, on the contrary, may use a time frame which goes back much farther when there were no Muslims and everything belonged to them. Among the Hindus, the Dalit identity is based on unfair denial of *X* (goods, status and power) which they deserved like any other group by the Manuvadi social structure. It would appear that social comparisons which yield feelings of relative deprivation or advantage at a particular time may be necessary for the development of social identity. There are studies which suggest that affect plays an important role in memory. The affect laden information is likely to be retained more than would be neutral information. Affect also acts as a filter so as to selectively choose information which is consistent with its nature. In view of this, what kind of collective memories will be recalled by Hindus and used for the construction of their social identity, *vis-a-vis* Muslims, may depend on the affect generated by a social situation and the cognitive cues which get released in the process and the cognitive frame which is used for meaning making. Emergence of some cognitive frames located in time, however, is more probable. In case of Hindus two cognitive frames, are more probable when they compare themselves with Muslims. First, relating to the days of 'Wonder that was India', and the second, when they became slaves in their own country as a result of the invasion of the Muslim rulers and later due to the colonization by the British. Hindu nationalists' identity seem to have developed as a result of meaning they have been able to make of such experience and of course of the experiences leading to the country's Independence and Partition of the country. Similarly, in case of Muslims, the cognitive frames chosen for sense making may vary. Even when they choose the same frames or events as chosen by Hindus, they may give them a different meaning. Partition has different meanings for Hindus of India, for Hindu and Sikh refugees who came to India after partition, then it has for the Muslims who stayed back when many of their kith and kins were migrating to Pakistan.

It will perhaps, not be right to explain the rise of Hindu Nationalism on the basis of Social identities which have roots in the politics and memory of the past alone. Probably one needs to reflect on the success or failure of the project of building of the Indian nation as a modern, secular, socialist and democratic republic guided by the British model of electoral democracy. It will also be pertinent to look at it in the context of rise in nationalism and ultra nationalism in the last few decades and particularly post September 11 and in the context of those famous words 'those who are not with us are against us.' The so called "soft states"' in the developing world, which harbour many nationalities hope to survive by creating one nationality through secular means but more often by harnessing religious identities than other kinds of social identities. After Iran and Afghanistan, it appears that nations with fractionated identities will have to make new efforts at creating a national identity by reinterpreting their pasts. It is another matter that this very process may result in their disintegration as the effort is likely to support rise of sub-nationalisms.

Just as the rise of caste identities today poses a threat to Hindu Social Identity, creating a national identity based on religious identity may inevitably lead to emergence of other regional and religious identities which may find accommodation identities within a national identity created on the basis of one religion. It appears to us that effort of the Hindu Political Parties and their sympathisers emanates from a belief that a strong national identity can be constructed on the basis of group beliefs of Hindus. They have sought to do it in contradistinction to Islam/Muslims in regions where they are numerically more in number, and to Christians, where they are the biggest minority. This has led to the development of different social identities of Hindus, which often come into contestations. This happens because groups use different pasts.

The Study

The study reported here was carried out to understand whether any differences will be seen in the social identities of the participants of the "Sankalp Rally" (October 15-16, 2004) and the still young non-politicised Hindus. Further what elements of the past are used in the construction of social identities and how by the two groups. Also how the nation of Ram Rajya (governance as per Ram) is constructed. Data collected from two settings based on a structured Interview Schedule are presented here. These settings were:

(a) *Temporary prisons*: Where the rallyists had been confined by the police, permission of the district authorities was obtained. Interviews took place only after the purpose of the study was explained to the respondent and the consent obtained. A total of 31 interviews were conducted here. These rallyists represented among themselves 11 States. However, a large number of them were from Assam, Maharashtra and Chhattisgarh.

(b) *University* : Data from Undergraduate students was collected on October 16. This was a day on which the rallyists had already congregated in town and the whole

> town was abuse with their presence. A total of 52 students participated in the study.

Data were also collected from rallyists who were staying in the VHP camps. These data have not been used here.

The structured schedule had largely open ended questions. The main questions sought to ask the respondents to answer questions like:

> (1) Who is a Hindu? (2) Who is an Indian? (3) Who is a Ram Bhakt? (4) What will Ram Rajya be like, if it were to happen? (5) Models used in personal life from: (a) the ancient times; (b) the modern times; (6) The contemporary leaders liked most and least; (7) Historical event from which lessons have been learned; (8) Historical events for which Hindus/Muslims cannot be forgiven; (9) Good and bad qualities of Muslims and Hindus; (10) Felt relative deprivation compared to Muslims; and (11) Desire to be reborn as what?

The data for the group of rallyists confined in Temporary Jails are compared with data gathered from the University students in order to understand how politically mobilised differ with respect to relatively politically neutral or uninitiated on the above questions.

We will turn to the responses to these questions in the next section. It will be more appropriate to describe the atmosphere which the city of Allahabad was experiencing during this period. We first visited the "Ram Bhakt Sewa Kendra" at the Royal Hotel. Approximately 3 thousand Ram Bhakts had collected there. Most of them had come from Maharashtra, Andhra Pradesh, Sikkim, Himachal Pradesh, and Chhattisgarh. We arrived to find a place, which though bustling with people, was well organized. The Bhakts were listening *bhajans* (religious songs), some of which had political overtones. The place was covered with banners which carried slogans. Some of these were:

"Awadhpuri ko jayenge
Mandir bhavya banyenge."
(We will go to Ayodhya and construct a beautiful temple)
"Gay nahin katne denge
Desh nahin batne denge."
(We will not allow cow slaughter and division of India)
"Jo hamare Ram ka nahin, Voh hamare kam ka nahin."
(One who does not belong to our Ram is of no use of us)
"Mandir ka kanoon banao, Varna gaddi se hat jao".
(Bring in a legislation for the construction of the temple or quit)

A little after we reached at the Royal Hotel, the Ram Bhakts were asked to collect and proceed to the station to board the train to Ayodhya. The group of Ram Bhakts started moving shouting slogans most of which had to do with the construction of the temple. These were largely the same slogans which had been raised in 1990 and 1992:

"Ram lala hum aayenge
Mandir vahin banayenge."
(Ram lala, we will come and construct the temple at the same place)
"*Eent pathar khayenge Mandir Vahin banayenge".*
(We will face stones but will construct the temple at the same place)

As the group moved towards the station, it came to a "*Majar*" (Grave of a Muslim saint) which was provocation enough for them to change gears. They now started shouting slogans which were anti-Pakistan and anti-Muslim:

"Neem ka patta kadua hai
Pakistan bhadua hai".
(Just as Neem leaf is bitter, like it Pakistan too is a bastard)

"Teen nahin hai tees hazar
Nahin rahega koi majar"
(It is not three (temples), it is thirty thousand we will not allow any *Majar* to remain)
"Talwar nikle myaan se
Mandir bane shaan se."
(Let the swords come out of the sheath and construct the temple with pride)

The procession of the Ram Bhakts arrived at the platform to find a train steaming in. However, it was not the train to Ayodhya. The Ram Bhakts stopped the train and did not allow it to leave. Most of the Bhakts were young and were in their 20s or early 30s. We returned to the camp to interview the Bhakts who were still camping.

The atmosphere in the temporary prisons was somewhat restrained compared to the one we witnessed at the camps. Some of the Bhakt's staying there had been separated from their kith and kin and felt concerned about them. They, however, were in high spirits and determined to proceed to Ayodhya, once released. Occasionally, they will shout slogans like:

"Ram ke Vaaste
Khali kardo raaste"
(For the sake of Ram, clear out the blockade)
"Ram yodhha, chalo Ayodhya"
(Rama's soldiers, proceed to Ayodhya)

The Bhakts were more upset about the treatment meted out to them by the authorities as there were no proper arrangements for toilets, water and food. Every now and then, a group of Bhakts would confront the officials and hot words were exchanged. For such Bhakts, the State was the enemy and not Muslims or Pakistan.

It was interesting to find that in almost all prisons the leaders who had mobilized these Bhakts were present. Communication was possibly only through them as no one talked, if they did not permit.

The Results

Who is a "good" Hindu?

This question was asked to understand how the Rallyists and the students will construct their Hindu identity and the elements which will go into its making. The attributes, which surfaced in the case of the politically mobilized Rallyists, were of a wide variety. Nevertheless, attributes related to Hindu Nationalism (Pride in Hinduism, Love for the Nation, Love for Ram) were more prominent. Performative characteristics related to religion too were mentioned, such as, offering of *Puja* (prayers), cow worship, idol worship, river worship. This differed greatly from the non-politicised sample of the students who put greater emphasis on the "Humanist" side of Hinduism and showing greater respect for other religions. They also emphasized *"Dharma Palan"* (performing moral duties) a little more than the Rallyists. It appeared that the Rallyists were using more of the external symbols to define a Hindu, although they also constructed a more varied and complex identity of Hindus compared to the students. When we asked them how many of the attributes mentioned by them, they themselves possessed, almost all of them said that they had all those attributes which they said a good Hindu ought to have. In this sense, they showed integration with their group. This, however, was not the case for the student sample where only half of them showed this kind of integration. In fact, more than half of them found themselves at some distance from an Ideal or proto typical Hindu.

Who is a Bharteeya (Indian)?

The construction of a 'Bharteeya' was done in a similar manner to a Hindu by the Rallyists. The attributes which got mentioned were one who believed in *Rashtravad* (nationalism), Hindu Nation, one who will stand up for the defence of the nation and religion, will sacrifice himself for the construction of a Ram Temple, honours the flag, defends its honour and also of Hindu religion. A *'Bharteeya'* also promotes Indian culture. Most of these attributes mentioned by the Rallyists are generally associated with the ideology propounded by the RSS and VHP. We did find, however, mention of other liberal attributes such as, respect for other religions, *"sarva dharma sambhav"*, "fraternal feeling" and "belief in social equality". In contrast to the Rallyists, the student respondents also used terms like *"Rashtra-Bhakti"*, "defending the nation", etc. What, however, was most striking in their case, was the greater emphasis they put on love and justice for all persons and religions, secularism, humanism, social equality and social conscience. As in case of attributes of a good Hindu, here too, we found, the rallyists attributing most of the characteristics of a *'Bharteeya'* to Self whereas in the student sample, the number was only a little more than 50 per cent. In fact, there were three respondents in the student sample who saw themselves as having few attributes of a *Bharteeya.*

Who is a Ram Bhakt (Devotee of Ram)?

As in case of their construction of a Hindu, the Rallyists presented a more differentiated picture of Ram Bhakt compared to the students. A Ram Bhakt, according to them not only follows Ram and his life as a model, but he also believes in making sacrifice, working for the welfare of living beings and obeying his parents. Along with this, he engages in doing "*sewa*" of Ram and engaging in his "*Bhakti*". The political side of the Rallyists surfaces when they choose attributes like making sacrifice for the sake of constructing Ram Temple, defence of Hinduism, and laying down life for the sake of truth. Ram Bhakts are also attributed humanistic qualities like not hurting others,' tolerance, etc. Students on the contrary, construct this identity on the basis of Ram's life and by accepting him as a role model. Apart from this they vest in a true Ram Bhakta humanistic qualities. Almost all Rallyists saw themselves as Ram Bhakt and as possessing these attributes. Only slightly more than half of the student sample saw themselves as possessing the attributes of the Ram Bhaktas.

Notion of Ram Rajya

Whenever the question of good governance gets raised in India, the memory of "Ram Rajya" is activated. Gandhi used it extensively for political mobilisation and after him, various political parties including Congress have used it. However, people make their own constructions based on their understanding of the Ramayana and what they have received as part of the oral tradition. The most prominent category to emerge for defining "Ram Rajya" in the case of Rallyists was the absence of physical, mental and spiritual ailments, peace and welloffness. Harmony, *"dharma palan"* (dutifulness), equality, Non-exploitation and influence exercised by the *"Praja"* (subjects of the state). As in previous cases, no one category was found preponderantly more significant than the other. However, in case of the students, the relationship between the ruled and ruler and influence the ruled exercise over the ruler emerged as more prominent than following the *'Dharma'* (duties). Both rallyists and the students find the Ram Rajya far away from being realized.

To the question, what should be done for Ram Rajya to be re-established, the Rallyists showed their political colours. Among the frequent responses made by them were construction of the Ram Temple, introduction of the Common Civil Code, abolition of "Talaq", end of Muslim appeasement, and punishment to "Ravanas" and corrupt officials. The students, however, differed on their strategy greatly. They would like an end to the Temple dispute, social and economic equality, removal of casteism, elimination of corrupt leaders, and their replacement with Ram like enlightened leadership. They also bring up various issues of development, such as, economic and social development, conscientization and literacy.

Historical Memories

The Rallyists and the students differ considerably with respect to the specific memories of historical events which bear lessons for us. In fact, students recalled fewer historical events. They also appear to use different time frames. The historical events which find mention by the Rallyists revolved around the Ayodhya temple. These are Babar's invasion, construction of the Babri Mosque, Temple demolition, firing at Ayodhya, Bombay Bombings, Godhra, and Akshardham besides partition of the country. Among the other historical events recollected were where Hindus had suffered because of their forgiving nature, like in case of Prithviraj and how they got duped by Pakistani leaders and in the Battle of Panipat. Students, on the other hand, recall the Violence due to Ayodhya dispute, and the partition more often. However, what was remarkable was the recall they made of the positive contributions made by the Muslims in the Independence struggle and also during the period of the Mughals. There are a number of students who do not want to remember as they say, history is for the scoundrels!

Other Findings

While it may appear that the Rallyists had become completely polarized, this may not be all together true. About half of them recognized the significant contributions of Muslim's in the struggle for India's independence against the British and in making of the culture of India. Their commitment to their religion, fraternal feelings towards other Muslims, faithfulness, organizational ability are some of the qualities which they admire. They also agree that India is basically multi-cultural and some of them concede that Muslims are no different from the Hindus as they were once Hindus and part of us.

As would be expected respondents in the students sample recount many more contributions of the Muslims and their good qualities. Only 11 out of 50 said that the contribution of Muslims had either been zero or negative. The rest of them said they had either made significant or as much contribution as other Indians had made in the development of India. They attributed many positive qualities to them like patriotic, good human beings, truthful, helpful, etc. to them.

Another interesting finding which throws light on the social identity differences between the politically mobilized Rallyists and the students was with respect to what they would like to be born as in their next birth. Out of 30 Rallyists, the 24 said they would like to be reborn as a Hindu or a Ram Bhakt and 5 said as Indians. The findings in case of the student sample were strikingly different. Not one out of 50 said that he would like to be reborn as a Hindu or an Indian (in fact, one said that he would like to be born as an American!). 22 student respondents said that they would like to be born as an *Insan/Manav*", 5 as women, 2 as men, and 3 said as birds!

Epilogue

This study provides some understanding of how the past has been used for political mobilization. It would appear that the Rallyists had accepted the constructions sent to them by the VHP organizers relating to the legitimacy of the claims of the Hindus over the land on which the temple of Lord Ram is to be constructed and the unfairness of the stand of the Government. In this discourse, the Rallyists not only see Muslims as enemies but also the state which has used power to suppress the Hindus. We found that there were a few Rallyists who mentioned Atal Behari Vajpayee as the leader who has damaged this country the MOST, besides Mulayam Singh. Both of them headed the governments at Delhi and Lucknow at the time of Rally.

Should one be hopeful that the non-politicised students are going to remain secular in their beliefs? One cannot be very certain. Much will depend on the kind of life experiences they are exposed to. We do feel optimistic, however. We need to create paces based on our positive recollections of our past. We need to build new frames, on the basis of intersection of the present and the past which will make it possible for strengthening the roots of a multi-cultural society. One is not suggesting for cultures to melt and become one homogenized lot but to assimilate and integrate to create a syncretic plural society in which multiple identities are possible.

REFERENCES

Bar-Tal, D. (2002). Collective memory of physical violence: Its contribution to the culture of violence. In E. Caims & M.D. Roe (eds.) *Memories in conflict.* London: Macmillan.

Bartlett, F.C. (1932). *Remembering: A study in experimental and social psychology.* Cambridge University Press.

Durkheim, E. (1965). Individual and collective representations. In *Sociology and philosophy* (trans. D.F. Pocock). London: Cohen and West (originally published in 1898).

Garry, M.; Manning, G.G.; Loftus, E.F.; & Sherman, S.J.; (1996). Imagination inflation: Imagining a childhood event inflates confidence that it occurred. *Psychonomic Bulletin and Review,* 3, 208-214.

Goff, L.M., & Roediger, H.L.; (1998). Imagination inflation for action events— Repeated imagining lead to illusory recollection. *Memory and Congnition,* 26, 20-33.

James, William (1890). *The principles of psychology.* New York: Holt.

Mead, G.H., (1934). *Mind, self, and society.* Chicago: University of Chicago.

Nandy, A.; Trivedi, S.; Yagnik, A.; & Mayaram, S. (1995). *Creating a nationality: The Ramjanmabhumi movement and fear of the self.* New Delhi: Oxford University Press.

Tajfel, H. (1972). *Social identity and intergroup behaviour.* Cambridge: Cambridge University Press.

Turner, J.C. (1987). The analysis of social influence. In J.C. Turner, M.A. Hogg, P.J. Oake, S.D. Reicher, & M.S. Wetherell (ed.). *Rediscovering the social group: A self categorization theory* (pp. 68-88). Oxford : Blackwell.

Worchel, S. (1999). *Written in blood: Ethnic identity and the struggle for human harmony.* New York: Worth.

Zavalloni, M. (1973). Social identity: A concept with research of a science. In S. Moscovici (ed.) *Introduction to social psychology* (pp. 245-266). Paris: Larousse.

5 Indian Immigrants' Perception of the French People

Looking Forward to Better Intercultural Relationships

Jyoti Verma

This qualitative data based chapter is part of a larger project on acculturative experiences of a sample of Indian immigrants in Paris which aimed at arriving at a worldview of the dominant host culture as represented in the respondents' perceptions, beliefs, experiences and observations. It is contended that the immigrants' worldview of the host culture takes shape as they interface critical issues of everyday life and meet the expectations and challenges offered by the country of settlement. However, the present chapter shall deal only with the Indian immigrants' perception of the French people and their experiences from their respective work life and educational environment. The objective at this point is to derive some insights from the represented narratives for developing better intercultural relations between the two interfacing cultural groups.

The Conceptual Frame

Immigrants are the group of people who come together with other groups voluntarily or because they have migrated to a new location (due to mobility), and some of whom are permanently settled in their new society (Berry, 1997). Rhee *et al.* (1996) observe that populations that are in cultural transition are particularly interesting because they may experience changes in their political, economic, religious, social and linguistic systems besides that in their social relationships with new relationships requiring redefinition of in-group and out-group and assigning different significance to ethnicity. Additionally, psychological changes may occur including shifts in attitudes, values, behaviour and life style.

It is contended that during the acculturation process a continuous effort is made by the immigrant groups to feel at ease and become functional in a new culture, experience social acceptability and equality and acquire material, social and psychological well-being. In this context a relevant question seems to be, 'at which level is navigation for better intercultural relations most important'? That is, should it be at the level of adapting to the values, norms and customs of the host culture group, at the level of understanding the host group in all its uniqueness, or at the level of choosing a particular acculturation strategy which is considered most advantageous for adapting amicably in the new culture? Therefore, asking the questions as to 'how people navigate between two cultures and whether they ignore, blend or transcend the conflicts between them' has practical implications. Similarly, any intercultural relations issue must look into the impressions of both the interfacing groups. In particular, one must address to the ethnic group's perceptions of and experiences with the host group and the impact these impressions have on their adaptation. The present researcher's interest in the acculturation process in general and intercultural relationship at this point led her to address to some questions of the following nature:

- How do the immigrants perceive the host country in terms of its system and culture?
- What are the immigrants' impressions of and experiences with the people of the host group?
- Whether the immigrants find the system and the people of the new country helpful in their adaptive efforts, feel accepted, welcome and treated equally?
- Whether the immigrants' adaptive effort and acculturative experiences are particularly hard and stressful due to discriminatory attitudes and practices of the host group?

In other words, any concern for improving intercultural relationship is likely to address to the 'sunshine spots' and the 'dark areas' of acculturative experiences of the immigrants with the purpose of understanding as to what might have gone wrong and what could possibly be the appropriate alternative for developing worthwhile and functional bonds? This is an important concern because imigration is a reality of the present day world which has become highly penetrable and extremely well connected for those who wish to shift and change their geographical locations for all kinds of reasons and purpose. The interest behind studying intercultural issues remains looking for the antecedents and the determinants of better intercultural relationships and a fair understanding of the ongoing relationship between the culturally different groups. However, it is desirable to study these issues from the point of view of the host culture as well.

Intercultural Relations Issue

Intercultural relations between immigrants and hosts are most often unequal. It is contended that cultural characteristics that accompany individuals into the acculturation process is necessary, partly for understanding where the person is coming from and in part to establish cultural features for comparison with the society of settlement as basis for establishing cultural distance. Furthermore, as a consequence of pervasive ethnocentric bias in intercultural relations, there is inbuilt ethnic tension between the immigrant and the host acculturation orientations. In line with the social identity theory, both sides will be inclined to favour the in-group culture over the culture of an out-group (Tajfel & Turner, 1986). In view of their dominant group position, the host community will demand some degree of adaptation from immigrant minorities, while their acceptance of culture maintenance will vary, depending on whether they perceive the minority culture as a 'threat' to group dominance (Bobo & Hutching, 1987; Montreuil & Bourhis, 2001).

Conversely, the minority status of the immigrants is associated with heightened ethnic self-identification which reinforces culture maintenance and at the same time, immigrant attitudes towards cross-cultural adaptation will vary depending upon whether they perceive the dominant culture as a 'threat' to group survival (Berry *et al.*, 1977). Some have shown, however, that on both sides ethnocentrism and perceived threat will decline with increasing levels of education (Scheepers, Verbeck & Coenders, 2001).

Objectives

As already mentioned the descriptive data of the study was generated through a long interview. The specific objectives for this chapter are:

1. To present some positive perceptions of the French system/ society as reported by a sample of Indian ethnic group members living in Paris,
2. To present the major problems suggested by the immigrants in adaptation with the host culture,
3. To present some experiences from the work life and educational institutions of the respondents, and
4. To present some suggestions for better relational outcomes.

METHOD

Sample

The sample comprised of 28 adults of Indian origin both males (16) and females (12) between the age range of 25 to 58 years. Fifty per cent of the women out of the total number of 12, were not working at the moment. All the respondents were at least Graduates with the exception of two (cases # 2, 8) who had only completed high school. The respondents came from a number of Indian states namely, Gujarat, Punjab, Bengal, Pondichery, Maharashtra, Kerala, Karnataka, Uttar Pradesh, Andhra Pradesh, Delhi, Kashmir, Orissa and Rajasthan. The sample was a heterogeneous one as regards to the occupations of the respondents and included students, personnel in jobs and business persons. There were at least two performing artists, one textile designer and a psychiatrist besides, two Indian Embassy staff and a highly qualified aeronautical engineer.

Years spent in the host country	*1–5*	*6–10*	*11–15*	*16–20*	*21–25*	*26–30*	*31–35*	
No. of respondents	7	9	3	5	1	1	2	28

Instruments

The Guiding Questions (Interview Schedule)

A list comprising of 18 guiding questions aimed at addressing to the contextual factors motivating migration and to get an impression of the acculturation experiences of the respondents was used. Accordingly, the respondents where requested to tell about their major aspirations and how far they have been realized, how they perceived the French culture and its people, what were the major hurdles faced during the adaptation process and what was good and nice in the host country. Further, they were asked to tell as to how did they find the job environment and in what ways the country of origin (India) still mattered to them. This chapter includes observations only against some selected questions for meeting its specific objectives.

The Questions

1. What is/are the major hurdle/s in adapting to the French society/culture?
2. What is that you like very much in this society?
3. Do you find French people friendly, unfriendly or indifferent towards immigrants?
4. Do you find your French co-workers/seniors/juniors helpful and cordial?

5. Do you think that the French co-workers/seniors/juniors keep a distance from you because you are not French?

OBSERVATIONS

1. Positive Perception of the French Society

Many good things were perceived in the French culture and its people. First, no one ever said that he/she repented her/his decision to come to France. It was mentioned invariably, that the system functioned very well and was more or less free of corruption. Every one agreed that France was a beautiful country; Paris was delightful and with a wonderful transport system and it was very convenient to travel in France. Aditionally, France had an excellent social security system which made each and every French citizen socially secure in this country. The "genuine moral freedom" of the French society was appreciated very well. For example, in Roshani's (# 16) opinion, France was completely secular, it was non-religious, intellectual, and Church was not behind religious, Calvinism". She also believed that meritorious and capable could go anywhere. Yesudas (#6) was fascinated by his new found freedom in France and Namrata (#9) felt "like a free bird." At least a couple of women believed (#9, 17), that women were much more protected and secure in France.

Strong nationalist feelings and the pride that French people took in their culture and heritage, were perceived as most remarkable features in the French character while their love for museums, concerts, art exhibition and fashion, was seen as unprecedented. French were perceived as intelligent, original and creative people with fine taste and good aesthetic sense. Their being possessive about the French language was justified as expression of their strong nationalist feelings and passion for preserving their cultural heritage. Even the popular tradition of eating out in restaurants and visiting cafe and bars, had a role in the continuation of a social life style which had the French signature.

One respondent appreciated that the French culture had a unique quality of maintaining a balance between the old and the new. It was amazing that there was 500 years old Louvre museum and an ultra-modern structure in front of it. France was not madly capitalist or very superstitious. In fact, the old and the new attitudes could survive in France side by side (# 9). Almost everyone seemed to agree with Dr. Preetpal (# 24) who observed that, France was a modern, successful country. The technology, the business and the system on the whole worked efficiently, there was huge achievement in different spheres and there was lot to like and respect in each field over here.

Barring a few exceptions, it was expressed that French people liked Indians, were interested in them and did not perceive them as threatening (# 16). India was perceived as a culturally strong country because of its performing arts, food, clothes and fashion fads that became popular in Paris. The young textile designer (# 9), Hariharan Iyer from the Indian Embassy (# 20) and Sanyukta Panda (# 23, who taught Indian cooking, Hindi language, and sold Indian accessories to her French acquaintances) had first hand information in support of the above observations. The two young performing artists (# 6, 27) admitted that, they had received enough affection and respect from the French art lovers and the general feeling was that Indians did not face much discrimination or came across racist attitude against their community (# 22). At least four respondents were full of praise for the French people and found them friendly, dependable and trustworthy (# 6, 10, 11, 23). These positive perceptions certainly offer hope and scope for developing good intercultural relationship between the French and the ethnic minority group of India.

2. Barriers in Developing Better Intercultural Relationships

(a) The Language Barrier

It appeared that the major hurdle in adaptation of the immigrants was two faceted. First, not knowing the *language* and second, a somewhat negative *perception of the French people.* In most of the cases, not knowing the language instantly created an "out group" feeling towards the immigrant groups by the host group. It was repeatedly mentioned that knowledge of French language was the very basic requirement for adaptation. Those who did not know the language and had recently arrived in Paris, looked for friends who could speak English and tried to get in touch with Indian people by joining Indian Associations. Often the students looked for accommodation at Maison de L'inde (#1) to remain in a familiar environment. It appeared that French were very possessive about their language because any compromise with the language was perceived as a step towards culture dilution. The immigrants generally felt that not knowing the language created an invisible 'close door' stopping possibilities for further interactions literally, and otherwise.

Some Examples from the Narratives

One of the respondents (# 14) made the following analysis: "what was commonly perceived in the French character as shutting up from others, could be a defence mechanism used by the French and since they were not very good in the English language, they did not want to express themselves in English". Talking of the greatest hurdle in adjusting to the French society, a mother of two small kids (# 26) narrated an incident about a "racist" doctor. Krishnavenu (# 12) observed that knowing the French language was not enough but one had to be an expert, for having a real impact on the other. Another person (# 5) said, "I might not say that they (French) are frigid but they are arrogant, not helpful nor friendly if you do not know their language. I cannot communicate in French and French do not accept this". It appeared that language was the real visa for entering France and without the same, efforts meant for developing closeness with the French people were likely to suffer. It was very common for the non-French speaking settlers to join French language schools as soon as they could.

(b) Immigrants' Perception of the Host Group: Examples from the Narratives

A film maker contended that often Indians were "unable to see what they did not saw." That is, they did not notice what the French liked and what they disliked. Furthermore, unfamiliarity with the norms, expectations, preferences, and life style of the people of the dominant group, was likely to lead to unfair perceptions and wrong conclusions, about them and their culture. Barring a few exceptions (# 6, 8, 10, 11, 17, 18, 23), in almost all the narratives, there was mention of the unfriendliness of the French people or their being closed to the outsiders. However, all such narratives had scope for alternative interpretations. Further, the immigrants' expectations from the dominant cultural group were likely to be guided by their own cultural orientation and, therefore, could lead to biased perception of the latter and setbacks in interpersonal relationships. Meenakshi (# 25) looked for Indian friends to help her in urgency because she realised that it was not the practice of the French people to "just drop in" at their neighbours place, or take the initiative for knowing the people around them.

She noticed that "nobody would come in to know or meet you just by pressing the doorbell". Vasundhara (# 7) was surprised that no one said 'hello' and felt like a stranger. Rani Mukherjee (# 2) found it difficult to make friends, while a number of respondents felt that French were formal, cold, uninvolved (meaning indifferent) and non-interfering in the lives of those around. Similarly, a "perceptible lack of warmth" was often marked as the cultural feature of the French society (# 3, 9 and 14). A young student (# 1) wanted to say that French were strong nationalists, and extreme people. They were either accepting or non-accepting, and there was no "in-between" for them while another young woman (# 9) remarked that French individualism was worse than the American individualism.

Some attitudes and gestures of the dominant group were perceived as discriminatory or seemingly racist. In the present sample of immigrants, at least two felt discriminated and marginalized (# 4, 8) while, there were a few more, who wanted to say that the non-French were not likely to reach top positions in jobs (# 5, 12, 14). Some were frank enough to say that there was racism in France which was perhaps, practiced in a subtle way. According to a recently arrived young student (# 3), French were not fond of people from other cultures who wanted to settle down in France or had lived under the French colonies. Therefore, one might come across racist attitude and expressions on trivial matters against such settlers. She observed further that French were not integrated even with the Indian groups who had been here for many years now and did not consider them to be part of the main stream.

Surjeet (# 22) believed that, "there were groups of French elite or bourgeois who were strict and unaccepting of others. However, towards the Indians, they had an open mind and not a negative attitude in particular." On the other hand, it appeared that French had some prejudice against the Algerians and the Moroccans. One respondent serving in the French Government's job (# 4), observed that French wanted to be in the dominating position and said, "French consider themselves as givers, providers, they look down upon you, and they do not look upon you as you were doing some service. They consider others as takers." It appeared that at least for the three cases (# 4, 8, and 12), adaptation apparently did not improve the "fit" between the individuals and their environment and there was some indication of resistance against the system which found vent in the negative feelings expressed in their respective narratives.

3. Representations from Work Life and Educational Institutions

The employed respondents had the general feeling that work facilities were good in France. Nevertheless, the respondents expected something like more salary, recognition, more personally fixed target realization and opportunity to grow from their respective jobs. What follow is the respondents' perceptions of and experiences from work life under the headings of:

- Job satisfaction and perceived discrimination at work,
- Importance of French degrees and diplomas, and
- Relationship with colleagues.

(a) Job Satisfaction and Perceived Discrimination at Work

Apparently at least a couple of immigrants (# 4, 12) were not particularly happy in their jobs. For example, the 45 years old accountant of a British company Krishnavenu (#12) had to say, "Before you come to a foreign land you have dreams but after you are there you are struck by the reality and the only possibility is compromise." Krishnavenu's personal opinion was that a decent guy with marginal intelligence should not choose a life like this. This man experienced little job satisfaction followed by a nagging feeling that by working hard one could have made it here or even in India. Unfortunately, he could come to this conclusion only after having walked the bumpy path to 'economic independence' in a foreign country. Moreover, the desired economic independence for this man did not come without a price. The cost included coming to join his wife's home in France contrary to what usually happened in India, leaving behind his near and dear ones and not being able to find a lot of job satisfaction. Further in his opinion, non-French could be paid marginally lesser than the French (as this was sometimes decided at the concerned company's policy level) but this could be perceived as the reason for feeling exploited by the non-French.

Krishnavenu believed that French society was not totally non-hierarchical. People maintained differences in their status and this seemed to be true in medium size companies. People preferred to do their own jobs and did not interfere with others' businesses. There was a sense of compartmentalization, people kept to themselves and there was less of human interaction. He added, "We can live as Indians but cannot perhaps be treated like French. If you have a French visa that is not enough reason for a rapport. In the office there is nothing to relate at the personal level."

Krishnavenu was somewhat bitter about all this and said that there were no alternatives but to accept what you have. However, he realized that India could have been bad too and for sure the physical working environment was good in France.

The Indian Embassy staff Hariharan Iyer (# 20) when asked whether he experienced job satisfaction, quipped "not really." He explained that job satisfaction was affected because "every three years the system changes at the Embassy and each new management has different expectations and different way of functioning." Similarly, Aparna Mahadevan (# 17) another office staff of the Indian Embassy who had worked for a fairly long period of time in this job and was earning enough, did not experience much job satisfaction. She admitted though, that job facilities were good in France in general and some companies offered a lot of fringe benefits to its employees.

Suneet Siddharth (# 5), the thirty-one years old male MBA who worked for UNESCO, considered UNESCO's job as nice as it was open to all the nationals. Though Suneet had some good experiences, he did not find his present job 100 per cent satisfying or "stimulating" enough but still "OK". Further, jobs were not easily available to the non-French persons and it was difficult for others to rise to the top. He observed that if you were perceived as "threatening" somehow by the people of the dominant group, (especially at the higher levels) then you could have difficulty.

The only psychoanalyst and psychiatrist in the present sample Dr. Preetpal Rajhans (# 24) was earning enough but was worried about his future. Since he started late, his security benefits were not going to be the best ones. He explained that to get the maximum benefit of the social security system in France one has to begin working as soon as 18 years of age.

Narratives suggesting Discrimination at Work

Aniket Pundit a company employee (# 21) pointed out that foreigners normally cannot reach the highest positions in offices or jobs in European countries. Moreover, non-European Union member countries were not likely to get employment easily in France. Similarly, Suneet (# 5) had observed, "In all over Europe it is difficult for people from other cultures to rise and be in high and very responsible positions... in France for example, one cannot get ahead of the French nationals. There might be very few exceptional cases in Europe when the non-dominant group's persons were placed at higher positions." On the contrary, mechanical engineer Mr. Sharma (#14) working in a multinational company observed that French were open to "racial integration" while racial intermixing was not popular in the United Kingdom or for that matter in Italy or in Germany.

Pradeep (# 4) a 45 years old male came to France in the year 1975 and worked in the French Government's job. He was a special case in the sense that he felt particularly unhappy in his present job situation. His suggested adaptive strategy was *marginalization* and it appeared to be linked to his job experiences, feeling of despair grounded in the observation that foreigners cannot reach the top, and his failure to be in the profession of his choice. Pradeep said, "You may be required to give up your values and become French. If you can ask questions, if you do not feel inferior than this may not be acceptable." There was something about Pradeep's general elusiveness and unwillingness to elaborate what he said and perhaps, one could see that there was fear of being punished (as a member of the non-dominant group) for being honest and vocal.

Pradeep observed that at the lower levels in the office you could get along well with the other colleagues and there was no problem. At the higher levels, however, there could be discrimination. He believed that being a person from another culture created hurdles for reaching the top positions in a job and perceived this as some form of discrimination against the outsiders. He nursed some hard feelings and observed, "French want to be in the dominating position, and even if you have the qualification and competence they would like to put you down."

The experiences of a small businessman Chiman Shah (# 8)

gave some vivid account of the discrimination experienced by a self-employed petty businessman due to the colour of his skin. However, this was the lone case which perhaps cannot be generalized. Chiman Shah was a 50 years old male who earned his living by raising a stall at the local 'marche' for selling small plastic articles and goods, toys and accessories used by women. He generally dealt with Chinese traders for buying his goods in whole sale and his relationship with the Chinese traders was more contractual but mutually respectful. Chiman Shah had limited contact with French people but his impression was that French first bought things from white skinned (French) businessman.

He observed, "Sometimes they would not like to acknowledge your presence, respond to you or talk to you." The white customers and shopkeepers would push his cart with foot which he found very disrespectful. He added that occasionally he got very angry with the French and told them that they were "inhuman devils". He reiterated, "French are not helpful to the outsiders and reserved their human touch for their own people. They do not like coloured skin people and in general maintained distance." Nevertheless, for practical reasons Chiman Shah wanted to choose France if he had to select a country to come back to.

A middle aged businessman Mr. Pankaj Patel (#15) believed that if people perceived racism it was perhaps, at the higher levels. That is, you or your children may not be able to get the highest positions in the jobs and the French would have this privilege. At the higher administrative levels you might be discriminated but not openly or in general. Mr. Patel wanted to say that if there was racism in France it was not obvious but quite "subtle". Vasundhara (# 7) a 39 years old non-working female shared something from her husband's experience at his job. Her husband worked with French people and she tried to give vent to his feelings by saying, "French people always kept a distance. They could make you feel like a stranger. They are not racist people but could make you feel small. They are subtle in their ways to suggest their racist attitude". At times her husband was in conflict with his co-workers or seniors.

On the other hand, there was belief in equality in this society in the sense that one could reach one's seniors or boss and discuss things with him/her. However, people will not go out of way to help you.

Mr. Rituraj Sharma (# 14) a well placed mechanical engineer employed in a multinational company observed that French were open to "racial integration". Racial intermixing was not popular in United Kingdom or for that matter in Italy. In France, however, there was evidence for marriages between blacks and whites. There was racism in Germany too, however, one cannot deny a subtle undercurrent of racism in France but there was some mixing as well. Language student Rani felt that (# 3) French do keep a distance from people of other cultures or groups.

(b) Importance of French Degrees and Diplomas

According to middle aged successful aeronautical engineer Mr. Diwakar Saxena (#10), the prospective job seeker's original degree was not treated at par with the French degree. He observed, "The French degree gets more respect. It was not like in England or in the USA where qualifications from Anglo-Saxon countries may be treated as equal". Mr. Saxena also sensed some competition between different educational institutions and alumni groups who helped their own members to study and speak exactly like them. Krishnavenu (#12) had argued too that, "Knowing French language was not enough and one had to be an expert in the language. To be recognized as competent, you have to have French degree and diploma. You may be very capable but that does not help without having French degree and qualifications. Here Anglo-Saxon people could have difficulty. Integration was faster in UK or in the USA than what we find in France."

Another case in point was Dr. Rajhans (#24) who had the MBBS degree but his basic degree was not recognised and he had to get the necessary qualifications again in England and France. This was the greatest hurdle faced by him and due to this he started off late in his profession. He believed that this made his integration more difficult and also delayed his professional success.

(c) Relationship with Colleagues

It would not be fair to conclude that all the respondents experienced discrimination or felt the absence of cordial relationship at their work place. In fact, it was frequently mentioned that the French colleagues, seniors and juniors did not maintain distance from their non-French colleagues (# 5, 9 and 10). Dr. Preetpal (# 24) occasionally met colleagues from the same profession in conferences and found them nice. The two members of the Indian Embassy Hariharan Iyer (# 20) and Aparna Mahadevan (# 17) felt that their French counterparts at the Embassy liked Indian colleagues and were friendly and helpful. Roshni (# 16) a research assistant shared similar feelings and Aditi (# 13) a school teacher, found her colleagues nice, friendly and cordial. Udayan Yesudas (# 6) a young male Carnatic music singer found his colleagues and team mates emotionally supportive. He had to say, "At times I was broken, depressed, but they were my strength. They were curious and wanted to know how I felt." He came across important persons at the concerts from the fields of judiciary, labour, films, literature and painting, etc. but did not find them "keeping distance" from him.

For 30 years old Parveen Sultana (# 19) a part-time school teacher, her two male colleagues were good, helpful and treated her well. Parveen could communicate with them and they did not mind sharing information with her. Sanyukta Panda (# 23), 56 years old female baby sitter had many good words to say for her French employers. She had arrived in France in the year 1980 and the French couple who employed her as a baby sitter trusted her well. Her employer worked as Air-France crew and occasionally had to leave their children with her for a day or two. In that case, Sanyukta stayed at their home and even cooked simple Indian food (*khichari*) for the kids and tried to speak in Bangla with them. On the other hand, the kids loved her too. Sanyukta's relationship with her employer's family had grown into an intimate one over time and she felt close to her employer's family. Businessman Mr. Pankaj Patel (# 15) employed French people for running his shop and found them helpful, cordial and nice.

Mr. Diwakar (# 10), however, wanted to point out that since hierarchy was prominent in France, therefore, French expected homogeneity with little apprehension. Suneet (# 5) was in UNESCO's job and the nature of his job did not give much scope for maintaining distance. Nevertheless, Suneet felt that one come across some "strong personalities". In company employee Aniket Pundit's (# 21) opinion, "You cannot put pressure on them (i.e., colleagues). You have to be careful about what you say. Labour laws were strict in France." Responding to the question 'whether co-workers and seniors maintained distance,' Aniket had to say that "distance depends, and it is up to you. I can go out to them. It could be different from person to person. If I want to talk to somebody I can." Similarly, Vineet a young job trainee found his French colleagues helpful and in fact more helpful and cordial than the Indian co-workers. He added, however, that good co-worker relationship also depended on the person concerned and could differ from person to person.

Jasvinder Singh (# 2) a 39 years old male chef of an Indian restaurant had arrived in Paris in 1983. Having moved little among the French group his observations were limited. Nevertheless, he had to say, "French people are not sacrificing, and they keep work relationship this, however, is good in the sense that you do not feel the pressure on you from their side (*bojh nahi parta*). In sum, French are not involved in you."

4. Some Suggestions for Developing Understanding and better Intercultural Relations

(a) Building on the Positive Perceptions

Efforts towards developing positive intercultural relations must begin by building on the positive perceptions of the respective cultural groups. For example, in the narratives barring a few exceptions it was expressed that French people liked Indians, were interested in them and did not perceive them as threatening. Similarly, India was perceived as a culturally strong country (due to its performing arts, food, clothes and fashion) and despite the impression that the French were apparently less friendly people they were seen as dependable and trustworthy and colleagues at work place cordial and accepting. It is argued that positive impressions of the host country and its people often help in locating the ground for developing good relations and bonds of friendship and must be focused upon.

Furthermore, the impression of the French society as "genuinely freedom loving", secular, non-religious and intellectual, opens up a whole vista for creative ideas and projects (Indo-French) and experimenting with the possibilities of developing better intercultural ties. Many Indian performing artists, designers and technical experts, who had made future and fortune in France for themselves individually, had an advantage over others for doing much towards strengthening of the Indo-French ties by introducing their country of origin powerfully to the culture sensitive French society.

Secondly, a genuinely appreciative stance for the striking qualities of the French character can always be taken by the ethnic groups as an inspiration for developing strong nationalist feelings, pride in one's culture and heritage and love for the country of origin instead of interpreting the seemingly 'Frencho-centric' ways of the host for categorizing them as unfriendly, closed and snob people. The unique quality of the French in maintaining a balance between the old and the new could be another point for learning and identification. France was perceived as a modern, successful country with huge successes in the fields of technology and business to name only two. The host culture's success story could be used as inspiration and translated into collaborative efforts by the Indian ethnic groups towards lasting international and intercultural relationships.

(b) Getting above One's Own Needs and Values for a Better Understanding of the Host Group

It may be argued that the immigrants' perception was not always fair but nevertheless true because it was grounded in their acculturative experiences. However, for a fair inter-cultural understanding it seems important that both the groups were willing to keep aside their own cultural standards for perceiving and evaluating the other culture and its people. Indians are known to be relationship oriented people; having strong social and affiliation needs (J. B. P. Sinha & Verma, 1987; Verma, 1992b). They prefer to seek help and social support from others, have concern for others' evaluation and would like to utilize interpersonal contacts. Consequently, they wish to relate with others at a personal level. However, they must realize that this may not be the 'need' or the 'cultural preference' of the host group and, therefore, eagerness towards making contact with the host group or spontaneous moves towards building friendship may not be reciprocated. It may be said that a large group of relationship oriented Indians were likely to misunderstand the reserve, formal, non-hypocritical, strongly nationalist, and straight forward attitude and expressions of the French people as unwelcoming, threatening, closed and unfriendly towards the non-French groups. Nevertheless, it is better to rely and initiate efforts for better intercultural relations with the belief that French were interested in Indians and remember that for knowing the French closely it was important to take the first step and learn their language.

(c) Realizing the Importance of the Time Factor for Better Understanding of the Host Group

Observations suggested that the time factor was important for a better understanding of the host culture and the immigrant groups need to realize this. Having long and intense experience of living in the host culture facilitated the development of sensitivity and competence to examine one's own acculturation experiences through the right and relevant perspective. This would help in realizing that the French life style was different than one's own in many respects but that did not make it wrong or deplorable. The narratives seemed to impress that the immigrants, who had lived in France for long, had developed the capability of looking beyond the manifest French ways and preferences. They could see that French people were not hypocrites or artificial people, but were genuine and straightforward; who did not pretend, and opened up only after the other person took the initiative to move towards them.

In general, the Indian immigrants carried an impression that French people were indifferent and unfriendly towards them. This impression too could undergo change and revision with the passage of time. Krishna who had lived in France since the late 60s had to say, "to integrate well, you have to have certain assets so that the French become willing to come to you...the prerequisite is to have a similar standard of living more or less at par with the French. People like to move in if you have that. Consequently, if you are receptive and begin to take their values, and entertain them, they come and try to mix with you".

(d) Realizing the Diversity in the Host Group

One group of respondents wanted to make a distinction between French people who were rich, snobs, lived in exclusive areas of Paris, belonged to a special age group, and were not ready to integrate with the outsiders, and those, who lived in the outskirts of Paris (or were non-Parisians), and had been exposed to other cultures. The latter group was perceived as willing to learn about other cultures and cultural groups and seemed to be more open to the outsiders. The realization that some French group of people are likely to hold relatively extreme negative attitudes and beliefs towards the minority groups due to their own whims and reasons (which should not be generalized) might help in becoming more tolerant towards such view points and opinions.

(e) Host Group need to put a Check on its Discriminatory Attitude and Practices

Finally, the subtle and sometimes obvious experiences of discrimination at work place could play a prominent role in the sustenance of hard feelings towards the French employers and colleagues. This issue has to be attended and dealt with caution and sensitivity when thinking of developing better intercultural relations. Certain discriminatory attitudes and beliefs showing disregard for human dignity (especially as suggested by the petty businessman) have to be contained because they can close doors that open in the direction of better inter-cultural ties. Here the major responsibility lies with the dominant cultural group. And lastly, if the host group leave some space for developing affinity, and possibilities for emotional bonds even in formal relations, things can improve for better and get the ball rolling.

CONCLUSION

The Indian immigrants perceived a number of positive qualities in the French system along with certain admirable characteristic in the French people. The respondents invariably agreed that French system functioned very well and was more or less free of corruption. France had excellent social security system while the "genuine moral freedom" of the French society was praiseworthy. Strong nationalist feelings, and the pride that French people took in their culture and heritage, were perceived as the most remarkable features in the French character. French were perceived as intelligent, original and creative people with fine taste and good aesthetic sense. Their being possessive about the French language was justified as expression of their strong nationalist feelings and passion for preserving their cultural heritage. French culture was exemplary for maintaining a unique balance between the old and the new. Almost every one agreed that France was a modern, successful, technologically savvy country and there were huge achievements in different spheres of

French and a fair number of respondents found the French as dependable and trustworthy people.

Regarding the hurdles in adaptation, the number one hurdle was stated as "not knowing the French language". Further, besides being perceived as culturally conscious, aesthetically oriented, nationalists and straight forward, Parisians were perceived as closed people. Some believed that there was subtle discrimination against outsiders and the non-French could not reach the top positions in jobs. Suggestions for improving intercultural relations include : (a) building upon the positive impressions and perceptions held about the host group; (b) going beyond one's own culture specific needs and values for perceiving the host culture and its people in a balanced way; (c) realizing that time was needed to develop a desired level of sensitivity and competence for understanding the host's ways and preferences; (d) having tolerance for the extreme views held against the ethnic groups by some segments of the host population; and (e) sincere and definite efforts to be made by the host group who ought to give up being unduly insensitive, unreasonable or unfair towards the ethnic minority groups.

REFERENCES

Berry, J. W.; Kalin, R.; and Taylor, D.M. (1977). Multiculturalism and ethnic attitudes in Canada. The Ministry of Supply and Services, Ottawa.

Berry, J. W. (1997). Cultures in contact: Acculturation and change. G. B. Pant Memorial Lectures, February 21-22, 1997. G. B. Pant Social Sciences Institute, Allahabad.

Bobo, L. and Hutchings, V.L. (1987). Perceptions of racial group competition: Extending Blumer's theory of group position to a multi-racial social context. *American Sociological Review*, 61, 951-972.

Montreuil, A. and Bourhis, R. Y. (2001). Majority acculturation orientations towards valued and devalued immigrants. *Journal of Cross-Cultural Psychology*, 32, 698-719.

Scheepers, P.; Verberck, G.; and Coenders, M. (2001). Recent Dutch research on ethnocentrism in an international perspective. In K. Phalet and A. Orkeny (eds.), Ethnic minorities and inter-ethnic relations in context (pp. 59-84) Aldershot: Ashgate.

Sinha, J.B.P. and Verma, J. (1987). Structure of collectivism. In C. Kagitcibasi (Ed.), *Growth and progress in cross-cultural psychology* (pp. 123-129). Amsterdam, The Netherlands: Swets & Zeitlinger.

Tajfel, H. and Turner, J.C. (1986). The social identity theory of intergroup behaviour. In S. Worchel and W. G. Austin (eds.), *Psychology of intergroup relations* (pp 7-24). Chicago: Nelson Hall.

Verma, J. (1992b). *Allocentrism and relationship orientation. In S. Iwawaki,* Y. and Leung (eds.) *Innovation in cross-cultural psychology* (pp. 152-163). The Netherlands: Swets & Zeitlinger.

6 Cognitive Artifacts and Education for All

A Concept at Community Service

Braj Bhushan

Human beings have always tried to use their intelligence to make things much more easier for themselves. Even though, people may not use jargons to denote certain actions but they do use small things to make bigger things easier. For example, we prepare a list before going for shopping, or we use calendar or year planner to remind us important events at right time. We present important things in the form of charts, or tables or graphs while drafting and presenting long texts. All these are physical objects or non-linguistic inscriptions that aid or enhance our cognition. Technically speaking these are cognitive artifacts which practically enhance the cognitive capability by breaking the task into simple representations.

Human beings have demonstrated unparallel ability to modify their environment by developing artifacts and transmitting the then modified accumulated knowledge to the forthcoming generations (Cole, 1990). The definition of cognitive artifacts include mental as well as material elements (Norman, 1993). The line of difference only lies in the fact that heuristics or mnemonics, the examples of mental artifacts, are clearly artifactual in nature whereas the material artifacts has to coordinate with the corresponding mental element to be cognitive artifact, i.e., the nature of their usage. Majority of the researches in psychology tells us about the functions of the unaided mind. We still need research backups for the mind supported by artifacts.

In the modern times technology has started dominating the knowledge transfer mechanisms. With the rise of complexity of task as well as the voluminous involvement of people in a particular operation the need for an artifact is desperately felt. Over a period of time technology has been integrated into curriculum but unfortunately the focus has been on the technical specifications at the cost of pedagogical concerns (Garland, 1999; Groves & Zemel, 2000; Clabaugh, 1993). Now-a-days we find vigorous use of artifacts such as figures, diagrams, charts, etc.

Categories of Artifacts

Though we, as species, have been intelligent and generous in manipulating our physical world according to our convenience, technically these modifications, i.e., artifacts, are categorized according to their nature. Ching, Levin & Parisi (2003) have cited five broad classes of artifacts:

Concrete Carriers

It includes 'physical objects in the classroom environment which cannot convey or display explicit meanings or knowledge directly, but may carry meanings based on their condition, size, and placement within physical space' (Ching, Levin & Parisi, 2003). For example, furnitures available in the classroom.

Concrete Conveyors

They are not representations of knowledge in themselves but simply display them. LCDs,VCRs, television monitors, other projection screens, black and white boards, etc. come under this category.

Instructional Artifacts

It includes inscriptions and texts. Inscriptions involve visual representation of information and are dependent upon another class of artifacts for its display. For example, using power point to project an illustration, or writing formulae on the blackboard.

Visual Artifacts

On-line materials are the prominent visual artifacts being used globally. Even in our country premier establishments responsible for regulating higher education such as AICTE has initiated projects for developing on-line course materials. This caters the needs of distant students as well as helps institutions effectively deal with the problem of insufficient experts.

Other than on-line materials use of gestures to drag attention of the students to a particular inscription (Roth, 2001) is another example of visual artifact. An interesting example comes from laboratory situations where scientists physically move their body to enact the movement of subatomic particles (Ochs, *et al.*, 1996).

Ambient Artifacts

A widely overlooked factors that has always been considered known to architects but has seldom dragged attention while designing a classroom such as sound, temperature, lighting, etc., are categorized as ambient artifacts. Presently we have hardly any research pertaining to this in behavioural sciences. It merits mention here that the physical environment has never been considered from an artifact point of view and one hardly finds researches done on teaching and learning space from a socio-cognitive perspective.

Theoretical Foundations and use of Artifacts

The justification for the use of cognitive artifacts lies in Vygotsky's (1978) activity theory which says that a learning child is not capable of doing certain cognitive activities all alone but can do so with others creating a "zone of proximal development" (Wertsch, 1985). This theory recognizes words and concepts as a powerful psychological tool that facilitates higher cognitive processing. Einstein once mentioned, "Words and language, whether written or spoken, do not seem to play any part in my thought processes. The psychological entities that serve, as building blocks for my thought are certain signs or images, more or less clear, that I can reproduce and recombine at will. The elements that I have mentioned are, in my case, visual and sometimes motor" (cited in Hadamard, 1945).

As described by Indurkhya (1992) the cognitive agent and the reality interact with each other and our concepts are not the reservoir of pre-existing structures rather they create the structure. The reality gets conceptualized as a *sensorimotor data set* that is determined by the perceptual and motor apparatus of the cognitive agents. The structural features, however, are based on reality. The cognitive agent also has the responsibility of forming cognitive relationship for which they probably use two mechanisms — accommodation and projection. In accommodation structural changes are made retaining the cognitive relation intact, whereas projection modifies the cognitive relations. The entire exercise is to maintain coherence of the concept network.

Both concrete and abstract artifacts can be used to construct, and hence convey multiple representations. The exploration of cognitive semantics, i.e., the construction of meaning through image schemas, conceptual metaphors and conceptual blends (Das & Bhushan, 2005)is desperately needed for coming forward with culturally appropriate artifacts. Studies prove that temporal sequencing can be understood with the help of spatial structures. Using the theory of conceptual blending (Fauconnier & Turner, 2002), Hutchins (2002) argues that for complex conceptual blends physical structure act as material anchor by giving representational stability to the elements in the blended space.

It is essential to deeply explore the psychological factors involved in the interplay between various processes in cognitive activities. We also need to look at the personal and the system view of an artifact. Every artifact imbibes both the system and the personal view. The system view expands the functional capability of the individual using it whereas it replaces the original task by a less difficult one from a personal point of view. Let us take an example from the aviation industry where artifacts are used in a big way. There are certain 'dos' before and during a flight takes off. Instead of overloading individual attendants and thus leaving points of anomalies a checklist has been formed which has been attested by the aviation authority. Now this checklist is an artifact which distributes needed effort and planning across time and people. Pilots have been using it without further modification. In fact, with repetition the whole operation involving the artifact is driven subconsciously thus making the task effortless (Bodker, 1989) and at times leading to serious consequences (Degani & Wiener, 1990; Norman & Hutchins, 1990; NTSB, 1989). An interesting example of personified artifacts can be traced in history. The medieval sailors of north Europe used to see the time of low and high tides at major ports using the compass card in a peculiar manner (Frake, 1985).

Artifacts might vary in terms of surface and internal representations. Slide rule and abacus contain only surface representations of information. Here 'the symbols are maintained at the visible surface of the device' (Norman, 1991). Few artifacts maintain the symbols within the device reflecting internal representations. Such artifacts need interface otherwise the internal representations would remain inaccessible to the users.

Stevens (1957) talks about two types of psychological representations–additive and substitutive. For example, loudness is the psychological percept of sound. Similarly brightness is the psychological percept of light. Here the representations can be ordered. These are the examples of additive scales or representations. However, the psychological percept of pitch (psychological percept of physical sound) and hue (psychological percept of wavelength of light) are examples of substitutive scales. According to Rustle (1961), "as one moves along the sequence of sets" in additive scale "one picks up new aspects, and one never loses any of the old ones.

Any such sequence of sets is ordered in a strict way, and distances are additive" (p. 49). Whereas in the substitutive scale "each step of the process involves discarding some elements from *A* and adding some new elements from *B*. Elements from *A* which have earlier been discarded are never reused and elements from *B* which have been added are never discarded.....each move along the scale involves substituting some elements from *B* for some of the elements of *A*" (p. 50).

Culture Specific Artifacts

As a social entity each and every aspect of human behaviour is supposed to be culturally coloured. According to Vygotsky (1981) during the culture development of a child functions appear on both the social as well as the psychological plane. Initially it is apparent as an inter-psychological operation between people and then as intra-psychological process within the child. Hence, by the virtue of socio-cultural means and methods a grown up child 'assimilates the experience of humankind' (Leont'ev, 1981). This becomes much more important in a world that is filled with culture specific artifacts.

However, the nature of man-machine interaction affects the artifacts and its use. The pilots look at the display panel in a particular way to know ± 5 knot deviations from the target speed instead of calculating it (Hutchins, 1995). Several studies confirm that interactions are affected by the choice of representations and the extent of interaction permitted by artifact (Hutchins, Hollan & Norman, 1986). Scribner (1984) has given the example of dairy workers who use the layout of standard dairy product cases in filling orders. The *dabbawalas* of Mumbai are famous for supplying meals to few thousand office-goers everyday with identifying and disbursing tiffin careers (*dabbas*) without error for last few decades. How do they identify the *dabba* of a particular customer amongst the thousands of careers? Just see the way your mother or wife or a cook in a hotel arranges the cooking implements and ingredients in the kitchen. Here the arrangement of artifacts itself is a cognitive artifact (Krish, 1995). What is interesting here is that the products are used for something it has not been designed for giving impression that human brain is capable of simplifying even the use of artifacts by personified strategy of using it.

Here only are highlighted teaching and learning of mathematics because of practical constraints.

Mathematical Ability and Artifacts

Usually while teaching a subject that heavily depends upon symbolism and abstraction, it is essential not to pour the information into the heads of the students leaving it completely on them to cognitively arrange them, but well-define a concept and link it to an already assimilated concept. Cognitive artifacts based on multimedia that can simulate a real life situation can be of great help. We must keep in mind that verbal representations are not suitable for explaining abstract concepts, and hence perceptual simulations can be used to reinforce cognitive relations.

The problem of teaching mathematics and the use of artifacts in so doing has attracted many researchers (Bhusan, 2004; Saxe, 2001; Sfard & McClain, 2001). The cognitive framework can be used to delineate the skills needed to learn mathematics as well as to identify learning difficulties and design effective intervention programmes to help the students. It would be wise to focus on certain specific operations such as arithmetic reasoning, spatial reasoning, geometric reasoning, logical reasoning, pattern sequencing, measurement, etc.

A close look at the mathematics syllabus indicates possible cognitive obstacles in the curriculum itself. In the light of Piagetian theory, cognitive obstacle comes in when a learner comes across a new idea that cannot be fitted into the existing cognition. This would then lead to incompatibility blocking the understanding and use of the information. This was introduced in the realm of science by Bachelard (1938). Usually students have to pick up a concept that helps solving a particular type of problems, but when a new situation comes into being conceptualization becomes difficult as the previous notion is well anchored in the mind. For example, while learning mathematical operations we learn addition, subtraction, multiplication and then division. We are rarely made to understand that multiplication is repeated addition and division is repeated subtraction. A step-by-step link between multiplication and repeated addition is never shown to a student. Similarly, when the student jumps from the number to fractions they face acute problem. The previous training has made it deep rooted that multiplication yields a bigger product. While working with the fractional numbers the students commit error, as the product of multiplication is not big. This is a dominant cognitive obstacle in the school years. Table 5.1 shows the contents of mathematics syllabi of classes two and three of CBSE. If you look at the mathematics syllabus of schools, usually fractions are taught before negative numbers. There have been viewpoints to reverse the order (Tall, 1989). There have been justifications to make the syllabi more complex. There have been advocacy for increased difficulty level. Hart (1981) went to the extent that "....the brain is.... an amazingly subtle and sensitive pattern-detecting apparatus" (p. 60) "....designed by evolution to deal with natural complexity, not neat 'logical simplicities'..." (p. 76).

If the curriculum has to accommodate more and more information, subsequently increasing the difficulty level, pedagogy needs to concentrate on basic cognitive mechanisms and artifacts can be designed to focus on these. Researches show that we all have the ability for instantaneous counting. Dehaene (1997) suggested that we have an innate tendency to count instantaneously up to 3 or 4 objects. Mathematical operations do make use of rote learning. Studies using brain imagery suggests that the area of the brain used for memorizing poems is also used for the memory of multiplication tables which is dominantly used during simple arithmetic operations (Dehaene, 1999). Further, these areas are

Table 5.1: Core concepts and its nature at class II and III level mathematics

Level	*Core Concept*	*Nature*
II.	Number	(Ordinal & cardinal)
	Addition-Subtraction	(Number line, tables, 10 × 10 grid, word problems),
	Multiplication	(Sign, tables)
	Geometric Shapes	(Spatial relations, solids, plane figures, lines)
	Measurements	(Length, non-standard units for measuring, arbitrary units, mass, capacity, time, money)
III.	Number	(Numeration system, In words and figures, Place value, Comparison)
	Addition	(Process, With/without regrouping, Alternative methods, Word problems)
	Multiplication	(Tables, Short-cuts, Solving and framing word problems)
	Geometric Shapes	(Basic shapes, Designs and models, Straight and curved lines, Closed and open figures)
	Time	(Read clock and tell time in hours, half and quarters, concepts of days, weeks, months)
	Subtraction	(Subtraction as comparison, with/without regrouping, word problems)
	Length, Mass & Capacity	(Standard and non-standard units)
	Division	(Equal sharing, grouping, checking using corresponding multiplication facts, word problems)
	Money	(Indian money, Conversion)
	Fractional Numbers	(Usage of active vocabulary, Identification of fractional parts of a whole and group)
	Pictorial	(Identification and interpretation of simple pictures,
	Representation of data	Symbols to represent specific number, Estimation of sum, difference, product and quotient of numbers)

spread throughout the brain. Symbols and abstraction are another important feature of mathematical operations. The concepts coming from a totally different sensorimotor ground are assigned symbols. Further, abstraction is an exercise of establishing cognitive relations between them.

Greater Social Responsibility

The behavioural scientists are supposed to play a much bigger social role as the diversity of cultural milieu demands different combat strategy for the larger social problems such as illiteracy. Studies show that with the increase in population and number of schools the number of illiterates as well as the drop-outs have not decreased. An interesting project was initiated by a NGO to promote self-prompted education in the non-school goers. Kiosks, i.e., the touch screen systems, were located in the remote villages of Maharashtra and the results were surprising. Without any background knowledge of computers and without any provocation young boys and girls started using kiosks.

Here the behavioural scientists have an important role to play. They can collaborate with the experts of communication design and computer science to develop concept and age specific artifacts that are also culturally acceptable. Here the whole traditional knowledge system can be incorporated to develop such artifacts.

One illustration is presented here. As shown in Table 5.1 one of the primary requirements of mathematics syllabus at class III is to read clock and tell time in hours, half hours and even in quarters. Experiences show that this is a slow and effortful task for the primary level students. To make youngsters learn this concept a suggestive artifact is given below (Figure 5.1).

Here figure 5.1 presents the time in a conventional clock with a digital marker in the centre. The child reads the time pronounces it and then the digital marker illustrates the right time. For kiosk users this becomes an auto correction device. After developing sufficient comfort the users can try their competence using prototype *B* and *C* with mentally rotating arms of the clock. In a teacher assisted situation the inclusion of overt action can make students and teachers develop their own artifacts to understand it better and transduce it into mental rotation. Once the entire concept of reading time is mastered *D* and *E* can be introduced. *D* projects shadow on the dial of the clock to reflect time. And then comes *E*, our cultural artifact used in ancient observatories to indicate time as well as eclipse. This entire display panel would

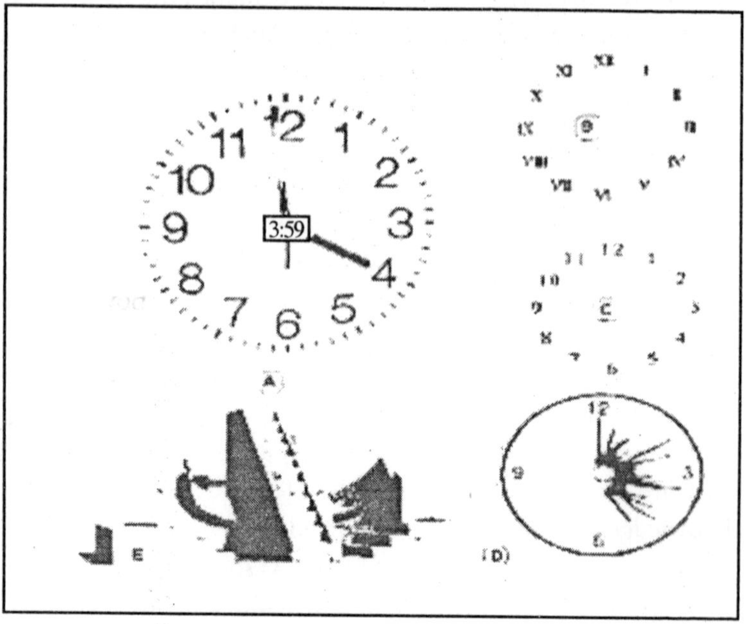

Figure 5.1

help a non-school goes learn what is needed at his/her age so that when he/she opts for open school pattern to clear high school examination the prerequisites are already clear.

This entire presentation also emphasize upon the development of thinking skills in students. A blend of modern technique suitable to a culture can be used to impart basic skills (reading, writing, arithmetic/mathematics) as well as thinking skills (creative thinking, decision making, problem solving, visualizing, reasoning).

The most attractive feature of this exercise can be curricular integration. Along with the focus on structure and method as well as factual content, the system can incorporate techniques facilitating higher-order thinking processes and casual reasoning, explicitly encouraging meta-cognition and meta-reasoning. The same illustration can be further used to make the concept of eclipse clear and so forth.

REFERENCES

Bachelard, G. (1938). *La Formation de l'esprit Scientifique,* J, Vrin, Paris: France.

Bhushan, B. (2004). Contemporary Cognitive Paradigms and Education: An Application Based Approach. Paper presented at Education and Social Science Paradigm, Jawaharlal Nehru University, New Delhi, India March 11-13.

Bodker, S. (1989). A human activity approach to user interfaces. *Human Computer Interaction,* 4, 171–195.

Ching, C.C.; Levin, J.A.; & Parisi, J. (2003). Artifacts of knowledge and practice in university teaching and learning. Paper presented at Perspectives on Artifacts in Physical and Virtual Learning Environmental, American Education Research Association, Chicago, April 22.

Clabaugh, S. (1993). *Design of general purpose classrooms, lecture halls, and seminar rooms: 2nd Edition.* University of Maryland at College Park.

Cole, M. (1990). Cultural psychology: A once and future discipline? Paper presented at the Nebraska Symposium.

Das, L., & Bhushan, B. (2005). From hard poetics to situated reading: A cognitive empirical study of imagery and graded figurative language. In H. Veivo, B. Petterson & M. Polvinen (eds.) *Cognition & Literacy Interpretation in Practice,* University of Helsinki Press.

Degani, A. & Wiener, E. L. (1990). Human factors of JQightdech checklists: The normal checklist (Contractor's Report). Moffett Field, CA: National Aeronautics and Space Administration, Ames Research Center.

Dehaene, S. (1997). *The number sense: How the mind creates mathematics.* Oxford University Press.

Dehaene, S. and associates (1999). Sources of Mathematical Thinking: Behavioral and Brain-Imaging Evidence, Science. 284, 970-974.

Fauconnier, G. & Turner, M. (2002) *The way we think: Conceptual blending and the mind's hidden complexities,* Basic Books.

Frake, C. (1985). Cognitive maps of time and tide among medieval seafarers. *Man,* 20, 254-270.

Garland, V. E. (1999). Improving computer skills in colleges of education. *Educational Technology Systems,* 28, 59-66.

Groves, M.M. & Zemel, P.C. (2000). Instructional technology adoption in higher education: An action research case study. *International Journal of Instructional Media,* 27, 57-65.

Hadamard, J. (1945). *The Psychology of Invention in the Mathematical Field.* Princeton University Press.

Hart, K.M. (ed) (1981) : *Children's Understanding of Mathematics* 11-16, John Murray.

Hutchins, E. (1995). *Cognition in the wild.* Cambridge, MA: MIT Press.

Hutchins, E. (2002) Material anchors for conceptual blends. Proceedings of The Way We Think, Symposium on Conceptual Blending, University of Southern Denmark.

Hutchins, E., Hollan J., & Norman D.A. (1986). Direct manipulation interfaces. In D.A. Norman & S. Draper (eds.), *User centered system design: New perspectives in human-computer interaction.* Hillsdale, NJ : Lawrence Erlbaum Associates.

Indurkhya, B. (1992). *Metaphor and cognition: An interactionistic approach,* Kluwer Academic Publishers.

Krish, D. (1995). The intelligent use of space. *Artificial Intelligence,* 72, 1-52.

Leont'ev, A.N. (1981). *Problems of the development of mind.* Moscow: Progress Publishers.

Norman, D.A. & Hutchins, E. (1990). Checklists. Unpublished manuscript, Department of Cognitive Science, University of California, San Diego.

Norman, D. A. (1993). *Things That Make Us Smart.* Reading, MA: Addison Wesley.

Norman, D.A. (1991). Cognitive artifacts. In John M. Carroll (Ed.), *Designing interaction,* Cambridge University Press, Cambridge.

NTSB. (1989). Aircraft accident report Delta Air Lines, Inc., Boeing 727232, N473DA, DallasFort Worth International Airport, Texas, August 31, 1988 (Report No: NTSB/AAR88/05, Govt. Accession No: PB 89/04. September 26, 1989). Washington, DC: National Transportation Safety Board.

Ochs, E.; Gonzales, P.; & Jacoby, S. (1996). When I come down, I'm in the domain state: Grammar and graphic representation in the interpretative activity of physics. In E. Ochs, E. Schegloff, & S. Thompson (eds.), *Interaction and grammar.* England: Cambridge University Press, pp. 328-369.

Restle, F. (1961). *Psychology of judgement and choice.* New York: Wiley.

Roth, W.M. (2001). Gestures: Their role in teaching and learning. *Review of Educational Research,* 71, 365-392.

Saxe, G.B. (2001). *Cultural and cognitive development: Studies in mathematical understanding.* Hillsdale, NJ: Lawrence Erlbaum and associates.

Scribner, S. (Ed.) (1984). Cognitive studies of work. *Quarterly Newsletter of the Laboratory of Comparative Human Cognition,* 6, No. 1 and 2.

Sfard, A., & McClain, K. (2002). Analyzing tools: Perspectives on the role of designed artifacts in mathematics learning. *Journal of the Learning Sciences,* 11, 153-162.

Stevens, S.S. (1975). On the psychophysical law. *Psychological Review,* 64, 153-181.

Tall, D. (1989). New Cognitive Obstacles in a Technological Paradigm. Research Issues in the Learning and Teaching of Algebra, *N.C.T.M.,* 87-92.

Vygotsky, L.S. (1981). The genesis of higher mental functions. In J.Wertsch (ed.), *The concept of activity in Soviet psychology* (pp. 144-188). Armonk, NY: M.E. Sharpe Inc. Publisher.

Vygotsky, L.S. (1978). *Mind in society: The development of higher mental processes.* M. Cole, V. John Steiner, S. Scribner, & E. Souberman (eds.) Cambridge, MA: Harvard University Press.

Wertsch, J.V. (1985). *Vygotsky and the social formation of mind.* Cambridge, MA: Harvard University Press.

7 Vedantic Approach to the Understanding of Human Mind, Behaviour and Karma

M.B. Sharan

Psychology : Gaining Conciousness

Psychology began as the study of consciousness, then turned to the study of observable behaviour. Today, it is the science of both: behaviour and mental processes. Thus, what psychology lost once (consciousness), it is gaining again with renewed vigour in the name of mental processes (Myers, 1986). Now, the question is: Why these swings of interest? Actually, in the beginning, the difficulty of studying consciousness scientifically led many psychologists to turn to direct observations of behaviour. But, by 1960, advances in neuroscience made it possible to relate brain activity to various mental states —waking, sleeping, and dreaming. As a result, today, many psyhologists are affirming the importance of mental processes and are looking afresh into the power of infinite mind.

Human Mind : Conscious, Subconscious or Unconscious?

The nature of human mind, however, is very difficult to understand because it is very subtle as well as hidden. Therefore, it has been defined in different ways by different thinkers. Since Freud originally defined the structure of personality in terms of the unconscious, preconscious, and conscious, we psychologists have also been talking about the same topographical model all these years — 'conscious' as the part of the psyche that includes material of which one is fully aware; 'preconscious' (or 'subconscious') as the part of the psyche that includes material which is not at the moment within one's awareness but which can readily be brought to the conscious mind; and 'unconscious' as the part of the psyche that includes material not within one's awareness and which cannot readily be brought to the conscious mind (Even, 1980). And thus, under the influence of Freud and his psychoanalysis, we have been recognizing unconscious factors as significant determinants of human behaviour.

Recently, however, a new debate between the "minds" has started and many of the thinkers and researchers are recommending to maintain a balance between the unconscious mind and the conscious/subconscious mind. They are just a way of describing events — 'conscious' as whatever we are aware of at a moment, and 'unconscious' as everything else—that are useful in the context of therapeutic change (Bundler & Grinder, 1979). Otherwise, as a whole, we have only one mind. This can be supported by an example. Suppose, we are driving along the highway returning home; on approaching the neighborhood, we start realizing that for the past several minutes our mind has been elsewhere. Daydreaming, thinking about things, our mind has been on anything but paying attention to the road. We wonder how we managed to watch out for cars, follow traffic signals, and make the right turns when we were "not there". Thus, there are a number of things we are doing without paying proper attention to all at a time and the pendulum of awareness swings between the "minds" without any difficulty.

Now, the question is : By which name should this one mind be known? Those who are working in the field of information processing say that conscious awareness is just the tip of the iceberg. It simply enables us to exert voluntary control and to communicate our mental states to others (Kihlstrom, 1987). Beneath the surface, actually, subconscious information processing occurs simultaneously on many parallel tracks. When we look at a flying bird, we are consciously aware of the result of our cognitive processing but not of our sub-processing of the bird's colour, form, movement, distance and identity. Therefore, from the functional viewpoint, it is the subconscious mind (including unconscious) which takes care of all the processes that are occurring out of conscious awareness. This one mind thus should be known as the subconscious mind.

Philosophers and some other thinkers, however, attach maximum importance to the conscious part of the mind. They say that it is the conscious part of the mind which does all the processing of information because it is logical, reasonable and can change its point of view at will. Since the subconscious mind is not logical and reasonable, it cannot take any independent decision of its own and it has to simply support the conscious mind. According to Vedanta (Ellis, 1994), the mind is called *antahkarana,* that is, "internal instrument" which perceives through five sense organs—eyes, ears, nose, tongue, and skin. It also instructs the five organs of action—the organ of speech, the hands, the legs, the organ of procreation, and the organ of evacuation. Thus, *Vedanta* recognizes the different functions of the mind—cognition, feeling and willing as the primary functions and memory, imagination, love, hatred, hope, fear, anger etc. as the other functions. All these functions are possible only through the power of consciousness. And thus, the 'one mind' should be known as the conscious mind because it has the power to be illuminated by consciousness.

Vedanta says further that the power of consciousness, however, is not the built-in-characteristic of the mind. This comes from some higher source known as *Soul, Atman* or *Self.* Since mind is not the real perceiver or knower of the mental phenomenon, Hindu religion differentiates between the mind and the Self—the mind as an object (the known) and the Self as a subject (the knower). Anything that falls into the category of the known does not have consciousness as its very essence whereas the subject or knower does. Thus, there is one ultimate observer or experience, and that is the Self. This is the reason why today many are also supporting the idea that there are three distinct factors of human personality—the physical body, the mind, and the soul. They are vitally connected and though they appear to be one single entity, they are distinguishable.

Recently, some Western psychologists (Reed, 1989) have also started talking about the 'super conscious' and the 'universal' parts of the mind which were accepted by Indian thinkers ages ago. Since Freud did not support Jung's collective unconscious mind, the transpirational mind remained neglected all these years. Otherwise, Jung was of the firm opinion that the unconscious mind gave us all the encouragement and help that a bountiful nature could shower on man. "It holds possibilities which are locked away from the conscious mind, for it has at its disposal all subliminal psychic contents, all those things which have been forgotten or overlooked, as well as the wisdom and experience of uncounted centuries which are laid down in its archetypal organs.....The unconscious can serve man as a unique guide, provided he can resist the lure of being misguided" (Ellis, 1994). Thus, the unconscious mind should not be treated as the 'forgotten' mind or the dark side of the mind. It has many spiritual and moral possibilities hidden within it.

Conclusion : Super Conscious Mind as the Soul's Mind

Now, the question is : What should we conclude from all these? We should not get caught by the words 'conscious', 'subconscious' and 'unconscious'. They are just to describe different functions of the same mind. There are conscious and considered thought, subconscious having recallable memories, habits, and old feelings, and unconscious having forgotten instincts, conditioning and collective or universal experiences. Each of these is accessible to us in some way because they communicate with each other in their own way. We should, therefore, try to develop such a mind which can perceive and judge things rightly making use of all the information—conscious, subconscious or unconscious. According to *Vedanta*, "The richest soil, the soil of the human mind, lies fallow. If it could be tilled well it would yield golden crops, but since it lies fallow, it yields brambles and thorny bushes and weeds" (Ellis, 1994). That means, if there are wrong tendencies lying within, they have to be weakened by constant effort. Since the subconscious and the unconscious mind work mechanically, such change is possible only by the conscious mind through its special power of self-determination. Thus, for the development of the mind, we have to feed the mind with rich food, nourish it regularly, strengthen it, and enrich it. As a result, we can have good understanding, peace, wisdom and joy. In this sense, our mind, illuminated by the Self, becomes the *Superconscious mind* and becomes the source of super-sensory perception, inspiration and creativity.

Human Behaviour : Physical, Mental or Spiritual?

American psychologists defined psychology as "the science of observable behaviour." For them, behaviour was an overt activity of the organism. Since sensation, feeling and emotion (or any other subjective matter) were not observable, they could not be the subject matter of psychology. As a result, many of the studies in psychology remained restricted to overt activities of an organism for many-many years in the hands of behaviourists. But, today, we are not agreeing with the behaviourists and are studying mental processes in psychology as well. Not only that, we also try to explain every human behaviour in terms of 'mind' involved in it. Since mind instructs the body to behave in a definite way, every resultant behaviour is having minimum two aspects—*the physical,* and *the mental.* In order to have an effective behaviour, we try to maintain a balance between the two. In this process, the effective behaviour, in which mind and body work together without dominating upon each other, becomes "spiritual" in nature due to Gestalt effect. We can take the example of understanding love in a laboratory. Is it not a fact that by putting love under scientific scrutiny, we are destroying its mystery? In reality, love includes affection and anger, excitement and boredom, stability and change, bond and freedom, etc. This, therefore, cannot be known by any scientific method. As a result, those researchers, who have tried to know about it by using all sorts of sophisticated instruments, have found it to be a 'triangle' of which the three sides represent physiological, psychological, and anthropological factors. But, outside the laboratory, the "true love" has emerged as a 'circle' which combines all the three kinds of factors into one. This organization as a whole is known as "spiritual love" in which all the parts are merged with each other. This is such a nice blend that no factor is dominating upon anyone. This kind of "true love" cannot be analyzed but can be experienced. Like this, every human behaviour needs to be effective (spiritual) and needs to be known as *karma.*

What is *Karma*?

Karma is a Sanskrit word which literally means action. But in Indian philosophy it also signifies cause and effect relationship. In the case of animals, instinct prevails but, in the case of human beings, reason prevails. Therefore, only human being has the freedom and capacity to judge rightly or wrongly about his/her behaviour. This exercise of judgement is known as *karma* and this makes human life as the *karma-bhumi.* All of us believe in the divine statement that 'As you sow, so you reap'. According to Newton's third law of motion, "Each action has an equal and opposite reaction." Edger Cayce proves with enough evidence that this law applies also to the moral world (McArthur, 1993). Thus, though the word "*karma*" is often used by us casually, it has many implications.

There is a strong belief in Indian culture, and more recently in Western culture, that the soul travels from one body to the next. The force that drives the process of rebirth of the soul is an element of *karma*. That means, the body is temporal and the soul is infinite. According to Harra (2002), "Human beings come into a body alone and when we shed our body we die alone. The only thing we take with us are our memories, our *karma.*" *Karma* is thus the mental and physical deeds that determine the effects of our life and rebirth and can be consequences from our previous lives or from actions in this one.

This shows clearly that our *karma* can be at least of three types: Present (*Agami*), Past (*Prarabdha*), and Accumulated (*Sanchita*). Present *karma* is everything we do today that creates cause and effect in future. Whether we realize it or not, everyday we are creating *karma* with every thought and action. Either we kill an insect, abuse someone, or are jealous of a friend, we are creating bad *karma*. All of this negative thinking and action creates negative memory in our subconscious mind and is stored in our brain. Thus, everyday, "there are a million activities in the brain that can create bad *karma*" (Harra, 2002). Similarly, every single thing we do each day that is positive-helping a person, aiding a beggar, or showing sympathy and love-creates good *karma*. In this sense, life is a constant balancing act of offsetting the bad *karma* with the good. Past *karma* is things we have already done either in this life or in past lives. This has already been set in motion and is the consequence that we are left to deal with. If our past thoughts and actions were positive, then we reap the rewards, and if they were negative, we are paying the consequences.

We have seen that everyday in our life whatsoever we do, *karma* is created. If we don't erase it or heal it at the end of everyday, it will accumulate and become bigger. Such accumulated *karma*—accumulated over time and sometimes over many lifetimes—work like the "snowball effect". Negative action will start multiplying from the moment it is committed. If a person tells a lie, he or she has to create more lies for protecting himself/herself from being found out. Overtime all of these lies can accumulate into one big lie and the consequences of not telling the truth will only get worse. We, therefore, need to resolve negative *karma* everyday by regular prayer (confession) and by more and more positive acts. Left unresolved, it may never be healed, and we have to live with the consequential suffering.

Laws of Cause and Effect

One of the great laws by which our lives are shaped is the master law of cause and effect. This law is so pervasive in our lives that many persons refer to our world as a causation world. Nothing that happens in our world or to us personally ever happens by itself or without cause. Thus, in the earth plane cause and effect is the natural law which decides everything.

If so, what about chance? Most of us believe that chance, luck and accidental events play a part, for better or worse, in our lives. But in reality, "*there is nothing by chance*" and this also follows from the law of cause and effect. It is a corollary of that law because it represents another way of stating "for every effect there is a cause." It is thus the reciprocal of that law. At times, there may be something which might be called accidents but, in reality, they too are governed by the same law of cause and effect. When one individual asked Edgar Cayce why he had an accident and what was its purpose, he replied that it was to create an experience from which lessons might be learned. In view of this realization it can be added that every accident can be made more meaningful by expressing it as:

Nothing Happens By Chance;
There Is A Purpose To
Everything That Happens.

Many time people confuse *karma* with fate or destiny. But *karma* is neither fate nor destiny; it is cumulative memory. There is a certain degree of preordained "facts" about our life which determine our parents, time and place of birth and death, certain elements of our health, etc. These are all unchangeable facts and we have to go through these events as lessons. Fate is thus something fixed like data in the computer. But destiny is the things we can change. We can decide to marry, to have children, to use our skills and talents, and to resolve our *karma*. Thus, "*Karma* is the combination of thoughts and actions that help us deal with our fate and create our destiny" (Harra, 2002).

Karmic Resolution

Every thought and action, whatsoever we do, creates memory and comes back either to bless or haunt us. This is what makes us unique and composes our lives. It also creates a field of information around us at the level of energy. We store this information in our field like data in a computer. This data or memory is either positive or negative. All the negative memory will resurface in our life again and again, and the only way to move forward is to resolve it. Reincarnation is thus one opportunity to repair what we did wrong. It is an opportunity to come back and repent, to ask for forgiveness and change what we did wrong. The attainment of elightenment removes the accumulated bad *karma* of the past and eliminates the need to reincarnate (come back). Thus ultimately, life is a process of introspecting our thoughts and actions and resolving the bad *karmas* everyday. This can be achieved through purifying the mind and following the *Karmic* Resolution Method as suggested by Harra (2002).

The mind is said to be one's greatest friend as well as one's worst enemy. If the mind is fully controlled, then it will prove to be his/her best friend, otherwise, it will be the worst enemy. Our strength and weakness, happiness and unhappiness, knowledge and ignorance, freedom and bondage, all depend on the condition of mind. Thus, unless mind is purified, we cannot have good *karmas*. Now, the question is : what are these impurities adhering to the mind? Patanjali (Ellis, 1994) says that there are five kinds of impurities:

(1) *Ignorance:* We do not know the truth but we always pose to about it.
(2) *Egoism:* We identify our true self with psychophysical system which is not the real one.
(3) *Attachment:* We feel attached to the physical world.
(4) *Aversion:* We have a strong dislike or antipathy for an object or a person.
(5) *Infatuation:* We are carried away by foolish or shallow love.

Releasing ourselves from bad *karma* is the only way to reach eternity, to achieve immortality. This can be accomplished only when we accept that "there are no coincidences" and our *karmas* are governed by the "law of consequences". When we acknowledge the divine in ourselves to resolve our *karmas*, we become honest to ourselves and view our life objectively. We use our new awareness to move forward by healing the past and making the right changes in our *karmas* for the future. This kind of realization helps us in attaining enlightenment which removes the accumulated bad *karmas* of the past and eliminates the need to reincarnate. Harra (2002) has suggested the following ten steps to resolve our *karma* in three important areas of life — relationships, health and fulfilling life purpose:

(1) *Deep Breathing:* Breath not only gives life, it also creates a bridge between the subconscious and conscious mind and connects the mind and the body.
(2) *Memory Meditation:* It is a powerful tool for allowing our conscious mind to access what is at work in our subconscious mind.
(3) *Expanding Emotional Awareness:* Sometimes we react in a heightened way because of *karmic* memory or connection that is hidden in our unconscious. Expanding awareness allows us to break the cycle of inappropriate emotions.
(4) *Recognizing and Breaking Negative Patterns:* When we understand which emotions are dominating our life and begin to view them objectively, we may recognize some negative recurring patterns. Such patterns or grip which they have on our life must be broken.
(5) *Restoring Equilibrium:* We should use our conscious mind in reprogramming of the subconscious mind by using imagery that replaces all negative thoughts and beliefs with positive ones.
(6) *Designing a Vision for the Future:* After breaking all negative thoughts and emotions and replacing them by positive ones, we can begin to visualize a new way of living.

(7) *Gathering Powerful Positive Energy:* In order to create a new reality we would need to recharge our batteries by tapping into the energy of the Invisible World.

(8) *Affirmations for the New Reality:* We need personal affirmations, which should come from deep within, to reinforce our vision and keep the energy of the Universe focused.

(9) *Prayers for Gratitude and Happiness:* The most important way of celebrating our new life is through acknowledging the universal life force and kindness of God.

(10) *Recording and Tracking the Progress in a Journal :* Writing things regularly help to clarify our thoughts and record our progress on different *karmic* issues.

We should always remember that the Universe wants us to be happy and fulfilled and to travel on the path of spirituality. There are many persons who have achieved *karmic* success on this path only through regular prayer and meditation.

How Prayer and Meditation Work Together

Daily prayer and meditation should be our way of life — a way of sharing ourselves with God, and God sharing Himself with us. Therefore, both play their own parts in total communication with God—Prayer talks to Him and Meditation listens to Him (Fields & Clement, 1998). Prayer is about connecting to the divine, recognizing and clearing the *karmic* events of the day, and speaking out about pains and desires, whereas meditation is moving beyond any interfering thoughts and entering a relaxed, attentive, receptive deep communication with Him. Thus, meditation fulfils a purpose that prayer alone cannot provide.

Conclusions

While describing the human mind, we should not get caught by the words 'conscious', 'subconscious', and 'unconscious'. They are just to describe different functions of the same mind which is 'one' as a whole. According to *Vedanta*, this 'one mind' should be best known as the conscious mind because it has the power to be illuminated by consciousness. *Vedanta*, however, says further that the power of consciousness is not the built-in characteristic of the mind. This comes from some higher source known as *Atma*, *Self*, or *Soul*. As a result, today, many are differentiating between the mind and the soul, and are maintaining that there are three distinct aspects of the human personality — the physical (body), the mental (mind), and the spiritual (soul). These three are different from each other but they are vitally connected. And, in order to have an effective behaviour, we have to maintain a balance between the body and the mind in such a way that no one dominates upon the other one. This will always result in making the behaviour effective because this becomes spiritual in character by Gestalt effect.

For Indians, human behviour is '*karma*' — not just an action as described by American psychologists — because it signifies cause and effect relationship. Human beings have the freedom and capacity to judge rightly or wrongly about their behaviours. Therefore, this exercise of judgement is known as *karma* and the human life as *karmabhumi*. We also believe that the soul travels from one body to the next. This force which drives the process of rebirth of the soul is an element of *karma*. *Karma* is thus the mental and physical deeds that determine the effects of our life and rebirth and can be consequences from our previous lives or from behviours in this one.

Many times people confuse *karma* with destiny. But *karma* is neither fate nor destiny; it is cumulative memory. Fate is something fixed like data in the computer. We cannot decide about our parents, place of birth and death, etc. But destiny is the things we can change. We can decide to marry, to have children, to use our talents, and to resolve our negative *karmas*. Releasing ourselves from bad *karma* is the only way to reach eternity, to achieve immortality. But for this, we have to accept that "there are no coincidences" and all of us are governed by the universal spiritual "law of consequences". When we acknowledge the divine in ourselves to resolve, our *karmas*, we become honest to ourselves and view our life objectively. Daily prayer and meditation become our way of life — a way of sharing ourselves with God, and God sharing Himself with us.

REFERENCES

Bandler, R., & Grinder, J. (1979). *Frogs into princes: Neuro-linguistic programming.* UT: Real People Press.

Ellis, R. (ed.) (1994). *Mind: According to Vedanta.* Madras: Sri Ramkrishna Math.

Ewen, R.B. (1980). *An introduction to theories of personality.* New York: Academic Press.

Fields. V.T., & Clement, S.G. (1998). *Beginning the search for God.* Virginia: A.R.E. Press.

Harra, C. (2002). *Everyday Karma.* New York: Ballantine Books.

Kihlstrom, J.F. (1987). The cognitive unconscious. *Science, 237,* 1445-1452.

McArthur, B. (1993). *Your life: Why it is the way it is and what you can do about it.* Virginia: A.R.E. Press.

Myers, D.G. (1986). *Psychology* (4th ed.). New York: Worth Publishers.

Reed, H. (1989). *Edgar Cayce on mysteries of the mind.* New York: Warner Books.

8 Changing Family Structure and Development of Self and Values

Abha Misra *and* Janak Pandey

Family is a primary social institution of mankind. As a social institution family has diverse functions resting upon man's biological, social and psychological needs. The relationship pattern in the family is unique. The child enters the world at large from the platform of family. It is the family, which teaches the child how to look at things and what is to be seen. Family provides the context in which the child's initial sense of self develops and basic identities, motivations, values and beliefs are formed.

Human child enters this world with no self-conception, with the help of social interaction through socialization he identifies himself. There is a wide range of processes and outcomes of socialization within the family, especially for the child. Socialization involves the process of teaching members of the society what they need to know to maintain social life. Socialization practices ensure that people understand the system of norms and roles developed by society and conforming to them. This involves teaching shared goals and means to achieve them and establishing a system of control over individuals. It is to accomplish these tasks that individuals are socialized into the culture of their society.

Cross-cultural psychologists have studied the concept of self-construal. They studied that most of the Western countries have developed independent self-construal whereas Eastern countries have developed interdependent self-construal. The reason behind it is that most of the Western countries are developed, economically strong and many Eastern countries are developing. In developing countries people are interdependent with their in-groups giving priority to the goals of their in-groups that shape their behaviour primarily on the basis of in group norms. On the other hand, people from developed countries have more opportunity to develop oneself.

Cross-cultural psychologists have also proposed the cultural concept that is individualism and collectivism that explains cross-cultural differences in behaviour over a wide range of situations. Generally Western culture is called individualistic culture whereas Eastern culture is called collective culture. Collective values are more concerned towards group goals, while individualistic values are more concerned to their own needs and desires.

Indian culture and traditions are unique in many ways. The joint family, institution of marriage, socialization of children, social values and norms, are some examples of this uniqueness. Respect for tradition and desire for change are very common in our society. Thus Indians are both traditional and modern. As studies have revealed that Indian's are neither fully collective nor fully individualistic. Some other studies have found that on the familial level, Indians show collectivism, but they have also strong tendency of individualism. The question arises that whether Indian's are collectivistic or individualistic, and whether they have independent self-construal or interdependent self-construal. Where are the roots of their psychological characteristics? Is it in their family or in location of residence (urban and rural)? To answer these questions, this study which focused on the changing family structure and development of self and values was planned. The main objectives were:

1. To study the relationships among the demographic and social psychological variables, i.e. self-construals and social values.
2. To study the urban and rural background variations and changes in family and their impact on development of self-construals and social values.

Definition of Variables

Family Structure : Here two types of family structure, i.e. nuclear family and joint family has been taken. The nuclear family consists of parents and their children. The joint family consists of at least two married couples and their children, and food cooked in one kitchen.

Self-construal is defined here as a constellation of thoughts, feelings and action concerning the relationship of the self to family members and the self as distinct to family members. Independent self-construal, which means the image of self as separate from family members. Independent self-construal is defined as a "bounded, unitary, stable self, that is separate from the social context". The constellation of elements composing an independent self-construal includes an emphasis on uniqueness, strong sense of identity, take their own decision, being direct in communication.

Interdependent self-construal means, "the image of self as connected with others". It is defined as "flexible variables". Interdependent self that emphasizes sacrificing self-interest for one's own group, respecting group decision, valuable relationships and believes in hierarchy.

Value means children's perception about their family preferences. From individualistic values children learn from their family to weigh private goals more heavily than collective goals. The constellation of elements composing an individualistic values emphasizes on power, self-direction, achievement and stimulation.

Collective values are defined as those, which are learnt from one's own family to weigh collective goals more heavily than private goals. The constellation of elements composing of collectivistic values emphasizes on conformity, universalism, tradition and benevolence.

Sample

The respondents were 200 young children of 9-12 years of age.

Half of the respondents belonged to rural areas and other half of the respondents belonged to urban area of Allahabad district. In both rural and urban areas, half of the respondents were of nuclear family and another 50 per cent respondents were from joint family. Half of the respondents were boys and another half were girls taken from both urban and rural and joint and nuclear families. All the respondents were school going children.

The SES scale contains items on five dimensions, respondent's mother's education, mother's occupation, respondent's father's education, father's occupation and household goods (assets). There was some problem in collecting information about family income because the respondents were too young to know the economic status of their family. Therefore, information about assets was collected. To assess the socio-economic status of respondents, the presence of household goods in the family (cycle, gas, T.V., scooter, fridge, car, A.C.) were recorded on the basis of the checklist. Every category has some scores; each of these variables was assigned weight (score) to obtain a total SES score for the subject (Table 7.1). The scores on the scale range from 5 to 41. On the basis of scores obtained on the scale three SES classes were identified viz. upper, middle and lower.

Table 7.1: Assets Description

Assets	Weightage value
AC	7
Car/Tractor	6
Fridge	5
Television	4
Scooter	3
Gas	2
Cycle	1

Measures

The first part of the survey questionnaire consisted of items related to family, social, educational and economic background of the respondents. In addition, the following scales were developed and/ or suitably adopted for use: (i) Self-Construal Scale, and (ii) Social Value Scale.

Self-Construal Scale

In order to tap the development of self-concept of a child, a scale of 24 items was developed. This scale was adopted from the Singelis (1994) test of Self-Construal Scale, but the children were too young to understand abstract thoughts related to test items, made for adults. To overcome this type of problem, short story type situation was given to the children, which was easier to understand and respond.

Since one objective of this research was to understand the strength of independent and interdependent selves separately, two dimensions of scale measured two aspects of self, namely independent self-construal and interdependent self-construal.

Each item was followed by a four point response scale ranging from 1 (disagree) to 4 (very much agree). Higher score indicated the higher level of self-construal. Reliability coefficient alpha was calculated for independent self-construal scale and interdependent self-construal scale. Cronbach alpha for independent self-construal was found to be .53. Alpha for interdependent self-construal was found .52. Two items were deleted in interdependent self-construal scale because they showed negative correlation with total self-construal scale.

Social Value Scale

In order to understand development of values in children, a scale consisting of 16 items was developed. Social Value Scale consists of individualistic values and collectivist values. The basic format of items was adopted from Schwartz's (1990) Value Survey. However, some changes were made to suit the present need in Indian context on the basis of pilot study. The cronbach alpha for individualistic value was found to be .71. Two items were deleted in individualistic value scale because they show negative correlation with total social value scale. Alpha of collective value was found to be 64.

Procedure

In order to ascertain communicability and appropriateness of the questionnaire pilot test was administered individually on 8 respondents (4 boys and 4 girls) who were selected from the schools of both urban and rural areas. The boys and girls belonging to rural and urban areas were selected for pilot test, because the final sample was to be drawn from these two areas and groups. Another purpose of the pilot study was to examine the clarity and effectiveness of the instructions and discriminability of items of the questionnaire.

The respondents were approached individually in their schools. After taking permission from their Principal, the investigator introduced herself as a research scholar from the University of Allahabad, and explained that the purpose of the study was to conduct a survey about changing family structure and development of self and values. After establishing rapport, the respondents were requested to volunteer for the study. Questionnaire was used as a schedule. Schools were chosen to approach for data collection by the investigator because children were found to respond more freely in a natural way, in comparison to their homes.

Results and Discussion

A number of demographic variables and urban rural background are examined to understand self and values. Results (Table 7.2) show that SES was significantly positively correlated with independent self-construal, both individualistic and collective values. High SES children developed more independent self-construal. Hofestede (1991) and Triandis (1988) have both hypothesized that the mechanism underlying this relationship is that wealth increaseas opportunities to do one's own thing, which is the main characteristic of individualistic value. Results show that SES had correlated with collective values also. The reason may be these two values are interconnected with each other.

Table 7.2 : Correlation of Psychological Variables with Demographic Variables (Details of SES)

	Demographic Variables				
Psychological Variables	*Mother's Education*	*Mother's Occupation*	*Father's Education*	*Father's Occupation*	*Asset Values*
Independent Self-Construal	.29**	.04	.32**	.29**	.14*
Interdependent Self-construal	.03	-.12	.02	.08	.06
Individualistic Value	.45**	.08	.42**	.39**	.23**
Collective Value	.33**	.08	.31**	.40**	.20**

*p<.05, **p<.01

Mother's education was positively correlated with independent self-construal, both individualistic and collective values, individualistic social behaviour and self-esteem. It may be due to education, which serve as a big factor to be independent. As Gore (1968) found in his study that where the head of the family was educated and had a new type of white-collar job, some changes in the family take place. The influence of mother's education and employment status on child rearing practice was observed and it was found that they permitted more independence.

The result of inter-correlation amongst psychological variables show (Table 7.3) that independent self-construal was significantly and positively correlated with independent self-construal, both individualistic and collective values. Interdependent self-construal was significantly positively correlated with both individualistic and collective values. Individualistic value was significantly positively correlated with collective values. The above trends show that these psychological variables are not different from each other instead they are interconnected.

Table 7.3 : Inter-correlation Amongst Psychological Variables

	1	2	3	4	5	6	7
Independent Self-Construal	–			–	–	–	–
Interdependent Self-construal	.01	–		–	–	–	–
Individualistic Value	.43**	.38**	–	–	–	–	–
Collective Value	.25**	.41**	.52**	–	–	–	–

**p<.01.

Correlation results reveal that parents' education is positively related to self and values of the children. It may be due to ambitious and encouraging nature of educated parents that such parents create an atmosphere for development of self and positive self-esteem. This supportive nature probably facilitates development of self and values in children. Education leads to individualism (Mishra, 1994). Education of parents shows high correlation with individualistic and collective values and individualistic social behaviour. Sinha and Tripathi (1994) proposed that in India individualism and collectivism are considered to co-exist in the same person.

Family Structure Differences

Insignificant mean differences of family structure (nuclear and joint) for independent and interdependent self-construals, individualistic and collective values, suggested that the family structure does not play any role in the development of self and values.

The score range of independent self-construal (Table 7.4) is found to be 12-48 and mean value for joint family is 23.51 and for nuclear family is 24.03. The score range of interdependent self-construal is found to be 10-40 and mean value for joint family is 29.06 and for nuclear family is 28.65. This trend shows that mean value are neither higher nor low in the development of interdependent self-construal and independent self-construal. An observation by Tripathi (1988) is very relevant in this context. He notes that Indian mind is governed by boundaries, which are constantly shifting. In other words boundaries are variables. In case of Indian, the self sometimes expands to fuse with the cosmos but in another moment it completely withdraws itself from it. For a Western mind, dichotomy between self and others, men and nature, subjective and objective exists. In Indian case the self does not relate to the other group but is included in it (p. 322).

Table 7.4 : Means and ANOVAS for the Main Effects of Family Structure

	Family Structure		*ANOVA (F)*
	Joint Family (Mean)	*Nuclear Family (Mean)*	
Independent Self-Construal	23.51	24.03	.77
Interdependent Self-construal	29.06	28.65	.61
Individualistic Value	16.63	16.67	.01
Collective Value	23.70	23.47	.38

The score range of individualistic values was 6 to 24 and the mean value for joint family is 16.63 and for the nuclear family 16.67. The score range of collective values is found to be 8-32 and mean value for joint family is 23.70 and for nuclear family is 23.47. The mean of collective values is higher than individualistic values.

One is generally observed reason that respondents who belong to joint family, sometimes perceive that they belong to nuclear family but structurally (sociological definition) they belong to joint family. On the other hand, if they belong to nuclear family they perceive that they are also from joint family. Sinha (1984) has argued that in India only one structure of family existed that is extended family (Gore, 1968; Gupta, 1978; Ramanujam, 1972). Joint family is neither fully joint nor nuclear. The only family structure, which is found in India, is extended family structure.

As Kapadia (1966) has found that many people are still not prepared psychologically to completely break away from the joint family. Such dissatisfaction, as exists, is not so much against the system itself as against the atmosphere generated by the behaviour pattern of the certain members of the family. Structurally, the joint family breaks into nuclear units, functionally all the members of the family maintain "jointness" in terms of family loyalty.

In other words, the Indian family is in a transitional phase. Though the joint family system seems to be on the way out, the Indian family is far from becoming completely nuclear. It is true that the kind of economic and emotional security that the joint family provided to its members is gradually being lost. But the individuals appear to be reluctant to give up the advantages of joint living.

The results of ANOVA show that family structure did not play any role in the development of self and values, social behaviour and self-esteem. Indian society is in the transitional phase. As many scholars found that in India there is only one structure of family existed which is extended family, therefore, clear-cut difference between joint and nuclear family could not be seen.

Location of Residence Differences

Result of ANOVA depicts (Table 7.5) significant mean difference of location of residence (urban and rural) for independent self-construal, individualistic and collective values. The respondents of urban areas had developed more independent self-construal, and individualistic and collective values.

Table 7.5 : Means and ANOVA's for the Main Effect of Residence

Psychological Variables	*Residence*		*ANOVA (F)*
	Rural (Mean)	*Urban (Mean)*	
Independent Self-Construal	22.40	25.14	21.23***
Interdependent Self-construal	28.69	29.02	.39
Individualistic Value	15.22	18.00	51.91***
Collective Value	22.60	24.57	27.64***

***p<.001.

The hypothesis based on Singelis (1994) work, that urban area is responsible for the development of independent self-construal, has been proved. But another hypothesis that rural area is responsible for the development of interdependent self-construal, has been rejected. Watkins and Regmi (1996) found that the rural, less modernized group, gave fewer individualist responses. The reason behind it could be that urban areas are the first who get influenced with western culture, which is predominantly independent self-construal. The Western culture emphasizes mostly on being unique, strong sense of identity, taking their own decision and being direct in communication, and these are the main characteristic of independence. As Triandis (1989) and Markus and Kitayama (1991) also found that ethnic groups at different stages of modernization or westernization are likely to differ also in terms of the nature of their self-conceptions, in particular that the more "modern" group will tend to describe themselves in a more independent, and individualistic manner.

In the case of social values, the results show that rural area is not responsible for the development of individualistic values. But urban area is responsible for the development of individualistic social values. Hofestede (1991) claimed that industrialized, wealthy, and urbanized societies tend to become increasingly individualistic (Misra, 1994), whereas traditional, poorer, and rural societies tend to remain collectivistic.

The study of urban rural difference has found that urban area is responsible for the development of independent self-construal, individualistic and collective values, but rural area is not responsible for the development of interdependent self-construal as studies has shown. The reason could be urban residents get firstly influenced with western culture, therefore, they have modernized view but on the other hand rural area also get influenced with urban area because every information, with the help of filter process, comes to rural people.

Gender Difference

Results of ANOVA depict (Table 7.6) male and female did not differ significantly on the self-construals and values. In terms of gender differences results reveal that male and female did not differ on the social values. Watkins and Regmi (1996) also found that males did not report a more individualistic self than females. Misra (1994) also found no high degree of either collectivism or individualism.

Table 7.6 : Means and ANOVA's for the Main Effect of Gender

	Male (Mean)	*Female (Mean)*	*ANOVA (F)*
Independent Self-Construal	24.22	23.32	2.29***
Interdependent Self-construal	29.36	28.35	3.69***
Individualistic Value	16.97	16.33	2.61***
Collective Value	23.68	23.49	.26

***p<.001.

Family, Residence and Gender Differences

The three-way interactions were not found significant for any of the variables like independent, interdependent self-construal, individualistic and collective values.

In order to analyze the unique contribution of each variable, univariate analysis of variance was computed. Development of independent self-construal as a function of two way interaction of family structure and residence of sample are shown in Fig. 7.1. The mean of both urban joint and nuclear family respondents are higher than the mean of the rural group. The results show that difference in nuclear rural and urban family is less than in joint family on the development of independent self-construal. Joint family of the urban is different from the joint family of rural area. In the urban joint family, generally one finds several nuclear families living in the same household. In this study, sociological definition of joint family that two couples with their children living in one accommodation and cooking food in one hearth was used. Everyone takes care of his own family (husband, wife and children) in spite of living together (two couples and their children), at one accommodation and using one kitchen. In the joint family there are more than one family units living together. They compare with each other and develop competition rather than co-operation. Rapid changes in both structure and functions of joint family are observed due to economic and socio-cultural processes. Thus, the child who belongs to urban joint family develops independent self-construal. In the rural joint family, money is in the hand of head of the family and the head of the family allocates it so they develop dependence and co-operation.

Fig. 7.1 : Development of Independent self-construal as a function of two-way interaction of Family Structure and Residence of sample

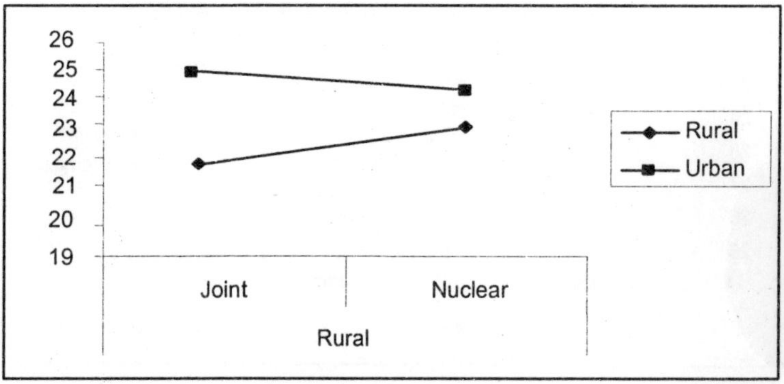

Development of interdependent self-construal as a function of two-way interaction of family structure and gender of sample are shown in Fig. 7.2. Males are shown low on interdependent self-construal and females high on interdependent self-construal in joint family but male are high on interdependent self-construal in nuclear family than females. Males and females of joint family differ less on interdependent self-construal but male and female of nuclear family differ significantly on the development of interdependent self-construal. The reason may be that in the nuclear family this primary group is very intact and concerned with others. All the family members understand each other and feel good whenever they are together. There is a lack of competitive environment and so they co-operate with each other. Nuclear family is, therefore, responsible for the development of interdependent self-construal but this phenomenon is only applicable for males only. Christakopoulou (1995) explored the social bonds in the life space of the community in the five cultural groups (Britain, Germany, Netherlands, Cyprus and Greece), emotional closeness to family members was shown to be a "strong universal dimension" (Leung & Bond 1989; Triandis, McCusker, Betancourt, Iwao, Leung, Salazar, Setiadi, Sinha, Touzard, & Zaleski, 1993).

Fig. 7.2 : Development of Interdependent self-construal as a function of two-way interaction of Family Structure and gender of sample

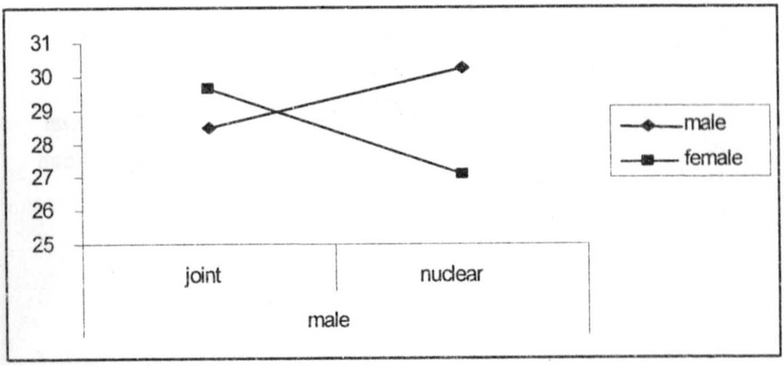

Another reason may be socialization practices. Males are trained as a future protector of the family. They show higher scores in interdependent self-construal in nuclear family. But girls show low interdependent self-construal in nuclear family. The reason may be that they are socialized in permissive manner. Increasing rate of literacy, to be independent is high in females. They get freedom for the first time and they want to enjoy all their freedom but boys have always freedom. This is the reason why joint family males show high interdependence and female show less interdependence.

Development of interdependent self-construal as a function of two-way interaction of residence and gender of sample are shown in Fig. 7.3. The results show that rural male and female differ less on interdependent self-construal but urban male and female differ significantly on the development of interdependent self-construal. Urban males were higher on interdependent self-construal as compared to females of urban areas. The reason may be that rural area had less opportunity to get education, and for jobs. But urban area has relatively higher opportunities. They understand that if they live jointly they would be more powerful. Males are socialized to consider as protectors and controller of the family (Dube, 1958), therefore, they develop interdependent self-construal. Money and feeling of security has played a very important role in joint living. This is applicable for urban area. In the rural area, people are poor. They are not able to fulfil their day-to-day needs, so they develop less interdependent self-construal. On the other hand, females show less interdependence in urban area; the reason behind it was that they have better opportunity to get education. Education is a big factor to increase independence.

Fig. 7.3 : Development of Interdependent self-construal as a function of two-way interaction of Residence and gender of sample

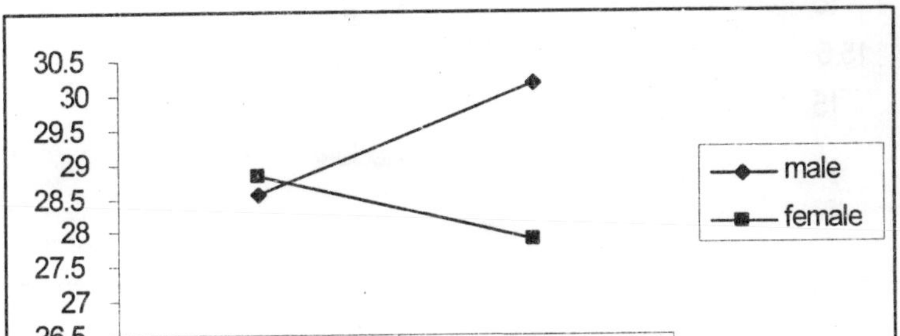

Development of individualistic values as a function of two-way interaction of family structure and gender of sample are shown in Fig. 7. 4. The results show that male and female of joint family did not differ on individualistic values but male and female of nuclear family differ. Nuclear families differ in individualistic values where male shows high individualistic values than females. Many studies by Cross and Madson (1997) and other scholars have found this type of phenomena. The reason as observed was that boys get more freedom and have more opportunity. On the other hand females from nuclear family have less individualistic values. The reason is that they are socialized in a restricted manner so individualistic values are suppressed in them. In the nuclear family they are in a position of getting attention of everyone hence they do not reinforce their individualistic values.

Figure 7.4 : Development of Individualistic Values as a function of two-way interaction of Family structure and gender of sample

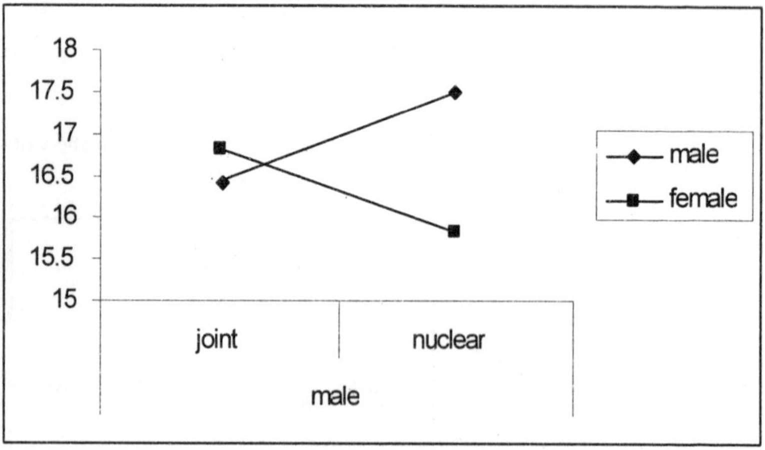

Development of collective values as a function of two-way interaction of family structure and gender are shown in Fig. 7.5. Fig. 7.5 shows that males of nuclear family show high collective values than males of joint family but females show less collective values in nuclear family than females of joint family. The reason is that male socializes as a protector and controller of the family so they take every member together. Therefore, on the familial level they show collectivism.

Fig. 7.5 : Development of Collective Values as a function of two-way interaction of Family structure and gender of sample

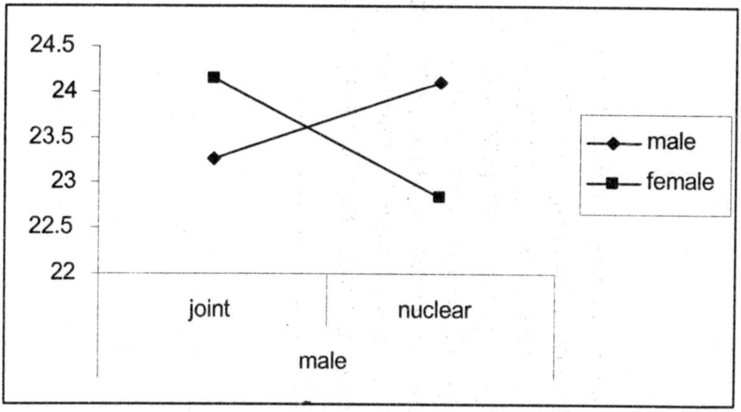

This study also found girls showing higher individualistic tendency in their behaviour. It can be explained with the help of increasing self-efficacy in girls. They think that they can do everything. They want to enjoy their freedom as maximum as they can. As Sinha and Tripathi (1994) have concluded that individualistic and collective values coexisted in a person. Therefore, here tendency was seen that boys are high in both individualistic and collective values and on the other hand girls show low individualistic and collective values. The reason may be in Indian religion or in the economic system. Young (1986) found that in order to understand the personality and self-construal of other cultures, it is necessary to examine the philosophical and religious underpinnings, traditional social structures and the economic system.

In India mostly individuals belong to Hindu religion. Their philosophy is whatever you have done you will be responsible for that. It shows individualism. Hindu religion is transcendental but traditional social structures are collective. As Verma (1996) also found that religion is a strong force, which guides Indian's co-operative and collective behaviours. Many of their rituals, customs and festivities are basically governed by canons of the God's and must be performed jointly by all the members by the community. All kinds of festivals they enjoy with each other. An Indian is, therefore, not surprised or shocked by coexistence of things, which are mutually contradictory either in his own mind or in reality. His morality is contractual and not absolute (Tripathi, 1988).

Japanese (collective society) and American (individualistic society) economic system are discussed here to understand how economic system affects value system. William Ouchi presented a popular view in the early 1980s. His analysis focused on characteristics of organizations as the basis for comparison. Ouchi listed such distinguishing features of Japanese organizations as lifetime employment, slow evaluation and promotion, non-specialized career paths, implicit control mechanisms, collective decision-making, collective responsibility, and holistic concern for employees. In contrast, qualities inherent in American organizations include short-term employment, rapid evaluation and promotion, specialized career paths, explicit control mechanisms, individual decision-making, individual responsibility, and a more segmented concern for workers.

All these characteristics have been seen in Indian economic system. Public sector is based on Japanese system and private sector is based on American system. This is the reason why Indian system is collective and individualistic also. In Indian society, individualism and collectivism act like figure and ground. Depending on the situation, one rises to form the figure while the other recedes into the background.

Conclusion

- The results of ANOVA show that family structure did not play any role in the development of self and values.
- The study of urban rural difference has found that urban area is responsible for the development of independent self-construal, individualistic and collective values, but rural

area is not responsible for the development of interdependent self-construal.

- The joint influence of family structure and residence results show that joint families from urban area were found to be more responsible for the development of independent self-construal.
- The interaction of family structure and gender results show that males from nuclear family show high interdependent self-construal as compared to females from nuclear family.

Policy Implications

The findings of the study clearly implicate role of family and culture in understanding of development of self and values, and the way self and values influence our social behaviours and self-esteem. The findings provide a lead for future research related to antecedents of self and values on the one hand and consequences of self and values on the other. Understanding complexity of social behaviour is quite a task and this study makes a positive contributions in that direction.

Future Trends

- These changing scenarios can be seen in a broad age range of child participants.
- For the participation of the non-school going children, different kinds of methods can be used.
- The study may be conducted at metro city Allahabad, a small city, and rural setting for the purpose of comparison.
- There is a need for psychological definition of family structure because these sociological definitions do not fulfil our need. Sometimes child belongs to joint family according to sociological definition but he perceives that he belongs to nuclear family and *vice versa*.

REFERENCES

Singelis, Theodore M. (1994). The measurement of independent and interdependent self-construals. *Personality and Social Psychology Bulletin.* 20 (5), 580-591.

Schwartz, Shalom H.; & Bilsky, Wolfgang (1990). Towards a theory of the universal content and structure of values: extensions and cross-cultural replications. *Journal of Personality and Social Psychology.* 58 (5), 878-891.

Hofestede, G. (1991). *Cultures and organizations: Software of the mind.* London: McGraw Hill.

Triandis, H.C. (1988). Collectivism and individualism: A reconceptualization of a basic concept in cross-cultural psychology. In G.K. Verma & C. Bargley (Eds.), *Personality, attitudes, and cognitions.* (60-95). London: MacMillan.

Gore, M.S. (1968). *Urbanization and Family Change.* Bombay : Popular Prakashan.

Mishra, R.C. (1994). Individualistic and collectivistic orientations across generations. In Uichol Kim, Harry C. Triandis, Cigdem Kagitcibasi, Sang-Chin Choi and Gene Yoon (eds.), *Individualism and Collectivism Theory, Method and Applications.* Thousand Oaks: Sage Publications.

Sinha, D. & Tripathi, R.C. (1994). Individualism in a collectivist culture A case of co-existence of opposites. In Uichol Kim, Harry C. Triandis, Cigdem Kagitcibasi, Sang-Chin Choi and Gene Yoon (eds.), *Individualism and Collectivism Theory, Method and Applications.*. Thousand Oaks: Sage Publications.

Tripathi, R.C. (1988). Aligning development to values in India. In D. Sinha and H. S. R., Kao (eds.) *Social Values and Development: Asian Perspectives.* (315-332), New Delhi.

Sinha, D. (1984). Psychology in the context of Third World development. *International Journal of Psychology.* 19, 17-29.

Gupta, G.R. (1978). The Joint Family. In M.S. Das and P.D. Bardis (eds), *The Family in Asia.* 72-88, New Delhi: Vikas.

Ramanujam, B.K. (1972). The Indian family in transition. In *The Indian Family in the Change and Challenge of the Seventies.* New Delhi: Sterling Publishers, 22-34.

Kapadia, K.M. (1966) (ed). *Marriage and Family in India.* Oxford University Press.

Watkins, David & Regmi, Murari (1996). Within culture and gender differences in self-concept : An investigation with rural and urban Nepalese school children. *Journal of Cross Cultural Psychology.* 27, (6), 692-699.

Triandis, H. C. (1989). Self and social behaviour in differing cultural contexts. *Psychological Review.* 96, 269-289.

Markus, H. S. & Kitayama, Shinobu (1991) Culture and self: Implications for cognition, emotion, and motivation. *Psychological Review.* 98, 224-253.

Hofestede, G. (1991). *Cultures and orgunizations: Software of the mind.* London: McGraw Hill.

Leung, K. & Bond, M.H. (1989). On the empirical identification of dimensions for cross-cultural comparison. *Journal of Cross-Cultural Psychology.* 20, 133-151.

Triandis, H.C.; McCusker, C.; Betancourt, H.; Iwao, S.; Leung, K.; Salazar, J.M.; Setiadi, B.; Sinha, J.B.; Touzard, H.; & Zaleski, Z. (1993). An etic-emic analysis of individualism-collectivism. *Journal of Cross-Cultural Psychology.* 24, 366-383.

Dube, S.C. (1958). *India's Changing Villages.* Routledge and Kagan Paul.

Cross, S. E. & Madson, L. (1997). Models of the self : Self-construals and gender. *Psychological Bulletin.* 122 (1), 5-37.

Verma, M. (1996). Values in Indian villages. In Hector Grad, Amalio Blanco and James Jeorgas (eds). *Key Issues in Cross Cultural Psychology.* Selected Papers from the Twelfth International Congress of the International Association for Cross Cultural Psychology.

William, C. Ouchi, (ed.) (1981). *Theory Z: How American business can meet Japanese Challenge.* Reading, Mass: Addison-Wesley.

9 Children's Theory of Mind
Implications for their Schooling and Social Competence

Bhaswati Patnaik

Cognitive development in human beings is not limited to growth of knowledge and reasoning about objects, symbols and concepts pertaining to the physical world. Our awareness about self, other people, social interactions and practices constitute a significant aspect of our cognitive process. Conceptualization of social phenomena differs from that of physical phenomena in one fundamental respect. Unlike physical objects, people are animate beings, capable of behaving rationally and purposefully. All our social interactions are determined by mental representations of reality that guides our behaviour. In other words, behavioural phenomena cannot be explained without the attribution of intention, purpose, plan or other mental concepts to the agent concerned.

In our everyday life, we make sense out of people's behaviour by taking what Dennett (1987) calls an 'intentional stance', i.e. we regard people as sentient creatures who behave intentionally. This stance or position makes human interactions truly dynamic and reciprocal. It involves the attribution of mental states like beliefs, thoughts, desires, intentions etc. to self as well as others for making sense of their actions or behaviour. This folk psychology is recently termed as theory of mind (Premack and Woodruff, 1978) to denote the ability to impute mental states to self and others for explaining action or behaviour of the agent in social situations. It is called a theory because the integrated and interrelated concepts of invisible mental states are used for explaining and predicting events in the referential domain of action, talk and behaviour.The theory of mind acquisition, however, does not take place overnight. It takes a few years after birth to become functional to a reasonable extent; the manifestations of which are reflected in children's language, play and social interactions.

Theory of Mind: Development in Children

At birth, all children show a preference for human faces to inanimate things. With the development of language, they can talk about people as thinking, knowing or feeling something. By talking about events gone by and things out of sight, solving problems by insight, finding invisibly displaced objects etc. children show us that they can think about absent and hypothetical situations. This ability to imagine a possible alternative reality is most clearly seen in young children's pretend play. According to Leslie (1988), representations, decoupled from the things they are representations of, become eligible for a secondary representation. These secondary representations can violate the normal reference, truth and existence properties of primary representation. For example, a stick can be represented as a telephone. Supported by an older and friendly sibling, even two-year olds take on make believe roles and can act out complicated scenarios in make-believe places (Dunn & Dale, 1984).

A remarkable development in children's sensitivity to mental world occurs around the age of 4 years when they can attribute a false belief to others (Perner, Leekam & Wimmer, 1987), i.e. they can predict that a person is liable to behave erroneously as a result of having an idea, which does not correspond with real state of affair. This reflects children's understanding that mental states are not just entities in mind but also are representations actively construed by the mind. For example, children can say that their father will mistakenly search for the pencils in the pencil box because he does not know about the transfer of pencils to the chocolate box. But a three years old is not capable of representing a false belief. When asked, she will predict that her father will look in the right place, even if the transfer has taken place in his absence. Thus, for explaining behaviour or action of somebody, a four years old can attribute a first-order mental state, i.e. describe somebody as thinking, knowing or wanting something to be the case.

Higher-Order Mental States

Around 6 to 7 years of age (Perner & Wimmer, 1985), children can attribute second-order mental states for explaining and predicting behaviour. They can conceive people thinking about the mental state of another person. For example, they can say, "Mummy thinks that I know that Dad has arrived, so she didn't call me." As mental representations have the unique recursive characteristics, i.e. a mental representation can contain several mental representations as its cognitive content, the attributions of second and higher-order mental states is possible. The sentence —"I think that you know that they feel that we want........" reflects the recursive character of mental states that they can be applied in an embedded manner.

The ability to attribute mental states recursively equips children for a richer variety of social interaction. Social interactions are primarily, if not exclusively, communicative and conversational discourses which are socially organized (Babu & Mohanty, 2001). In almost all social exchanges, mutual awareness of intentions and beliefs are common presuppositions. Therefore, social understanding of children in general is facilitated to a large extent with development of theory of mind.

Social Understanding

With the acquisition of competence of attributing first-order mental states, children are able to understand the see-know distinction, i.e. if one has seen something, one knows about it and one, who has not, is unaware. Thus, a relation between perception and knowledge is conceptualized at this stage. Similarly, children become aware of the fact that an object may appear different from what it really is. Tricking, cheating, lying etc. are based on intentional creation of false belief in others' mind. Children, in this period, also get better insight into the Machiavellian character of social situations — the world of lies and deception. In a study, children's performance in four standard false belief tasks was significantly correlated with their production of joint proposals and explicit role assignments during a play (Astington & Jenkins, 1995).

Various theorists have recognized the importance of higher-order mental states for social interaction. For instances, game theorists emphasized their role in strategic interaction and social coordination (Goffman, 1970; Rapoport, 1967); psychotherapists (Laing, Phillipson & Lee, 1966) have stressed their importance in the psychopathology of family dyads. Besides, in the formation of linguistic conventions (Grice, 1957, 1975; Lewis, 1969) and awareness of interpersonal relations (Selman, 1981), the role of knowledge regarding higher-order thoughts and intentions is nevertheless significant.

Shultz (1980) cites such examples of social interactions as strategic acts — acts performed to disguise one's own intentions or to lead others to misinterpret one's intentions — which reflect their truly interactive and essentially human character. In almost all dyadic relationships, the actual or possible mental states of one member must be seen as part of the intentional mental states of the other member.

Perner (1988) has indicated that children's attribution of second order belief is significantly related to their understanding of deceptive acts, the ability to distinguish between intended and accidental outcomes and the awareness about social commitment.

In an empirical study of 5 to 7 years old Oriya speaking children, Patnaik (2002) found that children's conception about friendship, communication skills and understanding of lying and joking distinction, varied as a function of their age and attribution of second – order mental states.

All these findings have implications for various educational and training ventures aimed at teaching social skills such as communication, cooperation etc. to children, who find it difficult to cope with everyday social experiences. There is a growing feeling that we should try to find ways to teach children from a very young age, the nature and management of communicative enterprises in a more direct and systematic manner. Incorporation of theory of mind skills in such ventures can make children's life socially more meaningful.

Children with Autism – A Special Case

The striking characteristic of the children with autism is their lack of normal contact with people, their complete self-absorption and emotional solitude. Moreover, there is impairment in their language development and more fundamentally, in their ability to communicate even without language. In other words, their pragmatic skill is seriously affected. That these children don't develop a theory of mind as normal children, was first demonstrated in an experiment (Baron-Cohen, Leslie & Frith, 1986) where children were asked to arrange four pictures in a sequence and tell a story. Autistic children aged six to seventeen could not attribute the mental state of surprise to a character for using it to make a sequence out of the pictures. Subsequent investigations (Leslie & Frith, 1988; Perner, Frith, Leslie & Leekam, 1989; Sodian & Frith, 1993) have confirmed and extended these findings.

The implications of acquisition of theory of mind for social and psychological competence can well be realized from the findings related to autistic children. For healthy socio-emotional development a reflective orientation towards the mental states of self and others is essential.

School Years and Learning

According to Bruner (1996), modern pedagogy is moving

increasingly to the view that the child should be aware of her own thought process and that it is crucial for the pedagogical theorists and teachers alike to help her become more metacognitive — to be as aware of how she goes about her learning and thinking as she is about the subject matter she is studying.

The period, during which children acquire a theory of mind, represents their early school years. This acquisition provides the base for the metacognitive skills required for their academic achievement. Attributing mental states to self and others is metacognitive too, as it involves the representations in mind, another mental state — a representation itself. Thus teachers can build on this foundation by consciously introducing and using language about thinking and other mental states in the classroom. This makes their understanding of mental and cognitive processes more explicit. According to Vygotsky (1962) control of a function is the counterpart of one's consciousness of it. A conscious understanding of thinking and learning can help children in constructing knowledge through their own actions and experience.

Building on the work of Tomasello, Kruger and Ratner (1993), Olson and Bruner (1996) have described four different conceptions of learner's minds held by teachers that lead to different kinds of pedagogical practice : (1) Conceiving of children as unable to do something leads adults to provide demonstration for them to imitate ; (2) Conceiving of children as ignorant of something leads adults to provide them with information about it ; (3) Conceiving of children as having their own ideas about something leads adults to engage them in discussion of it ; and (4) Conceiving of children as knowledgeable members of the culture leads adults to engage them in reflection on what is known in the world beyond what the children themselves knew.

These four models represent implicitly a developmental progression on the part of the learner. Children first benefit from demonstration, then from didactic instruction, then from participation in collaborative discourse, and finally, from participation in a world of objective knowledge. These benefits cumulate, rather than replace one another, so that eventually learning can occur in any of these ways. With the emergence of more complex social understanding, earlier forms of learning are subsumed by new forms of learning.

Thus, it has been argued that there may be a relation between the level of children's theory of mind development and their ability to learn by instruction and collaboration (Astington & Pelletier, 1996). This has particular relevance to method of imparting classroom instructions. Teaching methods, that tend to ignore the entering behaviour of the learner and the goals of teaching, can be detrimental for the education of a child. Teaching should be inevitably based on the teachers' notions about the nature of learner's mind. Children, who are capable of reflecting on the mental states of their own as well as others, may benefit more from collaborative learning methods rather than instructional methods. Collaborative learning requires appropriate metacognitive language to talk about mutual understanding and conflict. Therefore, a new conception of the reciprocity of teaching and learning can be formed by integration of research in children's theory of mind and teacher's awareness regarding it.

Furthermore, children's understanding of mental states has more specific and direct implications for their learning in school. In students' production and narration of literary and historical texts (Gardner, 1991), attribution of mental states is essential. According to Astington (1998), theory of mind development is also linked to the growth of scientific reasoning and critical thinking as they depend upon the ability to reflect one's own beliefs, to recognize where they are mistaken and to take another's perspective.

Recently it has been argued (Suddendorf & Corballis, 1997) that episodic memory, which requires travelling mentally into one's past and inspect one's history, and mentally disengaging from the present, depends on reflective awareness of mental states. Near absence of autobiographical memory in early childhood, when children's understanding of mental state is rudimentary, supports this argument.

Researchers have recently suggested links between peer-tutoring and theory of mind, arguing that the ability to tutor effectively depends upon the development of recursive perspective — taking skills or second order theory of mind. In a study of same age tutoring, it has been found that by 7 years, most children can teach contingently. Some 5 years old show contingent teaching but none of the 3 years old can (Tomasello, Kruger & Ratner, 1993; Wood, Wood, Ainsworth, O'Malley, 1995).

It has been argued (Kogler, 2001) that taking the perspective of others by attributing mental states is an essential cognitive mechanism needed to understand others. In the medium of language, we are able to articulate what constitutes other's view, and while stating what is different, we are at the same time united in the medium of common linguistic comprehension. This also enables students to move beyond an understanding of the other in terms of some alien, strange and unapproachable otherness. This has implication for the multicultural education and diversifying the curriculum which is a very important dimension of developing students' intelligence — assuming that there is a willingness in all of us to accept the complexity and richness that human social intelligence entails. This not only helps the students to develop a reflective understanding of themselves but also an open-minded worldview.

Conclusion

Social maturity of an individual is more fundamentally tied to the awareness of recursive nature of thought. Apart from academic and educational considerations, this awareness is significant with regard to the development of personality of the individual. Recursive reflection on one's own mental states has impact on one's self-conceptualization, self-control and self-esteem. Counting on one's own as well as other's impressions about self, makes self-esteem to become an important aspect of personhood. Self-assessment and self-control also become new means of restraints on behaviours.

In today's competitive world, individual's intellectual abilities alone do not stand him in a good stead. To make sense out of oneself, other people, interpersonal relations, social practices and institutions and to deal effectively in practical situations are important contributors to one's success in life. In short, the key is the need to direct one's attention towards the mental world of self and others. In fact, socio-emotional growth and maturity has been the focus of attention in recent times through the popularization of the concept of emotional intelligence (Mayer & Salovey, 1990). On the face of it, it appears that emotional intelligence of a person, in some degree, may be a function to the extent in which he or she is able to attribute higher-order mental states to self and others. Theoretical importance of recursive attribution of mental states would be enhanced if this relationship is experimentally established.

This reflection on mental states and higher-order mental states underlies children's pragmatic competence, conceptualization of relationship between people and interpretation of complex social interactions. Hence children's acquisition of a theory of mind can be regarded as a milestone in children's social-cognitive development. Significant departures from normative age of its acquisition may have adverse effect upon the socio-emotional growth of the child.

It has been found out that understanding of second-order mental states is achieved between 5 to 8 years of age. It is remarkable that the age between 5 to 8 years is indicated by Piaget (1972) as the period when children go through a transition from pre-operational to concrete operational thought. Therefore, at this age, a qualitative change in thought processes of children is evident regarding both social and non-social phenomena. Perhaps growth in metacognitive and other executive processes bring about a more abstract and hypothetical quality of mature thinking in children.

On the other hand, important links may exist in children's reasoning between social and non-social phenomena. According to Perner and Wimmer (1985), the observed change in how children answer Piaget's test of logical reasoning may be a function of what order epistemic intention they are able to attribute to the experimenter. Children who do not understand the experimenter's real reasons for asking the questions may be misled in the conversational context.

Further, it is argued that (Perner, 1991) the observation that children around age 4 become reasonable may not so much be a result of them becoming logical (in concrete operational thinking) but of them becoming rational about their own desires. Because acquisition of theory of mind makes them capable of reflecting on mental states like desires, intentions, feelings etc.

There are evidences regarding children's early acquisition of theory of mind which support Vygotsky's (1978) emphasis on investigation of origins of an individual's competencies in the interpersonal zone. Certainly, young children have the experiences of shared activities and conversations in their familial environment. The extent to which parents are conscious of the changes that take place in children in terms of awareness of mental world, determines the nurturing practices in a desired direction.

Future research, preferably naturalistic observation combined with intervention study, can throw more light on the relationship of theory of mind acquisition with other theoretical constructs and its implications in other areas of our social understanding.

REFERENCES

Astington. J.W. (1998). Theory of mind goes to school. *Educational Leadership, 56 (3), November*

Astington, J.W. & Jenkins, J.M. (1995). Theory of mind development and social understanding. *Cognition and Emotion*, 9 (2/3), 151-165.

Astington, J.W. & Pelletier, J. (1996). The language of mind: Its role in learning and teaching. In D.R. Olson & N. Torrance (eds.), *The handbook of education and human development: New models.*

Babu, N. & Mohanty, A.K. (2001). Language, theory of mind, and cultural construction of knowledge: A review. *Indian Psychological Abstracts and Reviews 8:1*, pp 3-47

Bruner, J. (1996). *The culture of education.* Cambridge, MA: Harvard University Press.

Dennet, D.C. (1987). *The intentional stance.* Cambridge, Mass: Bradford Books/MIT Press.

Dunn, J. & Dale (1984). I a Daddy: Two-year old collaboration in joint play with sibling and mother. In I. Bretherton (ed.), *Symbolic Play: The Development of Social Understanding* (pp. 195-217). Orlando, FL: Academic Press.

Flavell, J.H. (1977). *Cognitive development,* Englewood Cliffs, NJ: Prentice Hall.

Gardner, H. (1991). *The unschooled mind.* New York: M.I.T Press and Wiley Kogler.

Goffman, E. (1976). *Strategic Interaction,* Oxford: Blackwell Publisher.

Grice, H.P (1957). Meaning. *Philosophical Review,* 66, 377-388.

Grice, H.P. (1975). Logic and conversation. In P. Cole and J.L. Morgan (eds.), *Syntax and Semantics,* Volume 3: *Speech acts,* pp. 225-242. New York: Academic Press.

Kogler, H.H. (2001). *New arguments for diversifying the curriculum: Advancing students' cognitive development.* Retrieved November 3, 2001, from www.inform.umd.edu/diversity web/Koegler.html

Laing, R.D,; Phillipson, H.; & Lee, A.R. (1966). *Interpersonal perception: A theory and a method of research.* London: Tavistock.

Leslie, A.M. (1988). Some implications of pretense for mechanisms underlying the child's theory of mind. In J.W. Astington, P.L. Harris and D.R. Olson (eds.). *Developing theories of mind.* New York: Cambridge University Press, pp. 19-46.

Leslie, A.M. & Frith, U. (1988). Autistic children's understanding of seeing, knowing and believing. *British Journal of Developmental Psychology, 6,* 315-324

Leslie, A.M., & Frith, U. (1986). Mechanical, behavioural and intentional understanding of picture stories in autistic children. *British Journal of Developmental Psychology,* 4, 113-125.

Lewis, D. (1969). *Convention: A philosophical study.* Cambridge, MA: Harvard University Press.

Mayer, J.D. & Salovey, P. (1997). What is Emotional Intelligence? In P. Salovey and D. Slutyter (eds.), *Emotional development, emotional literacy and emotional intelligence: Implications for educations.* New York: Basic Books.

Miller, P.; Kessel, F.; & Flavell, J. (1970). Thinking about people thinking about people thinking about....: A study of social cognitive development. *Child Development, 41,* 613-623.

Olson, D.R. & Bruner, J.S (1996). Folk Psychology and folk pedagogy. In

D.R.Olson & N. Torrance (eds.) *The handbook of education and human development: New models of learning, teaching and schooling.* Oxford, England: Blackwell.

Patnaik, B. (2002). Recursive nature of thought in children's understanding of social interaction. Unpublished Doctoral dissertation, Utkal University, 2002, Bhubaneswar, Orissa, India.

Perner, J. (1988). Higher-order beliefs and intentions in children's understanding of social interaction. In J.W. Astington, P.L. Harris and D.R. Olson (eds.), *Developing theories of mind*, pp. 271-294. New York: Cambridge University Press.

Perner, J. (1991). *Understanding the representational mind.* Cambridge, Mass: Bradford Books / MIT Press.

Perner, J.; Frith, U.; Leslie, A.M.; & Leekam, S.R. (1989). Exploration of the autistic child's theory of mind: Knowledge, belief and communication. *Child Development, 60*, 689-700

Perner, J.; Leekam, S.; & Wimmer, H. (1987). Three-year old difficulty with false belief: The case for a conceptual deficit. *British Journal of Developmental Psychology, 5*, 125-137.

Perner, J. & Wimmer, H. (1985). "John thinks that Mary thinks that ….." Attribution of second-order beliefs by 5 to 10-year old children. *Journal of Experimental Child Psychology, 39*, 437-471.

Piaget, J. (1972). *The principles of genetic epistemology.* (W. Meys, Trans). London: Routledge & Kagan Paul. (Original work published 1970).

Premack, D. & Woodruff, G. (1978). Does the chimpanzee have a theory of mind? *The Behavioural Brain Sciences, 1*, 515-526

Rapoport, A. (1967). Escape from paradox. *Scientific American, 217*, 50-56.

Selman, R.L. (1981). The child as friendship philosopher. In S.R. Asher and J.M. Gottman (eds.), *The development of children's friendships.* New York: Cambridge University Press.

Shultz, T.R. (1980). Development of the concept of intention. In W.A. Collins (ed.), *Minnesota Symposia on Child Psychology,* (vol.13). Hillsdale, NJ: Lawrence Erlbaum Associates.

Sodian, B. & Frith U. (1993). The theory of mind deficit in autism: Evidence from deception. In S. Baron-Cohen, H. Tager-Flusberg and D. Cohen (eds.) *Understanding other minds: Perspectives from autism.* Oxford: Oxford University Press.

Suddendorf, R. & Corballis, M (1997). Mental time travel and the evolution of the human mind. *Genetic social and general psychology monographs, 123*, 133- 67.

Tomasello, M.; Kruger, A.C.; & Ratner, H. (1993). Cultural learning. *Behavioural and Brain sciences, 16* (3), 495-511.

Vygotsky, L.S. (1962). *Thought and language*. Cambridge, Mass and New York: MIT Press and Wiley.

Wood, D.; Wood, H.; Ainsworth, S.; & O'Malley, C. (1995). On becoming a tutor: Toward an ontogenetic model. *Cognition and Instruction, 13,* 4.

10 Role of Value of Children, Parenting Style and Attachment Pattern in Intergenerational Relationship

Shubhra Sinha *and* R.C. Mishra

Intergenerational relationships refer to the patterns of interaction between two generations. They may be formal or informal in nature. In nuclear family settings parents and children interact with each other. In a joint or extended family this interaction may include grandparents and children. Although these interactions seem to begin with the birth of a child, its preparation starts before the child birth in the form of value of children (VOC). VOC refers to the needs children serve for their parents (Hoffman & Hoffman, 1973). Two types of VOC are found : (a) traditional or social normative (TVOC), which refers to the economic and social normative reasons to have a child; (b) emotional VOC (EVOC) in which the pleasure and sentiments related with a child are greatly emphasized. However, VOC is not so simple as it sounds to be. It is a well known fact that need not only initiates behaviour, but also makes certain objects more attractive and satisfying as compared to others. In addition, it also decides the preferred way to achieve the goal. In the same way, once it is decided why parents want to have a child, it also gets decided what kind of persons parents would like to make their children. What would be the parenting goals they will set for themselves, and what kind of parenting strategies they will choose to implement their socialization agenda? The journey does not stop here. VOC also contributes to gender preferences held by parents. It is commonly seen that those who hold traditional VOC prefer boys over girls because they are seen as a social and financial support in old age. On the other hand, parents interested in emotional reasons view girls as better option, because they do not expect any financial aid but girls are supposed to help in domestic chores and provide parent with moral and emotional support when required. The phenomenon of rapidly changing quality of mother-daughter relationship is now termed as "*identical twin mother daughter*" relationship (Kashiwagi, 1999). It clearly depicts the changing needs and expectations of parents from their children.

Another issue deeply related to this is the number of offsprings people have and the variations found in the fertility rates across the world. In fact, the VOC study was originally started with the aim of addressing this issue. It was hypothesized that in societies where children were viewed as further earning members the number of offspring would be high as compared to those societies that believed in giving proper care and nurturance to children and making them efficient and productive members without being concerned about the future refunds. Education was thought to affect the fertility rate since urban families were supposed to have less children as compared to rural families. Studies fail to show any significant difference in the concept of ideal family size between parents having TVOC and EVOC and similarly between urban and rural families, but at the same time rural samples do show a higher fertility rate as compared to urban samples in India (Mishra, Mayer, Trommsdorff, Albert & Schwarz, 2004). It raises a potential question: If mother's VOC and demographic conditions do not have direct influence on the concept of ideal family size, and still one finds differences in actual number of offspring, there must be some other factors responsible for this discrepancy. In India there can be several factors such as husband's command or a desire for son.

Parental Intentions Interacting with Parental Actions

The roles that parents want their children to play also contributes in determining the way they will bring their children up. In technical jargon it can be said that it determines their parenting style. According to Baumrind parenting style depicts normal variations in parent's attempts to control and socialize their child. It has two main dimensions, namely acceptance and control. Based on these two dimensions four parenting styles have been identified: authoritative (high acceptance, high control), authoritarian (low acceptance, high control), indulgent (high acceptance, low control), and uninvolved (low acceptance, low control). They result in varied child outcomes. It is commonly seen that children whose parents are authoritative in nature develop both social and instrumental competencies properly and are least engaged in problem behaviours. Children of authoritarian parents develop instrumental competencies properly, but lack social competencies. Indulgent parents make their children very good at social competency, but not in instrumental competency. Children of uninvolved parents are found to be the biggest loser, because they do not develop any competency of the two. Most of delinquent children and those involved in drug abuse generally hail from families where parents are not involved in children's life.

In India both dimensions of acceptance and control fuse with other. The more mothers value the emotional reasons to have a child, the more they value the parenting role of obedience. It seems that in India acceptance generates control (Mishra *et al.*, 2004). Parenting has a pervasive impact on several aspects of life such as adolescent's involvement in problem behaviour and delinquency, acquisition of values and moral standards, emotional expressiveness and level of achievement.

Parenting Strategies: Communication *vs.* Control

Parental strategies, such as the use of reasoning and empathic statements, facilitate the development of internalization of values (Hoffman, 1975; Maccoby & Martin, 1983; Ryan *et al.*, 1995). The type of maternal control strategy used has been found to have a direct influence on the type of compliance and non-compliance strategies exhibited by the child. Power assertion techniques culminate in situational compliance, whereas committed compliance can be evoked by using reasoning and negotiation. Crittenden and Dihalla (1988) found that maltreated children showed compulsive compliance in which children suppressed negative behaviours and immediately complied with maternal directives not because of internalization but because of fear. Egeland, Sroufe and Erickson (1983) observed mother-child interactions during problem solving and teaching tasks at 24 and 42 months of age and found that children who had experienced physical or verbal abuse, neglect or psychologically unavailable mothers were more non-compliant and less compliant than non-maltreated children. Children were more likely to use less sophisticated form of non-compliances such as verbal refusals, anger, or other forms of overt opposition.

Findings often suggest that parent child communications are more beneficial than surveillance and control. One study tested the idea that attachment to parents lowers the likelihood of delinquency (Cernkovich & Glordano, 1987). Researchers used several indirect measures of attachment, some of which dealt with parent-child communication and the closeness of the relationship. The results suggested that delinquents had poor communication with their parents. They were lower than non-delinquents on caring and trust (intimacy in the parent-child relationship), identity support (parent's respect, acceptance and support), and instrumental communication (discussion of future plans). In another study of parental involvement and school performance, parent-child agreement and parent-child discussion predicted higher grade point averages and achievement test scores, but measures of surveillance or parental monitoring did not (Otto & Atkinson, 1997).

Parental warmth and positive expressiveness are indirectly related with child's emotional expressiveness as it contributes to the development of child's ego control. Warm positive parents may promote overcontrol behaviour in their children (particularly when parents are controlling), which predicts a lower level of children's emotional expressiveness. Cold negative parents may foster uncontrolled behaviour in their children (Eisenberg *et al.*, 2003). It is commonly found that adolescents having warm and affectionate relationship with parents in whom they can confide, are more willing to freely disclose their whereabouts and discuss various issues with the parents and become less engaged in substance abuse and delinquency as compared to those who are devoid of such privileges or whose parents are more interested in socialization and behavioural control.

All these studies portray a superiority of authoritative parenting style over authoritarian and permissive style in terms of likely child outcomes. But all children, whose parents are authoritarian or indulgent, do not lag behind others in social competency and instrumental competency respectively. Perhaps children having authoritarian parents do not suffer from any kind of confusion and indecisiveness. Rules are specified and clearly stated, the concept of right and wrong is well-defined and consequences of following or not following the parental socialization agenda are well known to them even before entering the situation. These may help the child in some way. It has been found that at least some of them do not turn into rebellions, make best use of parental instructions and guidelines, become successful in all fields and do have a social competency. In the same way, children of indulgent parents are usually high on empathic perspective taking and it is not at all essential that they fail in achieving anything. They are found to be successful and competent because they know what is right and what is wrong in spite of the fact that they never faced heavy demands from parents. In view of these evidences it may be concluded that parenting style is not the one and only determinant of child outcomes. Moreover, parenting style is also not a permanent trait. It changes across situations and over time. Characteristics of children can also moderate these effects. There are some areas in which parents can be satisfied with partial compliance; only for some, emphasis is placed on full committed compliance, whereas in some areas a negotiation between parents and children is also tolerable. Thus, the extent of strictness and strategies of parental control vary with time. It seems to be interesting and appropriate to look for cues and information that parents use to assess situations, child's willingness and capacity to adapt to parental agenda and the extent to which flexibility can be retained in situations.

Attachment : A Tender Feeling with a Strong Base

Another concept pertaining to VOC and parenting style is that of attachment security. Parental attachment is the process by which parents become the secure base from which one can explore the environment and – develop a sense of competence and mastery. Attachment remains important to one's emotional and identity development through adolescence and adulthood. The fundamental assumption in attachment research on human infants is that sensitive responding by the parent to the infant's needs results in an infant who demonstrates secure attachments, while lack of such sensitive responding results in insecure attachments (Lamb, Thompson, Gardner, Harnov & Estes, 1984).

Ainsworth originally proposed two types of insecure attachment: avoidant and resistant (ambivalent). This taxonomy was developed as a way of classifying infant behaviour in the "strange situation". All secure infants greet or approach the mother on reunion; if upset or crying they are comforted by physical contact, holding and interaction with the mother; they do not gaze, show signs of anger, or seek to be put down before they are ready to return to play. Accordingly, avoidant infants are predisposed to perceive the strange situations as normal. They do not become so panic in the absence of mother. Therefore, they do not feel a need to welcome or greet the other on reunion. Their cold responses also discourage mother and result in a dismissing and indifferent parenting style. On the contrary, the secure infants perceive the situation as difficult and greet their mothers warmly on reunion, actively engage in seeking proximity with the mother. All these reactions also provoke the mother to show warmth, support and affection.

Adolescent's Perception in Play

Studies also reveal that children engage in a number of interpretative and evaluative steps such as judgement of fairness or parental intentions in response to parental interventions (Grusec & Goodnow, 1994). Social comparisons within and outside the family are common. Children who perceive themselves as being in an advantageous position as compared to their siblings, or who feel that their parents are more supportive to them as compared to their siblings are more likely to have a better relationship with parents than their siblings.

Another important finding is that adolescents who come from families where there are frequent verbal disputes between parents and marital conflicts have more problems in all areas of life such as adjustment, emotional regulation, social competency and achievement as compared to those adolescents whose parents have taken divorce and they are able to maintain a close relationship even after divorce. This shows that psychological availability of the parent is more important than their physical availability. In the first type of families having frequent conflicts both parents are available physically, but they neither have time nor a right state of mind to be involved with their children. But in families where divorce has put an end to these conflicts and they maintain a close tie with their children, parents remain, psychologically available though physically separated.

Role of Parental Perception in Intergenerational Relationships

Parent's perception of the situation is not less important. Their ability to assess the cognitive and affective capacity of adolescents, situational demands and realities and accurate selection of parental strategies has great impact on instrumental and social outcomes of the child. It has been found that parents high on control view even simple misbehaviour of their children as an intentional disobeying of the parental commands. Parents who feel that they have lesser control of their child's life as compared to the child himself gradually become more and more controlling (Bugental *et al.*, 2000). Mothers who are high on empathic perspective taking are more likely to have mutually responsive relationships with their young children and to be more responsive to adolescents (Gondoli & Silverberg, 1997). Parents who accurately perceive adolescents thoughts and feelings during the course of a disagreement experience fewer conflicts overall in the case of fathers and greater satisfaction with the outcome of the disagreement in the case of mothers (Hastings & Grusec, 1997).

Parental Strategies to deal with other Socializing Agents

Besides parents there are other socializing agents present in the surroundings who are capable of moderating parent-child relationship, such as teachers, neighbourhood, and peer group. Their aims, ideologies and approaches can be markedly different from that of the parents. Parents have their own style to deal with the situation. Those who have good rapport and communication with their children usually pre-arm them about the possible ways of interactions and tip them off to deal with them effectively keeping their own ideologies intact. On the other hand, parents who lack such positive relationships are left with techniques of behavioural and psychological control which leaves a little opportunity for children to involve in situations and to be in company of those not liked by their parents.

Gender Differences and Parenting Style

A vibrant issue in intergenerational relationships is that of gender difference. As already mentioned, VOC has an effect on gender preference of parents. TVOC is related with a longing for a son because he is seen as a future support and being essential to keep the family sustenance intact. This phenomenon is referred to as a '*son preference*' (Anandlakshmy, 1994). However, generally no significant empirical evidence has been found which supports the existence of gender specific parenting style or attachment pattern. Empirically no difference is seen in parental monitoring as reported by either children or parents. However, according to both children's and parent's reports, girls freely disclose more than boys to their parents. Parents solicit more information from girls than boys according to children, but not according to parents. Although girls report being controlled more than boys, parents report controlling boys more than girls. The actual difference in this term is small. Boys report having better relationships than do girls with their parents (Stattin & Kerr, 2000). Other studies report that it is more important for females to retain close familial ties even when away from home as compared to boys (Allend & Stolltenberg, 1995). Thus, girls are better able to cope with an authoritarian style of parenting and less likely to turn into rebellions under high constraints.

Gender studies carried out in Indian settings show that Indian mothers (rural as well as urban) have high expectations from their grown up boys and girls, but rural mothers have comparatively greater expectations than their urban counterparts irrespective of their child's sex (Mishra *et al.*, 2004). Indian mothers in general have higher expectations from their sons as compared to their daughters. Rural mothers having high emotional VOC tend to expect more from their grown up children (boys and girls) than do their rural counterparts high on traditional VOC. On the other hand, urban mothers high on TVOC expect more from their sons, and a small positive effect of both TVOC and EVOC is found on the expectations from girls. In rural areas high economic status leads to higher expectations of grown up sons as well as daughters. In India EVOC is largely related with maternal expectation in both rural and urban areas, which clearly deviates from the common expectation that TVOC will lead to higher expectations. It seems that more the mothers accept their children, more they like to be accepted by them. As they are high in terms of social and emotional investment with their children, they want their child to be obedient and supportive in all respects in later life and these expectations are similar from boys and girls. Things would have been more transparent if maternal expectation had been divided in separate areas depending upon their nature and kind, because higher expectation does not give a clear idea about what kind of expectations mothers had.

The Nurturing Father

Another important change that has come in this research area is the increasing focus on father's role in child-rearing process and intergenerational relationships. Usually studies concentrate either on finding similarities or differences between the two generations. It was a usual trend to explore intergenerational harmony by using mother-child dyads and intergenerational conflicts by using father-child dyads. It could be because of the roles father would play at that time. They were primarily the earning members who neither had sufficient time nor interest to be involved in child-rearing. It was mainly the mother's responsibility. But now-a-days with changing social trends in which both parents share the responsibility of nurturing the offspring, things are changing. This change is prominently reflected in research trends, which are now focused on analysing the effect of father's presence on child's personality of overall development. This is promoting ideas that can help in maintaining warm and strong intergenerational relationship.

Unresolved Issues

Though parenting style and attachment patterns have been the central issues of investigation in child development studies for decades, much remains to be explored in this field. Research has extensively revealed the relationship between parenting style and child outcomes, but so many questions arise in mind regarding the cues that parents use in order to choose a particular parenting style, or to shift from one style to another style. How adolescents make social comparisons within and outside family? Are parents generally aware of children's perception of their strategies? If they are, how much value do they give to child's outlook? In spite of a long history of gender discrimination reported in India why does research fail to uncover those differences? What happens when the father's and mother's VOC differ? What would be the likely consequence of their interaction patterns? What are the factors that facilitate or inhibit intergenerational relationships other than parenting styles and attachment patterns? These are some crucial questions that need to be addressed in future studies of VOC.

All aspects of human life are multifaceted and so is the intergenerational relationship. They witness a dynamic orchestration of innumerable social, cultural and demographic factors. A full coverage of this is beyond the capacity of this chapter. Still it can be said that this area is rapidly enlarging and has tremendous scope and potentials for future research.

REFERENCES

Adam, E.K.; Gunnar, M.R.; & Tanaka, A. (2004). Adult attachment, parent emotion, and observed parenting behaviour: Mediator and moderator models. *Child Development,* 75, 110-122.

Albert, I. Trommsdorff & Mishra, R.C. (2004). *Parenting and adolescent attachment in India and Germany.* Paper presented at the 17 Congress of the International Association for Cross Cultural Psychology, August 2-6, Xi'an, China.

Eisenberg, N.; Zhou, Q.; Losoya, S.H.; Fabes, R.A.; Shepard, S.A.; Murphy, B.C.; Reiser, M.; Gutherie, I.K.; & Cumberland, A. (2003). The relations of parenting, effortful control, and ego control to children's emotional expressivity, *Child Development,* 74, 875-895.

Fei-yinng, F., Kenny-Benson, G.A.; & Pomerantz, E.M. (2004). Children's achievement moderates the effects of mother's use of control and autonomy support. *Child Development,* 75, 764-780.

Fletcher, A.C.; Steinberg, L.; & Wheeler, M.W. (2004). Parental influences on adolescent problem behaviour: Revisiting Stattin and Kerr. *Child Development,* 75, 781-796.

Grusec, J.E.; Goodnow, J.J.; & Kuczynski, L. (2000). New directions in analyses of parenting contributions to children's acquisition of values. *Child Development,* 71, 205-211.

Hasebe, Y.; Nucci, L.; & Nucci, M.S. (2004). Parental control of the personal domain and adolescent symptoms of psychopathology: A cross-national study in the United States and Japan. *Child Development,* 71, 1072-1085.

Jacqueline R.G.; & Feagans, L.V. (2004). Parental perceived control over care giving and its relationship to parent-infant interaction. *Child Development,* 75, 134-146.

Koenig, A.L.; Cicchetti, D.; & Rogosch, F.A., (2000). Child compliance/ noncompliance and maternal contributers to internalization in maltreating and non-maltreating dyads. *Child Development,* 71, 1018-1032.

Lewis, M., Feiring, C., & Rosenthal, S. (2000). Attachment over time. *Child Development,* 71, 707-720.

Mishra, R.C., Mayer, B., Tromssdorff, G., Albert, I., & Schwarz, B. Value of children and intergenerational relationships in India. In G. Trommsdorff & B. Nauck (Eds.), *National reports on the study of values of children and intergenerational relationships.* Lengerich: Pabst Science Publishers. (in press).

Sattin, H., & Kerr, M. (2000). Parental monitoring: A reinterpretation. *Child Development,* 71, 1072-1085.

11 Psycho-Social Dimensions of Gujarat Earthquake Disaster

T. Vijayakumar

Psychological trauma is the unique individual experience of an event or enduring stressful condition in which the individual ability to integrate his/her emotional experience is overwhelmed or individual subjectively experiences a threat to life, bodily integrity or sanity (Pearlman and Saakvitine,1995). We are living in an unpredictable world. Whenever a natural disaster or phenomenon occurs, the natural phenomena of human society immediately shattered. The devastating earthquake that stuck Gujarat on 26th January 2001 caused extensive damage to the standing concrete structure and houses of people in the urban and rural areas of the state. Worst being Kutch, the total damage caused in this district is estimated to about 70 per cent of the overall destruction in the state.

Disasters, whether man-made or natural, occur each day affecting the lives of many people psychologically, physically and socially. The impact a disaster has on a specific community had acute or severe effects on various individuals within their communities. The degree to which the disaster affects individual may depend on so many variables. And the trauma experiences occur across the entire population, certain people seem to be especially vulnerable in disaster because of several factors.

Several coping mechanisms are utilized to deal with such

traumatic experiences. The individual feels emotionally, cognitively and physically overwhelmed. The circumstances of traumatic events often include on going abuse of power, betrayal of trust, entrapment, helplessness, pain confusion and/or loss (Guiller, 1999).

In a situation where trauma is on-going and frequent such as childhood emotional, sexual or physical abuse and domestic violence, the symptoms of psychological trauma can be lasting and extreme. Often time's trauma related responses are diagnosed as psychiatric illness and given label such as dissociate disorder, borderline personality disorder or post-traumatic stress disorder. The symptoms of psychological trauma can be further exaggerated because they can co-occur with a variety of other disorders (Shaler, Friedman, Foa, and Keane, 2000). The present study has been undertaken to find out the psychological impact of trauma.

Objectives

1. To study the different psycho-social dimensions of the affected families.
2. To suggest measures for strengthening psychological rehabilitation.

Methodology

The methodology for the study was decided on the basis of objectives of the study. For intensive field study that was empirical in nature structured schedules were used. The first part of the schedule was intended to get information on demographic, socio-economic variables, relief, and reconstruction and rehabilitation process. The second part designated was meant to getting information on psycho-social dimensions of the respondents such as perception and attitude towards relief, rehabilitation, traumatic experiences, strain symptoms, coping styles, sensitivity, affective levels, and perception of decision making, adjustment to the trauma and to the new environment where they are to be rehabilitated.

Study Area

The study area was Kutch district of Gujarat where the epicentre of the earthquake was situated. The devastating earthquake that struck Gujarat on 26th January, 2001, caused extensive damage to the standing concrete structures and houses of thousands of people in the urban and rural areas of the states—worst being Kutch, the total damage caused in this district was estimated to be about 70 per cent of the overall destruction in the state. The area of Kutch district is 45,662 sq. kms, 21 districts out of 25 districts affected, 7, 633 out of 18,356 villages of the state were affected and the total population affected was 16.04 million.

Sampling

The study was undertaken in the randomly selected 150 families, from Bhuj, Anjar, Vondh, Indraprastha and Nandagaon. Within the district the most affected blocks, Anjar, Bachaav and Bhuj, were selected. From each block two villages were selected for canvassing the schedule.

Data Collection and Variables Studied

The entire data both, from primary and secondary, were collected in the month of November 2003. A field team consisting of faculty members from National Institute for Rural Development (NIRD) and six field investigators. The field investigators were put through an intensive guidance for proper collection of data. NIRD faculty members were also stationed in the field with the investigators for providing with day-to-day guidance in data collection. The team collected the secondary data from different official and non-official sources. Apart from collection of secondary data team also maintained notes of discussions held with officials and other members of the society.

The variables on which data were collected through personal interviews and group interviews are as follows:

1. Demographic variables details concerning (1) Caste, (2) Religion, (3) Education and Occupation of the family members, (4) Income and loss of property etc.
2. Psychological variables : (1) Perceptions and attitudes of the people, (2) Strain symptoms, (3) Sensitivity, (4) Coping mechanisms, (5) Phobic reactions, (6) Affective disorders, (7) Perception towards relief and rehabilitation.

Nature of Analyses

Most of the analyses done in the study was based on content analysis and frequency distributions and percentages. The information has been analysed in terms of caste, religion, education and occupation. An attempt has also been made to analyse the attitude and perceptional dimensions of the households to understand the relief, rehabilitation process using frequencies and percentages. The data have been presented in different sections, first dealing with the socio-economic characteristics for different groups and then psychological aspects by sectorial analysis.

Household Analysis

The household analysis reveals that the number of persons died in sample households (75) were 49 in urban areas and 63 in rural areas. The number of persons injured 74 in urban areas and 51 in rural areas. All the sample households' houses both in urban and rural areas were totally destroyed. The average value of house damaged in urban areas was Rs. 3,09,826 and in rural areas Rs.1,78,095. The average value of household items like furniture, TV and utensils etc. in urban areas was Rs.48,411 and in rural areas Rs. 35,500.

Graph 14.1 : Agency which did most of the help after earthquake in Anjar village of Gujarat

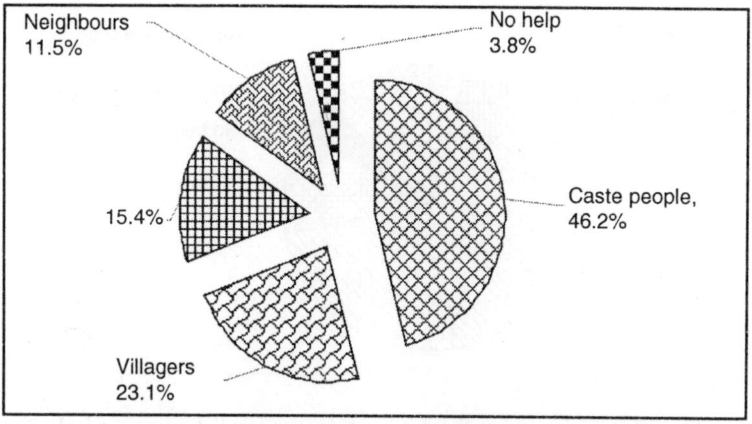

The above graph reveals that in Anjar village after earthquake 46.2% people said that caste people did most of the help, followed by 23.1% who said that villagers did help, 11.5% found helps from neighbours, whereas 3.8% people said that they have not received any help.

Graph 14.2 : Time taken to get the help in Anjar Village

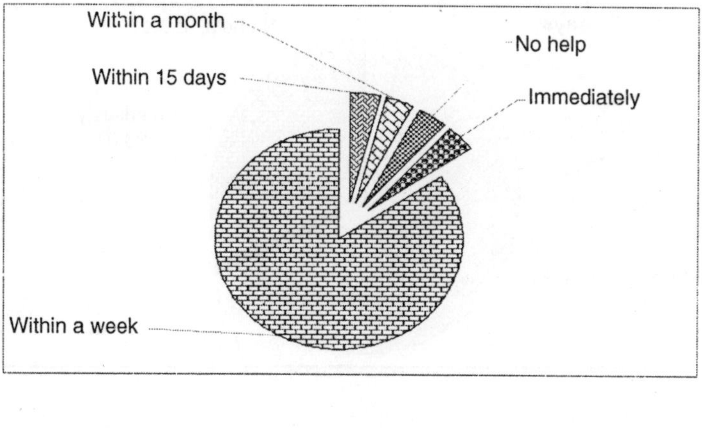

The Graph 14.2 indicates the time taken to get help in Anjar village. 84.6% people said that they have received help within 7 days whereas 3.8% people said that they have received help immediately within 10 days, and within 30 days no help.

Graph 14.3 : Agency did most of the help in Indraprastha village

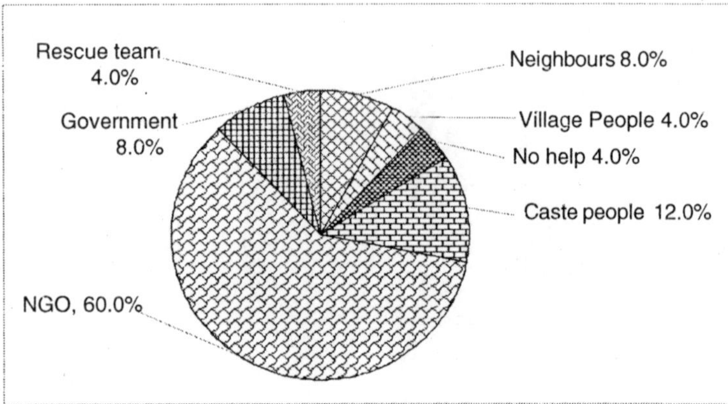

The above data reveals about the agency did most of help in Indraprastha village, 60% people said that NGO's did most of the help after earthquake followed by 12.0% caste people (Graph 14.3). It is said that in this particular village NGOs did most of the help.

Graph 14.4 : Time taken to get help in Indraprastha village

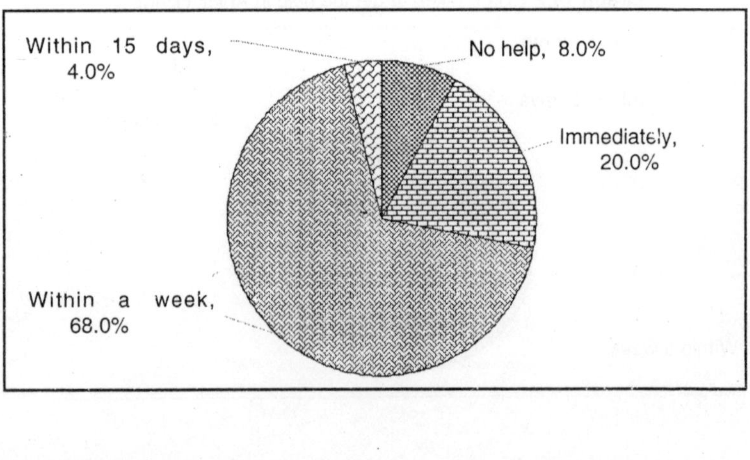

Graph 14.4 indicates the time taken to get help in Indraprastha village. 68.0% of the respondents said that they have received help within a week, 20% said that immediately they got help, whereas 8.0% said that they did not get any help.

Graph 14.5 : Agency did most of the help in Nandagaon village

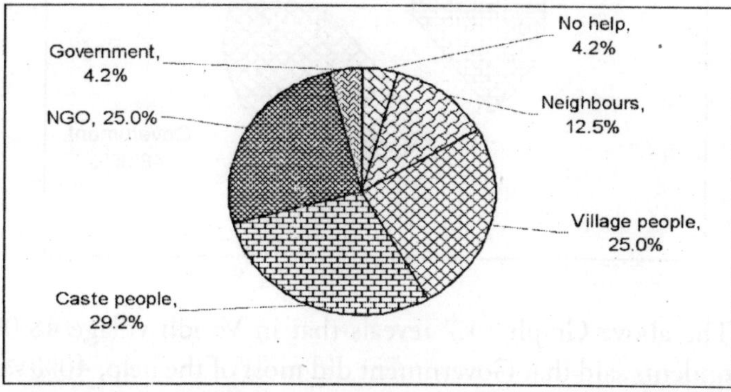

In Nandagaon village 29.2% respondents said that caste people did most of the help, 25.0% respondents said that NGO's and village people did help, whereas 4.2% said that Government did help, and 4.2% did not receive any help.

Graph 14.6 : Time taken to get help in Nandagaon village

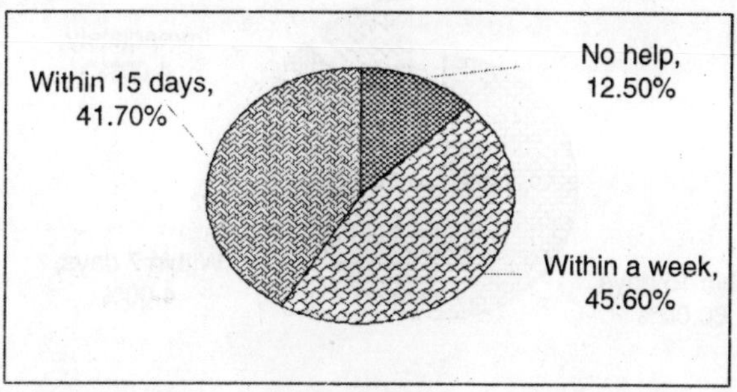

In Nandagaon village 45.6% respondents said that they received help within a week followed by 41.7% said that they got help within 15 days. Whereas 12.5% said that they did not have had any help.

Graph 14.7 : Agency did most of the help in Vondh village

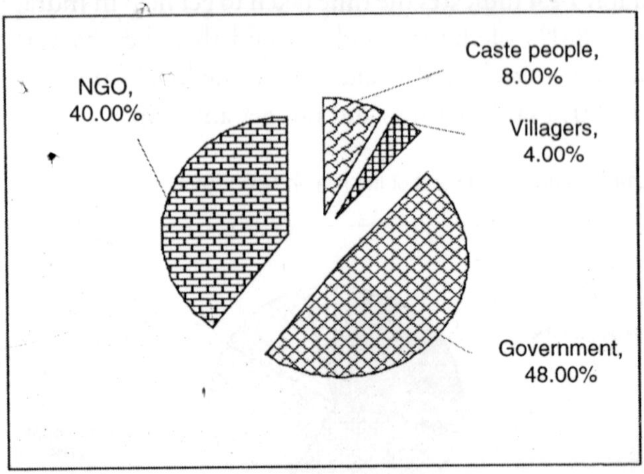

The above Graph 14.7 reveals that in Vondh village 48.0% respondents said that Government did most of the help, 40% said NGOs did help, whereas 40% respondents disclosed that villagers did most of the help.

Graph 14.8 : Time taken to get help in Vondh village

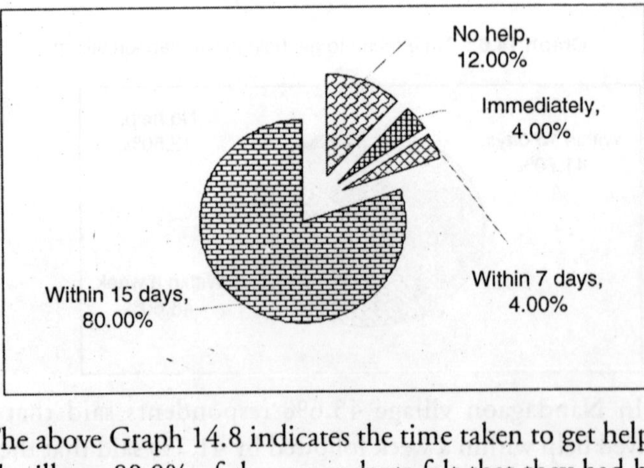

The above Graph 14.8 indicates the time taken to get help in Vondh village. 80.0% of the respondents felt that they had help

within 15 days, followed by 12% said that they did not get any help. Whereas, 4.0% respondents said that they received help immediately and similar percentage said that they have not received any help at all.

Graph 14. 9 : Agency did most of the help in Old Bhuj Town

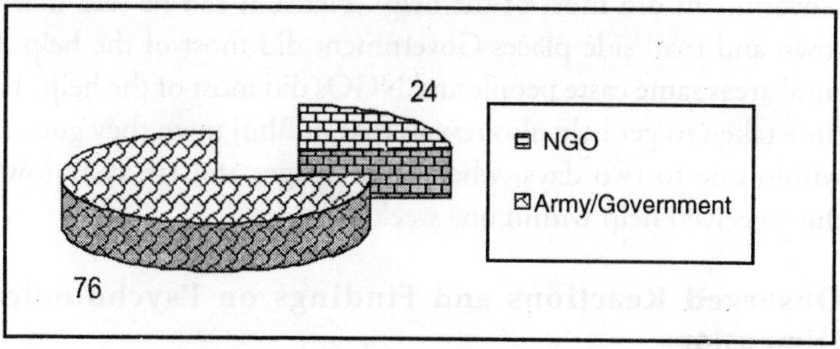

The above Graph 14.9 indicates that the Agency did most of the help in Old Bhuj town of Gujarat after earthquake. 76% respondents said that Government did most of the help followed by 24% who said that NGOs did help.

Graph 14.10 : Time taken to get first help in Old Bhuj Town

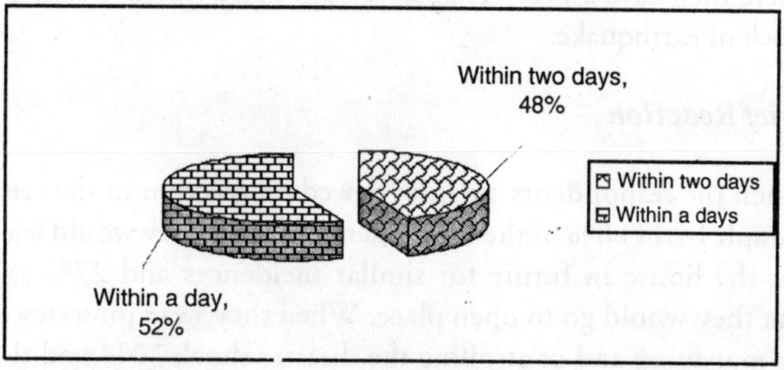

The data appearing in Graph 14.10, indicates the time taken to get first help in Old Bhuj town. 52% of the respondents said that they have received help within a day whereas 48% said that they have received help within two days.

Overall Observations on Help Seeking

After comparing all the graphs from 14.1 to 14.10 it became clear that in Anjar same caste people, Indraprastha NGOs, Nandagaon same caste people, in Vondh Government, and in Old Bhuj town Government did most of the help. Hence it can be said that in town and road side places Government did most of the help. In rural areas same caste people and NGOs did most of the help. The time taken to get help also reveals that in Bhuj town they got help within one to two days, whereas in villages and far away towns they received help within one week.

Observed Reactions and Findings on Psychological Dimensions

Sensitivity to Seek Help

On this item out of 100 respondents all the respondents said that they are sensitive towards seeking help and they told that for rehabilitation they have been given a choice to settle at a place where they have asked. They have been more sensitive after the shock of earthquake.

Grief Reaction

When the respondents are interviewed on reaction in the crisis (Graph 14.11) 8% of the respondents felt that they would leave out the house in future for similar incidences and 27% said that they would go to open place. When they were interviewed for managing and controlling the disaster shock 70% said that they would smoke whereas 30% said that they would run to safe place to control the shock. 50% of the respondents said that they would pray God to get rid off from fear, whereas 30% said that they would eat *gutka*, and 20% would look for peaceful atmosphere.

Graph 14. 11 : Grief reactions

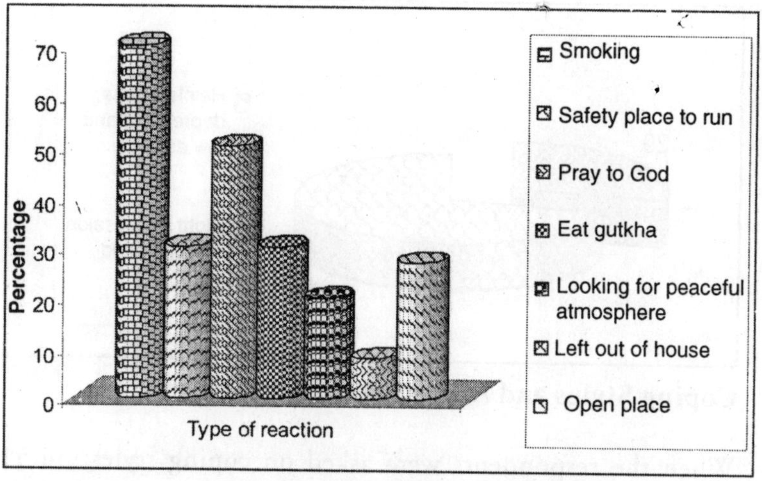

Perception and Attitude of the Respondents

Respondents were asked on perception and attitude towards earthquake relief rehabilitation, and effects on the people. 49% have expressed positive attitude whereas 51% expressed negative attitude towards relief, rehabilitation process. They said that the relief measures offered are only for eye wash. There is not much effects seen in growth and development of children, value changes, peer relationships, aversion in people. People are having slight negative attitude towards help what they received.

Affective Disorders

People were asked on affective disorders, hopelessness, helplessness, depression, low esteem and lack of concentration. As the Graph 14.12 reveals, 71% of the respondents said that they are having disorder of helplessness, depression and low esteem whereas 29% said that they do not have disorders but sometimes slightly depressed when that day was recalled.

Graph 14.12 : Affective disorders after earthquake

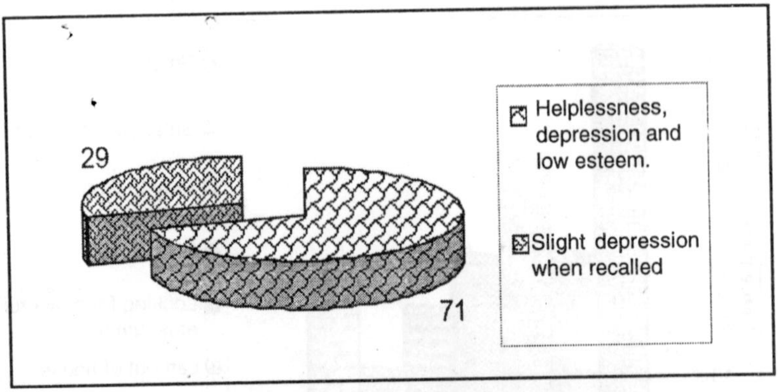

Coping Styles and Adjusting to Trauma Effect

When the respondents were asked on coping styles, 54.5% respondents viewed that they have adjusted to the trauma experience by helping each other, and taking responsibility and by eating tobacco and smoking. It is revealed that some persons especially women's experience negative emotions during the adjustment and most of them cope up without great difficulty. The uncertainty of adjustment is only because of anxiety. In some cases poor adjustment was also noticed by the following characteristics:

- Feeling of anger and confusion
- Rapid mood swings
- Withdrawal from significant others
- Fatalistic thinking (what can I do, this has to bear).

Strain Symptoms

On the strain symptoms, 52.8% respondents still have strain symptoms whereas 47.2% do not have any strain symptoms. They are having fear of loss of family member, fear of death, alarm, reactive to unfamiliar sounds, fear of darkness, frequent mood change, fear of tension. The women and children are experiencing these symptoms very frequently and to a larger extent. Fear of re-occurrence of earthquake, questioning of their ability to overcome were seen in a number of cases.

Health after Earthquake

The impact of traumatic experience on their health was interviewed through 6 questions. 70% respondents opined that they have developed anxiety disorder, 52% respondents said that they have developed both hypertension, and anxiety, whereas 30% respondents said that internal upset is the effect and sometimes they forget things, i.e. loss of memory (Graph 14.13).

Graph 14.13 : Ill health after earthquake

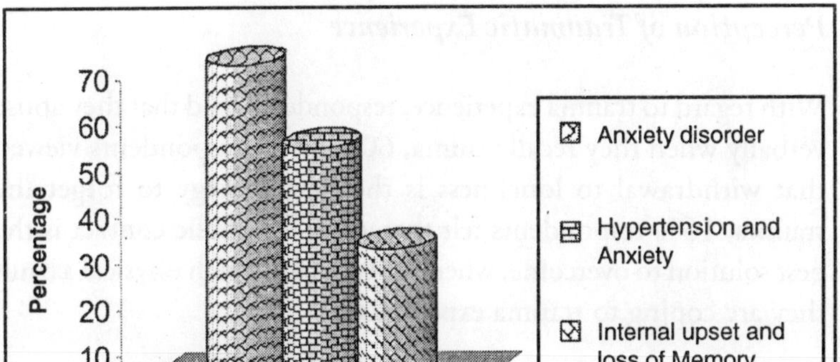

As far as eating habits are concerned out of total respondents, 60% said that after earthquake their diet has become irregular, followed by 18% light eating, 12 % no change in the food habit whereas 10% said that they are avoiding eating food as and when they recall the traumatic experience. It is reported in Graph 14.14.

Graph14.14 : Eating habits after earthquake

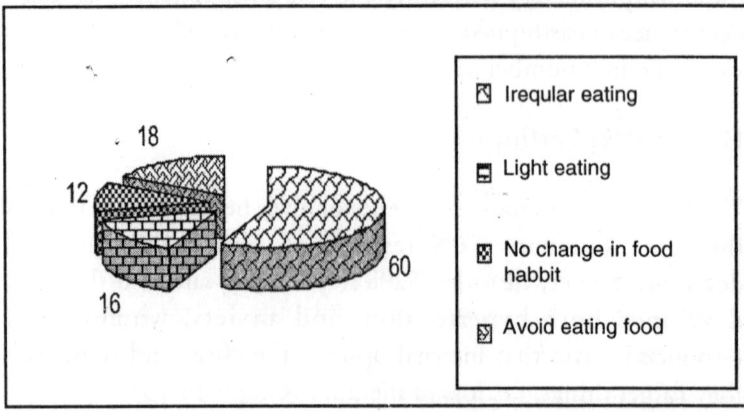

Conclusions

Perception of Traumatic Experience

With regard to trauma experience, respondents said that they abuse verbally when they recall trauma, 60% of the respondents viewed that withdrawal to loneliness is the best strategy to forget the trauma, 16% respondents felt that avoiding public contact is the best solution to overcome, whereas 9% said through physical assault they are coping to trauma experience.

- People have become more sensitive to help seeking.
- Majority of respondents felt that to get adjusted from the trauma experience, withdrawal to loneliness they are practicing.
- The coping styles of the respondents are: coming out from the house, going to open place. Eating *gutka*, smoking are some of the coping styles they are practicing but it varies from place to place.
- 52.8% respondents are having fear of death, fear of loss of family member, fear of darkness, they are reactive to unfamiliar sounds, frequent mood changes, fear and

tension, especially women and children are having seismic phobia. This clearly indicates their poor adjustment.

- 70% of the respondents are having anxiety disorders whereas 30% are having internal upset feeling and hypertension.
- 60% of the respondents are having irregular food habits whereas 18% are developed light eating habits after this earthquake.

Rescue and Relief Activities

Immediately after earthquake within three days before NGOs and Government reached, the caste people, neighbours and villagers helped the victims. They left their houses and stayed in open space and before getting food and other items they received medical aid. The Government with the help of military doctors and also some NGOs provided medical aid. Relief and rehabilitation was provided within 30 days and cooked food and potable water was supplied after 30 days. Regarding receipt of dry ration such as rice, wheat, pulses etc. and other items like lantern, kerosene stove, more people reported in urban areas than rural areas. It shows the urban bias in terms of distribution. There is no much difference in the average amount received under exgratia between urban and rural, but in terms of relief, urban respondents received more than rural.

- The phase of rescue work is rather dismal. The rescue agencies failed to reach the victims of the earthquake during first week. 60% of the respondents did not receive water, food, clothes and shelter during the first week following the disaster.
- Rescue came primarily from same caste people, neighbours, village people and NGOs while 10% respondents obtained aid from Government.
- NGOs and Government rescue was available in Bhuj and Bachhav but other affected parts were left out initially but later NGOs could attend the work in other parts.

- Proportionally the highest number of casualties occurred among the Muslim and ST communities.
- Proportion of females injured was slightly higher than the males.

Rehabilitation Activities

Construction of earthquake-proof houses is the most important activity both in terms of cost of the project and number of houses repaired and new houses constructed. The Bhuj town respondents were allotted house sites and sanctioned 20% of the amount for construction. They spent that amount for household consumption. But in Anjar town and in villages Indraprastha and Nandagaon all the respondents were satisfied with the quality of construction and all the new houses constructed were insured. In Vondh village 17 respondents and in Anjar town 6 respondents constructed their houses in their original house site.

- There is clear failure picture emerged in the communication of benefits available in the rehabilitation packages.
- Rehabilitation programmes were known to urban areas of Bhuj while rural areas don't have awareness.
- The decision of relocation of the village in the hands of Gram Sabha has been contested by the marginalized communities.
- The older generation in turn shared some of these reactions. Self help therapy was quite evident in the epicentre of the earthquake which distorted the whole townships. The difficulty facing the Kutch district still persists. Today, the earthquake tremors still continue, though sporadically with low intensity. There was not enough psychological assistance available. Therefore, there is a need of psychological interventions to cater the depression and psychosomatic disorders through psychological rehabilitation.

The psycho-social dimensions of Gujarat Earthquake disaster reveal that it is the peer groups, neighbours and NGOs who are involved in immediate relief and rescue operations. The time taken to receive help from outside was normally one week. About 70% of the respondents have felt anxiety disorders and coping mechanisms are leading to other addictions like eating *gutka* and smoking. People were provided relief in the form of dry ration such as rice, wheat, pulses and other items like lanterns, kerosene stoves etc. However, there was an urban bias in the distribution of these items. The rehabilitation package was in the form of cash and construction of earthquake-proof houses. Apart from it was used for household consumption. Since the people are the first respondents in any disasters they should be trained about disaster preparedness. Psychological interventions especially for treating depression and post-traumatic disorders are very much needed.

REFERENCES

Ashok K. Lahiri, Tapas K. Sen, R. Kavita Rao, Pratap Ranjan Jena (2001) Economic consequences of Gujarat Earthquake— *Economic and Political Weekly,* April 21,

Duregrov and Mitchell, 1992. Work with traumatized children, psychological effects and coping strategies. *Journal of Traumatic Stress,* Vol. 2.

Gujarat State Disaster Management Policy, 2002 .

Guus Van Deer Veer (1992) Counselling and Therapy with Refugees (Psychological problems of Victims of War, Torture).

Hardy, C.J. & Crace, R.K. (1990) *Dealing with injury.*

Interim Report of Gujarat Government on Reconstruction Support.

Lyla Mehta; Reflections on the Kutch Earthquake; *Economic and Political Weekly (2001).* August 4.

Mario Rutten, Involvement and Indifference, Gujarat Earthquake in Wider Perspective, *Economic and Political Weekly* (2001) September 1,

Sudhir Kuamr Katiyar, Rajiv Khandelwal (2001) Relocation in Kutch Bridging Old Fault Lines, *Economic and Political Weekly,* June 30.

Traumatic stress psychology and psychopathology, WPA section symposium on the psychopathology of Traumatic stress.

Vimal Ramesh Bhore (2003) Learning from Latur , *The Hindu,* October 26.

Part - II

Cultural, Social and Developmental Interface

12 Cultural Beliefs in Managing a Chronic Disease

Ajit K. Dalal

The prevalence of chronic diseases has increased rapidly in last two-three decades. Increase in life expectancy, life style, dietary habits, occupational and environmental stresses along with a host of other factors have led to a four-fold increase in the occurrence of chronic diseases in this century. The WHO Report (1998) shows that whereas the deaths due to acute and infectious diseases had come down from 36 per cent in 1900 to 6 per cent in 1980, deaths due to chronic diseases has gone up from 20 per cent to 70 per cent in the same period. In fact, if one is above 50 years of age, the chances are more than 80 per cent that he or she would be suffering from some chronic disease. Chronic diseases, particularly, those like cancer and heart attack are now central to the modern consciousness of what illness mean.

By definition, chronic diseases are long lasting diseases, often lasting for the lifetime. The symptoms may not be present all the time, but the prospects of recurrence of the symptoms means that recovery prospects are limited. In most of the cases the therapeutic intervention is limited to symptomatic treatment, not complete cure the diseases. Because of the long-drawn nature of the disease, people are required to integrate it in their lives. These diseases become part of their existence. The meaning these diseases acquire in one's life largely depend on — age, nature of occupations, achievements and responsibilities and social support one has. Severity, future course of the disease, its speed and directions are some other considerations. The afflicted person is required to comprehend the significance of the chronic diseases in terms of the nature of adjustments that are to be made to live with a disease in the world of healthy. Obviously, the person suffering from a chronic condition is required to take up major responsibility of managing his/her own disease. They are required to identify the symptoms, monitor progress of the disease and control its debilitating side effects. It becomes the responsibility of the people suffering and their families to manage medical, occupational, social and psychological after-effects and to restore one's sense of self-worth and meaning in life. They are not only required to live with the illness but also have to continue participating in everyday life; not as a patient but as a social being.

Cultural beliefs influence the whole gamut of health related behaviour, however, this article is primarily confined to discussing how these beliefs help people in appraisal and social construction of the experience of their illness, particularly in long term. These cultural beliefs may not play a predominant role in cases of acute and life threatening diseases where the immediate concern is to save a life, as in the case of heart attack. However, in the case of a long-term disease or disability the concern shifts to bringing about changes in one's life to adjust to the demands of the new situation. When do family, friends and social network play an important role in shaping a patient's perception of the disease and what are their implications for his or her life?

Not only there are wide cultural differences in the metaphysical beliefs which people have about the world and their own disease, these beliefs affect, in a complex way, the health status of people. Liven and Vanderpool (1991) reviewed a long list of about 300 articles published in this field from epidemiological, gerontological and behavioural sciences supporting a linkage of religious beliefs and practices with physical health outcomes. These studies have shown both, deleterious and salubrious effects of religion on health status. Most of these studies were of descriptive nature and no clear patterns of results were obtained. A process-oriented approach may probably be more appropriate in this field to make sense of the empirical relationships between religion and health (Dull & Skokan, 1995). The spiritual experience being multidimensional and context specific, the issue of relationship between religion and health has to be addressed within the larger domain of spiritualism and its relevance for the individual (Kier & Davenport, 2004).

In the traditional Indian society metaphysical beliefs, i.e., beliefs in *karma*, God, spirits, are presumed to be important determinants of many happenings in one's life, including illness and suffering. The theory of *karma* is invoked as an explanation for an array of undesirable life events. This theory holds that good and bad deeds accumulate over all previous lives and if people have done some wrong in this or previous births, then they have to suffer the consequences. The present suffering is frequently attributed to one's own misdeeds of this and previous lives. Another metaphysical belief: God's will is also frequently cited as an explanation for many happenings in life. As different from the principle of *karma*. God is seen as an external agent who controls reward and punishment, not always according to what ones deserves (Paranjpe, 1984). A person's bad deeds may be condoned by a benevolent God. The belief in fate implies that all life events are predestined and one can do little to alter them. Though conceptually different, these metaphysical beliefs are quite often used interchangeably in everyday parlance.

What is Belief?

Before proceeding further let us be clear about what does belief mean. Belief, in the psychological sense, is a representational mental state that takes the form of a prepositional attitude. In the religious sense, "belief" refers to a part of a wider spiritual or moral foundation, generally called faith. Belief is considered prepositional in that it is an assertion, claim or expectation about reality that is presumed to be either true or false (Hosen, Hosen and Stern, 2002).

The idea that a belief is a mental state is much more contentious. While some philosophers have argued that beliefs are represented in the mind as sentence-like constructs others have gone as far as arguing that there is no consistent or coherent mental representation that underlines our common use of the belief concept and is, therefore, obsolete and should be rejected. This has important implications for understanding the neuropsychology and neuroscience of belief. If the concept of belief is incoherent or ultimately indefensible then any attempt to find the underlying neural processes which support it will fail. If the concept of belief does turn out to be useful then this goal should (in principle) be achievable.

Why do Beliefs affect Health Status?

Beliefs mostly act on bodies in ways that an outside observer cannot measure. The human mind converts beliefs and expectations into biochemical realities. The mechanisms which link beliefs to the bodily processes are still not very clear. Most of the evidences are anecdotal suggesting that work, but no direct linkages are yet established. Perhaps the most compelling evidence is provided by the placebo studies. It is observed in a large number of studies that anticipation of physical effects as outcomes of medication placebos bring about actual physical changes. In one study (Feilding, Fag, Jones, Ellis, Hockey, Minawa, Craven, Mason, Timothy, Waterhouse & Wrigley, 1983) conducted in London on patients (n=411) were told that they should expect hair loss from the treatment of chemotherapy. Thirty per cent patients were placebos instead of chemotherapy who suffered hair loss to the same extent as other. As argued by Radley (1994) where doctor and patients subscribe strongly, where their separate roles are clearly defined, there placebos will have more therapeutic powers.

Expectations work in different/varied ways. One related phenomenon anniversary effect signifies that people are more likely to die around important dates in their lives. Philip, Van, Voorhees and Ruth (1992) surveyed the records of over 2 million people. It revealed that women are more likely to die within a week after their birthday, men peak just before their birthday. The interpretation was that women are more likely to believe that birthday are a time of celebration and meeting friends and relatives, whereas for men it is a time for taking stock of their accomplishments which they dread.

Bower, Kemeny, Taylor and Fahey (1998) have discussed some

of the important functions which beliefs serve for people. First, they provide explanations as to why they feel sick. It is important to have an explanation to make the life events predictable, no matter how aversive the life conditions are. It helps people in having mental preparations to face the hard truth. Second, beliefs about the causes of illness help people in deciding about the kind of treatment to be sought. People postpone decisions regarding the alternative medicine to be sought till they are sure about the causality. Third, beliefs play an important role in building hopes and expectations which trigger the healing mechanism of the body. People who expect to die on the operation table often fail the surgery. Beliefs help people in reintegrating within the culture they come from. Cultural beliefs help people find meaning in their suffering.

Most philosophers hold the view that belief formation is to some extent spontaneous and involuntary. Some people think that one can choose to investigate and research a matter but that one cannot choose to believe. On the other hand, most people have the impression that in some cases people don't believe things because they don't want to believe, especially about a matter in which they are emotionally involved.

Delusional Beliefs

Delusions are defined as beliefs in psychiatric diagnostic criteria (for example in the DSM). Psychiatrist and historian Berrios (see Wikipedia, 2005) has challenged the view that delusions are genuine beliefs and instead levels them as "empty speech acts", where affected persons are motivated to express false or bizarre belief statements due to an underlying psychological disturbance. However, the majority of mental health professionals and researchers treat delusions as if they were genuine beliefs, adversely affecting health of the patients.

However, this position is contested in recent times with convincing research evidences that many such beliefs play a positive role in the recovery process and in adjusting to adverse life conditions. Many psychologists (Lazarus, 1986; Taylor, 1989) referred to such beliefs as 'healthy illusions'— the beliefs that make life livable. Such beliefs (like, I am a good person) are essential to lead a healthy life. After reviewing the social psychological literature, Taylor and Brown (1988) concluded: "The overriding implication that we draw from our analysis....is that certain biases in perception that have previously been thought of as amusing peccadillos at best and serious flaws in information processing at worst may actually be highly adaptive under many circumstances" (p. 205). Three "pervasive, enduring, and systematic" (p. 194) illusions *about the self*—unrealistically positive self-evaluations, exaggerated perceptions of control or mastery, *and* unrealistic optimism—were said to be the key elements that help bring about and maintain psychological well-being despite the inaccuracy of these self-evaluations.

This set of positively biased illusions is associated with and fosters better life functioning as well as positive psychological adjustment. This is counter not only to traditional theories of mental health, but also to intuitive beliefs about adjustment. Even if one accepts the idea that overly optimistic beliefs foster psychological adjustment, it is compelling to believe that this would be a false happiness, that those living in a dream world would be unable to function as effectively in the long run as would more realistic persons. The reality is just the reverse (Taylor, Collins, Skokan & Aspinwall, 1989, pp. 115-116).

Managing One's Own Chronic Disease

How people live with chronic diseases is one of the most fascinating and challenging area of research in psychology. The research in this area has been growing in recent years, though there is still little consistency in the findings that have emerged. There are many reasons for this lack of consistency in the research findings. One, a bulk of research is from the medical perspective, where the emphasis is on the disease, not on the person. The effort is to understand the nature of the disease, to arrive at an accurate diagnosis, and to plan out the treatment procedure. Patient's own perspective, and their own perception and feelings are not much investigated. Second, patient's own role in managing the disease is still the least explored. Like the attending doctor, the patient is also actively involved in understanding the disease and trying out various remedial measures. Patients own beliefs about the illness play an important role in this venture. It is suggested in many studies that patient's own beliefs about their health and treatment regulate their health behaviour to a far greater extent than the doctor's beliefs or objective medical data (Roberts, Smith, Bennett, Cape, Norton & Kilburn, 1984). However, there are few longitudinal studies examining these aspects. Third, the role of cultural factors is relatively ignored in psychological researches in this area (Dalal & Ray, 2005). Though there is substantial anthropological and sociological work to highlight cultural differences in health practices and treatment modalities, psychologists have yet to provide an understanding of how these cultural beliefs gets translated into concrete actions. Psychological researchers may fall into some pattern if cultural beliefs and their psychological imports are more systematically investigated.

To put it briefly, research focusing on health beliefs shares some common understanding about the human nature. First, people are generally actively involved in understanding the meaning of their illness. This understanding is essential to appropriately react to the health crisis. Secondly, people differ widely in the way they subjectively construct the experience of even very similar illnesses. Their beliefs about the illness and life in general provide the basic inputs for these subjective constructions. Thirdly, these subjective constructions of the illness in terms of their meaning, causes and control influence their recovery (or adjustment) very significantly, at times more significantly than the real nature of the disease. Fourthly, people are motivated to make efforts to recover from the crisis situation. In fact, it is assumed that the efforts to recover begin with the onset of the chronic disease itself. Fifth, people are not only motivated but also possess a self-curing mechanism. In the crisis situation, this mechanism gets activated and people on very rare occasions need institutional support to deal with the psychological crisis. People not only recover or successfully adjust but also learn to be more resourceful in facing a similar crisis in future. Sixth, people can be helped and trained to cope with the adversities by bringing appropriate changes in their own beliefs and attitudes.

A REVIEW OF FIVE STUDIES

The five studies reported here were conducted at different time points by colleagues and this researcher at Allahabad. One of the major objectives of all these studies was to examine the beliefs the patients had about their own illness, particularly beliefs related to causes of the disease, factors contributing to recovery and beliefs about personal control. The linkages of these beliefs with effective reactions, psychological and medical recovery were also examined. The interest was in understanding the process through which these health beliefs influence recovery outcomes for the patients who were going through the acute phase of their chronic disease necessitating hospitalization. In all these studies the disease and recovery was studied from the patient's perspective.

The first of these studies (Dalal & Pande, 1988) was conducted on orthopaedic patients who were the victims of some major accident. These orthopaedic patients were classified as permanently disabled (e.g., amputees), or temporarily disabled due to the accident. They are interviewed two weeks and a month after the accident to map their beliefs and recovery. The second study was conducted by Dalal and Singh (1992) on tuberculosis patients convalescing in a local hospital. The patients were asked question about perceived causes of the diseases and beliefs about recovery. Their psychological and medical recovery was examined. The third study was carried out (Agrawal & Dalal, 1993) to investigate the recovery process of myocardial infarction patients. Their recovery was monitored at three time points, during hospitalization and later at home. Again the relation between their disease related beliefs and recovery process was the main objective of the study. The fourth study (Kohli & Dalal, 1998) was conducted on cervical cancer patients to study their explanatory models and psychological recovery. Women at different stages of treatment for cervical cancer were interviewed for their metaphysical beliefs about the disease. In the last study reported here (Dalal & Agrawal, 1999) studied the perception of hospital environment and its relation with affective reactions of patients getting treatment for different chronic diseases. Dalal (2000) has discussed major findings of these studies.

Major Findings

The major findings of these five studies are collated to find the overall pattern of the relationship between health beliefs and recovery from the disease. Since different questionnaires and measures were used in these studies, for the purpose of comparison the findings were in some instances further subjected to some transformation. Again, not all measures were included in these five studies and the comparisons were made wherever it was possible.

Causal and Recovery Beliefs : The mean ratings of causal and recovery attributions were rank ordered to compare findings across the first four studies conducted on different groups of patients. The highest mean rating was given the rank of 1 and so on. These ranks are presented in Table 12.1.

Table 12.1: Rank Order of Causal and Recovery Beliefs as Reported by the Patients.

	TB	*CHD*	*Cancer*	*Orthopaedic*
n=	*70*	*70*	*114*	*41*
Causal Beliefs				
Own Carelessness	3	1	5	4
Other's Carelessness	6	5	6	3
Family Conditions	5	3	4	5
Fate/Chance	4	–	3	–
God's Will	1	4	2	1
Karma	2	2	1	2
Recovery Beliefs				
Self	5	4	4	–
Family	7	2	5	–
Money	4	–	–	–
Fate/Chance	3	–	6	–
God	2	3	2	–
Karma	6	5	3	–
Doctor	1	1	1	–

The trends of ranks in Table 12.1 show that health problems were most frequently attributed to God's will and *karma*, except in the case of CHD patients. Other's carelessness was least used category of causes, except by the accident victims. CHD patients attributed the blame more to themselves than to any other factor.

The pattern was not that clear in the case of recovery attributions. Here, recovery was most frequently attributed to the attending doctor, may be because all the patients were in the hospital. After doctor, the recovery was most frequently attributed to God. The other attributions of recovery seem to be more contingent on the nature of illness.

Causal Dimensions and Treatment Decisions: The actual ratings of causal attributions as reported in Table 12.1 in the case of cancer patients were categorized along three causal dimensions and were correlated with delay in seeking treatment and perception of hospital environment. The three causal dimensions are internal (own carelessness), external (other's carelessness, family conditions), cosmic (Fate, God's will and *karma*). These correlations are reported in Table 12.2.

Table 12.2 : Correlations of Causal Dimensions with Delay in seeking Treatment and Perception of Hospital Environment

Causal Dimensions	*Treatment Delay++*	*Hostpital Environment Perceived. Threat*
Internal	.29*	–.21*
External	+.12*	.27*
Cosmic	.37**	.25*

* p<. 05
** p<. 01
\+ Perceived severity of the disease was partialled out.
++ Correlations derived on cancer patients only.

The results show that in case of cancer patients there was greater delay in seeking treatment when patients attributed their illness to internal and cosmic factors. It was also found that the hospital environment was perceived as less threatening when the disease was attributed to internal factors, and more threatening when attribution was made to cosmic factors.

Linkages of Health Beliefs with Recovery Measures: The two types of beliefs (causal and recovery), as taken in some of these studies were correlated with the measures of psychological adjustment. The indices of psychological recovery varied in these studies, but common among all the four studies were the items related to: disease appraisal, hope, mood state and positive attitude. The simple correlations between beliefs and psychological adjustment are given in Table 12.3.

Table 12.3 : Correlations of Health Beliefs with Recovery Measures

	TB	*CHD*	*Cancer*	*Orthopaedic**	
				Temp	*Perm*
n=	*70*	*70*	*114*	*20*	*21*
Causal Beliefs					
Own Carelessness	.22	.30**	.10	.30	.01
Other's Carelessness	–.24**	.01	–.14	.11	.25
Family Conditions	.26**	.02	–.31***	–.06	–.14
Fate/Chance	–.15	.–	.03	–	–
God's Will	–.09	–.37***	.15	–.05	.29
Karma	–.06	–.19	–.10	.39*	.29
Recovery Beliefs					
Self	.05	.24*	.28***	–	–
Family	–.03	–.06	.16	–	–
Money	.08	–	–	–	–
Fate/Chance	–.28**	–	.11	–	–
God	–.29**	.29**	.09	–	–
Karma	.18	.29**	.02	–	–
Doctor	–.12	–.18	.00	–	–

* p< .10
** p< .05
*** p< .01
* Temporary and Permanent disability

The results show that in general the correlations between causal attributions and psychological adjustment was found to be low and showed no consistent trend across different samples. Only in the case of CHD patients self-blame positively correlated with adjustment. Attribution to family conditions positively correlated with adjustment in case of TB patients and negatively in case of cancer patients. Cosmic beliefs also did not show any consistent pattern.

On the other hand, for CHD patients attribution to self, God and *karma* positively correlated with adjustment. The pattern of correlation was reverse in case of TB patients. Separate measures of control over self and disease, in general showed significant correlations with psychological adjustment of the patients.

Proposed Cultural Belief Model of Health

The above discussion and findings of the five studies, as reported above facilitates the formulation of a cultural belief model of health.

The formulation of this model is based on the following premises:

1. People are motivated to find the causes of their illness. The search for the causality is not in terms of medical causes but in terms of larger life perspective. The functional view of causality suggests that people search for those explanations which help them in making adjustments in their lives to deal with the aftermaths of a chronic disease. Such causal explanations are of value in integrating the illness experience in their larger world view.
2. People often resort to prevailing cultural beliefs as a wider framework to make sense of their illness. These are the beliefs which are readily accessible and are acceptable to the family and community to which the sick person belongs. In fact, making sense of a illness is a collective process in which family and support group of the patient are actively engaged. These explanations involve mundane and metaphysical beliefs; social and personal causality; traditional and biological causality consistent with the cultural belief system. A disease is thus understood and

interpreted within the existential domain of a socio-cultural system.

3. The main objective of viewing a chronic disease from such a broad socio-cultural perspective is to relocate one's place in the social matrix they belong to. A chronic disease dislocates a person and disrupts his/her old patterns of social interaction. The changed circumstances often call for redefining one's social relationships and relocating oneself in the social network. For example, a person after a major heart attack may no longer be an earning member of the family and may be very much dependent on others for daily routine. This is likely to affect his/her status in the family.

The cultural health belief model proposes that the way people make sense of their disease significantly influence their health-related behaviour. Specifically, two types of health beliefs are of significance. These are: causal beliefs and recovery beliefs. Causal beliefs are those which explains why a particular disease has occurred; whereas, recovery beliefs relate to the factors which are considered as contributing to the recovery process. The three types of causal beliefs are internal (attributing to self), external (attribution to outside factors) and metaphysical (attributing to cosmic, religious factors). The recovery beliefs are also categorized in these three types. In general, it is contended on the basis of the earlier studies that causal attribution are closely linked with decisions about the treatment mode and delay in seeking medical treatment. The recovery beliefs would relate with the emotional state of the patient's mood state and compliance with the course of treatment.

Of course, there are no direct linkages between cultural beliefs and recovery from the disease. This relationship is mediated by a number of background variables and illness conditions. This is an emerging area of research with many exciting possibilities. The work to identify mediating variables, and accordingly expand the cultural belief model of health is still in progress.

REFERENCES

Agrawal, M. & Dalal, A.K. (1993). Beliefs about the world and recovery from myocardial infarction. *Journal of Social Psychology,* 133, 385-394.

Bower, J.E.; Kemeny, M.E.; Taylor, S.E.; & Fahey, J.L., (1998). Cognitive processing, discovery of meaning, CD4 decline, and AIDS-related mortality among bereaved HIV-positive men. *Journal of Consulting and Clinical Psychology,* 66, 979-986.

Dalal, A.K. & Agrawal, M. (1999). *Reactions to hospitalisation.* Unpublished manuscript, University of Allahabad, India.

Dalal, A.K., (2000). Living with a chronic disease : Healing and psychological adjustment in Indian society. *Psychology and Developing Societies,* 12, 67-81.

Dalal, A.K. & Pande, N. (1988). Psychological recovery of the accident victims with temporary and permanent disability. *International Journal of Psychology.,* 23, 25-40.

Dalal, A.K., & Ray, S. (2005). Social dimension of health and well-being: An overview of research trends. In A.K. Dalal, & S. Ray (eds.), *Social Dimension of Health* (pp. 1-33). Jaipur : Rawat Publications.

Dalal, A.K. & Singh, A.K., (1992). Role of causal and recovery beliefs in psychological adjustment to a chronic disease. *Psychology and Health: An International Journal,* 6, 193-203.

Dull, V.T., & Skokan, L.A., (1995). A congnitive model of religion's influence on health, *Journal of Social Issues,* 51, 49-64.

Fielding, J.W.I.; Fagg, S.L.; Jones, S.; Elis, M.S., Hockey, A.; Minawa A.; Brookes, V.S.; Craven, J.L.; Mason, M.C.; Timothy, J.A.; Waterhouse A.H.; & Wrigley P.M. (1983). An interim report of a prospective randomized controlled study to adjuvant chemotherapy in operable gastric cancer. *World Journal of Surgery,* 14, 390-399.

Hosen, R., Solovey- Hosen. D., & Stern, L. (2002). The Acquisition of Beliefs that Promote Subjective Well-Being. *Journal of Instructional Psycoholgy,* 29, (4), 231-239.

Kier, F.J. & Devenport, D.S., (2004). Unaddressed Problems in the Study of Spirituality and Health. *American Psychologist,* 59, 53-54.

Kohli. N. & Dalal, A.K., (1998). Culture as a factor in causal understanding of illness: A study of cancer patients. *Psychology and Developing, Societies,* 10, 115-129.

Lazarus, R.S.; (1984). On the primacy of cognition. *American Psychologist,* 39, 124-129.

Levin, P. & Venderpool, D. (1991), Physical illness, the individual, and the coping process. *Psychiatry in Medicine,* 22, 156-168.

Paranjpe, A.C.; (1984). *Theoretical Psychology: Meeting of East and West.* New York : Plenum Press.

Radley, A. (1994), *Making sense of an illness.* London : Sage.

Robert, N., Smith, E.; Bennet, S. Cape, J.; Norton, R., & Kilburn, P. (1984). Health beliefs and rehabilitation after lumber disc surgery. *Journal of Psychosomatic Research,* 28, 139-144.

Taylor, S.E., (1989). *Positive illusions: Creative self-deception and the healthy mind.* New York: Basic Books.

Taylor, S.E. & Brown, J.D., (1988). Illusion and well-being: A social psychological perspective on mental health. *Psychological Bulletin* 110, 193-210.

Taylor, S.E.; Collins, R.L.; Skokan, L.A.; & Aspinwall, L.G.; (1989). Maintaining positive illusions in the face of negative information: Getting the facts without letting them get to you. *Journal of Social and Clinical Psychology,* 8, 114-129.

Wikipedia (2005), *Beliefs.* New York: The Free Encyclopedia.

World Health Report (1998). *Life in the 21st Century — A Vision for All.* Geneva: World Health Organization.

13 Living with HIV/AIDS
Coping Strategies of Young Widows

A. Mrudula *and* U. Vindhya

The World Health Organization estimates that nearly 5 million persons (4.2 million adults and 700, 000 children) are newly infected with HIV each year and more than 95 per cent of them belong to developing countries. Almost 50 per cent of newly HIV-infected adults in 2003 were women and 50 per cent were young adults in the 15-24 years age group. A global summary reveals that there are 40 million persons living with HIV/AIDS worldwide (WHO Report, 2003).

Despite increasing numbers of reported AIDS cases among women in the 1980s, during the early epidemic, women and women's perspectives were excluded from research (Amoro, Raj & Reed, 2001). Most of the research with women largely centred on them as mothers or prostitutes, i.e., as vectors of disease (Amoro, 1995; Cohan & Atwood, 1994; Corea, 1992; Sacks, 1996; Strebel, 1995; Welch, Cline & Mukenzie, 1996). In consequence, AIDS in women has remained less understood (Corea, 1992). Women have historically been underrepresented in medical research, therefore, it is not surprising that women have also been ignored in the development of appropriate diagnoses treatment and prevention of HIV/AIDS (Corea, 1992).

By the mid-1990s, researchers began to realize how decontextualized the models of explaining women's HIV-positive status were, and how little they offered for understanding women's risk for HIV infection (Amaro, 1995). Early HIV/AIDS treatment did not address the needs of women and clinical trials for HIV/

AIDS also did not include women (Fox-Tierney, Ickovics, Cerretta and Ethier, 1999). This general paucity of research on HIV among women led to a male-centred case definition of AIDS that did not include symptoms common among women (Berer, 1993: Cohan & Atwood, 1994; Strebel. 1995).

It is only in recent years that sexually transmitted diseases (STD) — including HIV/AIDS — have emerged at the forefront of current women's sexual health research and public health practice. The number of women contracting these infections is increasing each year. HIV rates are continuing to rise, particularly among adolescent girls, who now account for the majority of youth infected with HIV [Centre for Disease Control (CDC), Office of Women's Health website, 2000; Bryan, Fisher & Fisher 2002; UNAIDS. 1996; WHO, 2000]. The social stigma attached to sexually transmitted infections also extends to HIV/AIDS, even in a much serious manner. For this reason in some developing countries, AIDS is also seen as a "woman's disease" because of its perception as a sexually transmitted disease and its association with prostitutes who are regarded as the reservoir of STD and HIV infection (Songwathana & Manderson, 1998).

New research that has emerged has begun to gain a more contextual understanding of women's HIV risks (Amaro & Raj, 2000). More gendered perspectives have begun to be used in prevention research and AIDS diagnoses now include symptoms more common among women.

In India, the HIV/AIDS epidemic is 15 years old. Within this short period it has emerged as the one of the most serious health problems in the country. The initial cases reported were among the commercial sex workers in Mumbai and Chennai and injecting drug users in the north-eastern State of Manipur. Even though the officially reported cases of HIV infections and full-blown AIDS cases are in thousands only, there is a wide gap between the reported and estimated figures because of the absence of epidemiological data in major parts of the country [Andhra Pradesh State AIDS Control Society (APSACS), 2002].

The available surveillance data clearly indicates that HIV is present in almost all parts of the country. In recent years, it has spread from urban to rural areas and from individuals practicing risk behaviour to the general population. Studies indicate that more and more women attending antenatal clinics are testing HIV-positive, thereby increasing the risk of perinatal transmission [National AIDS Control Organization (NACO), 2003]. NACO's sentinel surveillance data shows generalized HIV epidemic in the States of Andhra Pradesh, Goa, Karnataka, Maharashtra, Manipur, Tamil Nadu and Nagaland, with 79.9 per cent of reported AIDS cases of the total recorded (Sen, 2003 : cited in Priya, 2003). About 89 per cent of the reported cases are occurring in the sexually active and economically productive age group of 18-59 years and one in every four cases reported is a woman (NACO, 1997-98). Sexual contact constitutes the single largest source of infections in AIDS cases in this country followed by contaminated blood transfusions (NACO, 2003).

In the Indian scenario, nowhere is gender discrimination so apparent than in the realm of health (Datta, 2003). Studies have revealed that women's subordinate position is perpetuated and reinforced by their limited access to and control over resources that includes access to health care services (Batliwala, 1993). While it is true that the poor in general have limited access to and control over resources in relation to those who own productive assets. Women have comparatively less control over such resources than men. Women thus get doubly marginalized—by virtue of being poor and of being women (Vijayanthi, 2002). Women also bear the brunt of multiple forms of exploitation that originate from class, caste, cultural and patriarchal systems of prejudice and discrimination (Gandhi & Shah, 1991).

Considering health in isolation without reference to these linkages leads to an improper understanding of women's health, and to clumsy and ineffective policy planning. Policy attention to women's health has so far been mainly addressed only to reproductive or maternal health and has not taken into consideration the impact of social factors on women's health. Such an approach circumcised all other aspects of women's health and highlighted the State's preoccupation with reduction of fertility in the early years of planning (Rao, 2000). Similarly, gender blind health programmes ignored social reality by overlooking important linkages between women's health issues and other aspects of their lives (Datta, 2003).

Women's vulnerability to STD and HIV infection is enhanced by several factors, including women's economic dependence on men, lack of access to education and information, poverty, sexual exploitation, coercion and rape, as well as the greater tendency of women to sell sex in order to survive (Aggleton & Rivers, 1999). Unequal gender relations are particularly visible in the special vulnerability of women to HIV and AIDS in countries like India where risk-taking behaviour among men is common.

Coping

In psychology, there has been a paradigm shift away from pathology and risk factors towards a focus on the positive aspects of human strength. Moving away from the existing deficit/vulnerability model, which focuses on the stress-illness relation, current research now aims at understanding the positive aspect of human strength, which has long been ignored in psychology, but is now receiving attention (Srivastava, 2000).

A direct offshoot of this shift is the significant increase in research on the role of psychosocial variables in the lives of those infected with HIV/AIDS. The literature on well-being and coping in general has identified achievement, social contacts, control, feeling of happiness with family, work satisfaction, spiritual quality, personal competence, social support, freedom from depression, autonomy, personal morale, interpersonal trust and freedom from anxiety as criteria for well-being and coping (Sahu & Rath, 2003).

In the case of adjustment and coping with chronic illness, literature in developed countries points to the role of psychosocial factors such as appraisal of illness, social support, symptom severity and adjustment to chronic illness (Bova, 2001). Coping strategies such as creating a meaningful life pattern, connectedness and self-care have been identified as having an impact on the coping ability of people living with HIV/AIDS (Mellors, Erlen, Coontz & Lucke, 2001).

High levels of social support, spiritual perspective, interpersonal conflict and perceived stress intensity are the predictors of mastery over stress in HIV-positive women (Gray & Carson, 2002). There was, however, no significant difference in the coping styles between HIV-infected and non-infected women and greater emotion-focused coping was associated with less general psychological distress. Problem-focused coping (along with the stage of illness) was found to be an important predictor of the patient's response in all areas of functioning (Ball, Tannenbaum, Armistead & Magnen, 2002).

Despite worldwide statistics pointing to the widespread prevalence of HIV/AIDS among women (UNAIDS, 1996; WHO, 2003) the category of widowed and infected women, *i.e.* those whose husbands have transmitted the disease and who are now dead, is a relatively under-researched one. The present study, therefore, made a modest attempt to explore the dynamics of how widowed women infected with HIV/AIDS cope and continue to live with the situation. The locale of the study is in the city of Visakhapatnam in northern Andhra Pradesh in south India. To the best of our knowledge, no such study has been conducted here so far. The importance of conducting such studies is underscored by the fact that Andhra Pradesh has been identified as one of the two most high-risk States in India so far as reporting and detection of AIDS cases are concerned (NACO, 2001; WHO, 2003).

Method

Participants

Participants consisted of 20 widows who had lost their husbands to HIV/AIDS. Out of a total of 87 identified widows who consulted a local Non-Governmental Organization, 20 of them were interviewed after ascertaining their marital status. The NGO conducts community based care and support programmes for people living with HIV/AIDS (PLWHAs) in Visakhapatnam city.

Only women who had been widowed due to HIV/AIDS and who were infected themselves were included in the sample. The mean age of the participants was 26.9 years and they ranged from 18 to 45 years of age. All of them belonged to the lower socio-economic category. A majority of them (n =13) had received primary education while the remaining had no formal education.

Measures

A personal data sheet aimed at obtaining the following socio-demographic information was used:

> Age, marital status and duration of marriage, education, occupation and income, religion and caste, number of children and their age and gender, type of family and number of family members, address and locality, referral, date of diagnosis and the duration of the illness. Information about the spouse included his occupation, income and education, his HIV status, and the date of his death were also obtained.

In addition to the socio-demographic data, the General Health Questionnaire (GHQ), a self-administered screening questionnaire designed for use in consulting settings and aimed at detecting those with a diagnosable psychiatric disorder was used (Goldberg, 1972). The test is concerned with two major classes of phenomena: inability to carry out one's normal "healthy" functions, and the appearance of new phenomena of a distressing nature.

This scaled version of the questionnaire comprising 28 questions is divided into four sub-scales consisting of seven questions each:

- A—Somatic dysfunction
- B—Anxiety and lnsomnia
- C—Social Dysfunction
- D—Depression

Results and Discussion

Sample Characteristics

The socio-demographic data of the sample yielded the following profile:

Table 13.1: Socio-demographic Profile

Variable	*Range*
Age	18-45 years
Education	No formal education; primary education
Occupation	Housewives, domestic help
Income	No income—Rs. 1000 per month
Residence	Urban slums
No. of children	1-3 children
Duration of marriage	10.65 years (average of the group)
Duration of illness	6 months—7 years.
Type of family	Nuclear

The age group of the sample (mean age 26.9 years) is representative of the global picture of the epidemic that occurs in the sexually active and reproductive age group of 15-45 years. 89 per cent of the reported cases in the country belong to this age group (NACO, 1997-98).

Education levels of the sample were found to be low. It is an acknowledged fact that the epidemic has reached its current proportions largely due to a lack of knowledge and awareness of the disease and high-risk behaviours. Though we cannot confirm a definitive causal relationship between formal education and knowledge of HIV and ASID, it is evident that education level does play an important role in the levels of awareness, recognition and prevention of high-risk behaviours.

The mean income of the group was Rs. 457 per month. Many of the respondents had no income (n = 6), while some of them earned Rs. 500 and less (n = 7). This inability to earn a minimum income per month can be attributed to their low education levels and lack of skills, which have a direct effect on the kind of employment that is available for them. Most of the women in the sample reported that they had never worked while their husbands were alive.

The components of socio-economic status, education, occupation and income, reveal that the sample is constituted entirely of the lower socio-economic class. Hailing from the lower socio-economic class, all the subjects reported that they experience severe financial constraints in not only getting treatment for their disease but in meeting day-to-day expenses as well. As recent studies have indicated, this means that the economic of the disease will be immense at the household level (Arunkumar, Rajan, Thimothy, 2004).

The sample consisted almost entirely of urban slum dwellers (n=15) from areas identified as high-risk for the transmission of the virus in the city of Visakhapatnam. The lack of awareness about HIV among infected individuals points to the fact that despite the increase in public awareness of HIV transmission, there has not been a resultant change in HIV/AIDS-related high-risk behaviour (Arunkumar, Rajan, Thimothy, 2004).

GHQ Scores

The cutting score of 4/5 was employed for GHQ (Goldberg & Hillier, 1979) to make a distinction of cases and non-cases. Using this cutting score, 12 of the respondents were found to be cases, i.e., they reported significant distress regarding their health. The remaining eight participants could be described as non-cases as their GHQ scores were below the cutting score. The widows who were identified as cases scored high on the depression sub-scale (D) followed by anxiety and insomnia (B) and somatic symptoms (A).

Subscale D of the GHQ 28 which measures depression, shows that many of the respondents have depressive features owing to the nature of the disease they are suffering from. These depressive symptoms are further compounded by their abject poverty. Poverty is one of the most consistent correlates of depression. Financial hardship almost doubles women's risk for the onset of depression (Brown & Moran, 1997). High levels of depressive symptoms are common among those with low incomes, especially mothers with young children. Discrimination also contributes to the poverty and economic inequalities that women endure and has direct and demonstrable effects on women's mental health and well-being (Belle & Doucet, 2003).

On closely examining some of the responses to the items in the depression sub-scale, it was found that most of the respondents had thought of suicide, and the idea had crossed their mind. This can be verified from the interview data, when respondents admitted that their initial thought, when they had been informed of their HIV-positive status, had been to commit suicide.

Anxiety and insomnia, measured by subscale B is also high in the respondents, considering the number of responses given them. Given the life circumstances of the women who participated in the study — HIV-positive, widowed, little or no income, and the responsibility of children — it is of little surprise that these women are more concerned with the economic hardships and with their conditions of poverty, which have a negative bearing on their mental health and well-being (Srivastava, 2000).

The subscale A, which measures somatic symptoms, shows that many of the respondents have complained of somatic symptoms. Though these responses cannot be considered completely true. Owing to the nature and symptoms of the virus, earlier studies have found that somatization is a commonly encountered complaint, especially among women (Goldberg & Huxley, 1980).

The respondents in the study did not indicate any social dysfunction measured by subscale C. This can be attributed to the overwhelming support from the natal family that each woman is receiving. Further, no respondent in the study reported facing any kind of discrimination or ostracization based on her HIV-positive status, though all of them feared having to cope with stigma and discrimination.

Coping Strategies

Todd and Worell (2000) in their study on resilience in low-income women found that the participants mentioned five factors which they felt contributed to their resilience: informal social support, children, religious/spiritual beliefs, determination to survive or prevail, and self-efficacy.

The in-depth interview revealed the presence of coping strategies such as social support, a strong sense of responsibility towards children, active acceptance of their illness and a strong belief in God. Other themes which emerged indicated the women's determination to keep occupied and the importance attributed to self-care including adherence to diet and exercise.

Social Support

Social support has often been shown to contribute to a person's psychological and physical well-being (Cohen & Will S., 1985) and to buffer the impact of chronic stress on well-being (Kessler & McLeod, 1985). In India, the collectivist society provides for a vast network of social support not only from the immediate family, but also from the extended network of friends, relatives and well-wishers. This network provides a strong buffer against the daily as well as life stressors. All the women experienced and enjoyed some form of social support. While some parents voluntarily looked after their daughters, some of the women were foisted onto them by the girl's in-laws after the husband's death.

> "...my mother-in-law doesn't care about my son and me. She said that my parents should look after us."

> "...they don't allow me to even see my children, I am not allowed into the house. They took my children and don't want me in their house because I'm having this (AIDS)."

Parents and the natal family support was reported by a predominant number of the women in the sample. Some of the women said that their parents did not know about their HIV-positive status and they preferred not to reveal this information, as they did not want to burden them further.

> "...they are old. My father has BP and my mother has arthritis. I don't want to burden them further by telling them about my illness. They are helping me as much as they can after my husband's death, this news will sadden them and they can't bear it."

All the women in the sample admitted that they received a lot of support financially and emotionally from their parents. This was cited as the major source of support for them even though some of them had not revealed their positive status to their family.

Responsibility towards Children

All the women in the sample had children, except for three women. None of the children had tested positive and this was a major relief to the mothers. One very strong and vehement reason all the participants in the study cited for continuing to live in spite of being infected was their children.

> "...I am bringing him up to think that he is going to stay with his (adopted) parents after I am gone so that he won't miss me too much. What can I do? I have to think of my son, if it had not been for his responsibility. I would have committed suicide."
>
> "...I want to get a job in an office and earn around

> Rs. 1000-1200, so that I can save a little money for my daughter for her future. I want her to go to school and study unlike me."
>
> ".......If something happens to me later, my children should be taken care of . I am trying to put them in a hostel for this reason."

All the subjects in the study had a futuristic goal, which they wanted to achieve for their children. This goal-directed thinking enabled them to plan and act in the present. The concern of their children's future was a source of great motivation and impetus for these women to think positively and make plans for the future of their children when they would not be there to look after their welfare. All the women exhibited a strong sense of responsibility towards their children.

Keeping Occupied

As the women were all from the lower socio-economic strata of the society, keeping themselves occupied with work was more a necessity rather than an active choice. Though they enjoyed a little financial support from their parents and, grudgingly from in-laws, all of them felt they had to make their contribution to their own and their children's walfare.

> "...I stay occupied most of the time. If I finish my work, I go to my brother-in-law's house and sit with his children, or I read some books."
>
> "...If I don't work, who will look after our needs? It's not sufficient, but we adjust I can't do any other kind of heavy work, as there's no one to look after my children and I get tired easily due to my illness."

Self-care

All the respondents in the study were aware of hygiene, a nutritious diet, and exercise. Adherence to the counsellor's instructions and guidance was high among all the participants in the study. They visited the NGO regularly to take the free vitamin supplements and other health enhancing products distributed there. Every respondent, during the course of the interview, emphasized on their diet and the multi-vitamin tablets that they used.

> "...the doctor told me to use medicines to keep it under control. But I don't use them, just these tablets which they give here. I maintain a good diet of leafy vegetables and protein rich food, as much as I can afford to."
>
> "...the doctor advised me to use homeopathy medicines, but there are too many diet restrictions. Whenever I can, I have eggs and milk, and walk to my house from the market. I can't afford to have rich food everyday, but whenever it's possible, I take a good diet."
>
> "...I feel nauseous if I see food. I am unable to eat properly. But I use the medicines which the doctor asked me to take and the medicines they give here."
>
> "...I use the tablets which they give here. Sometimes, I also go to the private doctors for tonics. I feel very weak."

The picture that emerged revealed that these women maintained their diet whenever they could afford the expenses involved. All of them used the food supplement tablets that were provided by the NGO. Personal hygiene was given due importance by all the respondents as was evident in their appearance and dress.

> "...she (the counsellor at the VCTC) told me to always be clean and dress nicely. I follow her advice. I wear clean clothes and take care of myself; how I look is important."
>
> "...after giving my son his bath, I also have a bath and light the lamp for God. I clean the house myself and mop the floors. My son is small and cleanliness is important for me also."

Active Acceptance

The striking feature among all the participants was that each of them, though initially hurt, angry and shattered, came to terms with their disease and continued with life after making adjustments in their previously organized lives. For all the women in the study, their lives changed with the positive test result of their husbands, and consequently, their own HIV-positive status.

> "...we all die sometime. I will die a little earlier than the others, knowing that I will die. That's the only difference."
> "...I have it. Now I can't get it out of my body. There's nothing anyone can do. So I continue with my work and my life."
> "...what can I do if I have it? There's nothing I can do about it. I don't think about the future, just today and tomorrow."
> "...I don't worry about anything, not even my children. I do what I can for them. I enjoy myself all the time. I don't feel sick at all. Even the usual symptoms which the doctor mentioned, I don't have."

These responses indicate action-focused or problem-solving strategies to alleviate the stress cussed by the disease. All of the widows have employed active coping strategies to deal with the illness and their perception of it. There was no evidence of any of the subjects in the study having resorted to avoid coping strategies such as denial, substance abuse or seeking refuge in dysfunctional mental states such as depression.

> "...yes, I do feel sad at times. But then I remember my children and I don't remain in that mood anymore."
> "...once in a while I wonder why I got this. At such times, I go to my brother-in-law's house or do some work, so that I don't continue with these thoughts."

Faith in God

Women with HIV face a number of challenges in living with this chronic, life threatening illness — economic, physical, social and emotional. When discussing their illness, the importance these women place on having a strong spiritual life is a consistent theme (Woodward & Sowell, 2001). The women in the present study explained their belief in God, particularly in Christ and Christianity, as having a positive and calming influence in their traumatic lives.

> "...after my husband's death, I went to the church. I felt a peace for the first time. I pray a lot, and I feel my prayers are being answered."
> "...I go to the church close to where I stay. I pray for my health, for my child's welfare, and for my friend who is giving me so much support."
> "...I believe a lot in Christ. I go regularly to church and pray. It is because of his grace that I am able to continue in life in spite of so many difficulties."

These statements show that these HIV-positive women are using their spiritual life to enhance their care rather than using their faith to avoid active care and coping. The respondents, who mentioned their spirituality, stated that their faith helped them gain inner strength and obtain reassurance from God.

Conclusion

A meta-analysis of recent studies of sex differences in coping showed that women were more likely than men to engage in most coping strategies. These studies revealed that women were more likely to use strategies that involved verbal expressions to others or the self; to seek emotional support, ruminate about problems, and use positive self talk (Tamres, Janicki & Helgeson, 2002). While examining the various coping strategies of widowed women living with HIV/AIDS, it is also essential to understand the psychosocial needs of HIV-positive women. Morrow, Costello and Boland (2001) found that women were interested in and perceived the need for psychosocial group intervention.

The present study paves the way for future studies that can focus on a need assessment of this particularly marginalized group of women battling with HIV/AIDS. For this reason, though small in sçale, this study assumes significance.

REFERENCES

Aggleton, P. & Rivers, K. (1999). Behavioural interventions for adolescents. In R. DiClemente and S. Vermund (eds.), *Preventing HIV infection in developing countries* (pp. 14-23). New York: Plenum Publications.

Amaro, H. (1995). Love, sex and power: Considering women's realities in HIV prevention. *American Psychologist*, 50, 437-447.

Amaro, H.; Raj. A.; Reed, E. (2001). Women's Sexual Health: The need for feminist analyses in public health in the decade of behaviour. Psychology *of Women Quarterly*, 25, 324-334.

Arunkumar,. T.S.; Rajan, S. Irudaya,; Thimothy, R. (2004). HIV Patients: Knowledge and Sexual Behaviour Patterns. *Economic and Political Weekly*, 29, 1208-1210.

Ball, J.; Tannenbaum, L.; Armistead, L.; Magnen, S.; *et al.* (2002). Coping with HIV infection in African-American women, *Women & Health,* Vol. 35(1), 17-36.

Batliwala, S. (1993). *Empowerment of women in south Asia*. Sri Lanka: Asian South Pacific Bureau of Adult Education and FAO's Freedom from Hunger Campaign/Action for Development.

Berer, M. (1993). *Women and AIDS: An international resource book*. London: Harper Collins Publishers.

Bova, C. (2001). Adjustment of chronic illness among HIV-infected women. Journal of Nursing Scholarship, Vol. 33(3), 217-224.

Bryan, A.; Fisher, J. D. & Fisher, W. A. (2002). Tests of the medtiational role of preparatory safer sexual behaviour in the context of the theory of planned behaviour, *Health Psychology*, Vol. 21(1), 71-80.

Centers for Disease Control. (2000). *HIV AIDS surveillance report: U. S. HIV and AIDS cases reported through December*. 1999. Year End Edition, Vol. 11(2).

Cohan. N. & Atwood, J. D. (1994). Women and AIDS: The social constructions of gender and diseases. *Family Systems Medicine*, 12, 5-20.

Cohen, S., & Wills. T. A. (1985). Stress, social support, and the buffering hypothesis. *Psychological Bulletin*, 98, 310-357.

Corea, G. (1992). *The invisible epidemic: The story of women and AIDS.* New York: Harper Collins Publishers.

Datta, Anindita (2003). Articulation of an integrated women's health policy using the life cycle approach. *Indian Journal of Gender Studies*: Vol 10(1). 25-43.

Fox-Tierney, R. A.; Ickovics, J. R.; Cerreta, C.; & Ethier, K. A. (1999). Potential sex differences remain understudied: A case study of the inclusion of women in HIV/AIDS-related neuropsychological research. *Review of General Psychology*, 3, 44-54.

Gandhi, N. & Shah, N. (1991). The Issues at Stake—*Theory and practice in the contemporary women's movement in India.* New Delhi: Kali for women.

Gray, J.; & Carson, C.L; (2002). Mastery over stress among women with HIV/AIDS. *JANAC: Journal of the Association of Nurses in AIDS Care*, Vcl. 13(4), 43-57.

Kessler, R., & McLeod, J. D. (1985). Social support and mental health in community samples. In S. Cohen & S. L. Syne (eds.), *Social support and health* (pp. 219-240). Orlando, FL: Academic.

Mellors, Mary P.; Erlen, J.A.; Coontz, P. D.; & Lucke, K. T. (2001). Transcending the suffering of AIDS. *Journal of Community Health Nursing*, Vol. 18(4), 235-246.

National AIDS Control Organisation (2001). *National Baseline General Population Behavioural Surveillance Survey.* Ministry of Health and Family Welfare, Government of India.

Priya, R. (2003). Health Services and HIV Treatment — Complex Issues and Options. *Economic and Political Weekly*, (December 13, 2003), 5227-5232.

Rao, M. (2000). Family planning programmes: Paradigm shift in strategy. *Economic and Political Weekly*. 35(49), 4317-4322.

Sacks. V. (1996). Women and AIDS: An analysis of media misrepresentations. *Social Science and Medicine*, 42, 59-73.

Sen, S. (2003). High prevalence states: An analysis of the HIV/AIDS scenario. *Health for the Millions*. 28(6) 20-30.

Songwathana, P. & Manderson, I. (1998). Perceptions of HIV/AIDS and caring for people with terminal AIDS in southern Thailand. AIDS Care. 10 (Suppl. 2) S155-S165.

Strebel, A. (1995). Whose epidemic is it? Reviewing the literature on women and AIDS, South *African Journal of Communication Disorders*, 25, 12-20.

Todd, J. L., & Worell, J. (2000). Resilience in low-income, employed, African American women. *Psychology of Women Quarterly*, 24, 119-128.

UNAIDS (1996). *Figures and trends about HIV/AIDS Worldwide*. Press release, 8 March. http: //WWW. undp. org

Vijayanthi, K. N. (2002). Women's empowerment through self-help groups: A participatory approach. *Indian Journal of Gender Studies,* 9(2), 263-274.

Welch Cline, R.J., & McKenzie, N.J. (1996). Women and AIDS: The lost population. In R.L. Parrott & C.M. Condit (eds.), *Evaluating women's health messages: A resource book* (pp. 382-401). Thousand Oaks, CA: Sage Publications.

World Health Organisation, (2000) Women and HIV/AIDS. http://www.who.int/en/.

World Health Organization. (2003). Facts and figures. http://www. Whosea. org/hivaids/fact 1.

14 Psychological Recovery of Cervical Cancer Patients during Three Therapeutic Phases of Treatment

Neena Kohli

Cancer is generally viewed as a dreaded killer disease, associated with the images of apprehension, incapacitation, intense physical pain, suffering and debilitating uncertainties. There are more than 100 discrete forms of cancer and cervical cancer is the most prevalent type of cancer for rural women (24%) [Biennial Report, National Cancer Registry, Indian Council of Medical Research (ICMR) 2000]. The exact cause of cancer of the cervix is unknown. But Herpes Virus B is the suspected cause. There are certain predisposing factors such as sexual intercourse before the age of 18, multiple sexual partners, marriage at an early age, poor male sex hygiene, more than five completed pregnancies, vaginal infections and venereal diseases. The symptoms of cancer of the cervix are unusual discharge and bleeding. Apart from physical harm, cervical cancer engenders a host of social and psychological crises for the patients and their families, in terms of interpersonal relations, mounting medical expenses, anxieties and loss of control over one's life.

Though appropriate treatment aims to provide good quality life, still cancer has a profound physical, social and psychological impact upon the patient. The physical implications and impact of the disease are best handled by the attending doctor. Nowhere is the blend of science and humanism more apparent than it is in medicine, and more so in the treatment of cancer, where the task is a challenging one. The doctor feels helpless if he or she cannot be of any help of the patient. But doctors experience satisfaction and happiness when they meet a patient who has been cured and has gone back to living a normal life.

The social impact of the disease is best dealt with by the family and the support network of the patient. The family member closest to the patient—spouse, parent or child— usually bears the strain of the illness with the patient. Illness often increases family solidarity and appreciation of each other emphasizing the commonplace occurrences of everyday home life. The converse may be true in a few cases where the relative unable to stand the illness abandons the patient. Social support provides the patient the assurance, that he or she is loved and cared for and this facilitates the process of bringing back the patient to normal functioning.

The psychological factors have a very close association with cancer. Such a connection was assessed as early as 200 A.D. by a Roman physician Galen that "melancholic" women were at greater risk for cancer than "sanguine" women (Goldfarb, Driesen, & Cole, 1967).

Psychological status and psychological adjustment have assumed a central status with the realization that patient's own initiative is crucial. Those patients who make conscious efforts and feel they can beat back the disease, not only adapt better psychologically, but show miraculous recovery. They are able to resume normal lives, as compared to those who resign themselves to prolonged and fatal illness.

Psychological Recovery

A review of the literature reveals that the term psychological recovery is treated as a multifaceted concept. The indicators of successful recovery or adaptation included in various studies are : keeping one's distress within manageable limits, having a positive self-concept, hopefulness, positive and realistic view of the situation and clarity of future plans (Haan, 1977; Hamberg & Adams, 1967).

However, many studies have cast doubts on the validity of some of these indices. For example, Workman and Dintzer (1978) have argued that relatively intense distress can play an important role in motivating individuals to initiate coping attempts. Consistent with this view, Goldsmith (1955) reported that patients with spinal cord injuries who were more distressed about their disability and who expressed anger and aggressive feeling about what happened to them, were subsequently judged as showing more progress in rehabilitation than patients who appeared to be less distressed. Derogates, Abeloff and Melisaratos (1979) obtained similar findings.

Whether called reorganization (Bowlby, 1980), recovery (Klinger, 1975, 1977) or acceptance (Kubler-Ross, 1969) it is commonly suggested that individuals will resolve their crisis, thus moving on to the next stage of their lives. This is assumed not only when the person encounters a single aversive event (e.g. rape, loss, permanent injury) but also in the face of one's deteriorating physical condition, when the next stage would be death.

It is difficult to postulate precisely how much time should elapse before recovery from a single traumatic life event. Yet an individual who has recovered would not be expected to experience a disrupted life style or extreme emotional distress after a rather lengthy period of time. Nevertheless, several studies on psychological reactions to mastectomy have found that many women show severe distress a year or more after surgery, even when the illness does not recur. For example, Maguire *et al.,* (1978) found that 39% of the breast cancer patients they studied were still experiencing levels of anxiety or depression one year after their mastectomy. In fact these problems were significantly more prevalent than those in a matched control group of women with benign breast disease. Similarly, Morris, Green and White (1977), found that one year after surgery, 30% of their breast cancer patients still appeared to be distressed by the operation and had "failed to adjust".

Investigators have found long-term negative effects from a

trauma in other populations as well. Kaltreider, Wallace and Horowitz (1979) report that following a non-elective hysterectomy without resulting malignancy or with excellent future prognosis, almost 30% of the respondents were still experiencing stress symptoms, including anxiety, depression, phobias and obsessive thoughts one year after the operation.

Clearly, the evidence reviewed suggests that a simple expectation of acceptance or recovery from a serious life crisis is unwarranted for a large majority of people. Most studies found significant levels of distress or disorganization after a year and those that have continued to follow their sample for a longer period of time have not typically found substantial improvement (Glick, Weiss & Parkes, 1974; Morris *et al.*, 1977; Parkes, 1975; Vachan, 1979). Nevertheless, many researchers have stressed that for most victims of life crises, emotional distress is reduced and lives are reorganized with time. Over time, the person is expected to achieve a state of recovery and return to normal role functioning. The impact of stressful events is governed by the manner in which the victim is able to cope with them.

The major objective of this study is to map the process of psychological recovery of cervical cancer patients.

Method

Sample

The sample comprised of female cervical cancer patients undergoing treatment at a local hospital in Allahabad. The sample included only stage III patients (in stage III, the carcinoma extends to the pelvic wall or to the lower third of the vagina). Only these cervix patients were selected, who were not suffering from any other disease or cancer related disability. All the selected patients were undergoing the same type of treatment at the Cancer Unit of Kamla Nehru Hospital, Allahabad.

The modality of treatment for all the patients was radiotherapy. Through all 132 patients underwent the same type of treatment, they were at different phases of treatment. Group 1 (Phase I) patients were those patients who had just begun radiation treatment (first week of radiation therapy). Group 2 (phase) patients were those who were towards the end of the treatment programme (last week of radiation therapy). Group 3 (phase 3) patients were those who came for their first routine check-up after the required treatment was over. The number of subjects in Groups 1, 2 and 3 were 50, 40, and 42 respectively. The demographic profile of these three groups of patients is presented in Table 15.1.

Table 15. 1 : Demographic Background of the Cervical Cancer Patients

Demographic Background	Groups 1 (n=50)	2 (n=40)	3 (n=42)	*Total sample (N=132)*	*F (2, 129)*
Age (in years)					
M	47.20	45.10	46.95	46.50	1.07
SD	7.45	7.85	6.76	7.37	
Number of Children					
M	3.90	3.70	4.40	4.00	1.32
SD	2.01	2.21	1.98	2.07	
Income*					
M	1.70	1.95	2.50	2.00	5.34**
SD	0.99	1.01	1.50	1.22	
Duration of Illness (in weeks)					
M	29.64	47.38	54.60	42.95	13.28**
SD	20.14	31.55	19.64	26.19	
Level of Education (Frequencies)					χ^2(df=2)
Illiterate	48	31	31	110	5.27
Literate	2	9	11	22	2.03
Residential Background (Frequencies)					
Rural	41	22	30	93	5.87
Urban	9	18	12	39	3.23

Note :

* Income 1=less than 500, 2=less than 1000, 3=less than 1500, 4=less than 2000, 5=less than 2500 and above.

** p<. 01

Design

Two types of design : cross-sectional and longitudinal were employed. The cross-sectional design comprised of three groups of patients at three distinct phases of treatment (initial phase of treatment (n = 50), intermediate phase of treatment (n = 40) and final phase of treatment (n=42). The longitudinal design (n=30) comprised of these patients of Group 1 of the cross-sectional design who reported for treatment at each subsequent phase.

Interview Schedule

An interview schedule in Hindi was prepared and it included items from two domains: (a) information about the history of illness and treatment and perception of severity of illness, and (b) measure of psychological recovery. The measure of psychological recovery was developed by Dalal, Kohli and Agarwal (1995). The indices of psychological recovery were related to the patients perceived recovery (8 items) and mood states (21 items). The indices were rated on a 5-point scale. The Cronbach alpha (α) for perceived recovery and mood states were .74 and .80 respectively. The Cronbach alpha (α) for the total psychological recovery scale was .90. Examples of items for perceived recovery scale and mood states scale respectively were (a) how worried are you that may fall ill again, and (b) you feel like crying.

Procedure

With the permission of the Head of the Oncology Department, each patient was approached individually. In a face-to-face interview lasting about 20 minutes, each patient was asked questions in a pre-assigned order. The responses were recorded verbatim. As majority of respondents were illiterate care was taken to ensure that they understood the rating scales.

Results

Information about the Illness

The findings showed that patients were aware that they were

suffering from cancer. Only two patients out of a total of 132 patients failed to name their illness. For them, their illness was associated with unusual watery discharge and blood. It was a general description of the symptoms of cervical cancer.

When asked, what happens in this illness, all the patients responded by listing the symptoms, which they had experienced or were experiencing at that particular moment. Out of total of 132 patients about 10 patients were apprehensive, nervous and hesitant at the mention of their illness.

As regards perceived severity of being ill, results of one-way analysis of variance (ANOVA) showed that patients across the three groups differed with respect to their perception of severity of being ill, $F(2, 129) = 22.02$, $p< .001$. Nearly all the patients (130 out of a total of 132 patients) reported relief as a consequence of radiotherapy.

With regard to the measure of psychological recovery, separate analysis were done for the cross-sectional and longitudinal groups. For the cross-sectional groups, one-way analysis of variance (ANOVAs) were computed for different measures of psychological recovery. The results are displayed in Table 15.2.

Table 15.2 : One-way ANOVAs and Mean Comparisons for Measures of Psychological Recovery

Measures	*Group 1*	*Group 2*	*Group 3*	*F-Ratio*
Perceived Recovery (Measure 1)	24.00a	26.68b	27.68b	4.24*
Reactions of Crises (Measure 2)	66.52	71.05	69.55	0.92
Psychological Recovery (Measure 1+2)	90.52	97.73	97.21	1.68

Note : Means with common subscripts do not differ significantly.
*P< .05

One way ANOVA result showed that patients across the three groups differed with respect to their perception of recovery, $F(2, 129) = 4.24$, $p< .05$. Mean comparison using Newman Keul's method revealed that patients in Group 1 differed significantly from patients in Group 2 and 3. No significant difference was found between patients in groups 2 and 3. Group difference (F values) were not significant for Measure 2 (reaction to crisis) and overall psychological recovery.

For the Longitudinal Group, the measure of Psychological Recovery was administered to patients at three time points (three phases of treatment). It was expected that patients would differ in their level of psychological recovery at three phases of treatment. Three one-way repeated measure analysis of variance (ANOVAs) were computed for different measures of psychological recovery. Results showed that patients differed across three phases of treatment, for perception of recovery, $F (2, 58) = 12.18, p< .01$; reactions to crisis, $F (2, 58) = 6.57, p<.01$ and overall psychological recovery, $F(2, 58) = 8.01, p< .01$.

A comparison of the cross-sectional and the longitudinal group on perceived recovery and reaction to crisis at three phases of treatment is presented in Figure 15.1.

Figure 15.1. shows the means of perceived recovery and the means of reactions to crisis for the cross-sectional and the longitudinal design patients at the three therapeutic phases. As is evident from the Figure, Group 3 patients of the cross-sectional design showed higher perceived recovery (M=27.7) than Group 1 patients (M=24.0) and Group 2 patients (M=26.7). A similar finding was observed in the longitudinal group. Patients showed higher perceived recovery (M = 29.5) when they were at phase 3 of treatment, than when they were at phase 1 (M=24.6) and phase 2 (M=27.3) of treatment.

With regard to reaction to crisis, findings from the cross-sectional and the longitudinal design were not similar. In the cross-sectional design, patients of Group 2 reacted to the crises in a better way (M=71.0) as compared to group 1 (M=66.5), and Group 3 (M=69.5) patients. In the longitudinal design, patients reacted to the crisis in a better way (M=78.2) when they were at phase 3 of treatment, rather than when they were at phase 1 (M=70.9) and phase 2 (M=69.3) of treatment.

To see the significance of these differences, mean comparisons

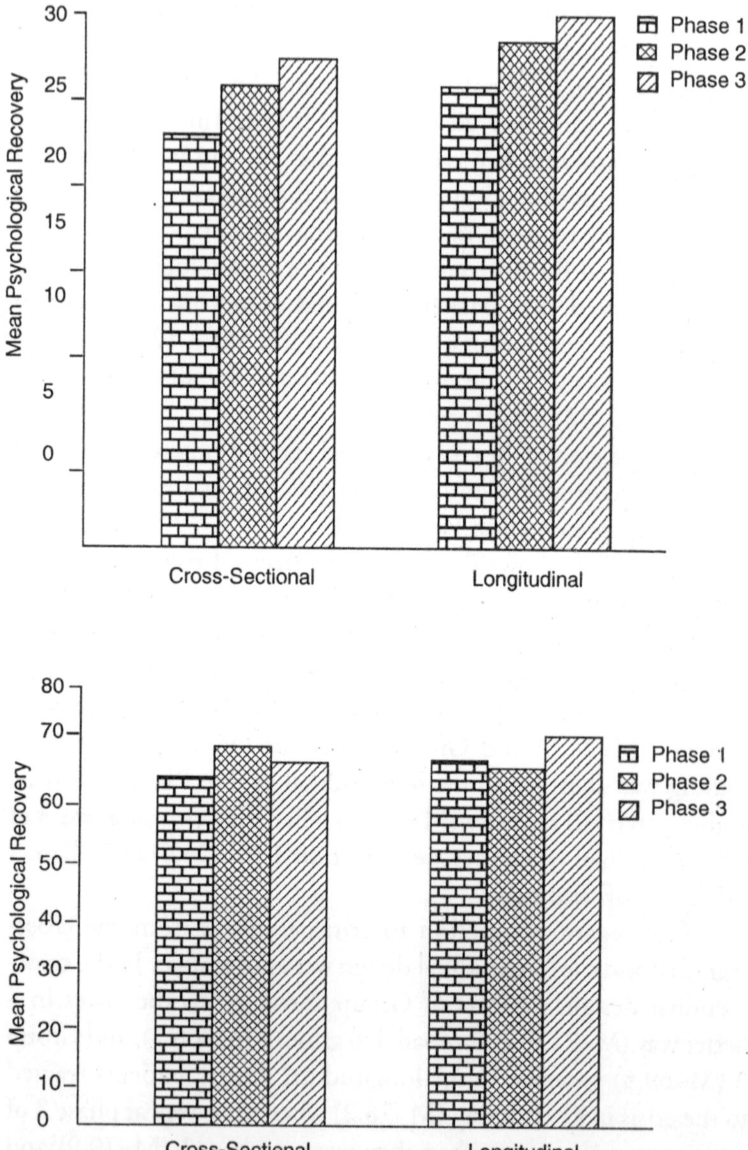

Fig. 15.1 : Showing the means of psychological recovery and reactions to crisis for the cross-sectional and the longitudinal group at three phases of treatment.

were performed with respect to perceived recovery and reaction to crises for the longitudinal group. Mean comparisons with respect to perceived recovery for the cross-sectional group are reported earlier. With regard to reaction to crisis no mean comparisons were performed for the cross-sectional group because the '*F*' value was not significant.

Mean comparisons using Newman Keuls' method for the longitudinal group showed that with regard to perceived recovery, patients reported less recovery at the initial phase of treatment, then at the intermediate and the final phases of treatment. Similarly, at the intermediate phase of treatment, patients reported more recovery than at the initial phase of treatment and less recovery than at the final phase of treatment. In comparison to phase 1 and phase 2 of treatment, patients reported greater recovery when they entered the final phase of treatment.

With regard to reaction to crises, mean comparison revealed that the way in which patients reacted to crisis was different when patients were at the final phase of treatment, than at the initial and intermediate phases of treatment. As compared to the initial and

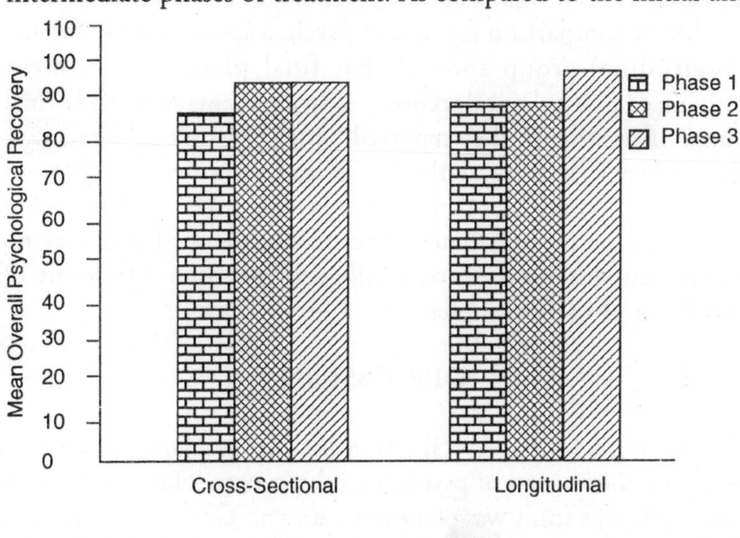

Fig. 15.2 : Showing the means of overall psychological recovery for the cross-sectional and the longitudinal group at three phases of treatment.

intermediate phases of treatment, patients reacted to crises in a better way, when they were at the final phase of treatment. The way in which patients reacted to crises was not influenced by the initial and intermediate phases of treatment.

A comparison of the cross-sectional and the longitudinal design patients on overall psychological recovery at the three phases of treatment is presented in Fig. 15.2.

Figure 15.2 presents the means of overall psychological recovery for both the cross-sectional and the longitudinal design patients at the three therapeutic phases. As is evident from the figure, Group 2 patients of the cross-sectional design showed higher (M=97.7) psychological recovery than Group-1 (M-90.5) and Group 3 (M=97.2) patients. The longitudinal design patients showed higher (M=107.7) psychological recovery when they were at phase 3 of treatment than when they were at phase 2 (M=96.6) and phase 1 (M=95.5) of treatment.

To see the significance of these differences, mean comparisons were computed. The mean comparisons were carried out only for the longitudinal group, because in the cross-sectional group, the '*F*' value was not significant for psychological recovery.

Mean comparison for overall psychological recovery for the longitudinal group showed that final phase of treatment influenced psychological recovery. When patients were at the final phase of treatment, they reported better psychological recovery than when they were at the initial and intermediate phase of treatment. Psychological recovery was not influenced by either the initial or intermediate phase of treatment. There was no significant difference in psychological recovery as a result of treatment of these two phases.

DISCUSSION

The interviews with cervical cancer patients primarily focused on mapping the process of psychological recovery. The classification variable in this study was phase of treatment. Groups were defined on the basis of their phase of treatment. Two research designs were employed. In one design (cross-sectional) three groups of patients at three distinct therapeutic phases were studied, and in another design (longitudinal) the same group of patients were studied at three time-points (three distinct therapists phases).

Nature of Psychological Recovery

Findings of one-way analysis of variance (ANOVAs) revealed that patients in the three groups did not differ significantly with respect to overall psychological recovery. It was expected that when the progress is treatment extended over a period of time, psychological recovery would be enhanced. But results presented a different picture. Further analysis, comparing two groups at a time, may have revealed differences between groups. However, one measure of psychological recovery (i.e., received recovery) showed significant differences across groups. Patients in Group 2 and 3 evidenced better-perceived recovery when the progress in treatment extended over time than patients in Group 1. Patients in Group 2 and 3 were relatively less distressed than patients in Group 1. Patients in Group 1 were at the initial phase of treatment and with a lot of symptoms, hence were more distressed. With the initiation of treatment (radiotherapy) there was symptomatic relief consequently, psychological recovery was enhanced.

The longitudinal analysis showed decrement in stress experienced and as a consequence better psychological recovery. Phase of treatment significantly influenced psychological recovery.

Findings revealed that patients perceived recovery was less at the initial phase and more at the final phase. At the intermediate phase, patient's perceived recovery was more than in phase 1 and less than in phase 3. With the progress in treatment, extended over a period of time patient's perceived recovery was enhanced.

With regard to reaction to crises, patient's response at phase 3 of treatment was different from phase 1 and 2. At the final phase of treatment, patient reacted to the crises in a better way. There was no significant difference in the way in which patients reacted to crises at phase 1 and 2 of treatment. The same trend was present for overall psychological recovery. Patients showed better psychological recovery at the final phase of treatment, than at the initial and intermediate phase of treatment. Though, there was no significant difference at phase 1 and 2, but the fact that the patient's level of psychological recovery was less at these phases than their psychological recovery at the final Phase of treatment, lends support to the fact that psychological recovery was accomplished, with the progress in treatment and mitigation in cancer associated problems.

This progress in psychological recovery over a period of time also enhances our faith in the common saying 'time is the best healer'. Explaining such a phenomenon, Bandura (1977) in his theory of self-efficacy stated that people devise their own coping strategies, which are likely to be successful. Over time, people acquire generalized cognitive skills for dealing successfully with stressful situations, thus restoring a sense of self-efficacy.

Arguing along similar lines, Rosenbaum and Ben-Ari (1985) suggest that a self-regulatory process is activated when the smooth flow of an ongoing behaviour is disrupted. In crises, a person strives to acquire a repertoire of behaviours and skills by which he or she self regulates internal responses (such as emotion, cognition, or feeling of pain). This phenomenon was termed as learned resourcefulness.

REFERENCES

Bandura, A. (1977). *Social learning theory.* Engelwood Cliffs, N.J.: Prentice-Hall.

Bowlby, J. (1980). Loss : *Sadness and depression* (Attachment and Loss; Vol. 3), New York: Basic Books.

Derogatis, L.R.; Abeloff, M.D.; & Melisaratos, N. (1979). Psychological coping mechanisms and survival time in metastatic breast cancer. *Journal of the American Medical Association,* 242, 1504-1508.

Glick, I.O.; Weiss, R.S.; & Parkes, C.M. (1974). *The first year of bereavement.* New York: Wiley.

Goldfarb, C.; Driesen, J.; & Cole, D. (1967). Psycho-physiological aspects of malignancy. *American Journal of Psychiatry,* 123, 154-1552.

Goldsmith, H. (1955). *A contribution of certain personality characteristics* of *male paraplegics to the degree of improvement in rehabilitation.* Unpublished doctoral dissertation, New York University.

Haan, N. (1977). *Coping and defending : Processes of self environment organization.* New York : Academic Press.

Hamberg, D.A. & Adams, J.E., (1967). A perspective on coping behaviour. Seeking and utilizing information in major transitions. *Archives of General Psychology,* 17, 277-284.

Indian Council of Medical Research (2000). *National Cancer Registry Programme: Biennial Report,* New York: Indian Council of Medical Research Publications.

Kaltreider, N.B.; Wallare, A.; & Horowitz, M.J. (1979). A field study of the stress response syndrome: Young women after hysterectomy. *Journal of the American Medical Association,* 242, 1499-1503.

Klinger, E. (1975) Consequences of commitment to and disengagement from incentive. *Psychological Review,* 82, 1-25.

Klinger, E. (1977). *Meaning and void: Inner experience and the incentives in peoples lives.* Minneapolis: University of Minnesota Press.

Kubler-Ross, E. (1969). *On death and dying.* New York : Macmillan.

Maguire, G.P.; Lee, E.G.; Bevingtón, D.J.; Kuchemam, C.S.; Crabtee, R.J.; & Cornell, C.E.; (1978). Psychiatric problems in the first year after mastectomy. *British Medical Journal,* 1, 963-965.

Morris, T.; Greer, H.S.; & White, P. (1977). Psychological and social adjustment to mastectomy: A two -year follow-up study. *Cancer,* 40, 2381-2387.

Parkes, C.M. (1975). Unexpected and Untimely bereavement. A statistical study of young Boston Widows and widowers. In B. Schoenberg, Gerber, A. Wiener, A.H. Kutscher, D. Peretz & A.C. Carr (eds.) *Bereavement: Its psychological aspects.* New York : Columbia University Press.

Rosenbaum, M., & Ben-Ari, K. (1985). Learned helplessness and trained resourcefulness: Effects of non-contingent success and failure on individuals differing in self-control skills. J*ournal of Personality and Social Psychology,* 148, 198-215.

Vachan, M.L.S., (1979, September). *The importance of social support in the longitudinal adaptation to bereavement and breast cancer.* Paper presented at the meeting of the American Psychological Association, New York.

15 Adjustive Demands of Physically Disabled Adolescent Girls and their Coping Style

A Qualitative Analysis

N. Tripathi

It is obvious that the disabled girl is trapped in a vicious circle — her low self-esteem, cultivated from birth by her immediate family or care-givers and reinforced by her wider community and the media, results in her having very low aspirations. She, therefore, makes few demands, or none at all, of those around her and of society for her rights and opportunities to break out of this vicious circle. There is a critical need for the creation of an enabling psychological and physical environment that is supportive of the ability of the woman with a disability to function, within the limits caused by the disability itself, as an equal member of society.

Disabled girls and women are at high risk of being regularly abused physically and mentally, most commonly by those around them — family members and caregivers — at home or in institutions for disabled persons. The disabled girl is not considered "marriageable" because her disability is seen as a "defect" and there is fear that her disability could be passed on to her children. There is doubt, too, whether she would be able to fully look after the home and family. Universally, the incidence of marriage for disabled women is lower than that for disabled men. Family shame, limited mobility or lacks of ability to communicate all serve to discourage a disabled woman from making contact with others outside the immediate family. Loneliness compounds the resulting sense of isolation and helplessness.

Around the world, women make up just over 51per cent of the population. Education is the key to the advancement of women and girls with disabilities; it provides access to information, enables them to communicate their needs, interests and experiences, brings them into contact with other students, increases their confidence and encourages them to assert their rights. Without a basic education, their chances for employment are almost nil.

Despite their significant numbers, women and girls with disabilities, especially in the developing countries of the ESCAP region, remain hidden and silent, their concerns unknown and their rights overlooked. Among women, the woman with a disability is seen as inferior, and even among other people with disabilities she is not their equal. In fact, women with disabilities are forced into being among the most isolated and marginalized. Disabled women face discrimination from birth. It is not unknown for children born with congenital disabilities to be killed or left to die. This is far more likely to happen in the case of a girl-child. If allowed to survive, the girl-child is likely to continue to face discrimination within the family, receive less care and food, and be left out of family interactions and activities. She will have less access to health care and rehabilitation services, fewer educations and employment opportunities, and little hope of marriage. She will also be more vulnerable to physical and mental abuse.

Psychologists have paid attention to the different aspects of the problems faced by physically handicapped persons. Cruickshank *et al.* (1951) and Hopkins (1973) have studied the self-perception of disabled persons. They found that handicapped children attribute their disability to themselves. Physical appearance serves as a critical variable in the process of personality development for the physically handicapped children. Dreikurs (1948) reported that nearly half of a sample of 40 severely crippled children deliberately used their abilities to appear inferior and more helpless than they really are. All of them showed poor self-concept. Their self-image was distorted and they blamed themselves. They experienced more fears and feelings of guilt than able-bodied children. All these showed their poor self-concepts. Shakespeare (1975) surveyed those studies of handicapped people in which better-adjusted and poorly adjusted people were compared. He found that better adjusted people have positive self-concept, more self-esteem and more readily see themselves as making a worthwhile contribution to society. His findings also showed that better adjusted people are less anxious and have less need of social approval.

Everything we do is shaped and defined by our unique life style; it determines which aspects of our total environment we will attend to or ignore and what attitudes we will hold. To understand how the style of life develops we must return to the concept of inferiority feelings and compensation, for they form the basis of our life style. The life style so formed becomes the guiding framework for later behaviour. The nature of life-style will depend on the nature of the relationship between parent and child as the child works to find a way to compensate for his or her sense of inferiority. For example, a girl who has been neglected may feel inferior in coping with the demands of life (negative self). Adler (1927) expressed that the individual creates the 'self'. Adler (1927) wrote that the person "does not relate himself to the outside world in a predetermined manner. He relates himself always according to his own interpretation of himself." This is the basis for the construction of attitude of the disabled person towards life.

Adjustive Demands (Stress)

Adjustive demands may be classified as frustrations, conflicts and pressure. Frustration is an important component of psychological stress. It occurs when one's strivings are thwarted, either by obstacles that block progress toward a desired goal or by absence of an appropriate goal. Physical handicap is also one source of frustration. It creates psychological barriers in the form of ethical or moral restraints. In the face of frustration, a person often tries to take direct action in an effort to solve the problem and remove the obstacle.

In conflict situations, the individual can attack the problem by analyzing the advantages and disadvantages of various options and making an objective, informed decision. Usually the individual resists undue pressure, especially when the pressure is seen as arbitrary and unwarranted. Resistance to pressure is an attempt by the organism to maintain its own integrity and to be in control of its own actions. Conflict with which everyone has to cope may be classified as approach-avoidance, double-approach and double-avoidance types. Stress may stem not only from frustration and conflicts, but also from pressure to achieve particular goals or to behave in particular ways.

The word 'stress' is sometimes used to describe a threatening situation or stimulus, and at other times to describe a response to a situation. Stress is thus most completely defined as a process by which a person both perceives and responds to events that are judged to be challenging or threatening. The most influential model describing stress as a process is the transactional model (also called the relational model), proposed by Richard Lazarus and his colleagues (Lazarus, 1993). The fundamental idea behind this model is that we cannot fully understand stress by examining environmental events (stimuli) and people (response) as separate entities; rather, we need to consider them together as a transaction, in which each person must continually adjust to daily challenges. When the demands of an event or situation do create stress, our response is not static but, rather, involves continuous interactions and adjustments, between the environment and our attempts to cope. Each of us is an active agent who can dramatically alter the impact of our potential stressor through our own personal resources.

The severity of stress is gauged by the degree of disruption in the human system that will occur if the individual fails to cope with the adjustive demands. Several objective factors influence stress severity. These are relatively independent of the individual involved or the situational context in which the demands occur. In terms of importance, it has been shown that certain stresses— such as the death of loved one, divorce, and serious personal illness or injury—

tend to be highly stressful for most people (Holmes & Rahe, 1967; Cochrane & Robertson, 1973). Often new adjustive demands that have not been anticipated and for which no readymade coping patterns are available will place an individual under severe stress. One factor that is often crucial in determining the severity of stress is the individual's own evaluation of the stress situation. Stress situation that are perceived as potentially damaging or threatening to survival— such as having a limb amputated carry a high degree of threat. The severity of given stress depends, too, on resources for withstanding stress in general and that stress in particular. If a person is marginally adjusted, the slightest frustration or pressure may be highly stressful. The term stress tolerance or frustration tolerance refers to one's ability to withstand stress without having integrated functioning seriously impaired.

Any stress reaction of course reflects the interplay of a combination of inner and outer determinants— some more influential than others, but all working together to make the individual react as he does. On a psychological and interpersonal level there are learned coping patterns and self-defenses. The failure of coping efforts on any of these levels may seriously impair an individual's adjustment. In coping with stress, a person is confronted with two problems: (a) to meet the requirements of the adjustive demand, and (b) to protect the self from psychological damage and disorganization. When the person feels competent to handle a stress situation, his behaviour tends to be task-oriented, that is, aimed primarily at dealing with the requirements of the adjustive demands. But when his feelings of adequacy are seriously threatened by the adjustive demand, his reactions tend to be defense-oriented-aimed primarily at protecting the self from hurt and disorganization.

Coping Style

Coping refers to the cognitive, behavioural, and emotional ways that people manage stressful situations (Moss-Morris & Petrie,

1997). Coping strategies—the ways people deal with stressful situations—are intended to moderate, or buffer, the effects of stressor on physical and emotional well-being (Ingledew, Hardy, & Cooper, 1997). Coping is the process of managing demands (external or internal) that are appraised as taxing or exceeding the coping resources of the person (Lazarus & Folkman, 1984). Coping consists of efforts, both action-oriented and intrapsychic, to manage (that is, to master, tolerate, reduce, minimize) environmental and internal demands and conflicts among them (Cohen 1987; Cohen & Lazarus, 1979; Lazarus & Launier, 1978). Coping processes can generally be divided into problem focused or emotion focused copings. Problem focused coping strategies involve changes in the situation to reduce aversive impact whereas emotion focused coping strategies alter individual's responses. In other words, problem focused coping efforts are attempts to do something constructive about the stressful condition. Emotion focused coping involves efforts to regulate the emotional consequences of the stressful events.

The way in which the person copes with stressful events and whether or not his/her coping efforts are successful in reducing stress are important for his/her health and well-being. The fact that individuals vary in the degree of stress experienced from the same stressful events and same individual may experiences different degree of stress from the same stressful events in the different situation has made the stress research more complex. This variability in the stress experience is due to many factors and moderates the impacts of stressors. It requires a lot of efforts to cope with stressors, especially uncontrollable ones. At each life stage, society within which one lives makes certain psychological demands upon individuals. Researchers have reported that adults experience greatest number of life changes and strains in early adulthood years (McLanahan & Sorensen, 1985; Pearlin 1980), and life strain decreases from early adulthood to middle adulthood perhaps because of adults settling into more stable lifestyle.

Task-oriented reactions may involve making changes in one's self or one's surroundings or both, depending on the situation.

Task-oriented reaction of all three types— attack, withdrawal and compromise— involve the same basic steps. These defense reactions protect the individual from both external threats, such as devaluating failures, and internal threats, such as guilt-arousing desires or actions. They appear to protect the self in one or more of the following ways: (a) by denying, distorting, or restricting the individual's experience; (b) by reducing emotional or self-involvement; and (c) by counteracting threat or damage. The action may involve attacking the problem directly; withdrawing from it or trying to find a workable compromise. In addition to withdrawing from danger physically, the individual may withdraw in various psychological ways, for examples, avoiding certain types of adjustive demands, or reducing emotional involvement in a situation and becoming apathetic. In these ways the individual can exercise considerable control over the nature and degree of stress to which he is exposed and thus keep pressures and other stresses from becoming excessive. Withdrawal serves to remove the organism from dangerous situations it cannot overcome, which can lead to panic and other maladaptive behaviour. A related form of compromise is the acceptance of substitute goals under conditions of severe frustration. When compromise reactions succeed, in meeting the essential requirements of the stress situation, the problem is resolved and the person can go on to other activities.

Each of us uses such defence mechanisms to some extent— singly and in various combination— for coping with the problems of living. For these reasons, ego-defence mechanisms are considered maladaptive when they become the predominant means of coping with stress.

These defence mechanisms are ordinarily used in combination, rather than singly, and often they are combined with task-oriented bahaviour. Because they are essential for softening failure, alleviating anxiety and hurt, and protecting one's feelings of adequacy and worth, we may consider them to be normal adjustive reactions unless they seriously interfere with the effective resolution of stress situations.

Indian Cultural View of Suffering and Coping

Cultural beliefs play an important role in shaping coping responses to tragic events in one's life. In each society there are beliefs about illness/disability, choices of treatment alternatives, sick roles and practitioner roles and health care-related institutions organized as a cultural system; the health care system. The way an individual experience and understand his or her cultural background largely determines his or her own condition.

The Indian scenario is different in many ways. In traditional Indian society a metaphysical belief, that is belief in *Karma*, God and spirit are presumed to be important determinants of many events in one's life, including illness and suffering. In the Indian setting, cosmic beliefs are presumed to be important determinants of all happenings in life, including illness and suffering. All the traditional system of Indian origin shares the concept of *Karma*. The theory of *Karma* is the cornerstone of Hindu religion and philosophy (Gokhale, 1961; Radhakrishnan, 1926). The doctrine of *Karma* is not fatalistic. The self-determination by an individual is evident, as the causes of the actions of the individual are thought to be due to the earlier actions of the very same individuals. The law of *Karma* is not a blind, mechanical law, but it is essentially ethical as it is justice, which is meted out. It is this conviction that there is in reality no injustice that explains the absence of any feelings of bitterness. Thus in the wake of pain and sorrow, when any misfortune occurs they blame neither God nor their neighbour, but only themselves. They hold their *Karmaphala* as being responsible for their condition. The *Karma* doctrine is concerned with inner control and there is no imposition of any constraint from outside. In India there is a greater degree of acceptance and rationalization. Studies on Indian patients (Dalal & Pande, 1988; Dalal & Singh, 1992) have shown that anger is less prevalent. This is due to cultural influences, where people accept and rationalize in terms of the theory of the *Karma*. Faith in *Karma* enables people to look for justification in something wrong they might have done in their previous birth, and thus helps them to accept.

Method

Sample

The sample consisted of 54 disabled girls. The age group of disabled girls was between 14 and 19 years of age. Their mean age was 16.5 years of age. Most of the disabled girls (62.96%) were from 11th to 12th standard and 37.04% disabled girls were from 8th to 10th standard.

Interview Schedule for Open-Ended Items

The interview schedule was conducted to tap the problems faced by the physically disabled adolescent girls and their own adjustments with these problems. Their stresses due to their disability and their coping style were also taken into consideration because all these play a significant contribution in the adjustment process and well-being of the disabled girls.

Demographic Information

This section of the questionnaire focused on eliciting the following demographic information:

Age

The age of the respondents were recorded in years and by rounding months. For example, if she reported that she was 16 years and 6 months old, then she was recorded as 17 years of age and if she reported that she was 16 years and 5 months old then she was recorded as being 16 years of age.

Socio-economic Status

For recording the socio-economic status as perceived by the respondent, four categories were given in the questionnaire: Higher SES, High middle SES, Low middle SES, Lower SES coded as 1, 2, 3, 4 respectively.

Education

The education of the disabled girls and their mothers were noted down. On the basis of the obtained educational information, a coding scheme was developed. Thus class VIII to X = 1, class XI to XII = 2, Graduate = 3, Post-Graduate = 4.

Family Structure

Family structure was recorded as joint or extended family =1 and nuclear family = 2.

Nature and Causes of Disability

Questions in this section were related to the identification of the disability, duration of the disability in years, causes and types of the disability. The respondents were also asked to rate their perception of the severity of the disability.

Adjustive Demands

Answers were also obtained on five open-ended questions (unstructured), dealt with the daily routine activities of the disabled girls, problems faced by them due to disability, activities which they can do well, and activities which they find difficult, their perception of disability as how they are different from the normal girls (their self-perception).

Coping Style

In this section items were related to coping style adopted by these physically disabled girls like coping strategies faced by disabled girls, worries and problems of the disabled girls, resolving worries and problems, and perception of future possibilities.

Procedure

On the basis of the pilot study, the main interview schedule was finalized for the study. Then these disabled girls were contacted through their class-teachers. On the basis of prior appointments, these disabled girls were contacted in their colleges. The interview took place in the college classroom. Before starting the interview, a good rapport was established with the disabled girls. Then they were told the objective of studies which was to understand the difficulties which disabled girls face.

The questionnaire was in Hindi. The conversation also took place in Hindi. All the respondents were individually interviewed. The interviewer writes the responses.

Results

Results were analyzed qualitatively and quantitatively both. The findings of the results indicated that the main cause of disability was Polio (89%) and accident (11%). Most of the disabled girls 65% were disabled by birth, 26.67% were disabled through diseases such as Polio (developed later on), and 8.33% were disabled from accidents. That is why most of the disabled girls reported that they were able to perform all types of work needed in the family wherein they did not need help of their mothers or others. As most of the disabled girls (87%) could do only those activities more efficiently in which they do not need the help of their lower limbs because most of these girls were having polio and their lower part was affected from the disease. Only 13% disabled girls reported that they could not do anything because their upper part was also affected from polio. It seems that most of the disabled girls had maximum difficulties in those activities, which required the use of lower limbs or affected part of the body.

The results further shows that most of the disabled girls were able to perform all types of work needed in the family wherein they did not need the help of their mothers but when the disabled girls were asked as to which daily routine activities they could do well, most of the disabled girls reported that they could do sewing, knitting, embroidery (40.7%), cooking (29.6%), their own personal activities (11.1%), studies (3.7%) and household activities (1.9%) efficiently. Few girls also revealed that they could not do anything (13%). Then again these disabled girls were asked about their difficulties due to their disabilities, it was found that most of the disabled girls (87%) reported that they had maximum difficulties in those functions which required the use of lower limbs for example wiping floor (61.1%), lifting heavy things such as water bucket and furniture (25.9%). 11.1% disabled girls revealed difficulties in their studies also because they could not sit for a long time to read and write.

Fig. 16.1: Perception of Severity of Disability

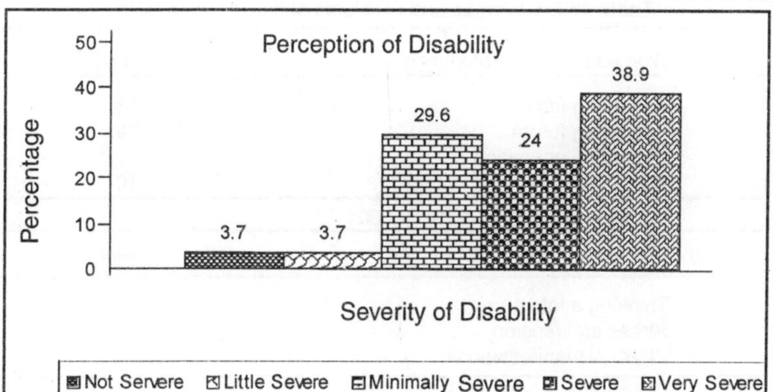

Fig. 16.1 shows that most of the disabled girls perceived their disability as being very severe (38.9%), followed by severe (24%), minimally severe (29.6%) and little severe (3.7%). Only 3.7% disabled girls reported that their problem was not severe.

Table 16.1 : Coping Strategies used by Disabled Girls in Facing Disability

Category	*Frequency*
Assistance from family	21
It was God's Will	7
With pain and sorrow	3
Deeds of past life	13
Accepted the disability that they are disabled now	2
With the help of medical treatment	8

Chi-square = 27.78, df =5, P< .001

Table 16.1 suggests that most of the disabled girls (38.9%) had faced their disability with the help and support of their family members. 24.1% disabled girls had accepted their disability as their deeds of past life, 14.8% disabled girls faced their disability with the help of medical treatment, 13% disabled girls accepted their disability as God's will, 5.6% disabled girls faced their disability with a lot of pain and sorrow and only 3.7% disabled girls faced their disability with accepting it that they were disabled now, they had to bear it throughout.

Table 16.2 : Worries and Problems of the Disabled Girls

(a)	*Worries of the disabled girls*	*Frequency*
	Regarding job	13
	Regarding future	29
	Regarding education	2
	No problem	10
	Chi-square = 28.52, df=3, P< .001	
(b)	*Problems of the disabled girls*	*Frequency*
	Thinking a lot	14
	Stress and tension	26
	Physical manifestations	14
	Chi-square = 5.33, df=2, P< .06	

Table 16.2 suggests that most of the disabled girls were worried about their future (53.7%), job (24.1%) and education (3.7%), only 18.5% were not worried. When asked further about their problems, 48.2% disabled girls reported stress and tension, 25.9% reported thinking problem and 25.9% have physical manifestation such as headache, anxiety, sleeplessness, and fatigue.

Table 16.3 : Resolving Worries and Problems by Disabled Girls

Category	*Frequency*
Taking help from parents	12
Taking help from family members	17
Individually	17
Taking help from mothers	8

Chi-square=4.22, df=3, P< .24

The findings, reported in Table 16.3 suggest that most of the disabled girls reported that they took the help of their family members (31.5%) followed by parents (22.2%) and mothers (14.8%) to solve their worries and problems. Only 31.5% disabled girls reported that they did not need any help, they tried to solve their problems themselves.

Table 16.4 : Perception of Future Possibilities

Category	*Frequency*
Wanted to do job	31
To get married	2
To be educated	8
God's will	6
No future plans	7

Chi-square =49.15, df=4, P< .001

Further, Table 16.4 suggests that most of the disabled girls (57.4%) reported that they want to do job (become independent). 14.8% disabled girls wished to be educated, and 3.7% disabled girls wished to be married. Only 13% disabled girls had no future plan and 11.1% left it on God.

Table 16.5 : Self-Perception of Disabled Girls

Category	*Frequency*
Dependent on others due to physical incompetence	2
Physically weak	11
No difference between disabled and normal (non-disabled)	3
Lonely, unhappy, shy, sad and emotional	3
Inferior to others	29
No future	6

Chi-square =77.96, df =5, P< .001

Lastely, Table 16.5 suggests that most of the disabled girls (53.7%) expressed that they were inferior to others (non-disabled). 20.4% disabled girls reported that they were physically weak. 11.1% disabled girls also said that they have no future, 5.6% disabled girls expressed that there was no difference between disabled and normal and 5.6% disabled girls reported themselves as lonely, unhappy, shy, sad and emotional. Only 3.7% disabled girls said that disabled persons were dependent on others because of their physical incompetence.

Discussion

It has been found in the present research that the disabled girls needed help, they are dependent on mothers for doing many functional activities so they are primarily cared and helped by the mothers and other family members. The results show that the disabled girls were in adolescent stage (14-19 years) and were studying in 8 to 12 standards as regular students. It is important to note that these girls despite their disability attended schools with other non-disabled girls. This suggests that these disabled girls were in frequent interaction with those who were different from them. There were only few girls in the colleges sampled who were physically disabled hence they were visible, easily identifiable and in a minority.

The results further show that the disabled girls were able to perform all types of work needed in the family wherein they did not need the help of their mothers. It is clear that physical disability interferes in the autonomous functioning of the disabled girls; they have to be dependent on others. It appears that due to disability there are functional limitations and these disabled girls have to depend always on others for doing small functions. This suggests a corresponding increase in their adjustive demands. That's why most of the disabled girls perceived their disability as being very severe (Fig. 16.1), it indicates that the extent to which a person feels that his/her disability is severe, likely to impact on adjustments to disability and related outcomes (Sacks, Peterson & Kimbel, 1988).

To overcome their adjustive demands they used different coping strategies as family support, consequences of their deeds of past life and God's will. It seems that family support system is more important than any other system. In a study of 100 American disabled people, Miller (1986) found that family support was significantly related to adjustment to disability. Its acceptance ensures that the world is a cosmos and not chaos: events are lawfully governed and not left to happenstance (Paranjpe, 1998). Beliefs in the law of *Karma* is one of the important aspects of this study that disabled girls considered the deeds of their past life were such that they have to inevitably undergo its negative consequences. There was no option or choice to escape from the consequences. Owing to firm cultural belief in the law of *Karma* these girls viewed their conditions with resignation of acceptance of its inevitability. The reason why some girls said that disability was God's will, nothing could be done even God is only a spectator, cannot do anything. Some girls, however, attempted to cope in a more realistic manner by seeking different forms of advanced medical treatment. It seems that by depending on the family support system or on the deeds of the past life, hoping for medical treatment had induced a tolerance in them. It also seems that these girls were worried and anxious and reported problems such as stress and tension, keep on thinking about their disability which is also manifested in psychosomatic symptoms such as headache, anxiety, sleeplessness and fatigue, but were not overwhelmed or overly disturbed by their disability. These worries were related to once future livelihood and one can think about one self only when one is not disturbed and threatened. That is why most of these disabled girls perceived themselves negatively such as inferior from the non-disabled, physically weak, have no future; dependent on others due to physical incompetence, and they could not do any thing in their lives as they felt lonely, unhappy, shy, sad and emotional. Bose and Banerjee (1969) also found that physically handicapped suffered from inferiority, shyness and emotional imbalance. This finding shows the acceptance of unpleasant reality (disability). In Belgrave's (1991) study, adjustment to disability is conceptualized as acceptance of disability. Acceptance of disability is based on Dembo, Levinton and Wright's (1956) and Wright's (1960) theory of acceptance of loss.

This indicates that these disabled girls were very sad and pessimistic regarding their disability and trying to accept it. The theoretical literature of adjustive demand also suggests that acceptance of any reality (disability) would contribute to adjustment (Coleman, 1982). The findings further suggest that these disabled girls needed less demands for adjustment. Most of these girls wished to become independent because apart from economic independence, work is an essential means of enabling a person to develop a sense of identity and self-esteem. Thus gainful employment is an important means of personality, the social integration of disabled girls. It seems that these girls do not feel optimistic regarding their future. It suggests that disability induces disappointment with life and people, therefore they cannot really see hope in their future that is why they depend on God's will.

This picture speaks for itself and brings out the grim reality that lies ahead in building the future and in rearing the disabled girls. The entire work of girl child welfare demands an integrated and scientific view. We must consider these disabled girls in their complexity and recognize their physical-mental-social needs. This fascinating adventure of promoting welfare services is not only in the interest of the family of disabled girls but also in the interest of their own future. The problem needs a multi-disciplinary approach. All branches related to physically disabled persons should integrate their activities in meeting the specific problem of this group. The world of disabled girls is a challenge not only to psychologist but also to all the social scientists and the social workers interested in their rehabilitation. These provocative ideas and findings suggest that problems related to the disability of the physically disabled girls must be explored within a very broad context of social and personality variables. Such investigations will help us not only to understand their adjustive demands, attitudes, beliefs but also coping mechanisms used by these disabled girls to reduce their stress.

In sum, this section of the discussion, which is focused on disabled girls, indicates that these girls are dependent by nature and necessity; they must be given help to the extent that they can be independent and mentally healthy. Physical appearance serves as a critical variable in the process of personality development for the physically handicapped children. As age increases the perceived severity of disability also increases, so older disabled girls would require additional support. Education is also one of the positive factors, which enhance self-concept of the disabled girls, and if their self-concept would be positive the adjustive demands would show a decline.

Implications of the Present Study

1. The study has significance of 'Talking Cure' of these disabled girls. They had been given an opportunity to express their grief and problems. The dialogue between the interviewers and subjects served a cathartic and therapeutic function, which enabled them to release their tension. They discussed their problems and difficulties in detail. They felt that at least people are willing to spend

time and listen their problems. They felt that they were given importance and social approval.

2. The study has significance for parents, teachers, social workers, rehabilitation psychologists, counsellors and planners in dealing with the problems of the disabled girls. If one knows the adjustive demands, attitudes, beliefs and strain of disabled girls and their mothers in meeting environmental demands, one may be able to help them properly.
3. Results may be applicable to orthopedically disabled girls of different institutions.

REFERENCES

Adler, A. (1927). *Understanding Human Nature.* New York: Greenberg.

Belgrave, F.Z. (1991). Psychosocial Predictors of Adjustment of Disability in African Americans, *Journal of Rehabilitation, 57,* 37-40.

Bose, S. & Banerjee, S.N. (1969). A Resolution of the Personality Make up of some Institutionalised Physically Handicapped Children by the Children Apperception Test. *Journal of Psychological Researches 13*, 32-36.

Cochrane, R., Robertson, A. (1973). The Life-events Inventory: a measure of relative severity of Psycho-social stressors. *Journal of Psychosomatic Researches, 17* (2), 134-140.

Cohen, F. & Lazarus, R. (1979). Coping with the stresses of illness. In G.C. Stone, F. Cohen & N.E. Adler (eds.), *Health Psychology. A Handbook,* 217-254, San Francisco: Jossey-Bass.

Cohen, F. (1987). Measurement of coping. In S.V. Kasi and C.L. Cooper (eds.), *Stress and health issues in research methodology.* New York: Wiley.

Cruickshank, W.M. *et al.* (1951). The Relation of Physical Disability to Fear and Guilt Feelings. *Child Development, 20,* 291-298.

Dalal, A.K. & Pande, N. (1988). Psychological recovery of the accident victims with temporary and permanent disability. *International Journal of Psychology, 23,* 25-40.

Dalal, A.K., & Singh, A.K. (1992). Role of causal and recovery beliefs in the psychological adjustment to a chronic disease. *Psychology and Health, 6,* 193-203.

Dembo, T.; Levinton, G.L.; & Wright, B.A. (1956). Adjustment to misfortune— A problem in social psychological rehabilitation. *Artificial Limbs, 3,* 4-62.

Dreikurs, R. (1948). The Social-psychological dynamics of Physical Disability: A review of the Adlerian Concept. *Journal of Social Issues, 4*(4), 39-54.

ESCAP Report (1993). *Asian and Pacific decade of disabled persons, 1993-2002: The starting point.* New York: United Nations.

Gokhale, B.G. (1961). *Indian thoughts throughout the ages: A study of some dominant concepts.* Bombay: Asia Publishing House.

Holmes, T.H. & Rahe, R.H. (1967). The social readjustment rating scale. *Journal of Psychosomatic Research, 11,* 213-218.

Hopkins, M.T. (1973). Patterns of Self-destruction among the orthopedically disabled. *Psychological Abstract, 50,* 6, 11509.

Ingledew, D.K.; Hardy, L.; & Cooper, C.L. (1997). Do resources bolster coping and does coping buffer stress? An organizational study with longitudinal aspect and control for negative affectivity. *Journal of Occupational Health Psychology, 2,*118-133.

Lazarus, R.S. (1993). From psychological stress to the emotions: A history of changing outlooks. *Annual Review of Psychology, 44,* 1-21.

Lazarus, R.S. & Folkman, S. (1984). *Stress, appraisal, and coping.* New York Springer.

Lazarus, R.S., & Launier, R. (1978). Stress-related transactions between person and environment. In L.A. Pervin & M. Lewis (eds.), *Perspectives in Interactional Psychology.* New York: Plenum.

McLanahan, S.S., & Sorensen, A.B. (1985). Life events and psychological well-being over the life course. In G.H. Elder, Jr. (ed.), *Life course dynamics: Trajectories, and transitions, 1968-1980.* Ithaca, New York: Cornell University Press.

Miller, S. (1986). Patients' perceptions of their adjustment to disability and social support in a community based teaching hospital. In S.Walker, F.Z. Belgrave, A.M. Banner, & R.W. Nicholls (eds.) *Equal to the Challenge-Perspectives, Problems, and Strategies in the Rehabilitation of the Nonwhite Disabled,* 28-38, Washington, D.C.: Bureau of Educational Research, Howard University.

Moss-Morris, R., & Petrie, K.J. (1997). Cognitive distortions of somatic experiences: Revision and validation of a measure. *Journal of Psychosomatic Research, 43,* 293-306.

Paranjpe, A.C. (1998). *Self and Identity in Modern Psychology and Indian Thought,* Plenum Press, New York.

Pearlin, L.I. (1980). Life strains and psychological distress among adults. In N.J. Smelser and E.H. Erickson (eds.), *Thesis of work and love and adulthood.* Cambridge, A.M.: Harvard University Press.

Sacks, C.; Peterson, R.A.; & Kimbel, P. (1988, April). The relationship between perception of illness, role disruptions and kidney dialysis treatment. Paper presented at Society of Behavioural Medicine Conference.

Shakespeare. (1975). *The Psychology of Handicap*. London: Methuen and Company Limited.

Radhakrishnan, S. (1926). *The Hindu View of Life*. Bombay: Blackie.

Wright, B.A. (1960). *Physical Disability: A Psychosocial Approach*. New York: Harper and Row.

16 Preschoolers Perceptions on being a Boy and a Girl

Gargi Singh Chauhan *and* Jigisha Shastri

The complete process of gender and sex typing has received tremendous attention by various theorists and researchers in the field of developmental psychology and allied disciplines. Gender identity forms a very important part of the self–perception of children. The main concern is how do children learn regarding their placement in a gender group, the frame in which they view themselves, and whether there are behavioural consequences associated with their self-concept.

View of Theorists on Gender as a Concept

The approach of various theorists varies as some emphasize on the cognitive aspect and other on the social aspects. The Gender Schema Theory and Kohlberg's Cognitive Developmental theory attribute the construction of gender through a schema or a cognitive structure. This schema is affected indirectly by the environment in which the child is born and reared (Maccoby, 2000). Once this schema is formed it guides the way; information from the environment is selected and remembered. It also provides a model for action. A gender schema, then can be considered a mental model containing information about males and females. On the other hand social learning theory emphasizes influences of differing "learning environment" especially with reference to children. This theory explains the acquisition of gender identity in the same way as the acquisition of other behvaiours : through a combination of observation, imitation and different reinforcement (Golombok & Fiyush, 1994).

Overall the gender schema and the external social influences help a child form their perceptions about their own gender as a male or a female. Children's perceptions regarding their gender are not formed in isolation. The gender concept of the child develops through the gendered environment by the children themselves (Chauhan, 2002). Children actively develop the concept of gender within the gendered environment.

Children's Perceptions

There are various factors which help in the development of gender concept in children and also their perceptions regarding their own gender. Children's own gender perceptions develop as they come in contact with the gendered environment, and also their interaction, observation, imitation within this gendered environment (Chauhan, Shastri & Mohite, 2002). The gendered environment consists of people within family, outside family and others. These people thereby contribute in constructing children's perceptions regarding their own gender.

Overall the child who is born with a biological gender forms her/his perceptions about the social gender through various variables in the gendered environment. All these variables together brings to a child, knowledge about various gender stereotypes. The gender stereotypes emerge within the gendered environment. Gender stereotypes are defined as a set of beliefs about what it means to be a male or a female. Gender stereotypes include information about physical appearance, attitudes and interests, social relations and occupations (Deaux and Lewis, 1984). The gender stereotypes pervade many cultures. Children as young as 2½-3 years start developing understanding for gender stereotypes and this understanding reaches its peak at age 5 (Rubin & Martin, 1998; J.E. Williams & Bert, 1982; Haugh, Hoffman & Cowan,

1980). Children of this age also believe very strongly in the stereotypes. Stereotypes for young children can include judgements about sex appropriate activities (e.g. girls play with dolls), sex specific characteristics (e.g. fearful and helpless) (Ruble & Martin, 1998) and sex related future roles (e.g. nurses are women) (Killen *et al.*, 2001; Kuhn, Nash & Brucken, 1978).

In India researches reflect gender stereotypes involved in toy selection for preschoolers in order to nurture gender stereotypic behaviour and traits in children. Research by Bhogle S. (1999) revealed that toys are selected and presented on the basis of gender rather than the interest of children. The nomenclature used for toys requiring active physical involvement is masculine and the ones that rotate around nurturing and caring lines are termed as feminine. The boys hold the privilege of receiving masculine toys (e.g. guns, trucks) and females all the feminine toys (e.g. dolls, homemaker toys). Even the games that require physical motor, active vigorous and outdoor involvement like cricket, kabaddi are valued as masculine. While nurturant, household, passive and indoor activities are labelled as feminine, like cleaning the house, playing "baby-baby", flower arrangement, cooking etc. The involvement in cross gender toys does not receive enough acceptance from the parents, peers and siblings.

Children's gender understanding is also influenced by occupational gender typing. The occupational gender typing is woven around the gender roles. Gender roles are the behaviours, interests, attitudes, skills and personality traits that a culture considers appropriate for males and females. Bhogle S. and Seethalakshmi (1992) revealed that in Indian context occupations are considered appropriate for individuals based on their sex, rather than on their ability and the gender typing of occupations begins at a very early age, e.g. boys always want to become pilot, engineer, cricketer whereas girls dream to be a teacher, nurse, doctor. As learning of gender concept takes place in a context, in an Indian context children from early years are exposed to gender stereotypic interests and preferences and develop gender concepts accordingly. It would be, therefore, interesting to look into specific variables that influence gender concept development.

Family

Within family parents play a very important role. The parental treatment affects children's gender knowledge (Fagot & Leinbach, 1993). Parents model gender roles and stereotypic behaviour for their children. Along with this they also direct their children to engage in gender stereotypic activities. For example, boys are asked to get things from the market and girls are asked to either help in the kitchen, or laundry. Through such activities boys and girls learn to associate certain chores with a particular gender (Elizabeth, 2000) and also form perceptions regarding their own gender. Parental involvement in creating a gendered environment is also seen when gender stereotypic toys are provided to children as discussed earlier. Specifically in the Indian context mothers of preschoolers revealed in a study that (Chauhan, Shastri and Mohite, 2002) parents portray certain characteristics which develop children's gender perceptions. They look different by dressing gender stereotypically, e.g. women in *salwar-kameez/sari* and men in pants and shirts. They also perform different roles as for majority of the families men go out and earn and women are usually involved in household chores. Even if the women are working outside home along with the men when it comes to work distribution the women is held responsible for the household work and caretaking.

The parents deliberately bring this to children's notice, through comparisons with same sex models and promoting gender stereotypic behaviour, dressing and activities thus providing children gender typed experiences and thereby contributing towards the perceptions of gender in preschoolers. In Indian context along with parents, grandparents also promote gender stereotypic roles, behaviour, activities and dressing in preschoolers. Their approvals and restrictions regarding cross, gender typed clothing, behaviour and activities help children follow the gender pattern expected in the Indian society (Chauhan, 2002). Many parents do state that they want their children to play with gender appropriate toys and they believe that boys and girls should be raised differently.

Siblings influence preschoolers about gender related attributes and interests. Preschoolers with older, opposite sex siblings have more opportunities for imitation and participation in "cross gender" play (http://www.fens.niv.edu/miller/280/p.social.html 12th December, 2003). Children who have same sex sibling are more rigid in their gender role preference than children from other family constellations, as having same sex siblings provides information in the form of modelling or reinforcement about gender appropriate behaviours (Katz and Boswell, 1986; Stoneman, Brody & Mac Kannon, 1986). Siblings thus may provide wider ranging experiences that facilitate flexibility or they may inhibit flexibility by providing information about behaviours to follow and avoid. They may actively reinforce gender typical behaviour and thereby heighten the salience of gender in the family.

Other than the within family influence children have some outside family influences like peers and the school.

Peers

Peer influence plays a very important role in preschoolers gender perceptions (Turner & Gervai, 1995 cited from *Psycho Social Development in Early Childhood* by Marie S.B.). As the children grow so does the reinforcement of gender typed behaviour by the peers. By the age of 3 and 4 years children develop the understanding regarding peer, attitudes towards gender appropriate behaviour and they start applying the same judgements on themselves (Bussy & Bandura, 1992). Studies conducted on preschoolers in Western and Indian context revealed children's preference for boys and girls who were more stereotypic in behaviour and were of their own sex (Nair, 2004; Emanuel, 2003; Kshetrapal, 2003; Zucker, Wilson, Smith, Kurita & Sterm, 1995 cited from *Psycho Social Development in Early Childhood* by Marie S.B.).

Even in a study on British and Hungarian preschoolers, the play preferences of children were found to be more influenced by peers and less affected by parents' gender typing. It is found that by age 3, same sex peers positively reinforce one another for gender typed play by praising, imitating, or joining in the activity of an agemate who shows a "gender-appropriate" response. When preschoolers engage in "gender inappropriate play" they receive criticism from peers (Ruble & Martin, 1998).

Maternal perceptions also reveal peers as sources of developing gender concept in children in Indian context, as they have different names, they wear different clothes and have different hairstyles. In Indian context peers play an important role at a representational level wherein children observe them and develop an understanding of being a boy or a girl (Chauhan, Shastri, Mohite, 2002).

School

Across decades much attention has been focused on schools and teachers as possible sources of gender socialization. Schools act as socializing agents which influence the development of gender schematic processing by increasing children's sex related knowledge and by assigning functional significance to gender as a social category for perceiving, evaluating and regulating behaviour (Meece, 1987; Martin & Halverson, 1981). For example, children are made to sit separately, use different toilets, play different games and engage in different activities (Chauhan, 2002; Meece, 1987).

Others

This category includes other important influences on children's perceptions regarding their own gender. It includes the media and cultural practices. Media plays a very important role in transmission of information. Media portrays each sex in terms of occupation, personality characteristics, social relationships, appearance and dress styles. Roles continue to be stereotypic and unbalanced, though some changes have been made, especially in portraying women involved in careers (Calvert & Huston, 1987).

Children come in contact with many real people who conform to traditional gender role expectations. In addition to imitating the gender-linked responses they observe, they also start to view themselves and the surrounding world in gender-biased ways (Putnam *et al.*, http://www.ncte.in.org/chapter2.html#ch23 2nd January, 2004). In Indian context girls grow up observing the centrality of males in the household rituals and festivals. Little girls fast to get a good husband, e.g. *Gauri* fasting in Gujarat. Women keep fasts to ensure long life of husband e.g. *Karva Chauth*. There are festivals centred around brothers, the *Raksha Bandhan* and *Bhaiya Dooj*, when sisters tie a colourful thread and apply vermillion to brothers, praying for their long life and, in turn, being assured of care and protection. The boys even younger, see it as their prerogative to pass strictures on their elder sisters. These are a few indicators in culture like ours which imbibe gender type behaviours and traits in boys and girls according to their gender (http://www.ncte.in.org/chapter2.htm#ch23 2nd January, 2004). Even the parents of preschoolers report such festivals as important events for gender learning and formation of gender perceptions in children (Shastri, Chauhan, Kshetrapal & Ray, 2004).

Overall the review suggests that the factors that create the gendered environment for children, help children conceive gender stereotypes which have basis for gender perceptions. As children grow so do their perceptions change regarding their own gender.

Various factors in a culture contribute towards this understanding and help children perceive their gender within the frame of that particular culture.

METHODOLOGY

Participants

The participants of the present study included 60 children spread across the age of 3 to 6 years. Within each age group sub-groups were formed. There were equal number of boys and girls at each age level (Table 6.1).

Table 6.1 : Sample Distribution

Age Group	*Boys (n=30)*	*Girls (n=30)*
3.1–3.5	5	5
3.6–3.12	5	5
4.1–4.5	5	5
4.6–4.12	5	5
5.1–5.5	5	5
5.6–5.12	5	5

The children participated in the study with the informed consent of their parents and the school authorities. All these children belonged to Gujarati Hindu middle class families of Baroda. The children attended a Gujarati medium school of Baroda. The family income of these children ranged from Rs. 8000-12000.

Design

The study was an exploratory research. In order to have consistency in the research constant variables were selected, they were religion – Hindu; Socio-economic Status – Middle; and community – Gujarati. Gujarati Hindus represent majority of the population.

Instruments

Data were obtained using a questionnaire-cum-interview schedule consisting twenty-five items. It assessed the three concepts of gender constancy, i.e. gender identity, gender stability and gender consistency. Each of these three concepts had items with reference to self, other children and adults; to which children were also given a scope to justify their responses. This tool is a compilation of items from scales developed by Patel (2001); Szkrybalo & Ruble (1999); Bem (1989). The scale was translated from English to Gujarati and back to English to validate the translation. The tool was content validated by experts from the field of Human Development and Family Studies and Psychology. This chapter deals with the data that has emerged through the justifications provided by children on each of the items.

Procedure

A pilot study was conducted on three boys and three girls. It revealed that the questionnaire-cum-interview schedule helped in eliciting appropriate responses. Children of 3 to 4 years of age group were interviewed at home in three sessions. Whereas the 4-6 years old were assessed in two sessions in their school itself. Entire process of data collection was done in two to three sessions.

Analysis

In this chapter the secondary analysis of children's justifications was done. The analysis was done both quantitatively and qualitatively. Quantitative analysis was done by calculating the frequencies. The qualitative analysis was done by data reduction and data categorization. It helped in forming broad categories for the similar specific responses. The responses of the children were translated in English. Wherever necessary Gujarati verbatims were retained, to maintain the original meaning.

Results

The results are discussed with reference to :

- Children's Perceptions on being a Boy or a Girl
- Age-wise differences in Perceptions
- Gender Cues as Basis of gender perceptions
- Perceptions Regarding Cross-Gender Children
- Gender Stereotypic activities and children's perceptions
- Gendered Environment
- Gender-wise Difference in Perceptions

Children's Perceptions on being a Boy or a Girl

The justifications provided by the children reflected their perceptions about being a boy or a girl. Different matrices for boys and girls based on responses of children were constructed. These matrices reveal that both the boys and girls describe their gender according to the gender stereotypic norms, activities, cross-gender typed things and the social others. The differences were evident in the kind of gender norms prevalent for boys and girls.

The responses of children revealed that they received cues from the three contexts of the family, the community and the media. Most of the perceptions were a contribution of the family. Within family, specific actions and directions of parents guided the children the most. It is across situations that children get exposed to both gender stereotypic and cross-gender typed cues, e.g. daddy never cooks in the home context and hotel cook is a man in the context of community. Children are active participants in the varied contexts. In the process of interaction they form conceptions of being a boy or a girl.

Boys defined themselves as being a boy because they had a boy's name, will become papa when they grow up, can play cricket, can not cook and play with dolls and everyone calls me a boy. The definition of being a boy thus emerged based on the name given by the family members, behaviours and actions promoted by parents specially play encouraged and mentioned by family and behaviours and actions of others in the community context.

— on the basis of the names provided to them by the family members.
— the behaviours and the activities promoted by the parents. For example, "Mummy says boys should not play with dolls."
— the games they play because they are boys and their future activities of earning or going to office were envisaged by them (Table 6.2).

Table 6.2 : Perception about being a boy : Specific Verbatims

Basis	*Household*	*Community*	*Market*
Gender Stereotypic Norms	• I am named according to my gender	• Boys grow up and become papa	
Gender Stereotypic activities	• I will go to the office, and daddy earns • Mummy says boys should not play with dolls so I will always stay a boy • Daddy never cooks food	• Only boys play cricket • Girls and boys sit in a separate line	• Tendulkar is also a boy and he plays cricket • When children play batman they are termed as boys
Cross Gender Types		• The Hotel cook is also a man, and stays a man only	
Social others	• Daddy says I am a boy	• Teacher says I am a boy	

Girls define themselves as being a girl because they had long hair, they wear frocks, and clothes which are different from boys and as all others call them a girl. Specific references were also made for cooking as an activity done by girls. Few girls also referred to cross-gender clothing and play patterns as the basis of their understanding of being a girl.

For example, to their hairstyles and accessories worn (Table 6.3)

— liking for stereotypic activities, like to cook food and work in the kitchen with mummy.
— opinion of social others.

The definition of being a girl thus emerged on the basis of the hairstyle they have, the clothes and the accessories they wear and the encouragement given to them within the home and community to follow gender stereotypic activities like helping in the kitchen and cooking.

These perceptions clearly indicate that gender is a social construct within which a child forms or perceive his/her gender and is able to identify, and stabilize concepts for the same.

Table 6.3 : Perceptions about being a girl : Specific Verbatims

Basis	*Household*	*Community*	*Market*
Gender Stereotypic Norms	• I have long hair and *Bhaiya* has short hair	• Boys and girls wear different clothes • Girls wear frock and boys wear pant, shirt	
Cultural cues	• I make pony so I am a girl	• Worn bangles, *bindi* and a *saree* which is worn by all women	
Social others	• Mummy says I am a girl	• All call them a girl so she will be a girl	
Gender stereotypic activities	• I like to do kitchen work and mummy does that	• Girls always cook and boys eat	
Cross gender activities	• *Didi* also wears both pant, shirt and frocks	• Both boys and girls play with all the toys • In school children play all games	

Children organise these body of knowledge into male and female categories, which develop in them a gender schema. This schema develops in the gendered world wherein a child associates between an object/behaviour and a gender label. The gender schema theory when laid in action gives the basis for gender identity. (Elizabeth, 2000, *Our Voices Psychology of Women*, U.S.A. Wadsworth).

Age-wise differences in Perceptions

The responses varied according to the children's age. The younger group (3-4 yrs.) children referred to social others as the basis for their identity.

For example, "Mummy says I am a girl"

As the age progressed children of 4-5 years of age started referring to the cultural cues. These cues included the mention about gender typed hair style and clothing as the basis of their understanding.

For example, "I am a girl because I make a pony, I have long hair".

"I am a girl because I wear frock".

Children of 5-6 years gave multiple responses. They reasoned on social others, cultural cues as well as those based on sex-conservation.

For example, "I know I am a boy, so I will be called a boy only".

Thus the understanding of their own gender or identification of self-based on gender changed with age. This reflects children's cognitive development and reasoning. The younger children reasoned with reference to the judgements or cues provided by social others and the older children reasoned by themselves.

Gender Cues as Basis of Gender Perceptions

Across age groups gender cues emerged as references for understanding of gender for self as well as for cross gender. According to children's perceptions gender cues refer to the dressing, accessories and hairstyles a person has. All (n=60) the children perceived their own gender as an attribute which was reflected through gender cues provided by the kind of dress a person wears, the hairstyle kept and also the accessories worn. For example, boys have short hairs and wear pants and shirts. Girls make a pony and wear frocks and skirts. Hairstyle and dressing were the most common gender cues referred by children. All the children perceived their own gender as an attribute which was reflected through cues of dressing and hairstyles "I am a boy so I have short hairs and wear pants and shirts and I am a girl so I have long hairs, make pony and wear frocks". Understanding about the other gender for majority of the children was also with reference to gender cues of hairstyle and dressing. For example, she is a girl because she wears a pony. He is a boy because he wears shirts and pants. An interesting point emerged wherein girls between 4½-6 years. (n=12) of age reflected on their openness regarding cross gender dressing and hairstyles. Whereas boys across all ages (n=24) were extremely rigid regarding their cross gender preferences. Boys (n=5) between the age group of five to six years revealed their rigidity regarding the cross gender dressing of girls and according to them even if they do, they have to behave like girls and not like boys. These results reflect that at this age both boys and girls are rigid about gender stereotypic hairstyles, dressing and traits.

Gender Stereotypic Activities and Children's Perceptions

The gender stereotypes mentioned by children, included cooking and playing as an activity. In the youngest age group very few children (n=3) referred to gender stereotypic activities. Children above four years and especially girls (n=14) referred to cooking as an activity done by women and cricket as a game played only by boys and men. As compared to girls, few (n=4) boys were also open to accept cooking as an activity done by males. Many boys (n=8) also said that cricket is a game which can be played by both men and women. This clearly reflects that boys were less rigid regarding gender stereotypic activities as compared to girls.

Figure 6.1 : Development of Perceptions regarding one's own gender

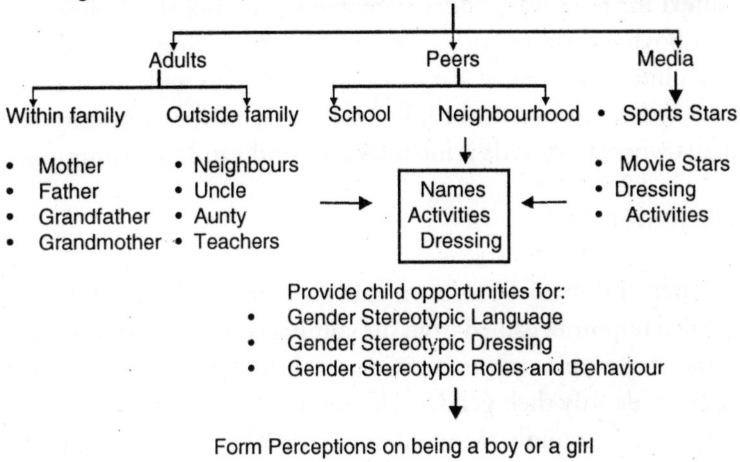

Gendered Environment

Children's perceptions, on being a boy and a girl, is explained through the framework (Fig. 6.1). This framework reflects on the gendered environment created by adults, peers and the media. The adults from family and outside family along with peers and media, provide children opportunities to get aware about existing gender stereotypes. These stereotypes are in the form of language, dressing, involvement in activities and also following certain roles and behaviours. In the process of socialization by constant orientations and interactions with these stereotypes and gender norms, children develop their perceptions of being a boy or a girl.

Gender-wise Differences in Perceptions

The basis of perceptions on being a boy or a girl is same. This was reflected in the responses with reference to gender stereotypes, gender norms and activities prevalent for boys as well as girls. The differences emerged in the reference children used for their perceptions. The context for the girls was gender stereotypic norms prevalent for them within the family and also community, e.g.

girls make pony, wear different clothes than boys. Whereas the context for boys was gender stereotypic activities they referred to their boyhood status with earning and not cooking, playing with masculine toys—guns, cars and batman. This reflects that the gendered environment for boys includes family, community and media whereas for girls it includes the family and the community.

Discussion

The perception of both boys and girls' regarding their gender revealed responses gained from the cultural context, as they referred to the stereotypic norms, activities and the social others as their guide to identify their gender. The gender schemata develops early and increases rapidly throughout preschool and early childhood years. The responses of the children manifested the context of their gender schema. Researches suggest that by 26 months children demonstrate knowledge of adult possessions and by 2-3 years they begin to form stereotypic views about gender activities and future roles (Kuhn, Nash & Bruckhem, 1978; Weinraub *et al.*, 1984). These things conserve in a child's mind and provides the basis for their understanding of being a boy or a girl. This group of 3-6 years children too have formed gender stereotypes with reference to dress, activities, roles and behaviours.

Boys and girls referred to the visual salient perceptual cues provided to them by the culture. This finding match with Bem's (1989) findings wherein she revealed that hair and clothing cues have been found to be the most commonly used cues in children making judgements about gender identity. These cues take a very important position in the gendered environment wherein children are socialized by parents, peers, teachers and relatives to abide by the gender stereotypic dressing, activities, and roles. All with reference to the prevalent gender norms and behaviours expected from them as a boy or a girl. Basically, if we look at definition it is interesting to note that both boys and girls defined themselves very stereotypically.

A very important aspect of discussion emerges in the children's perceptions regarding cross-gender dressing. Girls between 4½-6 years were very clear regarding the cross-gender dressing as compared to boys who had a rigid opinion for the same. The reason can be that for boys the gender environment is more rigid with reference to dressing. Even our everyday observation never trace a boy wearing frocks and skirts. This clearly indicates that the social forces – which includes the family, peers and also teachers help children to practice dressing according to their gender as is desired by the society and culture and it is more rigid for boys than for girls. Researches also indicate the same (Ruble & Szkrybalo, 1999), as they say that exposure of the cultural taboos, where male cross gender is not accepted by a culture, are learnt by the children at an early age.

Schools did not emerge as contributing factor in gender perceptions of children. Though the review suggests the importance of schools (Martin & Halverson, 1981) as socializing agents. As Indian preschoolers tend to spend less of a time in school and more with the family or non-family adults, therefore, they reflect their gender perceptions based on various judgements, cues and norms passed to them. The other reason can be at this stage children do not refer to school as a very important component to form their gender perceptions.

CONCLUDING REMARKS

This chapter reveals interesting findings on gender perceptions of preschoolers. In Indian context gender construction is widely influenced by the home environment. The gender stereotypic dressing, roles and responsibilities highlighted in the day-to-day chores by parents within the family influence the perspectives of children since the advent of age three. It can, therefore, be a mandate to understand the children's perspectives on gender in order to gain insight in the existing biases and gender gaps. Children's perceptions on gender also change with age, reflecting children's increasing reasoning. With increase in age of children the basis for gender identity changes from reliance on social others to cultural cues to sex conservation and reasoning.

Based on the present study certain recommendations can be made with reference to certain studies, which can be conducted.

(1) To examine the gendered environment across ages, i.e. 3-10 years. with changing context, across socio-economic status and also religions.
(2) The kind of conflicts children have when they are unable to follow the set gender stereotypes.

REFERENCES

Bem, S.L. (1989). Genital Knowledge & Gender Constancy in preschool children. *Child Development*, 60, 649-662.

Bhogle, S. (1999). Gender roles : The construct in the Indian context. In Sarswati, T.S. (ed.) *Culture, Socialization & Human Development*. New Delhi. Sage.

Bhogle, S.; Seethalakshmi, R. (1992). Development of Gender Constancy in Indian Children. *Journal of the Indian Academy of Applied Psychology*, 18(1-2), 49-56.

Bussey, K. & Bandura, A. (1992). Self regulatory mechanisms governing gender development. *Child Development*, 63, 1236-1250.

Calvert, L.S. & Huston, A.C. (1987). Television and children's gender schemata. In L. S. Liben & M. L. Signoriella (eds.), *Children's gender schemata*. San Francisco : Jossey-Bass.

Chauhan, G.S.; Shastri, J. & Mohite, P. (2002). Mothers perceptions on Development of Gender Constancy in Preschoolers. Paper presented at National Conference of National Academy of Psychology. Bhubaneshwar.

Chauhan, G.S. (2002). Development of Gender Constancy in Preschoolers. An unpublished dissertation at Deptartment of Human Development and Family Studies, M.S.; University, Baroda.

Deaux, K. & Lewis, L.L. (1984). Structure of gender stereotypes : Inter-relationships among components and gender label. *Journal of Personality and Social Psychology*, 46, 991-1004.

Elizabeth, A.R. (2000). *Our Voices : Psychology of Women*, USA : Wadsworth Publication.

Emanuel, P. (2003). Relationship between the social network and social competence of 5-6 years old children. An unpublished dissertation at Department of Human Development and Family Studies, M.S. University, Baroda.

Fagot, B.I.; Leinbach, M.D. (1993). Gender role development in young children : From discrimination to labeling. *Developmental Review,* 13, 205-224.

Golombok & Fiyush R. (1994). *Gender Development,* USA : Cambridge Publication.

Haugh S.S.; Hoffman, C.D. & Cowan G. (1980). The eye of the very young beholder : Sex typing of infants by young children. *Child Development.* 51, 598-600.

Katz, P.A. & Boswell, S. (1986). Flexibility and traditionality in children's gender roles. *Genetic, Social and General Psychology Monographs,* 112(1), 103-147.

Killen, M.; Pisacane, K.; Kim, J.L. & Rey, A.A. (2001). Fairness or stereotypes? Young Children's Priorities when Evaluating Group Exclusion and Inclusion. *Development Psychology* 37, 587-596.

Kshetrapal, N. (2003). Developmental pathways in social network of 3-6 years old children. An unpublished dissertation at Department of Human Development and Family Studies, M.S.University, Baroda.

Kuhn, D.; Nash, S.C. & Bracken, L. (1978). Sex role concepts of two and three years old children, *Child Development,* 49, 445-451.

Maccoby, E.E. (2000). Perspectives in gender development. *International Journal of Behavioural Development.*

Marie, S.B. (2004) *Psycho Social Development in Early Childhood.* (http:// highered.mcgraw-hill.com) 9th December 2004.

Martin, C.L. & Halverson, F.C. (1981). A schematic processing model of sex typing and stereotyping in children. *Child Development,* 52, 1119-1134.

Meece, J.L. (1987). *The influence of school experiences on the development of gender schemata.* San Francisco : Jossey-Bass.

Nair, M. (2004). Relationship between peer network and social competence of 3-6 years old children belonging to low socio-economic status. An unpublished dissertation at Department of Human Development and Family Studies, M.S. University, Baroda.

Ruble & Martin (1998). Gender Development in Damon, W. (ed.) *Handbook of Child Psychology,* Vol. 3 Eisenberg, N. (ed.) *Social, Emotional and Personality Development,* NY : John Wilers.

Shastri, J.; Chauhan, G.S.; Kshetrapal, N. & Ray, J. (2004). Parents

Perceptions regarding Development of Gender Concept. An unpublished monograph, Department of Human Development and Family Studies, M. S. University, Baroda.

Stoneman, Z.; Brody, G.H. & MacKinnon, C.E. (1986). Same Sex and Cross Sex Siblings : Activity choices, roles, behaviour and gender stereotypes. *Sex Roles*, 15(9/10), 495-511.

Szkrybalo, J. & Ruble, N.D. (1999). "God made me a girl" : Sex category constancy judgements and explanations revisited. *Development Psycholcgy*, 35(2), 392-402.

17 Exploring the Linkages between Dimensions of Self Knowledge and Empathy of 18-20 Months Old Infants

Ankita Mendiratta, Shruti Bhargava, Sucheta Jasrai *and* Prerana Mohite

Early years are very crucial since rapid changes take place in different developmental domains. The emergence of self as subject and object during the first 18-24 months of life suggests a growing appreciation of selfhood. Self-knowledge is acquired within different domains during the development phase within the first two years. For present study the domains included are:

(a) The featural knowledge refers to the categorical self or me (James, 1952; Pipp-Seigel & Foltz, 1997). By two years of age, the infants can understand self and acquire self-recognition, that is, are able to distinguish self from others (people and object) (Berk, 1994; Lindon, 1998; and Lewis and Ramsay, 1997). Phatak (1977) reported that by 14 months the infant can identify the named object belonging to him such as his/her shoes, socks, bangles etc. and shows it by touching, pointing or directly grasping. By 20 months the infant is able to identify the body parts of the doll.

(b) Agency refers to the self that recognizes the world as independent from interpersonal relationships and can act upon these aspects, although it emerges from early social relations (James, 1952). By 12-15 months of age, the infants acquire agency (Harter, 1983). According to Phatak

(1977), 18 months old infants follow direction. For example, when the infant is asked to sit the doll on the chair, give her milk from the cup and to wipe her nose the infants follow two out of the three directions. Culture and the child rearing practices shape this aspect of self. In Western cultures, where the socialization goal focuses on early autonomy and mother as primary caregiving person, there are few other social partners, the infants self-concept can be conceptualized as self as agent. In non-Western cultures, the infants self is regarded as co-agent, where the self development is explained not only in terms of mother infants interaction but also in terms of multiple caretakers and with respect to social relationship of caregiving persons with the infant (Keller and Eckensberger, 1998). Pipp, Easterbrooks and Harmon (1992), as per their study found that irrespective of age, the infants who felt more secured and attached with mother passed more self/mother tasks with varied complexities than the insecure infants.

(c) The third domain that defines self-knowledge is interpersonal self where the infant not only distinguishes, but also relates oneself to other primary caregiver. According to Keller (1999, unpublished manuscript), "interpersonal self is defined through the relational aspects within the matrix of primary relationships". Experience of warmth promotes this aspect of self. The concept of self and relationships with both people and things, that the infant acquires through early socialization situations shapes his/her ways of developing competencies in later years. Culture and the parenting style which also establishes intergenerational continuity and transformation define these early socialization situations (Keller and Greenfield, 2000). Super and Harkness (1994) postulated the idea of developmental niche to explain child's development. The three components that together make up the developmental niche include physical and social setting of everyday life, customs of child care and child rearing and psychology of the caretaker. These components together with the elements of larger culture shape the caretakers' interaction in which infant's development takes place which moulds the child into a culture specific child. Kagiticibasi (1996-97) in her functional contextual model of self development and family change differentiated the relational self and the separated self in terms of cultural and socio-emotional context, mediated by the family.The relational self develops especially in the family model of total (emotional and material) interdependence. This self is visualized in agrarian life styles, who value subsistence economies. This self is also dominant in collectivistic cultures which requires intergenerational interdependence for family livelihood. The authoritarian and obedience-oriented parenting contributes to the development of the relational self. On the other hand the separated self typically develops in the family model of independence. It is seen in the Western urban context, with individualistic cultures where inter-generational interdependence is not required for family livelihood. Relatively permissive and self-reliance oriented parenting contributes to the development of separated self. The third category of self is autonomous-relational self. This self is in combination with both collectivistic (relational) and individualistic (autonomous) elements, at the individual level. It develops in the family model of emotional interdependence. This self is dominant in the urban areas of societies with collectivistic cultures, where material intergenerational interdependencies weaken but emotional interdependencies continue. Combined autonomy and control oriented parenting contributes to the dimension of self. Kitayama and Markus (1995) and Kagistibasi (1997) similarly distinguished the "independent" and "interdependent" construal of self. According to Kitayama

> and Markus (1995: 369, 370), "under the independent construal of self, individuals tend to focus on their own internal attributes — their own preferences, traits and abilities". It is more prevalent in Western cultures. In the "interdependent construal of self, individuals tend to focus on their interdependent status with other people and strive to meet duties, obligations and social responsibilities". It is more prevalent in Asian cultures. Symbolic interactionists such as Cooley, Mead, and Baldwin (cited in Harter, 1998) are emphasizing on the role of social interaction, links between knowledge of self and others, the infant - caregiver interaction and the role of social, cognitive and affective processes on the development of the self. Moreover, there has been a shift from a focus on autonomy as an end point of self-development in infancy to a focus on the dual goal of autonomy and connectedness. Thus overall, the infant-caregiver interaction shapes those experiences of infants which differentiate his/her self according to prevailing cultural standards (Keller, 1999).

The other dimension that defines the infant's development of self is empathy, which defines the development of self in terms of emotional behaviour displayed by the infants. Empathy refers to not only understanding and becoming aware of other's emotions but also providing an emotional expression/responses to others emotional state. During the second year of life, the infants can interpret other's emotional expressions (Berk, 1994). There are individual differences in the way the infants respond to other's emotional state (Berk, 1994; Lindon, 1998). Toddlers try to provide an emotional response to the distressed person either by their own action/behaviour or by calling adults attention towards the person in distress. They tend to use clowning about and other means to make others, children or adults laugh. Zahn-Waxler, Radke-Yarrow, Wagner, and Chapman (1992) examined the children's (1-2 years) responses to distress that they witness and cause in others and the relation of children's emotional behaviour to self-recognition. It was found that the infants display prosocial behaviour (help, sharing, provision of comfort) and empathic concern (sad looks, sympathetic statements) towards others followed by an effort to understand and experience other person's distress. These emotional behaviours are supplemented by the social-cognitive changes in self-recognition. The infants displayed more prosocial behaviour to mother, and more empathic concern to experimenter. Similarly, Young, Fox, and Zahn-Waxler (1999) on the basis of their study on examining the role of infants and toddlers temperament in prediction of empathy concluded that infants were more responsive to the mothers distress than to that of the experimenter and the empathetic pattern were reflected in many ways. The infants were aroused (body tension reflected in postural freezing, attention to victim and disruption of play), they expressed emotional concern, got engaged in helping or in comforting behaviour. No gender differences were found for measuring of empathy. The factors that affect empathy displayed by the infants include advances in perspective taking, child rearing and parental intervention when negative emotions are displayed by the children (Berk, 1994). Children's emotional development is guided by the attention/ reaction displayed by the mother in response to child's behaviour which depends on the culturally guided beliefs and child-rearing goals (Friedlmeier and Trommsdorff, 1999). Shweder, Goodnow, Hatano, Levine, Markus, and Miller (1998) set forth encouragement and learning through examples as an important mode of development of empathy in Asian cultures.

The review clearly indicates that few researches related to understanding of self have been conducted in Indian context. The researches are conducted more in laboratory setting than in the natural setting. It thus becomes important to do researches in Indian context and in natural setting, to understand the influence of culture, child rearing practices and other variables like home environment, language that affects one's development of self in a given cultural context. The present study was a part of the Indo-

German Project, undertaken in the Department of Human Development and Family Studies, Faculty of Home Science, M.S. University, Vadodara. The project is a longitudinal study, which aims to study the developmental pathways of children from three months to six years. First stage of the study on the dimensions of self of 18 to 20 months infants has been done by Parikh (2000) where the major areas were similar to that of present study. The above study acted as a pilot for the present one. The primary analysis of the present study aimed to understand the development of "self" of 18 to 20 months old, "Indian" infants, with specific reference to self-knowledge, self-control, empathy and performing responsibility tasks. And to assess differences if any in gender and ordinal position.

The secondary analysis of the study focused on understanding the linkages between specific dimensions of self-knowledge and empathy of 18 to 20 months old infants. This chapter attempts to focus on the same.

Objectives

The main objectives for the study were:

(1) To understand the linkages between the dimensions of self-knowledge and empathy.
(2) To assess differences, if any, in development of self with reference to gender and ordinal position.

Method

Research Design

A descriptive research design with naturalistic observations was used to meet the objectives of the study. Observations and interviews were conducted in the home settings of 18 to 20 months old infants to get information on relevant aspects of the study.

Selection and Description of the Sample

The sample consisted of 20 infants (18 to 20 months), 11 boys and 9 girls, from Hindu-Gujarati families and their non-employed mothers. The sample was selected from the urban population of Vadodara city, belonging to middle and upper middle class, with income ranging from Rs. 8,000–20,000 per month. A purposive sample was selected through snowball technique, contact with pediatricians and hospital records.

Tool Description

Data were collected through :

1. Specific observations on various tasks performed by the infants.
2. Extensive field notes.
3. Interview schedule.

Specific Observations

Home observations were carried out by using the observation guidelines prepared by Keller (1999). These are described below:

Self Knowledge

It was assessed by three domains:

1. *Featural Knowledge*: The infants were involved in following tasks of self-recognition.

   (a) *Identification of body parts*: The infants were asked to identify (show, point to) his/her body parts (arms, legs, head, face, eyes, mouth, ears and nose) in a random order and the responses were noted.

(b) *Verbal labelling of body parts*: The infants were asked to label the above listed body parts and the responses were noted.

(c) *Rouge test*: A mirror was placed before the infant and the following procedure was carried out.

- The infant's reaction to the mirror image was observed and recorded.
- Next, the infant's reaction was observed and noted when the experimenter put rouge on infants nose/cheek, and
- Finally, when both mother and infant was in front of the mirror the infant's reaction towards the mother was observed and recorded (as part of interpersonal self).

2. *Agency*: Infants were asked to perform the following tasks. The observations were made and recorded.

- Experimenter pretended to eat and drink and asked the infant to do the same.
- Experimenter pretended to feed (eat/drink) the doll and asked the infant to do the same.
- Experimenter praised the infant and the reactions of the infant were noted down.

3. *Interpersonal Self*: Infant's relatedness towards mother and any other caretaker present during the entire assessment procedure (in terms of overt behaviour) were noted down.

Empathy

Episode I: The experimenter pretended to feed the doll and displayed sadness that the doll was not eating. The reactions of the infants were noted down. After some time, the experimenter pretended that doll had eaten and showed happiness. Again the infant's reactions were observed and noted down.

Episode II : The experimenter pretended to have a stomach ache and pretended to be sad. The reactions of the infants were noted. After some time the experimenter showed a sign of relief and happiness and again the infants reactions were observed and noted.

Field Notes

During the spot observations extensive field notes were taken regarding specific events (if any) along with infant's reaction to those. Field notes supplemented the observations for specific dimensions, like, physical environment which included presence of siblings, availability of play material and presence of other caretaker were also taken into consideration. Each infant was observed for 4-5 hours in 3-4 visits. Each visit lasted approximately for an hour or hour and a half.

Interview Schedule

To obtain in-depth information about mother-infant interaction and family background an interview schedule for mothers was prepared by the members of the Indo-German project team. The major components covered in the interview schedule were:

- Household information which included.

  - Background information of the household members (education, occupation and income)
  - Type of house (*pucca* house / semi-*pucca* house)
  - Household items (newspaper, television, vehicles, etc.)

- Daily Routine Schedule interview with mothers.

This section of the interview schedule focused on the routine of the mother, mother's activity related to self, infant and others in the home and the approximate time spent from dawn to dusk during the different activities.

Data Analysis

Data was analyzed in each of the areas by calculating scores, frequencies and percentages. Differences if any in terms of gender and ordinal position was also taken into consideration. The composite and individual profiles of the infants were also made.

1. *Self Knowledge*

(a) Featural Knowledge (identification and naming of body parts and rouge test)

- Frequency (0-8) / % were calculated in terms of how many infants named/identified body parts,
- Among 20 infants the common named/identified and not named/not identified body parts were also noted down,
- Frequency was calculated in terms of how many infants removed (score of 1 was given) and did not remove the rouge (score of 0 was given),
- The infant's reaction to the mirror image (before applying rouge) was noted down,
- Infant's reaction to mother (in mirror) was taken as part of interpersonal self.

(b) Agency

(a) Feeding self/doll
(b) Drinking self/doll
(c) Verbal praise

- Frequency (0-4) was calculated in terms of how many agency tasks the infants performed.
- Total frequency/percentage was calculated in terms of how many infants responded to Experimenter/mother or present caretaker.

- Specific categories were made for verbal praise in terms of the smiling and neutral behaviour of infants.

(c) Interpersonal Self

- Total frequency/percentage was calculated in terms of how many times the infant showed relatedness towards mother and other caretakers (father, grandfather, grandmother, siblings, etc.).
- Frequency/percent was also calculated for the most approachable caretaker.

2. **Empathy**

(a) *Feeding doll* (Episode - I)
(b) *Stomach ache* (Episode - II)

- Frequency/percentage was calculated for both the episodes in terms of how many infant showed Em / Cc / Cf (defined later).

Infants responses in Episode I (feeding doll) and Episode II (stomach ache) were analysed in three categories:

(1) EMPATHY (Em): It refers to when the infant makes an attempt on his/her own to make the others feel comfortable.
Example - If the doll is not eating and the experimenter displayed sadness, then the infant will himself/herself try to feed the doll. So herein the infant not only recognizes the emotional being of another person but also provides an emotional response to an other person situation and not simply shares the emotional expression. (Bischof Koehler, 1984, 1994 in Keller 1999 unpublished manuscript).
(Higher Level of Development).

(2) CONCERN (Cc): When the infant shows concern and anxiousness about the emotional being of other person

but does not provide an emotional response to the other person situation (personal communication, Keller, 2001). (Second Level of Development).

(3) CONFUSION (Cf): When the infant shows a state of mixed emotions (personal communication, Keller, 2001). (Third Level of Development).

3. Linkages between Self Knowledge and Empathy

Children were categorized into groups depending on their scores in the self-knowledge tasks. For each of the groups then children's reactions in the empathy tasks was qualitatively analyzed.

RESULTS AND DISCUSSION

The results and discussion were based on the data obtained through specific observations, field notes and interview schedule.

I. Self Knowledge

1. *Featural Knowledge*

(a) *Identification of body parts/ (b) Naming/verbal labeling of body parts:* The analysis revealed that the infants identified most of the body parts rather than naming them. 19 infants identified hands, legs, eyes, mouth, head and nose. The common unidentified body part was face followed by ear. 10 infants named the body parts. The most commonly named body parts were hand followed by legs, nose, eyes and ears. The common not named body parts were face followed by mouth and head. No significant differences emerged across gender.

(c) *Rouge test:* Out of 20 infants, 17 infants showed self-recognition. These infants not only identified the rouge on their nose or cheeks, but also tried to remove it. Gender difference was not significantly seen.

2. *Agency*

The data revealed that as per the agency tasks performed by the infants, out of 20 infants, 15 infants performed all the four tasks. (i.e., feeding self, feeding doll, drinking self and drinking doll). 18 infants responded to experimenter and two responded to the mother. Gender differences were not observed as six out of nine females and nine out of eleven males performed the tasks.

Verbal praise: On praising, infants showed either smiling or neutral reactions. In play related activities as compared to other areas, the infants showed more smiling behaviour than neutral behaviour. Girls showed more smiling behaviour in activities related to feeding and the boys showed more smiling behaviour in activities related to play. As per the observations infants besides, showing smiling and neutral behaviour also displayed other reactions/action, when praised by the experimenter, for example, went near mother, started moving/running in the room, continued doing the action, repeated the action/task again.

3. *Interpersonal self*

The infants showed more interpersonal self/relatedness towards the mother even when other caretakers were present. Gender differences were not significant. Certain interpersonal behaviour's were also shown by infants towards the mother during the rouge test, which were mainly smiling and turning towards mother.

II. Empathy

The infants displayed more concern in episode II (stomach ache) and more empathy in episode I (feeding doll). One of the reasons for displaying more empathy towards other object (doll) might be that doll is familiar object in the infants environment and feeding is a routine activity in daily living. The episode performed by the experimenter for the infant was easy to perform with the doll and more concretely observable. Similarly one of the reasons due to which the infants showed less empathy towards experimenter might be that experimenter is not a familiar person to the infant.

III. Linkages between Self-Knowledge and Empathy

Second level analysis revealed the linkages between the following dimensions of self.

1. Self-knowledge

(a) Featural Knowledge

The results on secondary analysis of data revealed that the infants who got the maximum score (8), that is, those infants who were able to identify all the body parts, indicating establishment of self – featural knowledge, their end point behaviour in rouge test was trying to remove the rouge. These infants before and after applying the rouge showed different behaviours like, smiled at the mirror image, turned towards mother, pointed towards mirror, pointed finger on nose, put hand on cheeks, started dancing looking in the mirror, press their nose on the flat surface of mirror, bring their head near mirror, cried looking in mirror, became scared and became shy and hide face in mother's lap.

The above behaviours/reactions indicated that these infants had firmly/clearly established knowledge of self and body parts and, therefore, could identify rouge as something that was not part of the body.

(b) Agency

The results revealed that those infants who had performed all the four tasks had identified at least six or more body parts out of eight.

(c) Interpersonal self

As per the aspect of interpersonal self the infants (N=20) displayed different behavioural responses towards the caretakers. The behaviours displayed were like, looked/gazed, held hands/saree of adult, came near, ran towards them, layed or sat on lap, touched, smiled, pointed, followed and played and called them.

The analysis revealed that the infants displayed these behaviours the more towards the mother even when the other caretakers were around. The maximum behaviour displayed was lying down or sitting on lap of mother followed by smiling, holding, looking, following, touching, pointing, running towards, playing and calling the mother respectively.

These behaviours were observed in all infants irrespective of whether they had attained or not attained featural knowledge.

2. *Empathy*

The infants who identified all the body parts and tried to remove the rouge that is had established the self knowledge displayed vast range of emotions like sadness, happy, serious, anxious, neutral and scared. For most of the infants two emotions were combined with a neutral reaction. Empathy emerged as a primary emotion, as per the tasks, i.e., feeding doll and stomach ache. The infants showed a shift from the state of empathy to concern across the two situations.

As compared to the infants who got the score of eight, the infants who were not able to identify all the body parts, their end point behaviours in rouge test cannot be directly demarcated as trying to remove the rouge. The behaviours these infants displayed included; just looked at mirror, smiled at the mirror image, pointed to mirror, put finger on nose and put hand on cheek.

These infants in the empathy tasks displayed less range of emotions like, being sad, happy, serious and neutral. For most infants two-three emotions were combined with a neutral reaction.

On the basis of interview schedule and observations regarding the mother-infant interaction, the results revealed that infants were never found to be all alone. Even while playing by themselves the mother were always around. The profiles of four infants were made, who were either at lower or higher level of performance. The results revealed that, the child rearing practices, language development, the home environment, presence of neighbours, exposure to natural setting, constitutes to the infant's development of self.

Thus infants acquire self knowledge by 18 to 20 months of age, as reflected in their ability to identify the body parts, but are unable to name them. They show concern towards others although empathy is not developed. The infants who scored more on the tasks related to self knowledge, displayed vast range of emotions as per the empathy tasks. The above shows that there exists a linkage between the self-knowledge and the empathy.

Similar results to some extent are also seen in other studies. Many studies revealed that infants by two years of age shows self-recognition, but the featural knowledge is not developed. That is, the infants can identify the body parts, but naming is not established (Berk, 1994; Phatak, 1977; and Parikh, 2000). One of the possible reasons for the above might be that by two years of age the infants language and/or vocabulary is limited and so the infant can identify more and naming is less. A study conducted by Pipp-Siegel and Foltz (1997) revealed that by two years of age the infant can distinguish self from others. 18 months old infants pass less self related tasks in terms of featural knowledge whereas opposite holds true in the agency tasks where the infants performed more self tasks than other tasks related to mother and inanimate objects. For mother and the object tasks, toddlers passed more tasks with increasing age. For the self version of the tasks, in contrast, 24 months old toddlers did not pass significantly more tasks than did the 18 months old toddlers. Moreover in both the domains: featural knowledge and agency girls passed more tasks than boys. In the present study most of the infants perform both self-related tasks (featural knowledge) and self and other related tasks (agency). No significant gender difference was there. According to Lewis *et al.* (1989), the infants by two years of age besides showing self-recognition also displayed self-conscious emotions like scared, crying etc. Similar behaviours were observed in the present study. As per the present study where mother being the most approached adult the infant showed minimal level of relatedness towards other caregivers. The above is very prominent in Asian cultures where the infants self is described in terms of multiple caregivers and the self is defined as relational self and interdependent self (Kagitcibasi, 1996-97; Kitayama and Markus, 1995). The Indian self is also defined in terms of different concepts. According to Roland (1988) (cited in Mishra and Giri, 1995) Indian self includes both familial self as well as spiritual self. He observed that 'private self' coexists within the 'we-self' in Indian context. The other concepts further characterize Indian self as both collectivistic and individualistic. Also as per the study by Parikh (2000), the infants interpersonal self is discussed in terms of infants maturity where the infants shows better interrelatedness towards caregivers and on the other hand the relatedness is discussed in terms of infants dependency on other caretakers. Moreover infants show different responses in terms of displaying empathy towards others and there are individual differences in responding to other emotional state. The above was reported by Berk, (1994), Lindon, (1998) and similar observations were noted for the present study and in study by Parikh (2000). Zahn-Waxler *et al.* (1992) on the basis of their study found that the infants displayed more prosocial behaviour (help, sharing, provision of comfort) to mother and empathic concern (sad looks, sympathetic statements) to experimenter. Girls showed more concern than boys. Similar was also found in study by Young *et al.* (1999) but no gender differences were there. In the present study both the episodes, that is, feeding doll and stomach ache was displayed by the experimenter and mother did not perform any task. Thus it becomes impossible to conclude to whom the infant was more responsive. But overall it was found that the infants displayed more concern than empathy. In terms of gender differences the girls showed more concern for the self-related task (stomach ache) than boys. In the study conducted by Parikh (2000) contradictory results to present study were found. In the earlier infants showed more concern for other than self. Researchers also concluded that there exists a connection between self-knowledge and empathy. According to Asendorpf and Baudomiere (1993), and Bischof–Kohler (1991) (cited in Berk, 1994: 436) "toddlers who pass the mirror self–recognition task are more likely to display empathy, pro-social behaviour and imitative play with peers". Zahn-Waxler, C. Radke-Yaroo, M and Wagner, E. and Chapman, M. (1992: 126), on the basis of their study on assessing, the development of pro-social and reparative behaviour and also finding linkages between the development of self-recognition in relation to children's response to distress found a correlation between self recognition and pro-social behaviour. As per their study "age changes in the early sign of moral development was accompanied by social-cognitive changes in self recognition". According to Lewis, Sullivan, Stanger, and Weiss (1989: 154) "the ability to consider one's self rather than the ability to differentiate or discriminate self from other is the cognitive capacity that allows for all self-conscious emotions such as embarrassment and empathy. Moreover, self-recognition behaviour represent an important milestone in the child's development of a self-system and in its general cognitive and emotional development".

REFERENCES

Berk, L.E. (1994). *Child development* (3rd ed.). New Delhi : Prentice Hall of India.

Crockenberg, S., & Litman, C. (1990). Autonomy as competence in 2-year olds : Maternal correlates of child defiance, compliance and self-assertion. *Developmental Psychology, 26*, 961-971.

Friedlmeier, W., & Trommsdorff, G. (1999). Emotion regulation in early childhood : A cross-cultural comparison between German and Japanese toddlers. *Journal of Cross-Cultural Psychology, 30* (6), 684-711.

Harter, S. (1983). Developmental perspectives on the self-system. In Mussen, P.H. (series Ed.) *Handbook of child psychology : Vol. 7. Sociolization personality and social development* (7th ed. pp. 275-385). U.S.A. published.

James, W. (1952). *The principles of psychology.* Chicago : Encyclopaedia Britannica.

Kagitcibasi, C. (1996). The autonomous - relational self : A new synthesis. *Journal of European Psychology, 1* (3), 180-186.

Kagitcibasi, C. (1997). Individualism and collectivism. In J.W. Berry, V. H. Poortinga & J. Pandey (Eds.), *Handbook of Cross Cultural psychology : Vol. 3. Social behaviour and applications* (pp. 1-49). Boston : Allyn and Balcon.

Keller, H. (1999). *Developmental pathways to individualism and interrelatedness.* Unpublished manuscript, University of Osnabrueck, Germany.

Keller, H. (1999). *Personality Formation in different cultures. A cross-cultural study program.* Unpublished manuscript, University of Osnabrueck, Germany.

Keller, H. & Eckensberger, L.H. (1998). Kulture and entwicklung (Culture and Development). In H. Keller (ed.), *Lehrubuch entwicklungs psychologie.* Bern : Huber Verlag.

Keller, H. & Greenfield, P.M. (2000). History and future of development in cross-cultural psychology. *Journal of Cross-Culture Psychology, 31* (1), 52-62.

Kitayama, S. & Markus, H.R. (1995). Culture and self : Implications for internalizing psychology. In N.R. Goldberger & J.B. Veroff (eds.), *The culture and psychology reader* (pp. 366-383). New York : University Press.

Lewis, M. & Ramsay, D.S. (1997). Stress reactivity and self-recognition. *Child Development, 68* (4), 621-629.

Lewis, M.; Sullivan, W.M.; Stanger, C.; & Weiss, M. (1989). Self development and self conscious emotions. *Child Development, 60,* 146 – 156.

Lindon, J. (1998). *Understanding child development : Knowledge, theory and practice.* London: Macmillan.

Mishra, G. & Giri, R. (1995). Is Indian self predominantly interdependent? *Journal of Indian psychology, 13* (1), 16 – 29.

Parikh, K. (2000). *Understanding psychological dimensions of self of 18-20 months infants.* Unpublished master's dissertation, M.S. University, Baroda.

Phatak, P. (1977). *A pictorial monograph of motor and mental development of Indian babies from 1 to 30 months* (1st ed.). Pune : Anand Agencies.

Pipp-Siegel, S., & Foltz, C. (1997). Toddler's acquisition of self/other knowledge : Ecological and interpersonal aspects of self and other. *Child Development, 68* (1), 69-79.

Pipp, S.; Easterbrooks, M.A.; & Harmon, R. (1992). The relation between attachment and knowledge of self and mother in one to three years old infants. *Child Development, 63*, 738-750.

Schneider-Rosen, K., & Wenz-Gross, M. (1990). Pattern of compliance from eighteen to thirty months of age. *Child Development, 61*, 104-112.

Shweder, R.A.; Goodnow, J.; Hatano, G.; Le Vine, Markus, H.; & Miller, P. (1998). The cultural psychology of development : One mind, many mentalities. In W. Damion, R. M. Lerner (ed.), *Handbook of child psychology : Vol. 1. Theoretical modes of human development* (5th ed., pp. 865-922).

Super, C.M. and Harkness, S. (1994). The developmental niche. In W. J. Lonner and R.S. Malpass, (eds). *Psychology and culture* (pp. 95–99). Allyn and Bacon.

Vaughn, B.E.; Kopp, C.B.; & Krakow, J.B. (1984). The emergence and consolidation of self-control from 18 to 30 months of age : Normative trends and individual differences. *Child Development, 55*, 990-1004.

Young, S.K.; Fox, W.A.; & Waxler, C. (1999). The relations between temperament and empathy in 2 years olds. D*evelopmental Psychology, 35* (5), 1189-1197.

Zahn-Waxler, C.; Radke-Yarrow, M.; Wagner, E.; & Chapman, M. (1992). Development of concerns for others. *Journal of developmental psychology, 28* (1), 126-136.

18 Sharing and Conflict Resolution Behaviour of Three to Four Years Old Children in the Preschool Context

Swati Shah *and* Hina Mankodi

Parents and other caregivers are always concerned about the development of young children. They make deliberate efforts for teaching their offsprings about what is good and bad. Learning about the needs of others and considering perspectives of others are very important for maintaining good relationship in the family and in the society. Even young children are expected to express certain value like sharing, helping, and cooperating. Hence during early childhood years moral behaviour is guided and controlled by adults. Also it is influenced by one's cultural norms and standards A true moral behaviour is not expressed only when the adult is present but children would also like to follow in various situation (Berk, 2001).

Literature on young children reveals that children are able to learn as well as internalize the standards of socio-moral behaviours. According to Torkington and Landers (1999) the newborn is also able to display prosocial and aggressive behaviours. There are certain other social factors that are also likely to affect children's development such as peer relationship because children can learn very easily from their peers. In connection with this Benenson, Markovits, Roy and Denko (2003) found that with increasing age children become more egaliatarian in their relationship with peers hence they would like to share with peers because of their enhanced negotiation skills. Also since children have more egalitarian relationship with peers, it provides them the opportunity to assert themselves, to present their own views and to freely argue upon different view points (Goffin, 1987).

The present study attempted to understand the sharing and conflict resolution behaviours of three to four years old children in the preschool context wherein there is scope to observe natural occurrence of behaviour during free play sessions. The study also focuses upon the gender dimension to gain more insight. Various other factors are likely to contribute in understanding the sharing and conflict resolution strategies such as cultural determinants, biological determinant and other factors.

Cultural Determinants

There are wide variations within the Asian culture such as culture of India and China, because of the practice of different philosophies, namely Hinduism and Confucianism. It influences upon the individuals belief and value system. Both cultures give emphasis upon sharing behaviour but for different reasons. In Confucianism emphasis is given on proper social conduct, therefore, sharing is encouraged whereas in Hinduism emphasis is given on the charity, which in a way leads to sharing (Rao & Stewart, 1999). In Hindu philosophy, the emphasis is given to *dharma, karma* and *moksha*. Individual's *karma* directs his/her current life as well as the life after death. Hence from the beginning of the life an individual's good social relations are valued more and given major emphasis.

With reference to sharing behaviour Rao and Stewart (1999) further found that Asian children shared more frequently than American children, whereas Chinese preschoolers shared more food in comparison with Indian preschoolers. Asian children expressed more spontaneous sharing while American children needed to be encouraged for sharing. The kind of environment provided within the school also differs from culture to culture. For example, in *Reggio Emila* preschool setting conflicts are viewed as an inevitable part of interaction through which children can get opportunity to share their different perspectives (Jones & Nimmo, 1999). Thus culture of school also plays very significant role in understanding of the sharing and conflict resolution behaviours of children in the early years.

Biological Determinants

Biology plays a significant role in determining development of the child. Each child indicates individual differences in one's behaviour and reactions. It is assumed and justified in the literature that children with their genetic endowments interact with various environmental elements. The actions, reactions of children even in the early years are influenced by their temperament, the nature and pattern of interaction with adults in the preschool and home context. Eisenberg and Fabes (1998) mentioned that human beings are biologically tuned for the development of prosocial behaviour but it is not true for young children.

Other factors such as expectation of approval, norms of responsibility, level of cognitive and social skill, feelings of well-being and socio-economic states and type of the family are likely to contribute in determining prosocial behaviours. At times prosocial behaviours are also influenced by immediate social circumstances (Torkington & Landers, 2000).

Sharing behaviour is the precursor to morality. According to Piaget, (1923/1965); Kohlberg, (1969), ability of sharing is one of the maturational milestones that can be achieved along with the ability of considering perspectives of others. Children like to share and cooperate with others when they relinquish their egocentricity (Harris, 1986). Sharing behaviour is an important source for learning about distributive justice, that is, notion about fair distribution of resources. Four years old children are able to give self-serving reason for sharing whereas five years old children are able to understand equality principle of sharing (Berk, 2002).

Interaction between peers encourages children to strike balance between the needs of one's own and of others. Sharing with peers is helpful in the achievement of one's own individual goals, and probably it is easier for the child to understand the perspective of same age peer because of similarity with one's own perspective (Benenson *et al.*, 2003). Thus peers play significant role in socio-moral development of children. They facilitate communication, cooperation, sharing and problem solving. Major objectives of children's friendship are to spend time with one another and to make common cause of activities that encourage them to share, to cooperate and to help (Hartup, 1989).

Regarding the age of children, older children are more likely to share because of their abilities to recognise sign of distress, language skill and to understand other's viewpoints (Kostelink, Smith, Wheiren and Soderman, 1998). Similarly Berk (1999) also mentioned that because of older children's increasing intellectual abilities they understand reciprocal nature of sharing behaviour that brings some kind of reward or future gains.

Sharing behaviour is less costly if the receiver is a known person. Rao and Stewart (1999) found that sharing behaviour varies for friends and acquaintances while comparing American children with Asian children. On the other hand they also found that Indian children made less distinction between friends and acquaintances in comparison with Chinese children. Rao and Stewart (1999) found that Asian girls are more generous while sharing than boys. Girls shared more with friends than with acquaintances while boys did not make any distinctions between friends and acquaintances. Gender may play crucial role because of differentiated adult's expectation towards children. Parents are concerned about appropriate behaviour of boys and girls that even reflect through the choice of gender typical play materials for their child.

Interpersonal relationships are not always based on agreements with other's viewpoints or actions. Social conflicts also play critical role in children's development because it provides scope for arguments and disagreements that help them to notice other's viewpoints, which also lead decline in the egocentrism (Piaget, 1923/1926). Thus the study on conflict provides more insight about individuals because for maintaining relationship with other people likely to use various conflict resolution strategies.

Conflicts between children can be viewed as an event where action of a child is opposed by others (Hartup, French, Laursen, Johnston, & Ogawa, 1993). Conflicts are not always negative or aggressive in nature. It has positive influences because it provided scope for children to recognize other's thoughts, feelings and views which are different from their own (Goffin, 1987). Conflicts within individual and conflicts between individuals are essential for personality development and for understanding of socio-moral principles that emerge from the situations. Several factors are responsible for conflicts. According to Killen and Turiel (1991), sources of conflicts mainly are physical harm (e.g. hitting, kicking), psychological harm (e.g. teasing, calling names), unfair distribution of resources (e.g. sharing), rights (e.g. using someone's space), and social order (e.g. not wearing apron while eating).

Conflict resolution is a strategy that is helpful to the person in order to interact with each other through resolving their differences (Stomfay-Stitz, 1994). Conflict resolution strategies are important for maintaining relationships and also for learning about the new ways of resolving conflicts. At the same time these constructive ways of resolving conflicts are helpful in promoting a cooperative psychological orientation (Boardman & Horowitz, 1994).

Preschool context is important for learning about sharing and conflict resolution behaviours with the same age peers. Both indoor and outdoor set-ups of the preschool also play significant role. Children get more opportunity to behave naturally during free play sessions. Children's conflict between friends are less intense in the open field situation, that is, free play situation than the closed field situation as given by Vespo & Caplan (1993). Also if the school environment is controlled by adults then it prevents scope for the emergence of conflicts and children will not be able to learn about conflict resolution skills. Hence an environment wherein children get the opportunity to resolve conflicts on their own would be important (Daros & Kovach, 1998). Selection of an appropriate strategy according to the need will guide further children's relationship. The selection of strategy is affected by various factors such as the behaviour of the peer, kind of relationship child share with peers, the material for which the conflict has occurred.

Thus both sharing and conflict resolution behaviours are interesting to study in the preschool context. There are possibilities that sharing may contribute as the source of conflict or conflicts may end with sharing. As mentioned by Deutsch, (1994), conflict resolution strategies are strongly associated with prosocial behaviour because it fosters the cooperative environment rather than competitive environment.

With reference to the age, younger children are able to resolve their conflicts with the use of bargaining, compromising, transforming and reconciliation stratagies on their own without any intervention of teachers (Killen & Turiel, 1991). Similar result is also found by Vespo and Caplan (1999). It has been found that children are able to resolve conflict through yielding such as crying and withdrawing from the activity. Among close friends children are also likely to continue their interaction through conciliatory gestures such as cooperation, offer and share objects. Vespo and Caplan also found that there were not any significant gender differences in resolving conflicts. One minor difference they found was that the boys were more likely to use conciliatory gestures in comparison to girls but they were unable to provide any clear reason behind this difference.

Teachers also play a very vital role in these behaviours. They provide social environment in the preschool where they can get opportunity to interact effectively with peers. Their support and guidance through verbal or non-verbal directive instructions are helpful to children for learning. It results into greater frequency of sharing behaviour among children than in the case of permissive instructions (Eisenberg & Fabes, 1997). Directly or indirectly adults influence on conflicts and their outcomes. Teacher's concern about child's safety, their beliefs about conflicts and negative outcomes of conflict, and their choices for resolving conflicts on behalf of children are contributing factors behind adult's intervention in the children's conflicts (D'Ros & Kovach, 1998).

Many times adults try to intervene before the resolution of conflict occurs. Killen and Turiel (1991) found that children received ready-made solutions from adults in their 91 per cent interaction with adults. Thus various outcomes of conflicts are possible such as child unwillingly accepts the dominance of others, drops conflicts, finds out mutually agreeable solutions and adult imposes the solution. Among all these aspects child's finding of mutually agreeable solutions is the only beneficial outcome for development of the child (Gillespie and Chick, 2001).

Theoretically it is evident that the period of 3 to 4 years of age is very important because developmental shift occurs during this period. Additionally children's entry to the preschool may also influence development of children. Children's social network expands from the immediate family members. Hence preschool set-up plays a major role in the development of children. Thus it was also relevant to examine their interactions in the free play situation and analyze the pattern of sharing behaviour and conflict resolution along the dimensions of gender, age and type of family. In the Indian context and specifically in the Hindu Gujarati family context there are limited studies about young children with reference to the early indicators of morality. Hence the present study is attempted to provide systematic understanding about the sharing and conflict resolution behaviour of children from Hindu Gujarati families with focus on the preschool context.

OBJECTIVES OF THE STUDY

The broad objective of the study was to explore the sharing and conflict resolution behaviours of 3 to 4 years old children in the preschool context. The specific objectives were as given below:

(1) Understanding the sharing behaviour of children in terms of nature, type of sharing and emerging pattern of sharing behaviour.
(2) Examining the conflict resolution behaviour of children with reference to source and nature of conflict, strategies of conflict resolution and the role of adult.
(3) Finding out the differences along the dimension of gender with special reference to sharing and conflict resolution.

METHOD

A descriptive research design was used.

Sample

The study comprised of 20 Hindu Gujarati children, 12 boys and 8 girls, in the age range of three to four years from younger group of Chetan Balwadi, Laboratory nursery school, the Department of Human Development and Family Studies, Faculty of Home Science, The Maharaja Sayajirao University of Baroda. The sample was identified purposively. The teacher of Younger group was also part of the sample.

Tools

The tools used for data collection were:

(i) *Observation guidelines*: It was developed for observation of sharing and conflict behaviours in the free play situations. Guideline regarding sharing behaviour consisted of nature and type of sharing whereas guidelines regarding conflict resolution comprised of nature of conflicts, strategies of conflict resolution and role of adults.

(ii) *Simulated tasks*: It consisted of four tasks about eatables, toys or play material and objects for knowing specifically about children's views on sharing.

(iii) *Teacher's interview*: Teacher's perception regarding sharing and conflict resolution behaviour and for seeking information about each child in terms of these behaviours.

Procedure

The investigator received training for one week in the local Gujarati medium school followed by the pilot study to find out applicability of the tool and to understand the process of data collection. The data was collected through observations during two indoor and one outdoor free play sessions. Each child was observed for 90 minutes wherein each session comprised of 30 minutes with the observation pattern of 10 minutes of observation and 5 minutes of break. Out of 30 minutes the net observation per session was for 20 minutes amounting to total 60 minutes. The running records were taken for each child who was considered as the focus child. Interaction with peers was also recorded in detail. During five minutes break field worker notes regarding the situations, location and other aspects of children's behaviour were noted. The major aim of observation in free play session was to understand the occurrence of behaviour in the natural everyday interaction and also to find out the effects of environmental resources on children's sharing and conflict resolution behaviours. Each child was observed within the period of ten days for maintaining consistency in the data. Simulated tasks and teacher's interview were done after completion of the children's observations.

The data was analyzed both qualitatively and quantitatively. Frequencies and percentages were calculated since the nature of data had in multiple responses.

RESULTS AND INTERPRETATIONS

Sharing Behaviour

Results regarding the sharing behaviour are computed on the basis of number of responses obtained and presented in the form of percentages. The data collected through observations was analysed quantitatively in terms of percentages. Information gathered from simulated tasks was analysed both quantatively and gualitatively, whereas the data obtained from teacher's interview was analysed mainly qualitatively.

The overall sharing behaviour of children with peers and adults indicates maximum sharing occurred with peers. Also sharing with adults was more in symbolic forms through pretend play (Fig.18.1).

Fig. 18.1 : Overall Sharing Behaviour

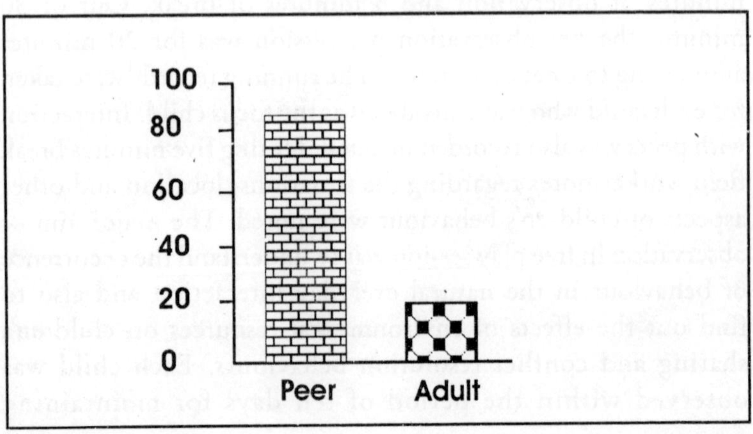

Boys shared maximum in the manipulative area, whereas girls preferred to share in the dollhouse, indicating almost twice the percentage of sharing in comparison with boys. These differences perhaps reflect the gender stereotypic choices of children for selection of toys and play material.

Children shared play material, space and adult's attention with peers, whereas with adults, children like to share play materials exclusively but it occurred through Pretend play of children where they would prepare some kind of food and on request of adults children would share with them.

Table 18.1 : Sharing Behaviour of Children in terms of Gender and Type of Family (N=20)

Type of Sharing	*Gender (%)*		*Type of Family (%)*	
	Boys (n=12)	*Girls (n=8)*	*Joint (n=12)*	*Nuclear (n=8)*
Play material	94.1	52.8	75.0	94.4
Adult's attention	—	7.7	3.6	—
Space	5.9	38.5	21.4	5.6

Note : Multiple responses.

Table 18.1 indicates that boys shared more play materials in comparison with girls, whereas adult's attention and space were exclusively shared more by girls. This is an interesting finding. One of the reasons could be the age of the boys because boys are little older than girls. Thus they are perhaps more able to consider demands of others.

With reference to type of family, it clearly shows that children from nuclear family shared maximum play material than children from joint family. Several factors like availability of resources and play materials, number of children present in the family, ordinal position of child and family income play major role behind sharing behaviour of the children. In case of boys it was found that they had same sex preferences for sharing while girls were found to share equally with boys and girls. It is also mentioned in the literature that during preschool years children would have more same sex preferences (Hartup, 1989). Though it is not present in case of girls. Perhaps girls were more open and also more girls belonged to joint families.

With reference to the outcome of sharing the data reveals that children responded positively to the demand of peer across gender and type of family variables. Although a high rate of sharing is found among boys, they also refused maximum to share though ignoring the demands of peers. Refusal was often verbal or non-verbal mode of behaviour.

Results obtained from the simulated tasks revealed that boys like to share eatables with others but surprisingly the boys would like to share more with adults in the preschool as well as in the home and that is not present in the case of girls. Boys expressed to share with the neighbourhood peers, whereas girls expressed to share with their relatives as the maximum number of girls is living in the joint family. In terms of sharing play material no clear difference emerged but girls showed preferences to share with close friends and boys also refused to share. With reference to favourite play material boys preferred to share manipulative kits followed by blocks and vehicles. Some of them also preferred to play with utensils and dolls. Whereas most of the girls preferred to play with various accessories of the doll house. The findings of sharing behaviour through observations are further confirmed by children's responses about sharing play material and context of occurrence of sharing, from the simulated tasks.

Conflict Resolution

The overall occurrence of conflicts among boys and girls is described in Fig. 18.2. It indicates that boys had more conflicts in comparison with girls.

Fig. 18.2 : Overall Conflict Occurrence

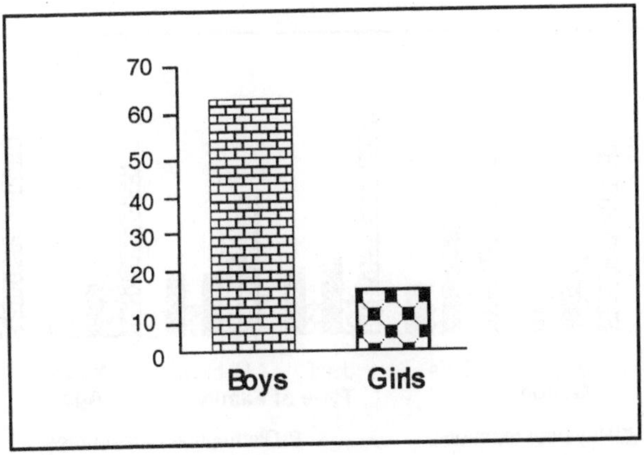

Context of occurrence of conflict in terms of areas indicates that girls had maximum conflict in the doll house whereas boys had more conflicts in the manipulative area. Results are similar to the sharing behaviour where girls found to share more in the doll house and boys found share more in manipulative area. Thus it reveals that the kind of materials available in various areas of the classroom tends to influence the children's sharing and occurrence of conflict.

With reference to the outdoor area girls had more conflicts than boys. During outdoor freeplay girls has more conflicts, as it demanded turn taking of the material and specifically on swings where many girls preferred to spend their time. Whereas boys had more conflicts in terms of hitting, kicking, throwing sand on each other. Thus boys tried to express their physical energies freely during outdoor freeplay whereas girls preferred to take turns and negotiate with peers.

Sources of conflicts in relation to gender, type of family and age of the child are presented in Fig. 18. 3. It clearly depicts that among children the most common conflict occurred that involved physical reaction followed by teasing and calling names.

Fig. 18.3 : Sources of Conflicts in terms of Gender, Type of Family and Age of the Child

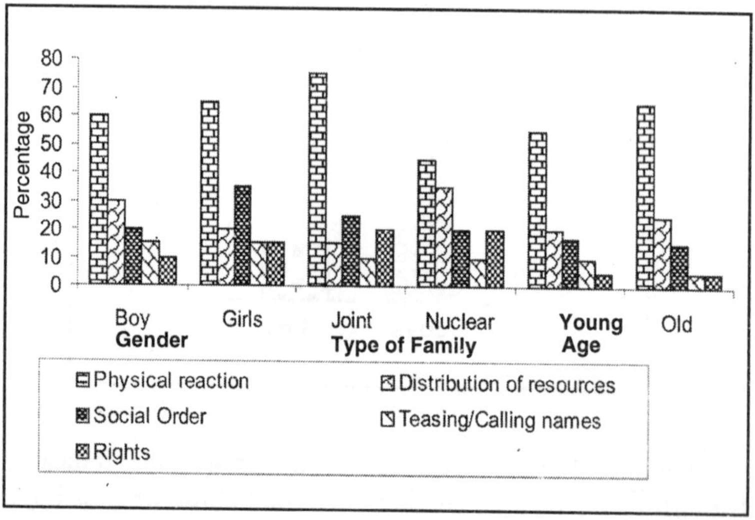

This was done more often by children for accessories of doll house. Distribution of resources such as sharing and turn taking were also responsible for conflicts among them. Whereas rights and social order was found to occur least among children. These categories of sources of harm were adapted from Killen and Turiel (1991).

With reference to gender boys had more conflicts in terms of physical reactions and teasing or calling names whereas girls had more conflicts because of physical reactions and distributions of resources. Children from the joint family had more conflicts because of physical reactions. The reason could be their socio- economic status where resources are limited, employment of mothers was about 16.6 per cent and/or 8.3 per cent of children had the previous experience of day care programmes. In terms of age, younger children has less conflict than older children. This finding also links with the variable of gender because 80 per cent girls were younger and girls had less conflict in comparison with boys.

Children used various strategies for resolving conflicts. Certain stratagies were child-generated, some are generated by adults whereas some are not resolved. It is presented in Table 18. 2 with reference to the variables of gender and type of family. It clearly reveals that children themselves resolved many conflicts. Physical stratagies were used maximum across both variables. Boys used verbal strategies maximum than girls. Whereas girls used strategies like reconciliation, seeking attention and giving back play material to the peer. So girls did not comply further against his or her actions. Perhaps the reason behind this could be the socialization of girl child where they are expected to be more obedient and follow instructions of parents and other elders.

Table 18. 2: Conflict Resolution Strategies in terms of Gender and Type of Family (N=20)

Resolution Strategies	*Gender (%)*		*Type of Family (%)*	
	Boys (n=12)	*Girls (n=8)*	*Joint (n=12)*	*Nuclear (n=8)*
Child-generated				
Bargaining, negotiating, compromising transforming	12.9	14.4	11.0	18.4
Reconciliation	4.3	9.5	8.2	2.8
Verbal strategies	14.2	4.8	6.9	17.9
Physical strategies	41.5	31.0	38.4	36.4
Seeks attention and gives play material	1.4	16.6	9.6	2.8
Sub Total	74.3	76.3	74.1	75.5
Adult-generated	15.7	16.6	19.0	10.3
Topic dropped	10.0	6.1	6.9	12.8

Note: Multiple responses.
Source: Terms are adapted from Killen & Turiel, 1991.

Children from joint family compromised relatively less. Generally in the joint family because of availability of limited resources and due to presence of more family members there are chances of equal distribution. Thus one has to compromise against one's wishes to get more is the general expectation among the people that is not always true. Maximum difference was also evident in children from nuclear families in terms of application of verbal stratagies for resolving their conflicts. Children from joint families sought more help of adults or peers for resolving conflicts that shows they had many adults for responding their need. In terms of adult generated strategies adults intervened for boys more often. In case of girls there was more adult interference. The reason could be that in the classroom apart from teachers there were about five student trainees from undergraduate and graduate courses offered by the Department of Human Development and Family Studies. Thus their orientation and ways of thinking and responding to conflict and conflict resolution strategies could be one reason. In terms of the topic dropped strategy with reference to the gender girls used moderately more times to drop their conflicts. Whereas boys were found to be dependent on others.

Various behaviours also emerged as an outcome after resolution of the conflicts such as positively agreeing, ignoring, changing place, starts playing again, stops playing, changing theme of play, and becoming upset. Majority of the children liked to change their place and start playing again after resolving their place and start playing again resolving their conflicts.

With reference to the role of adults, adult generated resolution strategies tried to direct behaviours of children. So that children can learn certain school rules, conventional rules or moral rules. The kind of strategies used by adults either by intervention or by interference.

Specific strategies like diverting children's interview revealed that boys preferred to share with close friends more in comparison with girls. The results obtained from the observations of sharing behaviour were similar with the results of the teacher's interview where boys had same sex preferences and shared more frequently than girls.

The perceptions of teacher in terms of conflict resolution indicated that both boys and girls were using physical strategies like pushing, pulling, hitting or biting the child more frequently than any other strategies. Again results are similar with the results of the observations where both boys and girls had used maximum physical strategies to resolve their conflicts. Gender differences for resolving one's conflicts is again evident in the teacher's perceptions that boys resolved their conflicts very actively through various strategies whereas girls preferred to take help from the peer to resolve their conflicts.

Discussion

Sharing behaviour among young children is necessary to understand specifically in the preschool setting for finding out the developmental trend. At the same time conflict and conflict resolution strategies are also essential to study for knowing about the individual and group dynamics of development (Ross & Conant, 1992). In the preschool context children have opportunity to learn about sharing and conflict resolution strategies from peers and teachers. Thus preschool is an important context for observing children's behaviours and development.

The study reveals that three to four years old children are able to share play materials, adult's attention and space with their peers as well as with adults. Thus the result of the present study are found to be consistent with the results of Rao and Stewart (1999) who found that Asian preschoolers are able to share more frequently in comparison of the American children. One major reason could be the cultural factor, the Indian tradition is also oral tradition and there is adequate scope for children to interact with a lot of people. The day-to-day interaction encourage children to relate to others and under-stand their needs.

With reference to the gender results show that boys shared more materials than girls. In connection to this Rao and Stewart (1999) did not find any gender differences in the Indian preschool.

There are very few Indian studies on sharing behaviour of young children.

Findings of the simulated tasks indicate that 75 per cent girls preferred to share with their relatives and it is interesting to note that most of the girls are belonged to the joint family. Thus it indicates that family's relatedness influences on the interpersonal relationship of the children. Culture influences the people in which they live. India is a collectivist society where individuals are related and bound with each other. In collectivist culture interpersonal relatedness is valued more rather than interpersonal separateness (Kagitcibasi, 1996). Thus for maintaining interpersonal relatedness with each other adults themselves encourage children for sharing.

Not only teacher or caregivers play significant role in guiding sharing behaviour but context is also important. Here in the laboratory school children are encouraged to express their needs, thoughts and feelings in verbal and other creative and graphic forms. The programme focuses on self-expression so children are encouraged to engage in role plays, creative movements and conversations.

Regarding the sex preferences boys have shown more sex preferences for sharing in comparison with the girls. With view to this Eisenberg and Hand (1979) found same sex preferences among girls for sharing. Thus during preschool years sharing behaviour of children is influenced by sex of the child. It is also evident that younger children found more difficult to share as it is reflected by their refusal to share or threatening peer for sharing.

With reference to the specific type of sharing especially about adult's attention it is evident that children from the joint families shared easily than children from nuclear families. Whereas regarding the overall sharing, children from the nuclear families shared more frequently in comparison with children from joint families. Sharing is often related to the conflict. Results revealed that two to three per cent request/demand for sharing behaviour of children led to conflicts among them. With reference to the conflict resolution behaviour the study reveals that preschool children in the age range of three to four years were able to resolve maximum conflicts on their own and certain conflicts were resolved by adults or some were dropped.

Gender differences were also evident. Boys had more conflicts than girls and reason could be age of the girls, who are younger than boys. While interacting with others boys tried to exert their power and status whereas girls tried to sustain harmonious interaction (Putallaz & Sheppard, 1992). It is very well reflected in the kinds of conflicts where maximum emerged due to physical reaction like hitting, kicking, etc. followed by teasing/calling name. Conflicts regarding rights and social order also occurred. The study done by Killen and Turiel (1991) found that conflicts in terms of teasing and calling names were occurred maximum among preschoolers. Gender differences were also evident during reaction of the conflict wherein girls used more physical reactions whereas boys more verbal reactions to oppose the actions of the focus child. One of the reasons could be age of the girls as they are younger to the boys so perhaps boys had good language facility.

In terms of conflict resolution strategies study indicated that children were able to resolve their conflicts on their own. Again boys had used more physical strategies and girls had used more physical strategies like seeking adult's attention, reconciliation and giving back materials for resolving their conflicts. With reference to this Vespo and Caplan (1993) found that boys had used more conciliatory gestures for resolving their conflicts.

The findings about the relationship of sharing and conflict resolution behaviour are quite interesting. The relation between sharing and conflict was evident as children who shared more frequently were engaged maximum in conflict also. The results also indicate that the school rules, moral and conventional rules are merged. Literature also reveals that in the Indian context often these rules are mutually inclusive (Menon, 2003).

Thus results of the present study indicate that young children are able to share and resolve their conflicts. The behaviours tend to be influenced by gender, family typology, age and classroom context. Since the study was conceptualized within the socio-moral domain of development sharing and conflict resolution behaviours were examined as the precursors of morality. In the contemporary context it is relevant to examine how children operate and respond to the demands of peers. These findings attempt to provide useful information for teaching and guiding children in the early years. The study has scope to expand the coverage of sample across different ages and variety of school settings both government and private sectors.

REFERENCES

Benenson, J.F.; Markovits, H.; Roy, R.; & Denko, P. (2003). Behavioural rules underlying learning to share: Effects of development and context. *International Journal of Bhavioural Development,* 27 (2), 116-121

Berk, L.E. (1999). *Development through the life span* (pp. 402-405, 461-465), MA: Allyn and Bacon.

Berk, L. E. (2002). *Development through the life span* (2nd ed.) (pp. 252-254, 326-328). MA: Allyn and Bacon.

Bordman, S. K. & Horowitz, S. V. (1994). Constructive conflict management and social problems: An introduction. *Journal of Social Issues,* 50 (1), 1-12.

DaRos, D. A. & Kovach, B. A. (1998, Fall). Assisting toddlers and caregivers during conflict resolutions interactions that promote socialization. *Childhood Education,* 25-30.

Deutsch (1994). Constructive conflict resolution: Principles, training and research. *Journal of Social Issues,* 50 (1), 13-32.

Eisenberg-Berg, N. & Hand, M. (1979). The relationship of Preschoolers reasoning about prosocial moral conflicts to prosocial behaviour. *Child Development,* 50, 356-363.

Eisenberg, N. & Fabes, R (1997). Prosocial behaviour. In N. Eisenberg & W. Damon (eds.), *Handbook of Child Psychology* (Vol. 3): Social, Emotional and Personality Development. New York.

Gillespie, C.W. & Chick, A. (2001 summer). Fussbusters: Using peer to mediate conflict resolution in a head start classroom. *Childhood Education,* 192-195.

Goffin, S. G. (1987, January). Cooperative Behaviours: They need our support. *Young Children,* 75-81.

Harris, A. C. (1986). *Child development.* (pp. 429-432). West Publishing Company.

Hartup, W.W. (1989). Social relationship and their developmental significance. *American Psychologist,* 44(2), 120-126.

Hartup, W. W.; French, D. C.; Laursen, B; Johnston, M.K. & Ogawa, J.R. (1993). Conflict and friendship relations in middle childhood : behaviour in a closed field situation. *Child Development,* 64, 445-454.

Jones, E.; & Nimmo, J. (1999 January) collaboration, Conflict, and Change : Thoughts on education as provocation. *Young Children.*

Kagitcibasi, C. (1996). The autonomous — relational self : A new synthesis. *European Psychologist,* 1(3), 180-186.

Killen, M. & Turiel (1991). Conflict resolution in preschool social interactions, *Early Education and Development,* 2(3), 240-255.

Kostelink, E.; Smith, B.; Wheiren, W. & Soderman, P. (1998). *Guiding children's social development:* Dalmar Publishers. (pp. 359-381).

Menon, U. (2003). Morality and Context : A study of Hindu Understandings. In Jaon Valsiner & Kevin J. (eds). *Handbook of Development Psychology.* New Delhi. Thousand Oks.

Puttallaz, M. & Sheppard, B.H. (1992). Conflict management and social competence. In C.U. Shantz & W. W. Hartup (ed). *Conflict in child and adolescent development.* Cambridge University Press.

Rao, N. & Stewart, S.M. (1999). Cultural influences on shares and **recipient** behaviour. *Journal of Cross-cultural Psychology,* 30(2), 219-241.

Ross, H.S. & Conant, C.L. (1992). The social structure of early conflict : Interaction, relationships and alliances. In C.U. Shantz & W.W. Hartup (ed). *Conflict in child and adolescent development.* Cambridge University Press.

Stomfay-Stitz, A.M. (1994, Annual theme). Conflict resolution and peer mediation pathways to safer schools. *Childhood Education,* 279-289.

Torkington, K. & Landers, C. (1999). *Enhancing the skills of early childhood trainers.* (pp.3.84 to 3.91). Bernard Van Leer Foundation/UNESCO, Oxford & IBH Publishing Co.

Vespo, J.E. & Caplan, M. (1993). Preschoolers differential conflict behaviour with friends and acquaintances. *Early Education and Development,* 4(1), 45-53.

19 Coping with Stress among Indian Adolescents belonging to the High Income Group

Jigisha Gala and Sangeeta Chaudhary

Adolescence can be a stressful time not only for adolescents but also for parents and adults who work with the adolescents. Adolescents are dealing with the challenges of growing. They are going through puberty, meeting the changing expectations of others, and coping with feelings they might not have experienced before. The most common sources of day-to-day stress for adolescents are school-related problems or pressures; problems with peers, family issues or problems with parents; their own thoughts, feelings, or behaviours, for instance feeling depressed or lonely, getting into trouble because of their behaviour. These problems are amply routine for most adolescents.

Nevertheless some adolescents may have to deal with things that their peers may not have to face depending upon the environments in which they grow. Adolescents from lower income groups may have to face different problems, for instance stress of participating in household chores or some income generating activities, compared to the adolescents from high income groups where the pressures would vary. Adolescents belonging to the high income groups are more influenced by the social changes caused due to westernization. Therefore not only the stresses but also the subsequent coping could also deviate across different groups.

In the present study stress refers to the demands made on the adjustive resources of the individual. The ability to adjust and adapt to the changes induced by the stress in order to reduce its harmful impact is coping. The study fathoms the different ways by which adolescents cope with stress. Such knowledge may give direction to what adults could do to help adolescents.

Review of Literature

The period of adolescence amongst human beings is a time when extensive changes occur in the physiological and biological systems and behaviours. Psychologists in the west have identified this stage as a phase of stress, strain and storm. However, in traditional India with the *Gurukula* system, this has not been the case. In recent years education systems seek to get a value for money and, therefore, have rigorous and inflexible curriculum based on narrow political vision overlooking the all-round human development: physical, mental and spiritual. Consequently, the present education system creates much stress as it encourages competition and comparison between individuals while the *Gurukula* helped pupils gain an understanding of interconnectedness of individuals and existence.

Recent historical events have drastically changed the experience of adolescence, in some ways making it more difficult than ever before. Hamburg and Takanishi (1989) account these changes and following are the considerations:

1. The period of adolescence has lengthened. In the United States 150 years ago, the average age of menarche was 16 years, and today it is 12 and half years. The trend for boys is similar but harder to document.
2. The disjunction between biological and social development i.e., they are reproductively mature (10-15 years) but social maturity lags behind.
3. Confusion about adult roles and difficulty in foreseeing the future.
4. Greater access to potentially life threatening activities—Adolescents are overpoweringly exposed not only to

> sexuality but also to alcohol and drugs, smoking, vehicles, and a variety of temptations to engage in health damaging behaviours that may appear tension relieving, however, the effects of which may endanger themselves and others.

In view of this we can discern that survival of the individual is based on how she/he perceives the stressor and cope with it. Hence in this study an attempt is made to gain insight into the ways adolescents cope with stress, along with consistencies and contrasts across the genders in ways of coping with stress and reasons for the same.

The review has been organized under sub-heads, beginning with grasping the concepts of adolescence, stress and coping and also recognizing the propinquity among the three constructs. Once this is understood, we move towards theoretical constructs related to coping and to few methodological considerations for studies related to coping, also apprehending the influence of gender and societal norms on coping and finally, to the conceptual framework of the study.

Adolescence —A Stage

'Adolescence' begins when hormones bring about physical changes to prepare the body for sexual reproduction, and ends in culture when one's status is defined by new role played in society as transition to adulthood begins (Grotevant, 2000 and Gardiner, Mutter and Kosmitzk, 1998). In many cultures, onset of each stage is marked by some ceremonies and the main purpose is public recognition (Gardiner *et al.*,1998).

Adolescence in the Western Context

Adolescence is as distinct phase has been recognized in the West, after 1900s. The factors accounting for this recognition are segregation of young people from adult and children, establishment of school and passage of laws for prevention of child labour due to the industrial revolution. The notion of adolescence was also strengthened by the works of Hall and Freud (Grotevent, 2000). Hall described this stage as a period of storm and stress (Arnett, 1999). In contemporary studies, Western scholars describe adolescence as a transition from childhood includes early, middle and late adolescence phases that concludes into young adulthood (Grotevent, 2000).

Adolescence in the Indian Context

In India 'adolescence' is a new term as compared to the West. Youth or Yuva are the common words used for adolescence in India (Singh, 1997 as cited in Saraswathi, 2002). The Hindu Model of *Ashramadharma* divides human life into four different stages, i.e. *Brahmacharya*, *Grihastha*, *Vrudha* and the *Vanaprastha Ashram*. Developmental progress through each of these stages necessitates acquisition of critical tasks associated with each of these stages in desired sequence and time frame (Pestonjee, 1997). *Brahmacharya* is a stage of apprenticeship, which is characterized by industry and acquisition of competence. However, the notion of industry in this context is in contrast with the western notion of identity crises and role confusion given by Erikson, conceding to the different time frame and the perspectives with which these theories were evolved. For example, in India the roles were duty based and predefined according to age, gender and class, therefore, there was no scope for role confusion. Nonetheless in the present scenario, this contrast has been reducing as roles become obscure due to westernization.

Another interesting feature as pointed out by Saraswathi (1999) is that the process of transition from childhood to adulthood is gendered and class based in India. For example, there is greater continuity between childhood and adulthood in traditional settings while in the contemporary Indian society for upper and middle class the discontinuity is greater. Upper class adolescents enjoy greater freedom due to less supervision of parents and have an easy access to material resources. They spend more time with peers as compared to adolescents belonging to other SES. Also child-adult continuity is more clearly evident in girls as the socialization to become good wives and mothers begins early in life.

Stress —A Concept

Today stress is a commonly used term. Stress is understood in relation to the stressor or with the feelings associated with it. Stress is both a physical as well as a mental condition, that pushes a person to change, grow, fight or adapt (Lazarus, 1976).

Stress in Indian Context

Stress in the modern sense is not found in the traditional Indian texts, two Sanskrit words, i.e. '*klesha*' (affliction) and '*dukha*' (pain, misery or suffering) approximate stress (as cited in Pestonjee, 1997). *Bhagwatgita* explains that '*Kama* or *Trishna*' (desires) are at the root of experiencing stress (as cited in Pestonjee,1997), as stress arises due to obstacles in fulfilment of desires. Palsane *et al.* (1986c) also notes that in contrast to the Western psychology where stress is believed to be produced by environmental events, in Indian psychology goals and expectations of the individuals bring to the potentially stressful situation. Personal goals and expectations indicate a separateness from the whole, i.e. is a feeling of '*aham*', which perceives the discord with the whole and hence is not in tune with it.

Coping — A Concept

Coping is management of stress or it can be explained as a process to overcome stressors or demands made on an individual. According to Lazarus, 1974, in stress literature word coping has two connotations:

1. It denotes the way of dealing with stress.
2. The effort to master the conditions of harm, threat or challenge when a routine or automatic response is not readily available (as cited in Pestonjee,1997).

Coping in Indian Context

The Indian tradition is characterized by a holistic approach to human phenomena. Behaviour is interpreted in terms of total body-mind relationship Palsane *et al.* (1986c). And since stress is a result of internal desires in the Indian context, then the management of stress will also be through internal control and understanding. The science of *Yoga* and meditation are Indian techniques that could relieve stress, however the design is to know '*advaita*' (non-duality), i.e. the transpositional level the '*Brahma*' or the ultimate reality.

Stress, Coping and Adolescents

According to Hamburg and Takanishi (1989), early adolescent period is characterized by experimentation that is developmentally appropriate and socially adaptive for most, but some of these behaviours carry high risks. In addition to these all youths are faced with a myriad of daily hassles such as preparing for exams, working through minor peer and family arguments, time-management challenges. Moreover the physical, social, hormonal and cognitive changes that accompany adolescence may lead to feeling of stress, anxiety and depression (Beta, 1994).

Although the experience of stress at some point during the adolescent years is common, most youth emerge through stressful periods without long-term negative effects. However, stress and depression are serious problems for many teenagers, as the 1986 study of Minnesota high school students reveals. These young people often rely on passive or negative behaviours in their attempts to deal with problems. Therefore, some adolescents are at a greater risk for the problems resulting from stress. Aaron T.E Bata (1994) has identified three types of factors that influence adolescent's vulnerability to negative effects of stress:

(a) The number of stressors that occur simultaneously in the life of a young person.
(b) The presence of internal and external assets in adolescents life such as self-esteem, feelings of competence, close friends, good social skills and trusting relationships with parents.
(c) Coping skills, adolescents who take specific and purposeful actions to change the source of the stress often fare better than those who use avoidance, denial, distraction or escape to try to deal with stress.

In the study conducted by Mehra (2003) and Kurian (2003) it was found that adolescents experience stress at home, school and peer and that there are gender differences in coping with stress and adolescents from different socio-economic states experience different stressors and cope differently. Also adolescents employ both effective and ineffective ways of coping. The Minnesota study of 1986 also reveals that certain coping behaviours doing something relaxing, trying positive and self-reliant problem-solving, or seeking friendship and support from others are appropriate for adolescents who are trying to become independent, take responsibility for themselves, and draw on friends and family for support. While others resorted to negative coping strategies such as yelling, fighting and complaining, drinking smoking and using doctor-prescribed drugs, sleeping, riding around in cars and crying more often (as cited in Mehta, Webb, 1996).

However, stress can be beneficial as well. In many instances stress encourages an adolescent to improve overall coping abilities and to concentrate on problem solving, mastery of a skills or learning various techniques to prevent similar triggers of stress from reoccurring in future.

Coping Research — Theoretical Constructs and Methodological Considerations

Theories of Coping

The identification of coping strategies used by individuals has led to the development of several theories for coping with stressors.

(1) First Lazarus and Folkman (1984) differentiated between problem focused coping and emotion focused coping.
(2) Second model proposed by Rothbaum, Weisz and Synder (1982) introduced the concept of primary control and secondary control.
(3) Cognitive-relational theory defines stress as a particular relationship between the person and the environment that is appraised by the person as taxing or exceeding his or her resources and endangering his or her well-being (Lazarus & Folkman, 1984b: 19). This theory has also been expanded recently to a meta-theoretical concept of emotion and coping processes (Lazarus, 1991, 1993a, 1993b; Lazarus & Folkman, 1987).

Methodological Considerations

There are three meta-theoretical assumptions: transaction, process, and context. Research has mostly neglected these meta-theoretical assumptions in favour of unidirectional, cross-sectional, and rather context-free designs. Hypothetical situations have been used in order to study the coping mechanisms of adolescents as these situations create a context and adolescents actively respond to the stressors. Also, on account of its complexity and transactional character leading to interdependencies between the involved variables, the meta-theoretical system approach cannot be investigated and empirically tested as a whole model. Rather, it represents a heuristic framework that may serve to formulate and test hypotheses in selected sub- areas of the theoretical system only. Thus, in practical research one has to compromise with the ideal research paradigm. However, stress has to be analyzed and investigated as an active, unfolding process rather than static states. Therefore, the use of hypothetical situations for the study of coping mechanisms offers to be the best alternative.

Classifying and Measuring Coping Processes

Although several attempts have been made to classify coping responses (Haan, 1977; Lazarus and Launier, 1978; Moos, 1976, 1977; Pearlin and Scholer, 1978), no accepted method has as yet emerged. For the present study the investigator has organized the dimensions of coping into three categories according to their primary focus, on dealing with the reality of situation; handling the emotion aroused by the situation or using recreation or entertainment in order to refocus on the situation after temporary digression.

Problem focused coping seeks to modify or eliminate the source of stress by logical analysis ("Introspect and analyze my mistake"), seek information or help ("take advice from my teacher"), take problem solving action("manage my time well"), this also includes negotiating, explaining, understanding, compromising to resolve the issue or developing alternative rewards ("I'll study for other subjects and score higher in them"). Emotion focused coping includes responses whose primary function is to manage the emotions aroused by stressors and thereby maintain affective equilibrium. For instance, affective control by suppressing ("I'll avoid fights") or maintaining a sense of pride("never apologize because I am egoistic"), resigned acceptance, i.e. deciding nothing can be done ("accept the way God has made me"), cognitive avoidance includes refusing to believe that the problem really exists or think unrealistically about the problem ("think my answers are not bad at all"), cognitive redefinition which includes accepting the reality of the situation and cognitively restructuring the problem to find something favourable in it ("think of my positive points"), emotional discharge which includes crying and talking out and engaging in impulsive act like shouting and getting angry. Digressing from the stressor includes engaging in some recreational or entertaining activity, i.e. taking a break away from the stressor for some time. This also includes alternative therapies and relaxation.

These categories are not mutually exclusive. Problem focused coping can help the person deal with the emotions aroused by a situation (studying for an exam may reduce anxiety; taking advice may generate emotional support), while emotional focused coping can provide the necessary sources to solve a problem (crying or shouting may communicate to the parents to stop nagging which was the source of stressor). Further more digression may reduce anxiety due to problem and help one in focusing on the problem (relaxing to reduce anxiety may help one in studying for an exam). The investigator shall use the preliminary classification scheme to categorize coping responses into three types, i.e. problem focused, emotion focused and digression. In using these categories the investigator has taken some liberties with the description provided by the original authors. These reformulation are justified by the need to develop conceptual domains of coping responses to understand the pattern of coping used by adolescents and also to form connections between coping responses and adaptational outcomes. There is a growing evidence that the use of such strategies such as logical analysis, cognitive redefinition, information seeking, problem solving action, emotional discharge such as crying can be positively related to adaptation while acting out on impulse,— cognitive avoidance may not lead to adaptation (Haan,1977; Valliant,1977; Weisman,1979).

Method

The central research question is : "What are the various coping ways that the adolescents perceive they would use to cope when under stress?" There is a focus on differences in these perceptions due to gender. This study is descriptive in nature.

Sample

Sixteen to eighteen years old adolescents studying in standard Xl and Xll belonging to the high income families, where their family's income ranges from Rs. 35,000-50,000 per month comprise the sample for the present study. Forty adolescents constitute the sample, out of which twenty are boys and twenty are girls. Academics emerged as a second major stressor in the previous study (Kurian, S., 2003), therefore, school-going adolescents belonging to standard Xl and Xll are studied. The income group is held constant so as to prevent this variable from intervening between the perception of the stress and subsequent coping. Sample was drawn by using purposive sampling technique.

Tool

Interview schedule using four hypothetical situations in the areas of stress related to academics, hetero-sexual relationship, teacher-student relationship and physical self-appearance was designed to yield indepth information regarding adolescents' perceptions of stress, major stressors, ways of coping with stress, parents attitude towards their coping ways and differences in these factors due to gender. The gender analysis framework developed by the Department for International Development (1999) [Guideline for the analysis of Gender and Health.U.K. DFID] was adapted and implemented, to provide information regarding gender differences in adolescents' perceptions of ways of coping with stress and parents attitude towards their coping ways.

Data Collection and Analysis

Adolescents were contacted and the permission to conduct and interview was sought from them and their parents. As per the appointments the investigator visited the adolescents at their homes and conducted an indepth interview. The language used was predominantly English while Hindi or Gujarati was used when preferred by the adolescents. Average time taken per interview was two hours. The responses were tape-recorded and transcribed. Data reduction charts, were formed for each interview and based on these charts, matrices were developed. Information related to the aspect of gender was incorporated into the Gender Analysis Framework for drawing interpretations and inferences.

Results and Interpretations

In general adolescents associate stress with tension or pressure, which is both physical and mental. Majority of adolescents report studies to be a major stressor. Adolescents adopt mind diverting or recreation related activities, when they respond to stress in general. Adolescents report awareness about a variety of alternative ways to cope with stress. The use of adaptive *vis-à-vis* maladaptive coping ways by the adolescents varies from situation to situation. Gender differences as well as similarities in coping ways of adolescents are noted which also vary from situation to situation. Most adolescents (58%) report coping with stress by indulging in some mind diverting or entertaining activity such as watching TV, reading or involving in some creative hobbies, when they are asked to respond to a stress in general. Few (5 %) adolescents also mention alternative therapies such as meditation and Reiki. Most (90%) of the girls prefer to break away from the stressor than to use problem focused or emotion-focused approach. Surprisingly only 30 % girls gave emotion-focused responses as compared to boys, who report 50 % emotion focused responses. Further, within emotion focused category, it is found that majority of the boys report forgetting about the problem or they deny anxiety caused due to it, while girls use emotional discharge positively by talking out or accepting the reality of the situation, therefore, indicating the use of more adaptive ways.

Adolescents' Perceptions about Coping with Stress in the given Situations

For the situation pertaining to academics similarities are observed between gender within the problem-focused category, i.e. negotiating with parents and managing time. Also responses of both boys and girls reveal understanding of parents concern. As explained by an adolescent "*I can understand their concern as these are our crucial years of studying. However, I will explain to them that relaxation is also important*" or "*Instead of doing things they don't like watching T.V., do what they like, i.e., talk to them or read newspaper*". However, in the emotion focused category adolescents state impulsive behaviour. More girls than boys reveal impulsive reactions towards parental restrictions. Yet, interestingly only girls mention unquestioned acceptance of parental expectations. Another gender difference is noted, where more girls report watching T.V. for taking a break from studies.

In heterosexual relationships 78% of adolescents have given problem-focused responses out of which 40% are given by girls. However, even though boys report apologizing to the girl for their mistake, they do it with 'qualifiers' such as "*apologize to her leaving my ego*" or "*apologize only once, if she does not understand I will forget about her*". While girls reveal that they would apologize and try to understand their mistake, so that they do not repeat it. This expounds that it is very difficult for boys to realize and accept their mistakes and further apologize for it. The egoistic temperament of boys may be a result of socialization. In contrast to boys, girls appear accommodative which suggest that relationships are very important for them. In heterosexual relationships surprisingly, out of the 30% emotion focused responses, 22.5% are given by boys. In all girls reveal impulsive emotional discharge while boys try to regulate emotions by maintaining false pride and not accepting the situations, both of which are not adaptive coping ways.

For the situation pertaining to teacher-student relation 59% of adolescents' responses are problem focused while 40% are emotion focused. Girls report 35% problem focused responses while boys report 25% for coping. Surprisingly, 4% more boys report emotion-focused responses in contrast to girls. Only boys express acting on impulse towards the teacher.

Seventy two per cent of adolescents' responses are problem focused, of which both boys and girls share 50% responses. More boys than girls have given emotion focused responses with stress caused due to physical appearance. Similarities are seen in the kind of responses within the categories, i.e. within the problem focused category, both boys and girls report taking some action to improve looks rather than seeking information about the problem. Within the emotion focused category most adolescent state accepting the reality and therefore, accepting one's physical appearance. However, more boys reveal this as compared to girls. This indicates that the social norm where girls are expected to look good affects the choice of coping here.

Across situations adolescents use problem focused approach more than the emotion focused approach. Taking a break away from the stressor is evident only in the domain related to academics. Most girls report problem focused approach of coping for the last two situations which are teacher student relations and physical appearance. Surprisingly more boys report emotional focused response across the last three domains that are heterosexual relationship, teacher student relations and physical appearance compared to the girls. In the domain related to academics, girls reveal more emotion focused responses, i.e. trying to see something good in the situation. This is more adaptive as one accepts the reality of the situation and restructures it. Also girls report using more of emotional discharge like "talking out with someone", i.e. expressing feelings more often *vis-a-vis* boys. Girls act on impulse only with parents while boys use it also with teachers. Girls also reveal more action-oriented coping towards the problem compared to boys. Cognitive avoidance is used more by girls for the physical appearance domain.

Awareness of the Various Alternative Coping Ways

As detailed in Appendices 75% of girls report awareness of the various alternative coping ways while 55% of the boys state the same. Adolescents' responses reveal that, they are aware about variety of coping ways. Strikingly, only one girl mentions about going to a psychologist. Also only girls mention the use of alcohol, drugs for coping while the boys mentioned about "eating to cope". Only two adolescents have given problem-focused responses when they are asked about coping alternatives in general. And, surprisingly both of them are girls.

Gender difference is observed here where girls reveal a number of entertainment and recreation activities. In alternate therapies, boys consider meditation and *yoga* as best ways, while girls have also added "aroma therapy". In activities girls mention gardening, cooking while boys mention more of physical activities like exercising and boxing.

Alternative Ways of Coping with Stress Across Situations

A variety of problem solving alternatives are reported across situations. Adolescents report various alternative ways of coping with stress. Across situations girls reported more number of alternative coping ways than boys. However, for the physical appearance domain, boys report more alternatives to cope. The teacher student relation domain includes 52% of problem focused responses. Again most of which are reported by girls. Under problem focused approach seeking help or advice from teacher, parents or friends is reported more by boys than girls. This is interesting because though more boys recount this alternative, they do not choose it as the best way to cope, which is in contrast to the girls. Girls also report more emotion-focused alternative than boys do, for the first two situations related to academics and heterosexual relationship. For the physical appearance domain boys report more emotion focused alternatives. This denotes that coping varies not only across gender but also across situations for the same gender.

Though there are differences in gender regarding the number of responses under each coping ways, similarities are observed in the kind of responses. For example, in domain related to teacher student relations, asking friends about effective methods to study is reported by both boys and girls under problem focused approach. Also it has the highest frequency for both genders. Similarly, focusing on other subjects is given second preference by both genders. Again digression is reported more for the situation related to academics similarly by both. For the physical appearance domain, similarities between gender is observed where both boys and girls reveal emotion focused responses compared to the other domains. The adolescents use affective regulation and cognitive redefinition i.e. they are working at their feelings regarding the stress and also trying to look at something positive in the situation, which is adaptive.

However, the emotion-focused responses in the teacher-student relations domain reveal more impulsive behaviours and avoidance by both genders which may not be adaptive.

Adolescents' Perception about Best Coping Alternative

For the academics domain, 63% adolescents report problem focused approach to be the best alternatives, 38% of which are girls. 5% responses are emotion focused out of which boys give both of them.

In the digression category, 40% adolescent report taking a break away from studies for some time, 22.5% of these responses are of boys. Here it can be noted that most adolescents have shifted from emotion-focused responses to problem-focused responses.

For the situation related to heterosexual relationship, 79% adolescents report problem-focused approach. Here girls report about seeking help from parents and elders, while boys report to seek help only from friends. Out of the 12% of adolescent who choose emotion-focused responses, girls (10%) reports most of them. Here girls display adaptive ways of emotional discharge while boys report denial.

For the domain teacher student relation as depicted in Appendices, 81% adolescent prefer problem-focused approach. Here 13% adolescent select emotion focused approach, where boys report maladaptive responses like avoiding the situation and rationalization, and girls report accepting the situation as it is. Boys (6%) report seeking recreation and entertainment as a best coping alternative.

As seen in Appendices, 74% adolescent select problem focused responses. More girls (43%) than boys give problem-focused responses. Here 27% of adolescent report emotion focused responses out of which 15% are boys. Boys report cognitive redefinition, i.e. looking for good points and accepting self more than girls. Girls prefer to remain passive in the emotion-focused category.

Adolescents' Perception about Need and Importance of Appropriate Ways of Coping and Reasons for the Same

Ninety eight per cent respondents felt that it is important for adolescent to be aware of adaptive coping ways. However one boy felt it was not important as *"adolescent is an age to experiment and so they need not be made aware of. They can experience and learn from it and cope on their own"*. Presence of too many stressors; existence of mal-adaptive coping mechanisms and the susceptibility of adolescents to both good and bad influences emerge as major reasons for the need and importance of adaptive coping for adolescence. Adolescents recognize that what they do for coping may not always lead to relaxation. For instance, *"watching TV would not relax our mind"*. This indicates adolescents seek support and guidance from adults and acknowledge that adults can suggest better strategies to cope with stress. Also they report *Adolescence is an age when you experiment different methods to cope, which may not be appropriate."*

Ideal Ways of Coping for a Boy and Girl

Both girls and boys feel that boys keep things to themselves, however, they must also talk out things to someone close to relieve stress. As a girl reports *"boys should also talk to parents or siblings but if not possible to friends"*. Another instance where a boy admits, *"under highly frustrating situations anybody would want to talk"*. Girls further explain that *"boys take to bad habits like smoking because they don't share things, they get frustrated by keeping things inside themselves"*. Talking things out with parents is considered best for girls by both genders and boys also feel that *"girls are more close to parents"*. Girls report crying for themselves as well as for boys. A boy also unveils that he would cry at times and not care when people say "*kya ladkio jaise rota hai*". This displays that adolescents feel the need of catharsis and consider it helpful and positive for relieving stress for both genders. Yet, social norms make catharsis difficult for boys. This manifests in other forms of aggressive behaviours observed in boys. Both boys and girls feel that girls prefer to watch T.V. while boys prefer going out with friends.

The study also includes the Gender Analysis Framework (Appendices), which depicts that difference in adolescents' coping ways are chiefly due to differences in temperaments of the boys and girls, activities preferred by them and due to social norms. Parental attitude towards adolescents' coping ways is also perceived to vary due to differences in temperaments of the boys and girls and social norms. Parents are perceived as understanding and supportive, in case of the academics and physical appearance domain by most of adolescence. However, in the two domains dealing with relationships most adolescents feel that parents will give suggestions as to how to cope. More number of adolescents perceive gender difference in parental attitude for domains related to the hetero-sexual relationship and physical appearance. Chiefly boys perceive this difference than the girls. Adolescents report "*conservatism*" as a factor for such differences. A girl relates *"They'll be less concerned if I were a boy as society always points out girl's mistake*". Or as boys reports *"Parents feel insecure with girls, because of which they'll be more strict".*

Discussion

Common understanding and scientific literature reveal that adolescence could be a difficult phase of life. The way in which individuals experience this stage today is different when compared with the earlier times. This may be attributed to the changing scenario especially where the traditional societies are undergoing transition. The more westernized these societies become, the more the adolescents experience role confusion (Thomas, 2001).

This transition can be illustrated by considering the changes in India. In traditional India, the problem of role confusion or Erikson's identity crisis did not exist. People belonged to the specific *'varnas'* and were prescribed specific roles and tasks. Notwithstanding the influence of the social changes due to globalization, modernization and more importantly westernization, Indian adolescents face similar problems like "role-confusion" as faced by adolescents in the West. In addition to this they also experience conflict between their traditional values and the Western values. Adolescents also report 'authority crisis' as reported by Kakar, S. and Chowdhry, A. (1970). 'Authority crisis' relates to the decreasing capacity of familial, educational, religious, social and political institutions to command Indian youth.

Influence of westernization is most evident among the high-income adolescents. This is so because they are particularly susceptible to western influences as a result of greater exposure to the western cultures. In addition to this the affluent groups have the necessary means and resources required to adopt the western life styles. The manner in which these adolescents dress; the kind of language used, for instance "*tell my parents to shut up as I know best what I am doing*" or "*If adolescents cannot cope with stress they would 'screw up' their lives*", peer culture and rebellion towards authority is evidence for the above. Another argument is related to the *status quo.* The low-income groups are susceptible to the influence of the middle-income groups while middle-income group compete with the higher income groups, and the high-income group contest with the West. However, western influence does not completely erase the Indian values or *'sanskars'*. In this case it is noted that, in spite of the rebellious attitude displayed by the Indian Youth or *yuva*, they also show concern and respect for the authority. For instance, though adolescents report *"I know what's best for me"* or "*Tell parents I am responsible enough*", these phrases usually precede "*I can understand their concern however...*" or "*parents tell us for our own benefit yet I would like to take my own decisions*".

Owing to the rapid changes and stresses associated with them we can conceive that this competitive environment may be hard on adolescents, as well as their parents and other concerned adults. Here again we can comment that the parental stress would vary across the different SES, as coping requires mobilizing different resources. The ability to mobilize these resources shall impact on parental attitude towards adolescent coping options and hence shall affect adolescent coping ways. In the present study adolescents have stated problem solving options such as "*Go to dermatologist to improve looks*" or *"Change my wardrobe and wear trendy clothes"* or *"my parents will provide me all that I need to improve my studies, such as good books, tuitions and everything"* which many of their peers belonging from middle or lower SES might not have considered practical as these options are expensive. One adolescent boy also considered going for a surgery for it is a sure way to improve looks!

"Stress war" business has already crossed $ 9.4 in America since 1996 (data compiled from internet sources). In India also we may expect similar trends where many people are investing time and money to learn about stress busters. Ancient Indian stress-relievers such as *yoga* and meditation have gained much importance and they attract the west also towards the east. *Yoga* and meditation are sciences that are concerned with all aspects of human functioning. *Yoga* science provides a unifying framework by which stress can be understood and eliminated and meditation is a systematic method that allows us to understand oneself and the environment at various levels, thus eliminating inner conflicts and creating peace (Pestonjee,1997).

The respondents of the present study have also acknowledged increase in the number of stressors experienced by the adolescents today. For instance, *"There is so much competition today. Life is much more complex because apart from stress due to academics we face stress in relationship, there is peer pressure and there is a need to be popular".* Further in the present study it is reiterated that adolescence as a stage itself is stressful, in words of an adolescent "*small things can worry an adolescent*".

Therefore one may ask, are the adolescents today able to cope and adapt to the rapid changes taking place within themselves and their environments? It is encouraging to note that in the present study, adolescents reveal awareness about a variety of coping alternatives which encompass action-oriented problem solving behaviours, information seeking behaviours, use of emotional discharge, affective regulation and cognitive restructuring of the problem. Other ways detailed are alternative therapies like meditation, *yoga* and *reiki.*

Moreover, adolescents also reveal knowledge about various maladaptive coping ways under a given situation, which means they are aware of the pitfalls as well. However, is the knowledge about the various coping alternatives and their benefits and pitfalls adequate? Probably not, as observed in the study, illustrations are as follows:

- Incomplete knowledge about the coping way. For instance, a boy reports that "*Meditation and Yoga are said to relieve stress, however I think it is good only for a while, ek,do minute aankhe band karne se kya hota hai, as one has to face the reality at some point".*
- Maladaptive strategy seems convenient or easy. As a boy illustrates *"Talking bad things about the teacher to the friends is easier than doing qualitative studying".*
- Rigidity in one's temperament: For instance, "*Frankly, I*

am egoistic. I'll never say sorry. I'll forget about her even if that makes me cry".

- Societal expectations/gender norms: The present study reveals that coping among adolescents is governed by societal expectations. As a girl illustrates *"It is better to change my attitude, but I'll change my appearance,"* i.e. though the girls prefer to use an emotion focused approach, like cognitive redefinition, they end up taking a problem solving action as in this case. This is because society expects girls to look good. In the same vein a boy tells "*boys are beyond looks, girls need to care more for it, so best is to not care"*. Here the boy instead of using a problem focused alternative like "*improving on looks*" prefers to use cognitive avoidance which may not be adaptive, because even for the boys physical appearance is a cause of concern at this age. Kurian, S. (2003) describes that more boys feel stressed due to biological changes and physical appearance, as they cannot share the anxiety caused due to it with their parents while girls can easily communicate their concerns with their mothers.

Therefore, awareness and knowledge about coping alternatives does not necessarily guarantee the choice of adaptive coping option as there are other factors that influence the selection of coping ways. Getting information about effective coping mechanisms is very easy in this age of information technology. In addition to this adolescents need guidance regarding how to use the knowledge effectively. Also at times the information available to them is inappropriate. As few adolescents felt that meditation is a form of escapism! One can understand this from the adolescent's perspective because he/she may be right in thinking that when one is stressed; one can use the stress for solving the problem rather than trying to relax in vain! However those who have known meditation would differ here and can help adolescents to use this stressful opportunity to not just do the best to understand the problem but also use it to gain an insight into the self, which is perceiving and experiencing the stress and simultaneously making efforts to cope with it. Moreover management of stress will actually be the by-product of meditation rather than the goal. As meditation, *yoga* are techniques that help the individual change from within, therefore, it may help the person to change the very perception of stress.

For the adolescents to cope in an adaptive manner, they need support may be in terms of appropriate role models especially from their parents and teachers. The present study shows that a number of adolescents prefer to turn to their parents and teachers for help, apart from their peers, as explained by an adolescent *"Parents can guide us better than friends, as our friends are as immature as us".* This finding is in contrast to earlier researches (Kurian, 2003) and the general notion that mainly their peers influence adolescents. Nevertheless adolescents' preferences regarding approaching parents over friends varies depending on the stressor. Yet, before we discuss about what parents and adults can do to assist adolescents, it is essential to understand the patterns of adolescent coping.

How do adolescents cope with stress? Some adolescents withdraw from others, some lash out at others, and some actively seek the comfort of others. Although adolescents cope with stress in different ways, there are general patterns in their coping behaviours. Adolescents' coping ways that emerge in the study can be categorized into: problem focused; which involves trying to deal with the problem by changing the situation or working towards the problem. Another way of handling stress is managing emotions; which involves handling the thoughts and feelings caused by the problem. Adolescents use both methods, and both can be effective, depending on what the problem is. The present study unfolds that people who deal with their problems, see the positive side of difficult situations, and take part in activities they enjoy are more likely to be well adjusted. Acting to solve problems often requires planning and learning new skills. For example, coping with poor grades might require learning study skills and managing time. Managing emotions can also be helpful in the early stages of coping with a problem. For example, talking out, crying out and positive thinking can be important ways of getting prepared to cope more directly with difficult situations. Another way of resolving stressful situations is to find meaning in the experience. It helps if youngsters can see that something good is coming out of the problem.

Finally, doing something enjoyable provides 'time out' from stress. It often "*recharges batteries*" so the person can go back to dealing with stress. Similar patterns of coping among adolescents has been reviewed by Ebata (1996).

Comparing coping ways between gender shows that some of the findings related to gender differences in coping ways are consistent with previous studies in this area. Biswas (1989) reveals that girls show greater patience in a frustrating situation while boys use denial more and tend to evade blame altogether. These emerging gender differences also matched with the perceived gender differences in the present study. For an example a girl narrates, *"As boy I would have not pursued the subject further, as a girl I am more patient."* A boy also confesses *"A girl can easily express her feelings to her beloved, as a boy I prefer forgetting the situation"*. Other illustrations are: a girl "*as a boy I would have been very immature*". A boy *"girls are more sensible at times"*. Boys reveal more problem-focused responses for some situations while girls for others. Similarly, boys are more prone to emotional focused coping under certain stressors. Girls reveal more adaptive use of emotion focussed approach' *vis-à-vis* boys. Similarities between the genders have also been observed. Overall across situations adolescents are more problem focused.

The social changes taking place also has affected the family structure and parenting styles. The present study reveals that adolescents' perceive that their parents are understanding and supportive. For instance, a girl reports, "My parents are very practical. They will understand my problems and bend rules for me". Parents deal with offsprings in a more responsive and democratic way than before as cited by Aggarwaly (2003). However broader social forces at work undermine the best intentions of both parents and teachers. Materialism and the focus on individualism, have both gained a dominance in Western culture which is undermining the best efforts of those seeking to offer a closer representation of the truth of being human.

Another aspect about adolescent coping as the study reveals is that adolescents coping ways vary under varying situations. As observed in the results for some situations, adolescents are more likely to use problem focused approach *vis-à-vis* the emotion focused approach. Also variation in responses is observed within the emotion focused approach, i.e. more adaptive responses like cognitive redefinition and restructuring of the problem, emotional discharge like crying etc. for some situations while more of cognitive avoidance, acting on impulse like getting angry for other situations.

Some investigators have tried to address this issue by assessing the same coping responses in different situations. For instance, Sidle, Moos, Adams, and Cady (1969) examined individual and situational consistence in coping strategies by obtaining information about the use of 10 coping responses in each of three problem-story situations. They found some individual consistency (respondents tended to use preferred coping responses irrespective of the problem situation), as well as some situational variability (the three stories elicited different coping responses). Folkman and Lazarus (1980) unroll that both problem-focused and emotion-focused responses are used in nearly every coping episode. There is some stability in the use of specific coping responses for a person across episodes, but in general individuals were characterized more by variability than by stability in coping patterns. This kind of individual stability and variance in coping across situation has not been examined in the present study.

Finally, we come to discuss the role of parents in facilitating adaptive coping. Adults can help adolescents to solve problems and manage their emotions in at least three ways. They can provide help, encouragement, and support during times of stress. They can help them develop the knowledge and skills to cope with future difficulties. And adults can get help for themselves when they need it. Parents may model effective coping skills and can encourage youth to develop a particular area of knowledge, talent, or skill to give them strong feelings of competence. They may help adolescents learn and practice problem-solving skills and develop social skills.

There are implications for future research. As pointed out in the present study, parents/teachers support is crucial for adolescents to cope with stress. Hence it becomes important to examine the coping mechanisms of parents and teachers. The correlation between parental coping ways with adolescent coping ways may be explored.

REFERENCES

Aggarwal, N. (2003). *Construction of Adolescence from the viewpoints of middle class Hindu-Gujurati adolescents and parents.* Unpublished master's thesis, Maharaja Sayajirao University, Baroda, (India).

Aldwin, 1984; Boss,1989; Doherty & Campbell, 1988. The coping and stress profile (pp. 2-5), Inscape Publishing Inc.(online) http\\www.inscape publishing.co.

Arnett, J.J. (1999), Adolescent storm and stress reconsidered, *American Psychologist,* 54 (5), 317-326.

Batra, P. (2001). *Simple ways to manage stress.* New Delhi: Think Inc.

Chauhan, S.S. (1983). *Psychology of adolescence,* Allied Publishers: New Delhi.

Craig, C.J. (1996). *Human Development* (7th ed.). New Jersey: Prentice Hall.

Davis, A. & Balladino (1997). *Psychology*-2 (2nd ed.). New Jersey, Prentice Hall.

Department for International Development, Social Development, Division (January 1999). *Guideline for the analysis of gender & health,* U.K.: Liverpool School of Tropical Medicine.

Dubois, D.L.; Frener, R.D.; Brand, S.; Adan, A.M.; Evans, E.G. (1992). A prospective study of life stress, social support and adaptation in early adolescence, *Child Development,* 63, 542-557.

Fontana, D. (1996). *Managing stress.* New Delhi: Excel Books.

Gardiner, W.H., Mutter, D.J. & Kosmick, C. (2002). *Lives across culture-cross cultural human development.* London. Allyn & Bacon.

Gelles, R.T. (1995). *Contemporary families – A Sociological view,* New Delhi : Sage.

Grotevant, H.D. (2000). Adolescent development in family contexts W. Daman & N. Elseuberg (5th ed.). *Handbook of Child Psychology* 5, (1124-1157), New York: John Wiley & Sons, Inc.

Greene, A.L. (1988). Early adolescents' perceptions of stress. *The Journal of Earlv Adolescence* 8(4), 391-403.

Hamburg, D.A.; Takanishi (1989), Preparing for life – The critical transition of adolescence, *American Psychologists Association,* 64(5), 825-827.

Joseph, K.S. (2002). Learning to cope with stress and distress. *Perspectives in education,*18(4), 217-234.

Kakar, S.; (1996) *The Indian Psyche,* New Delhi: Sage.

Katyal, S. & Vasudeva, P. (1996). Academic stress as related to parental attitudes and parental aspirations. *Personality Study and Group Behaviour,* 19,41-48.

Kashyap, L. (1996). India. In J. Gibson-cline (ed), *Adolescence from crisis to coping: A thirteen nation study* (pp. 103-117). Oxford London: Butterworth Heinemann.

Kirchner, E. (2000), Coping with Parental Depression. *The UCI undergraduate Research Journal.* (online) Http:\\www.tnpc.com/ adolescence.teens.html.

Kurian, S. (2003), *Stress and ways of coping: Perception of adolescents (15 –18 years) from the lower income group.* Unpublished master's thesis, Maharaja Sayajirao University, Baroda (India).

Lazarus, R.S. (1976). *Patterns of adjustment.* Tokyo: McGraw-Hill.

Mason, J. (1996), Qualitative Researching, ND: Sage.

Mehra, M.(2003), *Stress and ways of coping : Perception of adolescents (15 –18 years) from the lower income group.* Unpublished master's thesis, Maharaja Sayajirao University, Baroda (India).

Mehta, A. & Webb, L.D. (1996). Suicide among American Indian youths: The role of the school in prevention. *Journal of American Indian,* Edition 36(1).

Miles, M.B. & Huberman, A.M. (1994). *Qualitative data analysis: An expanded sources book,* (2nd ed.) New Delhi: Sage.

Moos, H.M. & Bilings, A.G. (1977). *Handbook of stress : Theoretical and clinical aspects.* (pp. 212 – 228)

Naughton, F.O. (1997). *Stress and coping,* Northridge California State University.

Palsane, M. N.; Bhavsar, S.N.; Goswami, R.P., and Evans, G. (1986). The concept of stress in the Indian tradition. *Journal of Indian Psychology,* 5(1), 1-11.

Pestonjee, D.M. (1997). *Stress and coping: The Indian experience.* New Delhi: Sage.

Punch, K.F. (1998). *Introduction to social research, quantitative and qualitative approaches*: New Delhi: Sage.

Roth, S; Cohen J.L. (1986) , Approach avoidance and Coping with stress. *American Psychologist Association.* 65(7), 813-819.

Saraswathi, T.S. (1999). Adult child continuity in India: Is adolescence a myth or an emerging reality. In T.S. Saraswathi. *Culture, Socialization and Human Development.* (pp. 213-233). New Delhi: Sage.

Stienberg, L. (1999). *Adolescence* (5th ed.) Boston: McGraw-Hill.

Verma, S. & Saraswathi, T.S. (2002). Adolescence in India : Street urchins or silicon valley millionaires ? In B.B. Brown, R.W. Larson, & T.S. Sarswathi. *The world's youth : Adolescence in eight regions of the globe* (pp.105-140). Cambridge: Cambridge University Press.

Verma, S.; Saraswati, T.S.; *An annotated bibilography on adolescent development in India: Contemporary perspectives.* (pp. 215 –219). Sage.

Verma, S. (2000). The Indian social reality of passage to adulthood. International Society for the Study of Behaviour Development. *Newsletter,* 2(37), 6-9.

Verma, S.; Sharma, D.; and Larson, R.W. (2002). School stress in India: Effects on time and daily emotions. *International Journal of Behavioural Development* , 20(6), 5003.

Wood, E.S. and Greenwood, E. (1996). *The World of Psychology* (2nd ed.). Boston: Allyn & Bacon.

APPENDICES

Awareness about alternate coping ways in general

Gender	*Categories of coping*		
	Problem Focused	*Emotion Focused*	*Digression*
Girls n = 15	Get information (1) Take psychologist's help (1)	Cry (1) Talk out with some one (1) Count blessing received (1)	Divert their mind (4) Listen to music (4) Read (3) Watch TV (3) Do *Yoga* and Meditation (3) Go out for drive (2) Gardening (1) Go to beauty parlour (1) Cooking (1) Painting (1) Meeting people (1) Learning Languages (1) Singing (1) Aroma Therapy (1) Help people in need (1) Join recreation clubs (1) Play sports (1) Go to sleep (1)
Boys n = 11		Eat to cope (1)	Meditation and *Yoga* are best ways (7) Exercise (3) Read books (2) Have Hobbies (1) Right Poems (1) Surf the Net (1) Watch Movies (1) Watch TV (1) Listen to music (1) Go for boxing (1) Take a walk (1) Go out for a ride (1)

n<40 because only 26 adolescents reported awareness about alternate ways of coping.

Adolescents' perception about best coping alternative
Situation 1

	Gender	*Categories of coping*		
		Problem Focused	*Emotion Focused*	*Digression*
Academics	**Girls n=20**	Reason out with parents (8) Explain to parents (4) Study with friends (1) Seek the support of parents (1) Study more (1)		Engage in hobbies (2) Go out (2) Seek entertainment (1) Joke with parents Sleep (1)
	Boys n=20	Discuss with parents (5) Use strategies (2) Start studying (2) Study with friends (1) Follow the same schedule (1)	Lie to parents (2)	Listen to music (4) Go out (2) Sleep (1) Would engage in sports (1) Divert other activities (1)

n > 40 multiple responses

Adolescents' perception about best coping alternative
Situation 2

Domain	*Gender*	*Categories of Copying*		
		Problem Focused	*Emotion Focused*	*Digression*
Hetrosexual Relationship	**Girls n = 20**	Apologize directly (7) Take parents' help (3) Analyze and talk to him (2) Patch up (1) Take friends' help (1) Talk to elders (1) Patch up or breakup for ever (1)	Talk to friends (3) Confess to GOD my mistake (1)	Engage myself in studies (1)
	Boys n = 20	Apologize directly (11) Apologize through letters or gift (2) Renew the relationship (1) Analyze the problem (1) Take friends' advice (1) Patch up (1)	Think it was her fault (1)	Hang out with friends (2) Listen to music (1)

Adolescents' perception about best coping alternative
Solution 3

Domain	*Gender*	*Categories of Copying*		
		Problem Focused	*Emotion Focused*	*Digression*
Teacher Student relationship	**Girls n = 20**	Take teacher's help (8) Follow teacher's advice (3) Work hard (3) Work hard in other subjects (2) Analyse and improve (1) Take advantage of good teaching (1) Pay attention to her to get attention (1) Help teacher in her other work (1)	Be neutral for some time (1) Not bother about the teacher-student relationship (1) Talk it out (1)	
	Boys n = 20	Talk to teacher and take her help (8) Take help from friends and toppers in class (6) Take guidance from parents (2) Work hard (2) Participate in class to gain attention (1)	Forget about it (1) Not bother about teacher student relationship (1) Rationalize that my answer were not bad (1)	Watch movies (1) Sleep (1) Hang out with friends (1)

Adolescents' perception about best coping alternative
Situation 4

Domain	*Gender*		*Categories of*	*Copying*
		Problem Focused	*Emotion Focused*	*Digression*
Physical Appear-ance	**Girl n = 20**	Working hard to improve (13) Stop comparing and carry myself well (2) Take parent's help (2) Get information from all sources (1)	Not react to people's comment (3) Accept what is given (1)	
	Boy n = 20	Work towards improving looks (7) Talk to parents (2) Discuss with friends (1) Go for counseling if all things fail (1) Get some treatment (1)	Not care for what people say (2) Focus on my good points (2) Accept myself (1) Excel in other fields (1)	

n > 40 multiple responses

Gender Analysis Framework

Categories	*Reasons for perceiving gender differences in*			
	Coping ways		*Parental attitude towards coping ways*	
	Girls	*Boys*	*Girls*	*Boys*
Temperament	Boys are immature and more aggressive (2)	Girls are more considerate (2)	More strict as boys are irresponsible (4)	Encourage me to talk to teachers as girls are shy (1)
Activities preferred	Boys play more sports to relax (3)	Girls prefer watching T.V. than playing (1)		
Social norms	Be able to go out more often (5)	Keep things to myself (5)	Less concerned about physical appearance (4)	More restrictions on going out (3)

20 Spirituality as a Predictor of Stress Vulnerability

Madhurima Pradhan and Padma Pandey

No one is immune to stress. No matter what our constitutional make-up, personality characteristics, coping style, social support or previous experiences, there might be situations that can bring about stress. But some individuals are more vulnerable to stress in certain circumstances than others. The resilience with which people encounter with stress has been termed as stress vulnerability. A person with low vulnerability to stress can withstand a huge amount of stress in life.

There have been a lot of researches seeking the relationship of stress vulnerability with different variables. It has been found that people with type A personality (Friedman and Rosenman, 1974), obsessional personality and people with external locus of control (Rotter, 1966), negative affectivity (Watson & Clark, 1984), pessimistic explanatory style (Burns & Seligman, 1989), low self-efficacy (Jerusalem & Schwarzer, 1992) are more vulnerable to stress while people with hardy personality (Kobassa, 1979), internal locus of control (Kanner & Feldman, 1991), sense of coherence (Bishop, 1993), coping flexibility (Cohen & Edwards, 1989), optimism (Taylor *et al.*, 1992), a sense of purpose or meaning in one's life (Visotsky, Hamberg, Goss & Lebovitz, 1961) are less vulnerable to stress. In addition previous experiences of lack of confidence, low self-esteem and fear of criticism may have repercussions in making people vulnerable to stress.

The findings of these researches imply that due to differences in personality characteristics, environmental effects and past experiences people differ in the appraisal of stress situation, selection and use of coping strategies and thereby in their resistance or vulnerability to the adverse effects of stress. Moreover the above mentioned studies reveal that no attempt has been made to study the relationship between spirituality and stress vulnerability.

Spirituality is now a much talked about subject all over the world. After a long period of heavy and soul-stifling materialism, people want to go beyond the mundane and material aims for seeking a higher meaning in their lives.

Currently, the term spirituality is used to devote 'certain positive inward qualities' and perceptions 'while avoiding implications of narrow dogmatic beliefs and obligatory religious observances' (Wulff 1996). It encompasses a search for meaning, for unity, for connectedness, for transcendence, for the highest of human potential (Pargament, 1997). It also refers to transcendent, meta empirical dimension of reality (Kelly 1995, Pargament and Park, 1995).

To be more specific, spirituality can be considered as a process by which people recognize the importance of orienting their lives to something non-material that is beyond or larger than themselves, so that there is an acknowledgement of and at least some dependence upon a high power or spirit. Adoption of such framework opens up all sorts of possibilities that have not been evident before. In other words, spirituality is that which gives meanings to one's life and promotes transcendence.

In the present study the humanistic and phenomenological perspective of spirituality as defined by Elkins *et al.* (1988) has been taken according to which spirituality, which comes from the latin "*spiritus*" meaning "breath of life", is a way of being and experiencing that comes through awareness of a transcendent dimension and that is characterized by certain identifiable values in regard to self, others, nature, life and whatever one considers to ultimate.

This view of Elkins forms the theoretical foundation on developing spiritual orientation inventory (SOI) which takes a multifaceted approach to spirituality. Spirituality is seen as distinct from religiosity and spiritual values are not necessarily grounded in a Christian belief system. There are dimensions of spiritual orientation inventory (SOI), i.e. transcendent dimensions of life, meaning and purpose in life, mission in life, sacredness of life, material values, altruism, idealism, awareness of tragic and fruits of spirituality.

The description of these dimensions is as follows :

Transcendent Dimension : The spiritual person has an experientially based belief that there is a transcendent dimension to life; the content can vary widely from a traditional view of a personal God to Greater Self.

Meaning and purpose in life : The spiritual person has known the quest for meaning and purpose and has emerged from this quest with confidence that life is deeply meaningful and that one's own existence has purpose.

Mission in life : The spiritual person has a sense of vocation, a responsibility to life, calling to answer.

Sacredness of life : The spiritual person believes that life is infused with sacredness and often experiences a sense of awe, reverence and wonder.

Material value : The spiritual person can appreciate material good but does not seek ultimate satisfaction from them nor attempts to use them as a substitute for frustrated spiritual needs.

Altruism : The spiritual person believes that we are our brother's keeper and is touched by the pain and suffering of others.

Idealism : The spiritual person is visionary committed to the betterment of the worlds.

Awareness of the tragic : The spiritual person is solemnly conscious of the tragic realities of human existence.

Fruits of spirituality : The spiritual person is one whose spirituality has born fruit in his/her life. True spirituality has a discernible effect upon one's relationship to self, others, nature, life and whatever one considers to be the ultimate.

A person's spiritual orientation can be of specific importance for people who wish to live stimulating and creative lives with specific goal in mind and strive to achieve optimum performance. Such people might face setbacks due to failure in their lives when their performance has not reached upto the satisfaction level of their expectations. To cope up of such setback they might require enhanced physical, emotional, psychological and spiritual resources. Apart from being physically strong, emotionally competent, psychologically healthy, they might require deeply based faith in God or Higher Power and its reflections (other human beings, nature and life). Such faith may empower them to face the stresses of the life and remain congruent and integrated even in the most undesirable circumstances.

In view of the above, it seems worthwhile to study how far spirituality of aspiring young adults is helpful in reducing their vulnerability to stress.

Methodology

Objectives of the Study

(i) To study the stress vulnerability of aspiring young adults.
(ii) To explore how spirituality and its different dimensions predict stress vulnerability.

Variables

Nine dimensions of Spirituality, namely Transcendent dimensions, Meaning and purpose in life, Mission in life, Sacredness of life, Material value, Altruism, Idealism, Awareness of the tragic realities of life, and Fruits of spirituality have been taken as Predictor variables. Stress vulnerability was criterion variable. It has been operationalized in terms of coping techniques a person employ for combating stress. It has been considered that the greater the use of these coping techniques the lesser would be his/her vulnerability to stress.

Sample

The study was conducted on 40 aspiring young adults (26 males and 14 females) preparing for various competitive exams (medical, engineering, administrative services and management). The age range of the subjects was between 17-26 years with the mean age of 21-23 years.

Tools

1. Spiritual Orientation Inventory developed by Elkins *et al.* (1988) to measure spiritual orientation. It consists of 85 statements to be rated on 7 points scale and has nine dimensions, i.e. transcendent dimension (13 statements), meaning and purpose in life (10 statements), mission in life (9 statements), sacredness of life (15 statements), material values (6 statements), Altruism (7 statements), Idealism (10 statements), awareness of tragic realities of life (5 statements) and fruits of spirituality (10 statements). The reliability coefficient for this inventory ranges from .75 to .95.
2. Stress Vulnerability Scale developed by Lyle H. Miller and Alma Dell Smith (1985) at the Boston University Medical Centre. It has 20 statements to be rated on 5-point scale.

Data Collection and Analysis

Spiritual orientation inventory and stress vulnerability scale was individually administered to each respondent. Descriptive Statistics (Mean, Standard Deviation) and regression analysis were used for the analysis of data.

RESULTS AND INTERPRETATIONS

Table 17.1 shows mean and standard deviations of different variables. It also reveals the level of scores obtained by the respondents. It is to be noted that these levels have been given on the basis of scale values. The scale range of the nine dimensions of spirituality is 1 to 7 while the obtained mean of all these nine dimensions are of high level (4.63 to 5.67). The sum of the total of spirituality score ranges from 4.29 to 5.85 with the mean of 5.19. On the other hand the scale range of stress vulnerability scores is 0-80 while the obtained mean of stress vulnerability scores is 29.37, which indicates very low level of stress vulnerability of the respondents. It seems that high level of spirituality of the respondents is increasing their resilience against the experience of the stress and as a result they are least vulnerable to stress. Previous studies also reveal that when facing a crisis person often turn to their spirituality as a means of coping (Pargament, 1997). In addition different spiritual/religious variables have been found to help in coping with significant negative life stress and daily stress (Fabricatore *et al.*, 2000).

Table 17.1 : Showing mean and standard deviation

Sl. No.	*Variables*	*Obtained range*	*Obtained mean*	*Scale range*	*Level*	*Standard deviation*
1.	Transcendent dimension (TD)	3.69 - 6.54	4.99	1 - 7	High	.72
2.	Meaning and purpose in life (MP)	4.50 - 6.60	5.57	1 - 7	High	.59
3.	Mission in Life (ML)	3.66 - 6.77	5.67	1 - 7	High	.60
4.	Sacredness of life (s)	3.86 - 6.60	5.26	1 - 7	High	.69
5.	Material values (Mv)	2.66 - 6.66	4.63	1 - 7	High	1.04
6.	Altruism (Alt)	3.71 - 6.86	5.32	1 - 7	High	.68
7.	Idealism (I)	4.30 - 6.40	5.27	1 - 7	High	.53
8.	Awareness of tragic (AT)	2.40 - 6.40	4.85	1 - 7	High	.96
9.	Fruits of spirituality (F)	4.10 - 6.70	5.42	1 - 7	High	.71
10.	Spiritual Orientation (SOI)	4.29 - 5.85	5.19	1 - 7	High	.41
11.	Stress Vulnerability (SV)	7.00 - 56.00	29.37	0 - 80	Low	13.95

The proportion of variance of the criterion measure (stress vulnerability) attributable to joint action of the predictor variables (spiritual orientation and its nine dimensions) is depicted by R. Table 17.2 reveals all independent variables studied are accounted for 37% in stress vulnerability among aspiring young adults. It follows from the above finding that spiritual aspect of the person should be acknowledged in stress researches.

Table 17.2 : Summary of regression analysis

R	*R Square*	*Adjusted R*	*Standard Error of the estimate*	*Duration — Watson*
.608	.37	.15	12.85	2.17

Criterion Variable: Sv
Predictors: TD, MP, MI, S, Mv, Alt, I, AT, F, SO

Different dimension of spirituality namely spiritual beliefs, spiritual practices and spiritual behaviours can be proposed to affect stress process differently. Following the model of stress and coping suggested by Lazarus and Folkman (1984a) spiritual beliefs may influence the event and resource appraisals of the person during stressful encounter and also to the choice of relevant and adequate coping activities as well as their constant evaluations regarding effectiveness in current situation. Sometimes, spiritual experiences can be a consequence of highly stressful life experiences (James & Samuel, 1999). Some of the crises of life that leads an individual towards inner search may be personal illness, death of a spouse, parent or child. This search might challenge previously held views about the meaning and purpose of life and lead to changes in spiritual beliefs, values and practices. The level of spiritual involvement (included in spiritual practices) may also affect the way in which an individual handles the stress. Those people who attend religious/spiritual services may feel more support because of the social network of those with similar beliefs (Schniker, 2001).

It seems that spiritual strivings are likely to meet basic organismic needs for self-transcendence, thus are likely to be inherently satisfying and growth promoting (Sheldon & Kasser, 1995). Spirituality may thus reduce stress vulnerability through a reduction of overall conflict and promotion of spiritually oriented life style facilitating congruence, integration and wholeness of the person.

Table 17.3 depicts beta coefficient, standard errors it values and level of significance. Beta coefficients reveal the relative weights with which each independent variable predicts the criterion variable. We find that transcendence, sacredness, material values, altruism, idealism, and awareness of tragic negatively contribute to stress vulnerability. It follows that respondents who has an experientially based that there is a transcendent dimension of life, believe that life is infused with sacredness and experienced a sense of awe, reverence and wonder towards God's creation in the form of self, others, nature and life, do not seek ultimate satisfaction from material values, believe that they are their brother's keeper and are touched by the pain and sufferings of others, are visionary committed to the betterment of the world and are conscious of tragic realities of human existence are less vulnerable to stress.

Table 17.3 : Coefficients

Model	*Unstandardized Coefficients*		*Standardized Coefficients*	*t*	*Significance*
	B	*Standard Error*	*Beta*		
TD	- 3.782	3.704	- 1.97	1.021	.316
MP	- 4.876	6.187	.207	.788	.437
ML	- 5.514	5.446	.241	1.012	.320
S	- 3.182	4.798	- .158	-.663	.512
MV	- 3.449	2.636	- .258	- 1.308	.201
ALT	- 1.620	3.819	- .080	- .424	.675
I	- .892	4.898	- .034	- .182	.857
AT	- 5.298	3.854	- .366	- 1.375	.180
F	4.500	4.231	.232	1.064	.296
SO	13.961	17.060	.416	.818	.420

Note :(a) Criterion Variable : SV

(b) Predictors : TD, MP, ML, S, MV, Alt, I, AT, F, SO.

Additionally, the results also reveal that meaning and purpose in life, mission in life are positively contributing to stress vulnerability. It follows that respondent's tendency to always look for meaning and purpose in life and their sense of responsibility to life, calling to answer might make them more vulnerable to stress. This is to be kept in mind that respondents of the study are young adults aspiring to get success in different competitive examinations. They might be trying to meet the challenges of cut throat competitions. Moreover this age of young adulthood is characterized by stamina, vigour and enthusiasm in which people strive to prove themselves through achieving the highest desired aspirations of life. But if they are not able to manage their enhanced level of stress through positive, appropriate and life enhancing coping strategies (i.e., proper diet and exercise, positive thinking, having self-confidence and self-esteem, developing and maintaining social support network) they might get a victim of stress. Stress load of respondents was not measured in the study; but the study suggests that it should be checked and managed by the respondents, once in a while to optimize their performance.

Results also depict that fruits of spirituality dimensions is also contributing to stress vulnerability positively. It follows from this finding a possibility that if spirituality of the respondents has an effect upon their relationship to self, others, nature, life and the ultimate power they might get vulnerable to stress. This finding can be explained in terms of motivation to be spiritual. Two aspects of religiosity/spirituality have been mentioned, i.e. intrinsic and extrinsic (Hovemyr, 1998). A person with intrinsic spiritual orientation lives out "spiritual faiths for the sake of the faith" (Gorsuch, 2000). He /she is deeply committed to such beliefs and values in a self-sacrificing manner (McFarland and Warren, 1992). Social aspects of spirituality are not as important for him/her. Such person is motivated to be spiritual at the core of his/her being. The person with extrinsic spiritual orientation uses religion as a tool to achieve non-religious ends (Nielson, 1995) like social standing and endorsement (Hunsberger, 1999). Previous findings suggest that extrinsic spiritual orientation was found to be positively related to cope with negative life events (Pargament *et al.*, 1992). Although the spiritual orientation of the respondents of the study was not measured in the present study, it seems that they possess extrinsic spiritual orientation which is hampering their self-confidence to cope up stress of life. Several other studies also support the postulate that extrinsic religiousness is maladapted form of religiousness and is predictive of negative outcomes such as mental illness as opposed to mental health (Richards and Bergin, 1997).

Conclusions

(i) Spiritual orientation of a person might cast a positive influence upon the capacity of the person to face the stress of life and decrease his/her vulnerability to stress.

(ii) In addition to having meaning and purpose in life and a responsibility to life, people need to follow some positive strategies that might enhance their resources to cope up with stress.

Implication and Suggestion

Model of stress vulnerability should include protective factor such as spirituality in addition to other variables for psychological interventions to those who are vulnerable to stress.

REFERENCES

Bishop, G.D. (1993). The sense of coherence as a resource in dealing with stress, *Psychologia, 36;* 259-63.

Burns, M.O. & Seligman, M.E.P. (1989). Explanatory style across the life span: Evidence for stability over 52 years, *Journal of Personality and Social Psychology, 56*; 471- 477.

Cohen S. & Edards, J.R. (1989). Personality characteristics as moderators of the relationship between stress and disorder. In R.W.J. Neufeld (ed') *Advances in the investigation of psychological stress* (pp. 235-283*)*. New York;Wiley.

Elkins, D.N.; Hedstrom, J.L.; Hungness, L.L.; Leaf, J.A.; and Saunders, C. (1988). Toward a humanistic-phenomenological spirituality: Definition description and measurement, *Journal of Humanistic Psychology, 28,* 5 - 18.

Fabricatore, A.N.; Handal, P.J.; Fenzel, L.M. (2000), 'Personal spirituality as a moderator of the relationship between stressors and subjective well-being'. *Journal of Psychology and Theology, 28(3),* 221-228.

Friedman, M. & Rosenman, R.H. (1974). *Type a behaviour and your heart,* Greenwich, C.T. Fawcet Press.

Gorsuch, R.L.; Miller, W.R. (2000). "Assessing Spirituality", in W.R. Miller (ed.). *Integrating Spirituality into treatment,* Washington DC : American Psychological Association.

Hovemyr, M. (1998). The attribution of Success and Failure as related to different patterns of Religious Orientation. *International Journal for the Psychology of Religion,* 8(2) 107-124.

Hunsberger, B. (1999). Social-psychological causes of faith, new findings offer compelling clues, *Free Inquiry,* 19(3), 34-38. Expanded database : http://web7. infotrac.galegroup.com

James, B.J. & Samuel, C.A. (1999). High stress life events and spiritual development. *Journal of Psychology and Theology, 27*(3), 250-260.

Jerusalem, M. & Schwarzer, R. (1992). Self-efficacy as a resource factor in stress appraisal processes. In R. Schwarzer (ed.) *Self-efficacy: Thought control of action.* London: Hemisphere.

Kanner, A.D. & Feldman, S.S. (1991). Control over uplifts and hassles and its relationship to adaptational outcomes. *Journal of Behavioural Medicine, 14*(2):187-201.

Kelly, E.W. Jr. (1995). *Spirituality and religion in counselling and psychotherapy,* Alexandria, VA, American Counselling Association.

Kobasa, S.C. (1979). Personality and resistance to illness. *American Journal of Community Psychology, 21,* 595-598.

Lazarus, R.S. & Folkman, S. (1984a). *Stress, appraisal and coping.* New York: Springer.

Lyle, H. Miller & Alma Dell Smith (1985). At the Batson University Medical Centre in *Interventions in Occupational Stress* by R.R. Ross & E.M. Altmaier, Sage 1994, 144.

McFarland, S.G., and Warren, J.C., Jr. (1992). Religious Orientations and Selective Exposure among Fundamentalist Christians. *Journal for the Scientific Study of Religion, 31* (2), 169 - 174.

Moore, T. (1993). Care of the soul: The benefits and costs of a more spiritual life. *Psychology Today,* May - June 28.

Nielsen, M.E. (1995). Operationalizing Religious Orientation : Iron Rods and Compasses. *The Journal of Psychology, 129*(5), 485-494.

Pargament, K.I. and Park, C.L. (1995). Merely a defense? The variety of religious means and ends, *Journal of Social Issues, 51,* 13-31.

Pargament, K.I.; Olsen, H.; Reily. B.; Falgout, K.; Ensing, D.S.; and Van Haitsma, K. (1992). God Help Me (II) The Relationship of Religious Orientation to Religious Coping with Negative Life Events. *Journal for the scientific study of religion, 31(4),* 504-513.

Pargament, K.I. (1997). *The psychology of religion and coping.* New York; Guilford Press.

Richards, P.S.; and Bergin, A.E. (1997). *A Spiritual Strategy for Counselling and Psycho Therapy. Washington, D.C.* : American Psychological Association.

Rotter J.B. (1996). Generalised expectancies for internal *vs.* external control of reinforcement. *Psychological Monograph,* 80 (1 Whole No. 609).

Schnittker, J. (2001). When is a faith enough? The effects of religious involvement on depression. *Journal for the Scientific Study of Religion, 40* (3), 393 - 411.

Sheldon, K.M. & Kasser, T. (1995). Coherence & congruence : Two aspects of personality integration. *Journal of Personality and Social Psychology,* 68.

Taylor, C.J. & Scogin, F. (1992). Dysphoria and coping in women : The effect of threat and challenge appraisals. *Journal of Social and Clinical Psychology, 11,* 26 - 42.

Visotsky, H.M.; Hamburg, D.A.; Gore, ME; & Lebovitze, B.Z. (1961). Coping behaviour under extreme stress. *Archives of General Psychiatry, 5,* 423 - 428.

Watson, D. & Clark, L.A. (1984). Negative affectivity: The disposition to experience aversive emotional states. *Psychological Bulletin, 96,* 465 - 490.

Wulff, D.M. (1996). The psychology of religion: An overview, in E.P. Shapraspse (ed). *Religion and the clinical practice of psychology,* Washington DC; American Psychological Association.

21 Keeping Security-Service Personnel Functional

The Role of Some Organizational Level Variables

Sweta Srivastava *and* Arvind K. Sinha

The present study attempts to make explorations regarding the relationship of organizational level variables such as organizational justice, perceived organizational support, supervisors' support, and political interference with certain outcome variables. The variables included in the study were evaluated for their interrelationships in the context of a security-service organization, owned and run by the government in India, popularly known as the Indian Police.

The Variables under Consideration

Organizational Justice

Though the study of work place justice has been proliferating in recent years, the pioneering work in the area was proposed by Adams way back in 1963, which gave rise to the establishment of the Equity Theory. The theory states that men and women are in a continual and never ending state of social comparison with a referent group of individuals. Adam's traditional theory assumes that responses to injustices are more dynamic in form and entail a need to reduce that level of distress or dissonance created by the inequitable state. Individuals constantly measure their perceived "inputs" and their "outcomes" as a ratio in comparison to a referent individual. Adams defines the "inputs" in social exchange as qualities and characteristics that a person possesses such as age, seniority, social status, education, effort, ability or skill. The "outcomes" are defined as items or privileges received in social exchange such as rewards, money, increased status, authority, or enjoyable work/assignments/duties.

The basic belief in equity theory is that when someone is in the inequity state, he or she will then be moved or motivated to do something that will help the person regain a perception of equity in the situation. When equity is present, the belief is that the person is at peace with the social exchange and is not moved by any action other than contentment.

Greenberg (1990) described organizational justice as a literature "grown around attempts to describe the role of fairness as a consideration in the workplace". An organizational justice perspective is concerned with how perceptions of fairness impact on behaviour in organizations. It has been found that individuals appraised both what they receive and how they receive it. In work settings, employees often gauge whether the rewards they receive match their contributions to the organization or the rewards received by their colleagues (Adams, 1963, 1965 and Leventhal, 1976). Employees also judge the fairness of decision-making procedures used by organizational representatives. They also consider interpersonal treatment as important in fairness processes (Bies & Moag, 1986 and Greenberg, 1993).

The study of organizational justice has largely focused on three variables. They are:

1. Distributive justice is the pursuit fairness of outcome.
2. Procedural justice is the perceived fairness of process by which outcomes are arrived at.
3. Interactional justice is focused on inter-personal side of organizational practices, specifically, the inter-personal treatment and communication by management to employees.

Distributive Justice

Equity Rule : Distributive justice is the perceived fairness of the outcomes or allocation that an individual receives. According to Adams, what people were concerned about was not the absolute level of outcomes *per se* but whether those outcomes were fair. Adams suggested that one way to determine whether an outcome was fair was to calculate the ratio of one's contribution or inputs to one's outcomes and then compare that ratio with that of comparison with others. He was clear that this process of evaluation was completely subjective.

Equality rule : According to this rule, people evaluate fairness in terms of whether they obtain equal outcomes. The rule dictates that the receiver should obtain similar outcomes regardless of differences in their contributions or needs.

Needs rule : This rule dictates that the receiver outcomes should be sufficient to satisfy their legitimate desires and prevent sufferings.

As distributive justice deals with the perceived fairness of outcomes, it has the organizational controls, of which distribution of outcomes is an integral part. Due to its focus on outcomes, distributive justice is predicted to be related mainly to cognitive, affective and behavioural reactions to particular outcomes. Thus when a particular outcome is perceived to be unfair, it should affect the person's emotions, cognition and ultimately their behaviour. Empirical tests suggest that employee who feel under-benefited, experience anger and a desire for restitution.

Procedural Justice

People's perception justice also involves questions of procedural fairness. Every organization has procedures for regulating the distribution of outcomes to receivers.

Thibaut and Walkers' (1975) pioneering work suggested that people care at least as much about the procedures used in making allocation decisions as they do about the outcomes themselves. Their explanatory model emphasized two types of control or input into decisions: process control or voice (i.e., the opportunity to present information or evidence as input the decision) and decision control (i.e., the opportunity to influence the decision itself). Decisions resulting from procedure offering process control work perceived as fairer.

Leventhal and colleagues can be credited for extending the notion of procedural justice into non-legal contexts such as organizational sittings (Leventhal, 1980; Leventhal, Karuza & Fry, 1980). In doing so, they also broadened the list of determinants of procedural justice far beyond the concept of process control. Leventhal's theory of procedural justice judgments focused on six criteria that a procedure should meet if it to be perceived as fair. Procedures should (a) be consistent, (b) should suppress the bias information, (c) correctible, (d) representative, (e) ethical, and (f) should be accurate.

Procedural justice is predicted to be related to cognitive, affective, and behavioural reactions towards the organization. Accordingly, when a process leading to a certain outcome is perceived to be unfair, the person reactions are predicted to be directed towards the whole organization, rather than his or her task or the specific outcome in question. This differs from predictions made for distributive justice, which emphasizes outcome focus rather than organization focus reactions.

Interactional Justice

Bies and Moag (1986) introduced what may be treated as one of the most recent advances in the justice literature by focusing attention on the importance of the quality of the interpersonal treatment people receive when procedures are implemented. Bies and Moag referred to these aspects of justice as "interactional justice". When an employee perceives interactional injustice, he/she is predicted to negatively react towards his/her supervisor rather than negatively react towards the organization as the whole, as is predicted by procedural justice models, or towards the specific outcomes, as is predicted by distributive justice theory. A different conceptualization of interactional justice has been recommended by Greenberg (1993). Greenberg suggested we look at interactional justice as composed of two facets: interpersonal justice and informational justice. Interpersonal justice reflects the degree to which people are treated with politeness, dignity, and respect by authorities involved in determining outcomes. Informational justice, focuses on the explanation provided to people that convey information about why procedures where used in a certain way or why outcomes were distributed in a certain fashion.

Happiness

Happiness is a common goal towards which people strive, but for many it remains frustratingly out of reach. Psychologists have attempted to define happiness over the past 30 years. Initial attempts have been to identify happiness with the subjective well-being of an individual. Several landmark studies have been done in this regard.

Bradburn and Caplovitz (1965) conducted a pioneer study on American people's quality of life and their psychological well-being. They found that positive and negative feeling states were not correlated with each other, though both were correlated individually with general measures of happiness. Here, happiness was taken as the outcome variable.

Happiness is a pleasant emotional experience, the affective component of subjective well-being (Andrews & Withey, 1976; Bradburn, 1969). Researchers have also shown that happiness is actually composed of frequent positive affect and infrequent negative affect.

Myers and Diener (1995) have suggested that happy individuals not only have specific traits but also have strong relationships. Two aspects of social networks family (relationship with parents) and school (peer relations and school performance) have been found by various studies to be important to young people's mental well-being and social adjustment (Argyle, 1987). Many researchers like Herz and Gullone (1999) argued that the quality of the parent-child relationship has a significant impact on the long-term confidence, resilience and well-being of individuals.

Organizational Citizenship Behaviour

The current interest in organizational citizenship behaviour can be traced back at least to Katz (1967), who identified the following dimensions of discretionary and spontaneous behaviour that are beyond the explicit role requirement, and these are (1) cooperating with others, (2) protecting the organization, (3) volunteering constructive ideas, (4) self-training, and (5) maintaining favourable attitude toward, the company. This concept was subsequently made more explicit by Smith, Organ, and Near (1983) and was called "organizational citizenship behaviour" (OCB), later defined by Organ (1988) as "individual behaviour that is discretionary, not directly or explicitly recognized by the formal reward system, and that in the aggregate promotes the effective functioning of the organization". By discretionary, we mean that behaviour is not an enforceable requirement of the role or the job description that is the clearly specifiable terms of the person's employment contract with the organization, the behaviour is rather a matter of personal choice, such that its omission is not gradually understood as punishable. Organ noted two critical component of OCB: (a) the behaviour is not part of the employee's job description and is not rewarded explicitly, and (b) the behaviour is not usually obvious but does, in aggregate, benefit the organization.

Podsakoff, Mackenzie, Paine, and Bacharach (2000) had organized more than 30 potential forms of OCB into seven common themes or dimensions. In a very recent article on citizenship behaviour, Farh, Zhong, and Organ (2004) have stressed upon nine dimensions of OCB and these are as follows: (a) Altruism or helping behaviour, (b) Conscientiousness, (c) Sportsmanship, (d) Courtesy, (e) Civic virtue, (f) Functional participation, (g) Advocacy participation, (h) Loyalty, and (i) Voice.

Four major antecedents. Social scientists have identified four antecedents of OCB and these are: (a) Individual or employee characteristics, (b) Task characteristics, (c) Organizational characteristics, and (d) Leadership behaviours such as leader-member exchange, and supportive leader behaviour (Kumar, 2002).

Job Satisfaction

In the field of organizational psychology, there is increasing recognition of the fundamental significance of the concept of job satisfaction. Job satisfaction is perhaps the most widely studied work orientation over the last four decades of organizational research. Job satisfaction has been considered as a function of the perceived relationship between what one expects and obtains from one's job and how much importance he or she attributes to it (Kemelgor, 1982; Mobley & Locke, 1970). Job Satisfaction has been defined as "positive emotional state resulting from the appraisal of one's job or job experiences" (Locke, 1976). Therefore, Job Satisfaction emphasizes upon the specific task environment where an employee performs his or her duties (Mowday, Porter, & Steers, 1982).

Judge (2004) has suggested that one clear aspect of work environment that consistently influences job satisfaction is the intrinsic challenge present in the work. He suggested some ways of increasing mental challenge in the job and these are: (a) by introducing job rotation in the organization, (b) by job enlargement, sometimes called horizontal loading, which means expanding the number of tasks with a particular job, and (c) by job enrichment or vertical loading, where more responsibilities are assigned to each job level.

Judge (2004) points out some of the outcomes that job satisfaction has been linked to, and these are: (a) job satisfaction correlates moderately to strongly with life satisfaction, (b) the relationship between satisfaction and performance may be reciprocal. Productive employees are not only those that are happy with their jobs but performing the job well may also lead to job satisfaction, and (c) job satisfaction displays weak and negative correlation with turnover and absenteeism.

Organizational Commitment

Organizational commitment is a construct that is reflected in an individual's identification with and involvement in his or her organization as well as in willingness to exert effort and remain in the organization. It has been defined as the nature of individual's relationship to an organization so that a highly committed person will indicate a strong desire to remain a member of a particular organization and would be willing to exert high level of effort on behalf of the organization, and would have definite belief in and acceptance of the values and goals of the organization (Mowday, Porters, & Steers, 1982).

Personal Effectiveness

Various definitions have been offered to explain the concept of personal effectiveness. Personal Effectiveness is understood in terms of individual goals, he has in his life to achieve. According to Sutton and Ford (1982), personal effectiveness refers to an ability to perform the job effectively. According to Campbell, Dunnette, Lawler, and Weick (1970), the effective manager is one who is an optimizer in utilizing all available and potential resources—material, human, and financial—both, within and without the organization, toward its sustained long term functioning.

Views of Rao (1985) and Pareek (2004) may be taken as representative of conceptualization of effectiveness by Indian scholars. According to Rao (1985), the manager who understands his job and job requirements well, is aware of his own and his subordinates' strength and weakness utilizes his own and his subordinates' strength in performing the tasks, overcome weaknesses and acquire new capabilities though continuous learning on the job may be considered effective. Pareek (2004) focused more upon the aspects that led to personal effectiveness. He maintained that an individual's performance depends on his or her potential effectiveness as a person, technical competence, managerial experience, as well as the way role, which the person performs in the organization is designed. Therefore, effectiveness depends upon individual's own potential effectiveness, the potential effectiveness of the role, and the organizational climate. Interestingly, an attempt has been made to distinguish between role efficacy and personal efficacy. Personal efficacy would mean potential effectiveness of a person in both personal and interpersonal situations. Role efficacy is the potential effectiveness of an individual occupying a particular role in an organization.

Perceived Organizational Support

Perceived organizational support (POS) refers to people's global beliefs concerning the extent to which an organization's management values their contributions, cares about their well-being, considers their goals and values, listens to complaints, helps them when in a problem situation, and can be trusted to treat them fairly (Eisenberger, Huntington, Hutchinson, & Sowa, 1986). POS develops through multiple exchanges between employees and their employer over time.

Some mechanisms seem to underlie the positive relation between POS and work-related outcomes. First, Eisenberger, Fasolo, and Davis-LaMastro (1990) proposed that POS would increase performance by conveying to employees the organization's propensity to notice and reward increased performance (i.e., performance-reward expectancies). Second, just as perceived support from friends and relatives may fulfil socio-emotional needs in interpersonal relationships, POS was assumed to meet important socio-emotional needs in the work place such as those for respect, caring and approval (Eisenberger *et al.*, 1986). Third, norm of reciprocity too seems to play important role in POS. Social exchange theorists argue that the organization's fulfilment of socio-emotional needs should create an obligation to reciprocate with greater work effort. Fourth, POS increases employees' inference that the organization judges them as superior performers and is proud of their accomplishments, which satisfies their need for esteem.

Supervisors Support

The concept of perceived supervisor support was derived from perceived organizational support. Using the framework of perceived organizational support perspective as suggested by Eisenberger *et al.* (2002) developed the concept of perceived supervisor support, which refers to subordinates' general views concerning the degree to which supervisors value their contributions and care about their well-being.

Theory suggests that, just as notions of reciprocity affect employees' perceptions of their organization, notions of reciprocity will also affect the interpersonal relationships that employees develop with their supervisors. When employees perceive supervisors to be supportive, they become more committed to the supervisor and, perhaps, to the organization (Smith, 2005).

Political Interference

Viewing organizations as political entities is not a recent phenomenon. March (1962) suggested that organizations are political coalitions in which decisions are made and goals are set by bargaining processes. In the early 1980s, researchers also began to investigate the importance of perceptions of organizational politics by organizational members. These early studies found that the frequency of perceived political behaviour varied depending on the organizational level or function and that certain conditions are more likely to promote political behaviour.

Mayes and Allen (1977) postulated that (a) behaviour referred to as politics takes place in varying degrees in all organizations, (b) not all behaviour in organizations can be categorized as political, (c) the organizational political process can be described in non-evaluative terms, and (d) while many variables involved in describing organizational politics may be familiar to other organizational behavioural concepts, a combination of these variables constitutes a unique process that cannot be described adequately by existing paradigms. This unique process is organizational politics. Major attempts to define organization politics fall under four heads. They are mentioned as: (a) Claims against the resource sharing systems, (b) Conflict over policy preferences, (c) Relationships of controls and influence, and (d) Self-serving behaviour.

The Conceptual Scheme

The study included the variables in two broad categories, (a) The organization level variables, and (b) The Organizationally Relevant Outcome Variables. The first category included the variables of organizational justice, political interference, perceived organizational support, and the supervisor support. The second category included the variables of organizational citizenship behaviour, organizational commitment, personal effectiveness, job satisfaction, and happiness. It was conjectured that the organization level variables would be related to the organizationally relevant outcome variables. Schematically, the idea may be represented as depicted in Fig. 21.1.

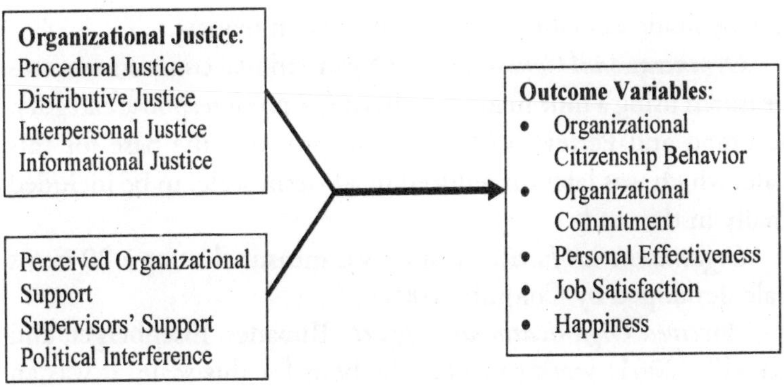

Fig. 21.1: The conceptual scheme

Hypotheses

1. All the organizational level variables, except Political Interference will be positively related to the Organizationally Relevant Outcome Variables.
2. Political Interference will be negatively related to the Organizationally Relevant Outcome Variables.

Method

Sample

The sample consisted of 270 male respondents from the lower and middle hierarchical levels of Police organization. The respondents, at the time of data collection, were located in four cities situated in the eastern (one city), middle (two cities), and western (one city) parts of a large State of north India.

Measures

The following measures were used for data collection. The measures may be made available from the authors on request.

Organizational Commitment: Organizational commitment was measured using a nine items scale having 5-point response category. Bozeman and Perrewe's (2001) work provided the base for this scale, which was later on reduced to a 9-item scale, to be included finally in the study.

Organizational Justice : Justice was measured using a 20 items scale developed by Colquitt (2001).

Perceived Organizational Support : Rhoades, Eisenberger, and Armeli's (2001) work provided the basis for this scale. It was an eight items scale having a 5-point response category.

Supervisors' Support : This scale was based on the works of Rhoades, Eisenberger, and Armeli's (2001). Supervisors' support was measured with the help of four-item scale having 5-point rating category.

Happiness : Happiness was measured through a 'face pattern' pictorial measure based on the work of Andrews and Withey (1976).

Job Satisfaction : Job satisfaction was measured through a three-item, 5-point scale questionnaire that was adapted from the work of Cammann, Fichman, Jenkins, and Flesh (1983).

Personal Effectiveness : This was measured by a fourteen item scale having a 5-point rating scale. The scale was developed by Sinha (1998).

Political Interference : Political interference was measured by a scale having nine items with a 5-point rating scale, developed by Maslyn and Fedor (1998).

Organizational Citizenship Behaviour : Kumar (2002) found a shorter version of the scale consisting of 22 items with a 5-point scale to be more useful in Indian settings, which was used for the present work.

Procedure

Structured questionnaires were used for data collection. Data were collected individually and on a few occasions also in small groups of 3-4 respondents during off duty hours.

Result and Discussion

The present work may primarily be considered as exploratory in nature. The major part of the research analyses was done using SPSS-X (3.0). Since the present study was conceptualized in a multivariate framework, it was imperative to unravel the underlying dimensions of the constructs in the study; consequently all the multi-item measures were subjected to factor analysis. Only those items were taken up for factor analysis that had an item-total correlation of more than or equal to 0.121, which is the magnitude required for .05 level of significance of a correlation coefficient given the sample size of 270, and Cronbach's alpha value equal to or greater than 0.70. Remaining items were dropped for the purpose of further analyses. The basic statistics pertaining to the measures and respective variables may be had from the author on request.

Exploring the Underlying Dimensions of the Construct: The Factor Analysis Results

This section presents a description of the measures in the study, their relevant properties and the corresponding factor— analytically derived dimensions. The names of factors extracted by factor analysis based on principal factoring with iterations and oblique rotations using the PA 2 option of the SPSS-X statistical analysis package programme. The details of the factor analyses in tabular form are presented below. Brief description of the factor structure and their names would follow right after the tables. The Table 21.1 shows mainly the factor names as well as the number of items that were retained after meeting the criteria successfully.

Table 21.1: Showing the Factor Analyses Results

Table 21.1a: Factor and Loadings of Organizational Commitment Questionnaire

Original item No.	*Serial No.*	*Factor 1: Organizational commitment Items*	*Loadings*
1	1	I am willing to put in a great deal of effort beyond that normally expected in order to help this organization be successful.	.49
2	2	I talk up this organization to my friends as a great organization to work for	.46
5	3	I am proud to tell others that I am part of this organization.	.57
6	4	I am extremely glad that I chose this organization to work for over others I was considering at the time I joined.	.73
7	5	Often, I find it difficult to agree with this organization's policies on important matters relating to its employees.	.68

STANDARDIZED ITEM ALPHA = .7251

Table 21. 1b : Factors and Loadings of Organizational Justice Questionnaire

Original item No.	*Serial No.*	*Factor 1: Procedural Justice Items*	*Loadings*
2	1	Have you had influence over the (outcome) arrived at by those procedures?	.74
3	2	Have those procedures been applied consistently?	.74
5	3	Have those procedures been based on accurate information?	.54
STANDARDIZED ITEM ALPHA = .7060			
		Factor 2: Distributive justice Items	
8	4	Does your (outcome) reflect the effort that you have put into work?	.72
9	5	Is your (outcome) appropriate for the work you have completed?	.75
10	6	Does your (outcome) reflect what you have contributed to the organization?	.65
11	7	Is your (outcome) justified, given your performance?	.59
STANDARDIZED ITEM ALPHA = .7733			
		Factor 3: Interpersonal justice Items	
12	8	Has (he/she) treated you in a polite manner?	.75
13	9	Has (he/she) treated you with dignity?	.82
14	10	Has (he/she) treated you with respect?	.88
STANDARDIZED ITEM ALPHA = .8539			
		Factor 4: Informational justice Items	
16	11	Has (he/she) been candied in (his/her) communications with you?	.62
17	12	Has (he/she) explained the procedures thoroughly?	.83
18	13	Were (his/her) explanations regarding the procedures reasonable?	.59
STANDARDIZED ITEM ALPHA = .7200			

Table 21.1c: Factors and Loadings of Perceived Organizational Support Questionnaire

Original item No.	*Serial No.*	*Factor 1: Perceived Organizational Support Items*	*Loadings*
1	1	My organization really cares about my well-being	.83
2	2	My organization strongly considers my goals and values	.88
4	3	My organization cares about my opinions.	.70
5	4	My organization is willing to help me if I need a special favour	.82
6	5	Help is available from my organization when I have a problem	.84
7	6	My organization would forgive an honest mistake on my part	.70

STANDARDIZED ITEM ALPHA = .9104

Table 21.1d: Factor and Loadings of Supervisors' Support Questionnaire

Original item No.	*Serial No.*	*Factor 1: Supervisors' support Items*	*Loadings*
1	1	My supervisor cares about my opinions	.90
2	2	My work supervisor really cares about my well-being	.89
3	3	My supervisor strongly considers my goals and values	.90

STANDARDIZED ITEM ALPHA = .9268

Table 21.1e: Factor and Loadings of Job satisfaction Questionnaire

Original item No.	*Serial No.*	*Factor 1: Job satisfaction Items*	*Loadings*
1	1	Working for this organization is very satisfying to me	.74
2	2	I am satisfied with my job	.91
3	3	All things considered, I am satisfied with my current job	.74

STANDARDIZED ITEM ALPHA = .8352

Table 21.1f: Factors and Loadings of Personal Effectiveness Questionnaire

Original item No.	*Serial No.*	*Factor 1: Effective Dealing with Individuals* *Items*	*Loadings*
5	1	During my stay I have focused on learning and growth of people by giving them individual attention and support	.54
9	2	I have reasons to believe that my group members look up to me for ideas and motivational strength.	.68
11	3	I have enough of expertise to change myself to meet environmental requirements	.64
12	4	Even if my organization ventures into a totally new area of operation, I am confident I will be one of the last ones to be laid off	.45
13	5	I have been able to discover my potentials for greater effectiveness in the organization	.61
STANDARDIZED ITEM ALPHA = .7183			
		Factor 2: Effectiveness in Dealing with Group, Environment and Human Growth Issues *Items*	
1	6	I am able to deal with problems related to individuals who work with me.	.62
2	7	I am quite effective in taking care of the problems that arise due to my own way of doing things.	.69
3	8	I can take care of two individuals simultan eously even if they approach me with mutually conflicting proposals.	.67
STANDARDIZED ITEM ALPHA = .6991			

Table 21.1g: Factor and Loadings of Political Interference Questionnaire

Original item No.	*Serial No.*	*Factor 1: Political interference* *Items*	*Loadings*
2	1	Rewards come only to those who work hard in this organization	.68
4	2	Pay and promotion decisions are consistent with existing organizational policies	.63
6	3	There is no place for 'yes-people' in my work group, good ideas are desired even when it means disagreeing with superiors	.50
7	4	My immediate officer does not apply pay and promotion policies in a political manner	.63
8	5	Employees are encouraged to speak out frankly even when they are critical of well-established ideas	.64
STANDARDIZED ITEM ALPHA = .7554			

Table 21.1h: Factor and Loadings of Organizational Citizenship Behaviour Questionnaire

Original item No.	*Serial No.*	*Factor 1: Organizational citizenship behaviour Items*	*Loadings*
7	1	I am willing to stand up to protect the reputation of the organization	.74
8	2	I show pride when representing the organization in public	.63
9	3	I produce highest quality of work, regardless of circumstances	.80

STANDARDIZED ITEM ALPHA = .7637

Note : The original item numbers refer to the numbers with which the items appeared in the questionnaire circulated to the respondents. The serial numbers indicate the number of items in a particular sub-section of the questionnaire corresponding to a variable or a dimension thereof.

After the initial factor analyses and the correlation findings, Multiple Regression Analyses (MRAs) were carried to test the hypotheses in question. Only those MRAs are being discussed here that came out to be significant.

Table 21.2 : Summary of Regression Analysis for Variables Predicting the Dimension of Organizational Citizenship Behaviour (N = 270)

Variables		*b*	*SE b*	*β*	*t*	*p*	*Adj R^2*	*F*
Predictor	*Criterion*							
IFJ	OCB	-.010	.06	-.11	-1.58	.12		
POLI		-9.00	.03	-2.00	-.00	.10		
DJ		.06	.04	.10	1.39	.16		
IPJ		-.10	.06	-.13	-1.67	.10		
PJ		-.04	.07	-.04	-.52	.60		
POS		-.06	.04	-.16	-1.55	.12		
SS		.22	.07	.34	3.29	.00		
Constant		12.89	1.00		12.87	.00	.0355	2.41 $p \leq .02$

Note : OCB = Organizational Citizenship Behaviour, POS = Perceived Organizational Support, POLI = Political Interference, SS = Supervisors' Support, PJ = Procedural Justice, DJ = Distributive Justice, IPJ = Interpersonal Justice, IFJ = Informational Justice.

Table 21.2 showed that Organizational Citizenship Behaviour is predicted by a number of organizational level variables. The overall regression came out to be significant. However, variables shared 3.55 per cent of variance with Organizational Citizenship Behaviour. Supervisors' Support was the most significant predictor for this outcome variable. The results pointed to the fact that for the chosen sample, compared to the other variables, it is the supervisors' support that makes the most difference in terms of organizational citizenship behaviour. This also makes sense because when employees perceive supervisors to be supportive, they become more committed to the supervisor and, perhaps, to the organization. We also get similar finding from the literature. Eisenberger, Stinglhamber, Vandenberghe, Sucharski, and Rhoades, (2002) found in their study that Supervisors' Support was positively related to Perceived Organizational Support. They suggested that supervisors, to the extent that they are identified with the organization, contribute to Perceived Organizational Support and job retention.

Table 21.3 : Summary of Regression Analysis for Variables Predicting the Dimension of Organizational Commitment (N = 270)

Variables		*b*	*SE b*	*β*	*t*	*p*	*Adj R^2*	*F*
Predictor	*Criterion*							
IFJ	CMM	-.26	.11	-.18	-2.45	.01		
POLI		-.01	.06	-.01	-.17	.87		
DJ		.01	.07	.01	.08	.93		
IPJ		.18	.10	.14	1.76	.08		
PJ		.04	.12	.03	.31	.76		
POS		-.01	.06	-.02	-.19	.85		
SS		.17	.12	.15	1.47	.14		2.08
Constant		18.82	1.76	–	10.67	.00	.0274	$p \leq .05$

Note : CMM = Organizational Commitment, POS = Perceived Organizational Support, POLI = Political Interference, SS = Supervisors' Support, PJ = Procedural Justice, DJ = Distributive Justice, IPJ = Interpersonal Justice, IFJ = Informational Justice.

Table 21.3 showed that the overall regression was found to be significant for organizational level variables predicting the Organizational Commitment. The predictor variables shared 2.74 percent of variance with the criterion variable. Informational Justice turned out to be as a significant, but a negative predictor for Organizational Commitment. Keeping in view the nature of sample of the study, it makes sense to believe that Informational Justice acts as negative predictor. The structure and dynamics of the police organization is such that the reward system is based on not so well defined grounds and whatever feedback people receive in the organization is rather negative in nature. Probably, it is due to this reason that Informational Justice emerged as negative predictor for Organizational Commitment.

Table 21.4 : Summary of Regression Analysis for Variables Predicting the Dimension of Effective Dealing with Individuals (N = 270)

Variables		*b*	*SE b*	*β*	*t*	*p*	*Adj R^2*	*F*
Predictor	*Criterion*							
IFJ	EDI	-.02	.09	-.01	-.18	.86		
POLI		.03	.05	.05	.66	.51		
DJ		.26	.06	.28	4.07	.00		
IPJ		-.19	.09	-.17	-2.09	.04		
PJ		.01	.10	.01	.10	.92		
POS		.06	.06	.12	1.16	.25		
SS		.01	.10	.01	.08	.94		3.19
Constant		14.72	1.54		9.57	.00	.0539	$p \leq .00$

Note : EDI = Effective Dealing with Individuals, POS = Perceived Organizational Support, POLI = Political Interference, SS = Supervisors' Support, PJ = Procedural Justice, DJ = Distributive Justice, IPJ = Interpersonal Justice, IFJ = Informational Justice.

Table 21.4 showed that the overall regression turned out to be significant. The organizational level variables shared 5.39 per cent of variance with the criterion variable. Two, out of the four dimension of organizational justice, came out as the significant predictors, namely Distributive Justice, and Interpersonal Justice. However, owing to the negative beta-weight, Interpersonal Justice turned out to be a negative predictor.

Table 21.5 : Summary of Regression Analysis for Variables Predicting the Dimension of Job Satisfaction (N = 270)

Variables *Predictor*	*Criterion*	*b*	*SE b*	*β*	*t*	*p*	*Adj R^2*	*F*
IFJ								
IFJ	JS	-.08	.07	-.07	-1.09	.28		
POLI		-.05	.04	-.08	-1.22	.22		
DJ		.08	.05	.11	1.68	.09		
IPJ		.04	.07	.04	.57	.57		
PJ		-.11	.08	-.11	-1.42	.16		
POS		.07	.04	.17	1.82	.07		
SS		.21	.08	.26	2.70	.01		9.33
Constant		9.58	1.138		8.41	.00	.1782	p ≤ .00

Note : JS = Job Satisfaction, POS = Perceived Organizational Support, POLI = Political Interference, SS = Supervisors' Support, PJ = Procedural Justice, DJ = Distributive Justice, IPJ = Interpersonal Justice, IFJ = Informational Justice.

For Job Satisfaction, the variable which turned out as a significant predictor was Supervisors' Support. Table 21.5 shows that the overall regression was found to be significant with variables sharing 17.82 percent of variance in the criterion variable. Here again, the importance of Supervisors' Support was evident for the criterion variable of Job Satisfaction. Employees generally turn to their Supervisors' Support for any kind of support they need in the organization. A large segment of their experience/affect toward the organization is determined or channelized through the support of immediate supervisor. Hence it is not surprising to find that Supervisors' Support positively relates to Job Satisfaction.

To conclude, the study could identify some variables that make significant contributions to the outcome variables. They were: Organizational Justice, Political (non) Interference, Perceived Organizational Support, and Supervisors' Support.

REFERENCES

Adams, J. (1963). Toward an understanding of inequity. *Journal of Abnormal and Social Psychology*, 67, 422-436.

Adams, J. (1965). Inequity in social exchange. In: L. Berkowitz (ed.), *Advances in experimental social psychology* (Vol. 2, pp. 267-299). San Diego, CA: Academic Press.

Andrews, F. M., & Withey, S. B. (1976). *Social indicators of well-being.* New York: Plenum Press.

Argyle, M. (1987). *The Psychology of Happiness.* London: Methuen.

Bies, R. J. & Moag, J. F. (1986). Interactional justice: Communication criteria of fairness. In R. J. Lewicki, B. H. Sheppard, and M. H. Bazerman (eds.), *Research on negotiations in organization* (vol. 1, pp. 43 - 55). Greenwich, CT: JAI Press.

Bozeman, D. P. & Perrewe, P. L. (2001). The effect of item content overlap on organizational commitment questionnaire — Turnover cognitions relationships. *Journal of Applied Psychology.* 86, 161-173.

Bradburn, N. M. (1969). *The Structure of Psychological Well-Being.* Chicago: Aldine.

Bradburn, N. M. & Caplovitz, D. (1965). *Reports on happiness.* Aldine, Chicago.

Cammann, C.; Fichman, M.; Jenkins, Jr.; D. & Flesh, J. R. (1983). Assessing the attitudes and perceptions of organizational members. In S. E. Seashore, E. Lawler, P. H. Mirvis, and C. Cammann (eds.). *Assessing organizational change* (pp. 71-138). New York: John Wiley & Sons.

Campbell, J. P.; Dunnette, M. D.; Lawler, E. E.; III. & Weick, K. E. Jr. (1970). *Managerial behavior, performance and effectiveness.* New York: McGraw-Hill.

Colquitt, J. A. (2001). On the dimensionality of organizational justice: A construct validation of a measure. *Journal of Applied Psychology.* 86, 386-400.

Eisenberger, R.; Fasolo, P.; & Davis-LaMastro, V. (1990). Perceived organizational support and employee diligence, commitment. and innovation. *Journal of Applied Psychology*, 75, 51-59.

Eisenberger, R.; Huntington, R.; Hutchinson, S. & Sowa, D. (1986). Perceived organizational support. *Journal of Applied Psychology*, 71, 500 - 507.

Eisenberger, R.; Stinglhamber, F.; Vandenberghe, C.; Sucharski, I. L. and Rhoades, L. (2002). Perceived supervisor support: Contributions to perceived organizational support and employee retention. *Journal of Applied Psychology*, 87, 565 - 573.

Farh, J. L.; Zhong, C. B. & Organ D. W. (2004). Organizational citizenship behavior in People's Republic of China. *Organizational science,* 15, 241 - 253.

Greenberg, J. (1990). Organizational justice: yesterday, today and tomorrow. *Journal of Management.* 16, 399-432.

Greenberg, J. (1993). The social side of fairness: Interpersonal and informational classes of organizational justice. In R. Cropanzano (ed.), *Justice in the workplace: Approaching fairness in human resource management* (pp. 79-103). Hillsdale, NJ: Lawrence Erlbaum Associates.

Herz, L. & Gollone, E. (1990). The relationship between self-esteem and parenting style. *Journal of Cross-Cultural Psychology*, 30, 742-761.

Judge, T. A. (2004). Promote job satisfaction through mental challenge. In E. A. Locke (Ed.) *Handbook of principles of organization behavior* (pp. 75- 89). Oxford, UK: Blackwell Publishing Ltd.

Katz, D. (1967). The motivational basis of organizational behavior. *Behavioral Science.* 9, 131-146.

Kemelgor, B. H. (1982). Job satisfaction as mediated by the value congruity of supervisors and their subordinates. *Journal of Occupational Behavior*, 3, 147-160.

Kumar, A. (2002). *Essence and consequence of organizational citizenship behavior.* Unpublished doctoral dissertation, Indian Institute of Technology, Kanpur.

Leventhal, G. S. (1976). The distribution of rewards and resources in groups and organizations. In L. Berkowitz and W. Walster (eds.), *Advances in experimental social psychology* (Vol. 9, pp. 91 - 131). New York: Academic Press.

Leventhal, G. S. (1980). What should be done with equity theory? New approaches to the study of fairness in social relationships. In K. Gergen, M. Greenberg, and R. Wills (eds.), *Social exchange: Advances in theory and research* (pp. 27-55). New York: Plenum Press.

Leventhal, G. S.; Karuza, J. & Fry, W. R., (1980). Beyond fairness: A theory of allocation preferences. In G. Mikula, (ed.), *Justice and social interaction* (pp. 167-218). New York: Springer-Verlag.

Locke, E. A. (1976). The nature and causes of job satisfaction. In M. D. Dunnette (ed.), *Handbook of Industrial and Organizational Psychology.* (pp. 1297-1349). Chicago: Rand McNally.

March, J. G. (1962). The business firms as a political coalition. *Journal of Politics*, 24, 662 - 678.

Maslyn, J. M. and Fedor, D. B. (1998). Perceptions of politics: does measuring different foci matter. *Journal of Applied Psychology.* 83(4), 645-53.

Mayes, B. T. & Allen, R. W. (1977). Toward a definition of organizational politics. *Academy of Management Review*, 2, 672-678.

Mobley, W. H. & Locke, E. A. (1970). The relationship of value importance to satisfaction. *Organizational Behavior and Human Performance*, 5, 463-483.

Mowday, R.; Porter, L.; & Steers, R.; (1982). *Employee-organization linkages: The psychology of Commitment, absenteeism, and turnover.* New York: Academic Press.

Myers, D. G. & Diener, E. (1995).Who is happy? *Psychological Science*, 6, 10-19.

Organ, D. W. (1988). *Organizational citizenship behavior: The good soldier syndrome,* Lexington, MA Lexington.

Pareek, U. (2004). *Understanding Organizational Behaviour.* New Delhi: Oxford University Press.

Podsakoff, P. M.; Mackenzie, S. B.; Paine, J. B.; & Bachrach, D. G. (2000). Organizational citizenship behavior: A critical review of the theoretical and empirical literature and suggestions for future research. *Journal of Management*, 26, 513-563.

Rao, T. V., (1985). Psychological factors in managerial effectiveness. In U. Pareek and D. M. Pestonjee (eds.) *Behavioral process in organizations,* pp. (15-26) New Delhi: Oxford & IBH Publishing Company.

Rhoades, L.; Eisenberger, R. & Armeli, S. (2001). Affective commitment to the organization: The contribution of perceived organizational support. *Journal of Applied Psychology.* 86, 825-836.

Sinha, A. K. (1998). *A new instrument measuring personal effectiveness.* Unpublished manuscript, Department of Humanities and Social Sciences, Indian Institute of Technology Kanpur at Kanpur, (India).

Smith, B. D. (2005). Job retention in child welfare: Effects of perceived organizational support, supervisor support, and intrinsic job value. *Children and Youth Services Review,* 27 (2), 153-169.

Smith, C. A.; Organ, D. W.; & Near, J. P. (1983). Organizational citizenship behavior: Its nature and antecedents. *Journal of Applied Psychology.* 68, 653-663.

Sutton, R. I.; & Ford, L. H., (1982). Problem solving adequacy in hospital subunits. *Human Relations*, 35, 675-701.

Thibaut, J. & Walker, L. (1975). *Procedural justice: A psychological analysis.* Erlbaum, NJ: Hillsdale.

22 Cognitive Behavioural Interventions for Emotional Wellness

Archana Shukla

Emotional Wellness— What is it?

Some emotions are pleasant, while others are not. We do not resist or complain about being too happy, but we all grudge and crib when stressed, lonely, sad, disappointed, pressured, cornered, disobeyed, annoyed, rejected, looked down upon, hurt, anxious, guilty. The list of negative emotions is long. These emotions diminish our sense of worth, decrease our competence and destruct our interpersonal relationships.

Anger, anxiety, guilt, etc. are some very unpleasant and destructive emotions. Experiencing such emotions could be like being in a tsunami. We cannot think straight, cannot problem-solve. We are not in control. We are not even aware of the way we happen to think, feel, and act when in the grip of an emotional tsunami. We simply get swept away. If we could, we would not choose to experience them.

These are strong negative emotions and are hence difficult to handle. They negatively affect not only us but also those around us. An occasional burst of anger, for example, may at times be perfectly OK as it could assist us in various instrumental ways but if we experience these emotions often enough we need to sit back and ask if we are being emotionally well. The answer would probably be in the negative. If so, we are likely to score in the direction of low EQ. Thus, although we very much want to be, we are usually far from being emotionally well. Emotional wellness would mean feeling happy, eager, alive and thriving. When we are emotionally well we develop greater authenticity. We have the courage to accept challenges and the security to admit our ignorance. We are also able to expand our circles of trust and stretch our capabilities. And, when mistakes happen, we are able to readily forgive others and ourselves. How we feel emotionally at any given point in time depends, in large measures, on how we happen to be thinking then or what cognitions were predominant at that time.

Thinking about thinking !

We think about various things, but we seldom think about thinking. This is one primary cause for being relatively insensitive to how we think. If we develop awareness about the content of our thinking, we could also become aware of the consequences that these thoughts have for our psychological well-being.

Point to Ponder–1

"People seldom think about what they think about. They think about how they feel. They think about what they do. But what is causing what they feel and do is what they seldom think about. What do you think about that?"

Dr. Maxie Maultsby

Cognitions are ideas, thoughts, internal communications or self-talk that make up an individual's belief system. Consider viewing our bodies like an ecosystem. An ecosystem contains everything in the environment, such as water, land, cars, people, animal, vegetation, house, landfills, etc. A negative thought is like pollution to your system. Just as pollution in the densely populated cities affects everyone who goes there, so, too, do negative thoughts pollute your limbic system, your mind and your body. That is why emotional upsets can manifest itself in physical symptoms such as headaches and stomachaches.

Alternatively, you can consider experiencing negative thoughts as being caught in a traffic jam. Nothing is able to move there.

Everything is put stayed. Besides, there is a probability of getting scratched by the uncontrollable rush of a variety of vehicles, being driven by impatient, irritated people. The only way out of this 'traffic jam' is to breathe, relax and examine your thoughts and then to weed out the negative, unwanted, unworthy thoughts. Only then can the traffic (or, the bodily organs) start to function happily again.

The two major categories of *problems* in an individual's belief system could be (i) distortions, which represent wrong, unreasonable or irrational thinking, and (ii) deficits, which refer to a lack of reasonable, constructive or positive thinking.

Internal Communications

Internal communications are our self-talk, or, thoughts that we think about us. Thoughts matter. Thoughts are biologically based and have a real impact on how one feels and behaves. Stimuli are processed and interpreted by an internal cognitive system. A good thought makes our brain release chemicals that calm our deep limbic system and help our body feel good. When people are happy, their muscles relax, their hearts beat slower, their hands are drier, and their breathing steady. During an angry, sad, unkind or cranky thought our hands get colder, heart beats more rapidly, blood pressure goes up, breathing quickens, muscles tighten, and hands sweat more. The deep limbic system is responsible for translating our emotional states into physical feelings of relaxation or tension. No matter who you are, your body reacts to what you think. Usually a person regards these thoughts as reasonable even when they appear to be in contradiction with objective evidence. These thoughts are negative and emerge automatically and extremely rapidly. They are, therefore, called 'automatic negative thoughts'. They are so lightening swift that you have difficulty catching them. They are 'too fast and too furious'– from 0 to 60 in a second! Such thoughts are characterized by an illogical logic. Internal communications thus often represent cognitive distortions. They are a negative judgemental voice. By bringing these automatic negative thoughts into the open and examining them on a conscious level one can realize how little sense it makes to think these thoughts. Although people are usually not aware of or ignore these thoughts and, therefore, do not report them, they can be taught to observe them introspectively while experiencing a negative emotion.

Activity 1 — Beware of ANTs

- Become aware of what you can do to your thoughts. You can choose to think good thoughts and feel good, or you can choose to think bad thoughts and feel lousy. If you think a negative thought without challenging it, your mind believes it and your body reacts to it.
- Our 'automatic negative thoughts' or *ANTs*, are very much like those red/black insects called ants. Ants invade our kitchen and ruin our food. *ANTs* invade our minds and ruin our mood, our sense of internal calm, our relationships, and our self-esteem and personal power.
- When you feel sad, blue, anxious or mad, acknowledge that you are having an *ANT* invasion in your head.

We need a strong, internal *ANT eater* to get rid of the *ANTs* and the bad feelings that follow. We need to 'turn down' the volume of our irrational, emotional mind.

Two Types of Minds?

We can think of ourselves as having two types of mind: an irrational, emotional mind and an objective, data processing, wellness mind. How we feel emotionally at any given point in time depends, in large measures, on how we happen to be thinking (or, what cognitions are predominant) at that time. Thus our cognitions (or thoughts, beliefs, ideas, attitudes) determine whether in a given situation our emotional mind or else wellness mind is likely to be in control. Our cognitions are what we speak to ourselves. These are our internal communications or self-talk.

Emotional wellness comes from working intently and effortfully to turn down or switch off the volume of dysfunctional self-talk every time it starts to play. Understanding the connection between thoughts, feelings and behaviours is crucial in our continued journey toward emotional wellness. Remember, thoughts generated by your wellness mind are positive and learned. They, in turn, cause positive feelings and constructive behaviours. Thoughts generated by your emotional mind, however, are automatic and negative. They, in turn, cause negative feelings and destructive behaviours.

The Emotional Mind

Irrational ⇒ Unpleasant ⇒ Undesirable
Thoughts Feelings Behaviours

The Wellness Mind

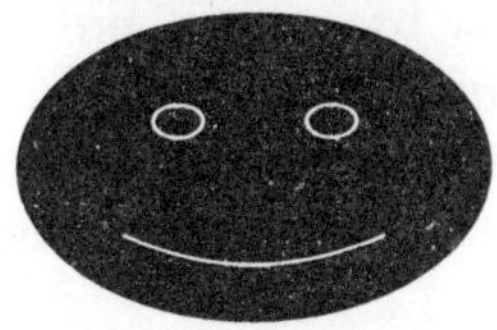

Rational ⇒ Pleasant ⇒ Desirable
Thoughts Feelings Behaviours

Activity 2 – Challenge Your Emotional Mind

Recall some painful event from your life and do a 'thought record'. Then, analyze your thought record using the guidelines listed below :

1. *Recognize your triggers.* What difficult events you have had?
2. *Listen to your emotional mind.* Listen for automatic thoughts generated by your emotional mind.
3. *Identify your core beliefs:* What is it that your emotional mind is trying to get you to believe about yourself, your future, and your world?
4. *Examine your feelings:* Observe what you are feeling in response to your self-defeating, automatic thoughts and core beliefs. Rate pleasantness of your feelings on a 10-point rating scale from 'most unpleasant' to 'most pleasant'.
5. *Stop:* Don't respond to your emotional mind. Disconnect physically as well as mentally. You can try wearing a rubber band around your wrist that you snap every time you happen to think a negative thought. This will shake you out of your downward emotional spiral.
6. *Re-evaluate your thought:* Look and listen. Ask for proof? Scan your environment for evidence that support, or else, contradict your self-defeating thoughts. Look for objective reality (something that a camera can see).
7. *Re-Think:* Replace your automatic, negative thoughts and core beliefs with realistic, positive thoughts from the wellness mind.
8. *Re-examine Feelings:* Compare your here and now feelings with what you were feeling earlier while thinking automatic negative thoughts.
9. *Re-act:* Respond now, thinking positively. Notice the change in the way you feel when you think positive thoughts.
10. *Rehearse:* Practice steps 1 through 10.

Some Fairly Standard Errors in Thinking

Cognitive distortions take place when people are egocentric. They see everything that happens only from their perspective. Using 'shoulds', and 'musts' in our utterances and 'catastrophizing', or viewing life in 'absolutistic', 'exaggerated' ways indicate a crooked, irrational thinking.

In many studies of problem solving, it has been observed that people frequently make a 'rush to judgement', or 'over-generalize' on the basis of too little evidence, or, stick rigidly to one (their!) interpretation of the facts to the point of avoiding or denying contradictory objective evidence. Some such common errors in thinking are illustrated below:

- *Overgeneralization or 'Always Thinking'* – 'I *never* have any self-control', '*No one* is concerned about me', '*Everyone* takes advantage of me', 'You are *always* angry', 'You turn away *every time* I touch you'.
- *Personalizing* – '*I am* such an idiot for not practicing safe sex'.
- *Blame* – 'Why didn't *you* warn me before?' 'How am I supposed to know?' 'It's *your* fault that I...' 'That would not have happened if you had...'
- *Black and white thinking* – an 'either/or' reasoning which categorizes everything into extremes. 'I have blown my diet *completely*',
- *Fortune telling* – Predicting that bad or negative things would happen. 'I am *going to* fail my exam', 'That party *would be* a disaster', 'I *would* make a fool of myself', 'I *would* say something stupid', 'I *will* forget...'
- *Catastrophizing and labelling* – It is also called 'awfulizing'. This kind of thinking focuses on extremely negative outcomes. 'It will be a *disaster* if I...' 'I am an *idiot*'; 'I am a *failure* in life'.
- *Guilt Beatings* – are represented by 'should' and 'ought' statements — CBT trains people to avoid statements such as 'I *should* have got the job' or 'I *ought to be* earning a good wage by now' and mind reading 'She *is going to think* I'm an...'.
- *Focusing on the negative* – having a negative mental filter

which *does not* let us *notice positive* things, or makes us *play down* their significance. Thus, we are left with focusing only on what has gone wrong in a situation. On receiving a compliment some one may react by uttering that 'you are only saying this to be nice', 'oh dear, I must be… if he is commenting on…' This kind of thinking is well illustrated in the famous Disney movie, Pollyanna.

- *Mind Reading* – is believing that one can read whatever it is that goes on in others minds: They are talking about me', 'He does not like me', and 'They think I will never amount too much'.
- *Thinking with your feelings* – is wrongly mixing your feelings with your thoughts, or, using feelings to think. 'I feel nobody will ever trust me', 'I feel like you don't love me', 'I feel stupid ', 'I feel like a failure'.

Refuting Irrational Ideas

There are five steps (*A* through *E*) to refuting and eliminating irrational ideas. An individual's emotional reactions and behaviours appear to be caused by some *activating event (A)* such as a rejection, a critical comment from another person, low grade on an exam, a medical report etc. This significant activating event may seem to be the *consequence (C)* of an individual's reactions but it is not. An individual's reactions or behaviours are caused by his or her cognitions or the *belief system (B)*. These cognitions are the internalized sentences a person utters about *A*, and, about the self in relation to *A*. Emotional difficulties are caused when a person's beliefs are irrational and self-defeating. These irrational beliefs *(iB)* can be replaced with rational, healthy beliefs. A person can learn to *dispute* (*D*) the irrational talk by challenging, that is, asking for proof/support for the irrational idea. Next, he/she is encouraged to *evaluate/examine (E)* the irrational idea, compare it with a rational thought and substitute the dysfunctional selftalk with a positive, verifiable thought. The central technique of Rational Emotive Therapy, RET, is disputing (Ellis, 1979).

Point to Ponder–2

"Get out of the forest of your feelings and emotions and examine your thinking from 30,000 feet. Then sort through what is rational and *what is irrational and make better decisions.*

— Albert Ellis

Preferential RET is an elegant cognitive therapy as it seeks to provide a philosophy of living and a reconstruction of personality.

Many of us have a pattern of internalized negative self-talk. These stressful thoughts may be said to yourself, perhaps even several times a day, as in the following examples:

"I can't do anything right".
"I am not a good person".
"I always foul up".
"I should have done better".

Activity 3 – Thought Stopping

Ask the following questions about each of your negative thoughts-

- *What error applies to this thought?:* Engage in critical thinking or an analysis of errors / fallacies in your thinking.
- *Examine the evidence*: Look for actual, objective evidence for or against beliefs and explanations. Re-assess your beliefs.
- *Treat yourself as you would be a sympathetic but honest friend*: Or otherwise, you must be applying a double standard. Be honest as well as sympathetic to yourself. Rationalizations and wishful thinking is no route to emotional wisdom.
- *Avoid loaded emotional language*: Distinguish a word's emotive meaning from its descriptive one. Try to use words that stick to facts. Instead of saying 'I am a disgrace' say 'I am disappointed with myself over this act'.
- *Avoid black and white, all-or-none thinking*: Try to see how things usually are somewhere in between. Think in terms of probabilities and percentages. Say, for example, 'There is a 50% chance I have failed in my exam', 'I am 100 calories over my limit today'.
- *Examine the long term consequences of emotions, attitudes and behaviours*: Ask, does getting angry actually do you any good? Does it protect your health and happiness?
- *Be careful about using 'should' and 'ought' statements:* Ask yourself if the action you are commending is something that the person can do? Remember that 'ought' often implies 'can'. Also ask if the 'ought' a universal law or just a parental/societal prescription or a personal preference?

One can embark on the journey to emotional wellness by asking, "What are some of my recurrent areas of negative self talk?" Having identified these areas, evaluate the possibilities for thought stopping by following the steps outlined in the Activity 3.

Thought stopping is a fun, quick, and easy-to-learn technique that can help you overcome everyday, nagging worry and doubt.

Other Cognitive Behavioural Interventions

The Cognitive-Behavioural Therapy (CBT) has grown out of developments in behavioural and cognitive psychology. The behavioural origins of the approach emphasize process of learning through classical and operant conditioning, direct observation of behaviour (modelling), and a scientific attitude of behavioural change. A cognitive dimension of this approach is added through attention to dysfunctional thought processes and irrational beliefs. CBT employs a range of intervention techniques to achieve the behavioural objective. CBT proposes that psychological problems result from (1) faulty learning, (2) making incorrect inferences on the basis of inadequate or incorrect information, and (3) a failure to distinguish between imagination and reality. In short, thinking can be unrealistic because it is derived from erroneous and inadequate premises; behaviour can be self-defeating because it is based on unreasonable and unrealistic thinking. Internal communications thus are the basis of emotional disorders. An important element of CBT is that the beliefs are not just specific to a particular situation: there may also be very general 'core' beliefs at work. The 'downward arrow' technique is used to be into the initial automatic thoughts in order to explore and later challenge the underlying core belief.

Cognitive approaches to counselling tend to take a logical, intellectual approach to the solution of client's problems or difficulties. They argue that emotions do not cause wrong thinking. Rather, wrong thinking causes disturbing emotions. Thus it is demonstrated that irrational thinking is the basis of emotional disorders. By correcting the distortions and the deficits in the thought processes, CBT aims at enabling people for rational thinking, acceptance of uncertainty, tolerance of human fallibility, flexibility and openness to change, risk taking and willingness to try new things, self-direction, independence and responsibility, and self-acceptance.

> **Point to Ponder– 3**
>
> "Finally, brothers, whatever is true, whatever is noble, whatever is right, whatever is pure, whatever is lovely, whatever is admirable, whatever is excellent and/or praiseworthy— think about such things. Whatever you have learned or received or heard from me, or seen in me— put it into practice. And the God of Peace will be with you..."
>
> **— Letter from Paul to Philippians, 4:8-9**

Various techniques are used to cure unreason by reason, rehearsal, and reinforcement. Counsellors using this approach do a great deal of talking, persuasion and argument to take the person out of his/her firmly held irrational beliefs and unhesitatingly confront his/her neurosis creating ideas or attitudes.

There are at least four main avenues for producing change in the existing belief system: disconfirmation or confrontation, reconceptualization, process insight, and repetition and rehearsal. Some specific CBT procedures utilizing these are being outlined below:

Self-Instructional Training – It combines graduated practice with elements of RET. The key process here is that of repetition. It is a sequence in which overt verbalizations are transformed into covert self-verbalizations or thoughts.

Stress Inoculation Training – It combines a skill training acquisition phase with an opportunity for later practice or rehearsal. It is done in three steps: educate, rehearse (coping statements, relaxation) and apply.

Problem Solving Therapy – It is a five step procedure.

Multi-modal Therapy – It combines explicit cognitive changes with behavioural interventions.

Relapse Prevention – First the 'awful catastrophe' of 'relapse' is redefined as 'lapse'. Then, the clients are encouraged to identify the situations, which are likely to evoke a lapse, and acquire social skills in order to deal with them. Three types of experiences have been identified as being associated with high rates of relapse: 'downers', 'rows', and 'joining the club'.

Eye Movement Therapy – This method may interrupt negative thoughts by sequentially stimulating opposite sides of the brain. By moving one's eyes rapidly back and forth while vividly imagining a stress-inducing event, painful patterns of thinking can be broken and associated distress relieved.

Activity 4 — What is in the words?

First, complete the following sentences	(You could have completed like this)
• I *can't live without...*	*...smoking.*
• I *need...*	*...money.*
• I *can't ...*	*...let you use my brush.*
• I *won't...*	*...ever lie.*
• It will be *terrible* if...	*...I lose my job.*
• ...is *awful.*	*...Missing my flight is awful.*
• My boss will *kill me* if...	*...I am late for this meeting.*
• My spouse would be *mad at* me if...	*...found me taking money from his/her wallet.*
• I *want...*	*...to be rich.*
• I *must* be...	*... successful.*

Next, substitute the underlined words in the ten sentences that you just completed with words that more accurately describe what you are trying to state. For example, learn to discriminate between things which are inconvenient *vs.* awful; things that you prefer *vs.* need; things that you can and/or cannot live without. Everything that is inconvenient is not awful or terrible. Similarly, everything that you desire/prefer is not what you need or cannot live without. Also, missing a flight could be inconvenient, not awful; bosses don't kill, they become irritated and displeased; spouses don't get mad, they express dislike and/or anger; you don't have to be rich and successful, rather you prefer to be that.

Re-read the changed sentences:. Notice the tremendous difference that results in the way we feel when we use accurate, more appropriate words.

Diary writing – The common feeling of depressed individuals that they don't get anything accomplished can be challenged by encouraging them to keep weekly activity schedule on an hourly basis. By so doing, people can be made to acknowledge that they do of course accomplish several things in the course of daily living, and also that good things happen to them too, but they fail to notice these because of their erroneous perception regarding the same being trivial. (See Activity 4).

There are several areas for negative thoughts such as guilt feelings, procrastination in which you might "over-think" the situation, worry over details, fear that things will only get worse, anger that others "never get it right", repetitive thinking about past failures, and/or always needing the approval of others. Each of these could be likened to an ants' invasion, for which you need to employ an efficient ant-eater (see Activity 5).

Activity 5 – ANT eaters (Kill ANTs by talking back)

One way to crush these ANTs (the *A*utomatic *N*egative *T*hought*s)* is to bring them into the open (or, write them down) and talk back to them. Challenging is an advance skill that requires constant practice. By challenging, you take away the power from your irrational thoughts. Therefore, dispute each of your negative thoughts by following these steps:

- *Engage in critical thinking*: Analyze the fallacies in your thinking.
- *Do objective data processing:* Look for actual, objective evidence for or against beliefs and explanations. Think in terms of probabilities and percentages. Do a cost benefit analysis. Re-assess your beliefs.
- *Use correct (not loaded emotional) language*: Distinguish a word's emotive meaning from its descriptive one. Instead of saying 'I am a disgrace' say 'I am disappointed with myself over this act'.
- *Practice stopping ANTs*: Experience an ANT, shout 'STOP'. Another ANT, 'STOP'. Yet another ANT, 'STOP'.

We often drive into the future looking in the rearview mirror. We tend to make choices and decisions based on what has happened to us in the past, without stopping or challenging whether our choices are rational or relevant. Recall Victor Frankl's statement that 'we have the freedom and accountability to make choices'. We have the freedom to choose how we respond. We cannot control the events that happen to us. Sometimes, we can influence them but life is too capricious to be controlled. All we can truly control is our thinking, our feelings and how we respond. And, the crucial place to start is by controlling — disputing and changing — what we think.

Activity 6 – 'The snake made me do it'

- Imagine 3 people, *X, Y,* and *Z,* from different socio-cultural, geographical background in a room.
- A 5-foot-long snake enters the room.
- *X* is out of the door, if there is no door, she will make a door. *Y* goes right for the snake and picks it up. *Z* freezes.
- What caused these different responses? The obvious answer is.the snake! Think again. It's not 'the snake', but our beliefs/thoughts about the snake, which makes us, do anything!!
- Think about your thinking and grow up emotionally. Certainly, good things, bad things, and tragic things happen to us. Life shows up. 'Snakes' keep appearing. We cannot control the events. What we can control to a great extent however is what we think about those events, how we interpret what happens to us.
- By controlling our thinking, we can better manage our emotions and better control how we respond to the events.
- Remember, *emotions are the fuel of behaviour.*

At the root of all irrational thinking is the assumption that things are done to you: 'That really got me down...She makes me nervous...Places like that scare me...Being lied to makes me angry'. Nothing is done to you. Things happen in the world. You experience those events *(A)*, engage in self-talk *(B)*, and then experience an emotion *(C)* resulting from the self-talk. A does not cause *C, B* causes C. Snakes don't make you run, your belief about snakes makes you run. If your self-talk is irrational and unpleasant, you create unpleasant emotion. Remember, neurotics are not emotionally sick, they are cognitively wrong.

Point to Ponder–4

'Grant me the serenity to accept the things I cannot change, courage to change the things I can (and should), and wisdom to know the difference'.

–The Serenity Prayer

The Brain Physiology of Change

Conservative estimates inform us there are at least ten billions neurons in the human brain, which by seven years of age is almost adult in weight and size. Thereafter, complexity is the result not of the growth of more cells but of connections between cells. There are from ten trillion to one hundred trillion such connections.

The neuron has three parts: (1) The cell body, which contains the nucleus; (2) the dendrites, which are the branches of 'receiving wires' that pick up messages from other neurons; and (3) the axon, or 'sending wire' through which messages are passed on after being evaluated by the nucleus.

The sending wire of one cell does not touch the receiving wires of the other cells. They are separated by a chasm that is a millionth of an inch wide. The messages must jump the chasm, called the synapse. Brain messages can perform this 'leap' 500 to 1,000 times per second, with the average speed or frequency of firing being about 100 times per second.

The sending wire of the cell ends in little protein vesicles called boutons. When an action is repeated, stimulating cells at frequent intervals, boutons at the synapse increase both in size and number, shortening the span over which the messages must jump. Habits are formed thus.

Next time when you think of your habit, think of your boutons. How are you to change your habits if you cannot get rid of your boutons? The encouraging discovery is that even though we cannot destroy old boutons, we can grow new ones and build new neural pathways around the old ones. The most important element in building new habits is thus not time but energy. The more frequently we start doing something, the quicker we start developing the synapse of a new habit path. The same holds true if we are to develop the habit of more rational, positive thinking.

Insight

In order to become emotionally well, it is desirable to move through the following three levels of insight, which are necessary for any change:

1. Knowledge that you have a problem, and awareness of some of the events that may have caused the problem.
2. Seeing clearly that the irrational ideas you acquired early in life are creating the emotional climate you live in now, and that consciously or unconsciously you work fairly hard to perpetuate them.
3. The strong belief that after discovering these two insights, you will still find no way to eliminating the problem other than steadily, persistently, and vigorously working to change your irrational ideas.

Without a commitment to this last insight, we will experience difficulty altering our habitual emotional responses.

Emotional Wisdom

Emotional wisdom lies in daily reminding us that life is such that things often do go wrong. Besides, excessively high standards and expectations are not compatible with our all-too-human day-to-day performance and, therefore, imply continual failure and bad feelings. Some disappointment with oneself, as well as guilt, shame, frustration and anger with others is inevitable. Yet, it can do a lot of good if we develop the habit of doing a 'cost-benefit' analysis of our emotional reactions. For example, a cost-benefit analysis would be more favourable to the emotion of 'remorse', where one tries to atone for one's wrong doings, than for that of 'guilt', where one may punish oneself without any gain to anyone. Making use of appropriate words in our day to day living could be the key to doing such an analysis and arriving at more healthy versions of some emotions.

Activity 7 – Healthy Versions of Emotions

Unhealthy	*Healthy*
Anxiety	Concern
Depression	Sadness
Anger	Annoyance
Guilt	Remorse
Shame	Regret
Hurt	Disappointment
Jealousy	Concern for one's relationships
Frustration	Irritation

Words help us think. And, thinking is powerful. If emotions involve beliefs about what has happened, evaluations about their personal significance, and evaluations about the appropriate ways to react, then emotions can be influenced by dialogue about these beliefs and evaluations. Therefore, think about thinking. 'We need to understand more and condemn less'. CBT provides a technology for changing people's worldviews and for altering emotions. The title of the book by the American philosopher and counsellor Elliot Cohen — *Caution: Faulty Thinking Can Be Harmful To Your Happiness* — is a case in point.

Index